Arduino™ for Musicians

Arduino™ for Musicians

A Complete Guide to Arduino
and Teensy Microcontrollers

Brent Edstrom

OXFORD
UNIVERSITY PRESS

OXFORD

UNIVERSITY PRESS

Oxford University Press is a department of the University of Oxford.
It furthers the University's objective of excellence in research, scholarship,
and education by publishing worldwide. Oxford is a registered trade mark of
Oxford University Press in the UK and in certain other countries.

Published in the United States of America by Oxford University Press
198 Madison Avenue, New York, NY 10016, United States of America

Library of Congress Cataloging-in-Publication Data
Edstrom, Brent.
Arduino for musicians: a complete guide to Arduino and teensy microcontrollers/Brent Edstrom.
pages   cm
Includes bibliographical references and index.
ISBN 978-0-19-930931-3 (hardcover: alk. paper)—ISBN 978-0-19-930932-0 (pbk. : alk. paper)
1. Electronic musical instruments—Construction.   2. Arduino (Programmable controller)
3. Microcontrollers—Programming.   4. MIDI controllers—Construction.   I. Title.
ML1092.E37   2016
784.190285—dc23
2015024668

9 8 7 6 5 4 3 2 1

Printed by Webcom, Canada on acid-free paper

This book is dedicated to my brother, Brian.

Contents

x

xiv

Preface

It's just that the digital revolution has now reached the workshop, the lair of Real Stuff, and there it may have its greatest impact yet. Not just the workshops themselves (although they're getting pretty cool these days), but more what can be done in the physical world by regular people with extraordinary tools.[1]

Chris Anderson, author of *Makers, the New Industrial Revolution,* makes a good point. We live in an era of almost unimaginable creative potential where a $3.00 microcontroller is capable of doing 16-million instructions per second, 3-D printers can bring an idea into the physical realm, and the Web can connect creative people from around the globe. This book is about tapping into the creative potential of Arduino—one of the most popular tools of the maker movement.

What is Arduino?

Arduino is the name of an open-source electronics platform built around microcontrollers that are functionally similar to a small computer. Although you won't use an Arduino to balance your checkbook or run music notation software, Arduino microcontrollers are perfectly suited to an incredible range of musical applications from sound synthesis to custom MIDI control systems. With the proper tools and knowhow, it is possible to connect circuits to the microcontroller and use a programming language to tell the "brains" of the microcontroller what to do. In this sense, you might think of an Arduino as an autonomous device that can function as a digital/analog synthesizer, MIDI controller, pitch converter, or for any number of other musical applications.

An Arduino UNO (one of the most popular Arduino microcontrollers) is shown in Figure 1. (You will learn more about different types of Arduino microcontrollers and how to use them in Chapter 1.)

FIGURE 1

Arduino™ UNO.

Extension of the Creative Process

One of the things I most enjoy about exploring Arduino technology is the vast creative potential. Where a piece of blank manuscript holds the potential for an unlimited number of musical expressions, Arduino (and related microcontrollers) provide a nearly limitless potential for creating new performance control systems and sound sources. This extension of creative potential into the physical realm has profound implications: It is now possible

FIGURE 2

Stella synthesizer.

to not only envision but to actually *create* devices that respond to breath, touch, proximity, light, or other forms of input. Figures 2 through 4 illustrate just a few of the many creations I have enjoyed developing with Arduino microcontroller technology:

FIGURE 3

Emote MIDI breath controller.

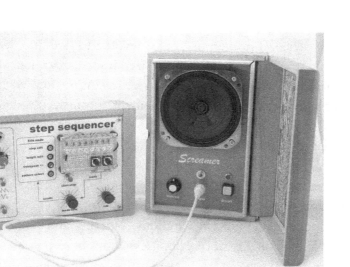

FIGURE 4

Step sequencer/ synthesizer.

The Road to Parnassus

In the chapters that follow, you will learn how to program an Arduino and how to create circuits that will interact with the device. You will also learn about concepts such as MIDI, direct digital synthesis, and audio input and output that will help you to unlock an Arduino's musical potential. By the end of the book you will be rewarded with a newfound ability to envision and create your own Arduino projects.

How to Use the Book

The book is organized in three primary sections consisting of building-block chapters, intermediate concepts, and demonstration projects. Readers who are new to programming or circuitry will want to take the time to read through the building-block chapters before attempting projects in the final section of the book. Readers with a background in electronics will likely want to skip to specific concepts that are of interest such as MIDI input and output or direct digital synthesis.

Programmers often talk about *object-oriented* design, and that is a good metaphor for using the book. As you read, consider how concepts such as force sensitivity, MIDI, or audio output could be utilized and combined as building blocks for your own projects; and be sure to experiment and adapt the concepts to your own use. This approach will foster a deeper understanding of the material and will help you to more easily utilize the concepts in your own work.

Why I Wrote the Book

When I started exploring the potential of Arduino several years ago, I did not envision that my work would lead to a publication. After all, there are dozens of good websites and numerous books devoted to Arduino. However, I was frequently frustrated by a lack of centralized information that would enable me to tap into the musical potential of the Arduino. As my knowledge and confidence grew, I realized that there must be many other musicians who would benefit by a book that focuses on the musical potential of the platform, and the seed for the book was planted.

While most of the concepts in this book can be found in books and various websites, the sheer volume and complexity of information can be daunting: Arduino projects not only involve programming and circuitry, they require specific components, design considerations, soldering, and many other skills to bring a project to fruition. My sincere hope is that this book provides a useful introduction to the topic that will enable you to realize your own creative projects. Although the process can be challenging at times, rest assured that it is not unduly difficult. There is no false modesty when I say, "if I can do it, you can, too."

Safety Tips

Although the risk of bodily injury is slight for projects involving low-voltage circuitry, potential hazards such as an exploding battery or fire could result from a short circuit or other problem. Further, it should be understood that there is a potential for damage to components including (but not limited to) computers, microcontrollers, integrated circuits, and other components when experimental circuits are connected to such devices.

Readers should use common sense and take precautions including (but not limited to):

- Never connect any of the circuits in this text to a high-voltage (e.g., "mains"/household) power supply.
- Always wear appropriate safety equipment.
- Never connect circuits to expensive components including (but not limited to) devices such as computers, cell phones, or microphones.
- Always disconnect battery or Universal Serial Bus (USB) power before working on a circuit and double-check the circuit before applying battery or USB power.
- Always disconnect battery or USB power before leaving a circuit unattended.
- Never leave a hot soldering iron unattended.
- Always disconnect power from soldering irons and other tools after use.
- Always keep tools and soldering irons out of reach of children.

Acknowledgments

I am grateful to Tom White from the MIDI Manufacturers Association for reading and providing valuable feedback on the Music Digital Interface chapter. I am also grateful to Evan Edstrom for reading and commenting on large portions of the manuscript and for numerous photographs: your feedback helped me in innumerable ways. Thanks, too, to Jennifer Edstrom for photographing many of the illustrations and for your patient support of this project. I am also deeply grateful for the time and effort of the (unknown) peer reviewers who provided advice that helped me to clarify and improve the text in many ways and to the production team at Oxford University Press including Richard Johnson, Senior Production Editor, and Diane A. Lange, copyeditor. Finally, I want to express my heartfelt thanks to Norman Hirschy, editor, Music Books, Oxford University Press, for his support of this project, sage advice, and patience.

Arduino™ is a trademark of Arduino LLC.

About the Companion Website

www.oup.com/us/arduinoformusicians

Oxford has created a website to accompany *Arduino for Musicians*. Material that cannot be made available in a book, namely videos demonstrating some of the techniques in the book, is provided here. The reader is encouraged to consult this resource in conjunction the chapters. Examples available online are indicated in the text with Oxford's symbol.

Arduino™ for Musicians

Getting Started

This chapter provides a "cruising altitude" overview of the Arduino platform. By the end of the chapter you will have a conceptual understanding of what an Arduino is and how musicians and other creative individuals can use the platform to create custom instruments, controllers, and sound-making devices. You will get a sense of the design cycle that is at the heart of most projects, and you will consider some of the components that can be purchased to bring your designs to life.

Who This Book Is For

This book is aimed squarely at musicians and other creative individuals who want to expand their palette of artistic resources. Until recently, musicians have relied on instrument manufacturers and software companies to produce the tools that are used to create and manipulate sound. Arduino is starting to change that model so that makers of art can also envision and implement their own instruments and instrument controllers. In a sense, Arduino is the perfect marriage of hardware and software in that it provides an incredible music-making potential for anyone who is willing to roll up their sleeves and learn the basics of programming and electronics.

I would stress that no previous experience with programming or electrical engineering is required—all the basics are covered in the relevant chapters—so the only necessary background is an interest in music technology and a curiosity about the vast music-making potential of Arduino and related platforms.

2

What Is Arduino?

The quick answer that I give to friends when I describe my recent work with Arduino is that Arduino is an electronics platform built around a small and very inexpensive computer called a *microcontroller*. An Arduino can be programmed just like a personal computer, and circuits can be connected to the device to expand its functionality. At the heart of the Arduino is an inexpensive chip (the "brains" of the unit) such as the ATmega328 (see Figure 1.1). Although Arduino specifications aren't impressive when compared to modern personal computers, it is important to remember that the chip at the heart of a typical Arduino is capable of about 16 million instructions per second—more than enough speed for many musical applications. Even more to the point, the ATmega328 chip costs less than five dollars, so the chip can be used for any number of embedded applications for which a full-fledged computer would be impractical or cost-prohibitive.

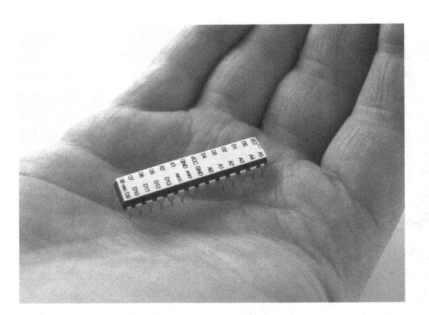

FIGURE 1.1

ATmega 328 chip.

What You Can Do with Arduino

Arduino microcontrollers are well suited to many musical tasks. For example, you could use an Arduino to a detect touch, sense the proximity of a hand, or respond to changes in ambient light; and those same inputs could be translated into Music Instrument Digital Interface (MIDI) messages. An Arduino can also be used to play samples or generate waveforms such as sine, triangle, square, or sawtooth through a process called *direct digital synthesis*. Not only can an Arduino be used to convert digital signals to analog, it can also digitize incoming analog signals. This opens the door to certain types of effects processing and analysis. Through the work of some very clever people, it is even possible for an Arduino to do Fast Fourier Transforms to analyze the frequency spectrum in real time.

In addition to MIDI and audio, an Arduino can be used to control actuators and motors with appropriate circuitry. This makes it possible to create control systems that interact with traditional acoustic instruments. A virtual marimba or velocity-sensitive vibraphone motor are just a few of the ideas that come to mind.

What You Can't Do with Arduino

The modest speed of an Arduino UNO can be challenged with some operations. For example, floating point math (operations that involve numbers like 1.23 or 5.67) is notoriously slow.[1] As you will see in Chapter 9, there are some workarounds. However, one of the biggest limitations of Arduino devices is the relatively small amount of RAM. Given that a minute of digitized uncompressed audio requires about 5 MB *per minute* at a sample rate of 44.1kHz (the standard CD sample rate), the 32KB[2] of available RAM is too scarce to be useful for many forms of real-time audio effects processing. With that said, I have spent a great deal of time working on the Arduino platform over the past few years, and my enthusiasm for its musical potential is even stronger than when I started.

The Lay of the Land

Like any new concept, a primary challenge in learning to use the Arduino platform is getting a sense of the "big picture." In this section I will describe how the primary pieces of the puzzle fit together and the items you will need to purchase or borrow to get started.

The Arduino Family

Although it is common to refer to Arduino in the singular when referencing an Arduino device, Arduino can also refer to a family of devices. For example, the Arduino UNO is a modestly priced microcontroller that is a good choice for most new users. The Arduino UNO, built around an ATmega328 chip, provides a small amount of memory and female headers that provide access to its digital and analog pins. Using musician terms, small patch cables (called hookup wire) are used to connect a variety of electronic components to the female headers (see Figure 1.2).

Shields

One of the benefits of starting with an Arduino UNO is that you can attach a variety of *shields*—premade circuitry that can be used to easily expand the

4

FIGURE 1.2

Arduino UNO (directly connecting a switch to the Arduino headers).

functionality of the base unit. A wide variety of shields have been developed for everything from digitizing audio to connecting to an Ethernet network. All that is usually required to incorporate a shield is to attach the shield to the top of the Arduino, download an associated library, and incorporate the library code into your project.

Other Arduino Flavors

Other Arduino flavors built around the ATmega168 or ATmega328 chip include the Duemilanove and Diecimila. Another option is the Arduino Leonardo, which is similar to the UNO but includes a built-in USB interface. (Although the Arduino UNO also sports a USB connection, the port is only used to program the unit and for serial communication and power.) One of the benefits of the Leonardo is that it can emulate a USB keyboard. For this reason, the Leonardo could be a good choice as the basis for keyboard control projects that are used to control software or automate keystroke-intensive tasks.

There are also larger Arduino boards such as the Mega 2560 and Due. The Due, in particular, will be of interest to musicians given the additional memory and digital-analog converters. However, these boards are not compatible with most shields, so the ubiquitous UNO will be the primary focus of this book. Rest assured, though, that the concepts you learn can be readily applied to other types of Arduino and related microcontrollers as well as credit card–sized computers such as the Beaglebone and Raspberry Pi.

Unofficial Arduino Microcontrollers

There are also a number of unofficial variants such as the Teensy series of microcontrollers. Teensy microcontrollers, including Teensy 2.0, Teensy++2.0, and Teensy 3.1, are manufactured by PJRC. I am very fond of the Teensy microcontroller boards because not only are they relatively inexpensive, Teensy boards can emulate a MIDI interface with just a few lines of code and require *no drivers*. This is a truly plug-and-play solution that is very attractive for any number of MIDI projects. The newer Teensy 3.1 microcontroller and Audio Adapter Board will also be a good option for many musicians (see Figure 1.3).

FIGURE 1.3

Teensy 3.1 microcontroller with audio shield. (Photo based on one by PJRC Electronic Projects. Used by permission.)

Purchasing a First Arduino

My recommendation is to start with an Arduino UNO. Not only is the UNO compatible with the most Arduino shields, it is the version that is referenced in many books and online articles. Another benefit of the UNO, which will not be apparent until Chapter 12, is that UNOs with removable ATmega328 chips can be used as a sort of low-budget programmer should you want to take the plunge and create "standalone" projects around the underlying ATmega328 microprocessor. With this approach, you can use the UNO to prototype and debug your project and simply swap chips when you are ready to upload the program to another chip. This provides an inexpensive way to utilize the core functionality of the Arduino platform without purchasing a new Arduino for every project.

If you have the budget for two microcontrollers, a Teensy microcontroller such as the Teensy 3.1 is a good choice for most musicians. As previously stated, Teensy microcontrollers are a terrific choice for many MIDI applications, and microcontrollers like the Teensy 3.1 offer additional processing power and RAM, making them a good choice for direct digital synthesis applications.

Programming and the Arduino IDE

In order to do something interesting with an Arduino, it is necessary to program the unit. Although it is possible to directly program an ATmega chip using specialized hardware programmers and software, one of the benefits of the Arduino platform is that some of the low-level details of the process are hidden. Arduino provides a free Integrated Development Environment (IDE), a special type of text editor that can be used to program the microcontroller. The process is simple: download and install the Arduino IDE, connect the Arduino to a computer via a USB cable, write some code, and click a button to compile and upload the program to the device. In this way, musicians and other individuals can expand their creative expression into the realm of silicon and electrons.

Compiler

The compiler takes the human-readable text commands you type in the program editor and converts the instructions to a machine-friendly format. Although there are a few downsides of programming solely in the Arduino IDE—Elliot Williams, author of the excellent book *Make: AVR Programming*, compares the Arduino IDE approach to programming with oven mitts—the Arduino IDE *does* simplify the process and is a good choice for most people, particularly those who are new to programming and/or circuitry.

Circuitry

Although it is possible to write useful programs, called *sketches*, without connecting an Arduino to external circuitry, the combination of custom programming and circuitry provides a vast creative potential. Don't worry if you don't know the difference between a resistor and a capacitor; those components are easy to understand and will be explained in the building-block chapters that follow. For now, understand that you can connect custom circuits to the Arduino that will enable the microcontroller to respond to sound, light, pressure, and other sources of input. Similarly, circuitry can be connected to the Arduino that will make it possible to flash an LED, output sound, turn on a motor, or use any number of interesting applications.

Solderless Breadboard

During the prototyping phase, circuits are typically mocked up using a solderless breadboard like the one shown in Figure 1.4. With a solderless breadboard, components such as resistors and transistors can be temporarily connected in order to test the functionality of a design without committing to a permanently soldered version. You will find that, with some practice and hands-on experience, the solderless breadboard will become a sort of electronic sketchpad.

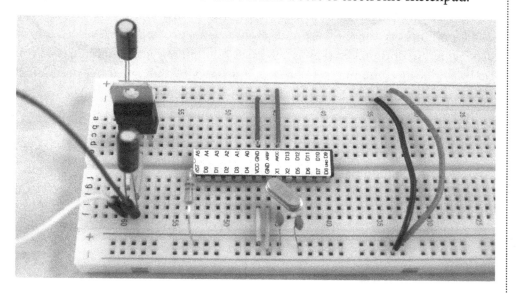

FIGURE 1.4

Solderless breadboard.

Review

Let's review the primary points thus far:

- Arduino is an open-source *microcontroller* that is akin to a small computer.
- A special type of text editor called an IDE is used to write programs, called *sketches*, which are compiled and uploaded to the microcontroller.
- Custom circuits can be connected to the Arduino to enable it to interact with users and the environment.
- A solderless breadboard provides a way to temporarily connect electronic components as you experiment with circuits.

Design Cycle

A project will necessarily start with an idea. Maybe you would like to use light or hand pressure to control the cutoff of a filter, or you envision a new type of synthesizer that responds to breath control. Once the seed of an idea starts to take shape, it is time to consider how the idea could be implemented with hardware and software. In the case of the first example, you will learn that a *photoresistor* is

8

an electronic component that responds to light. Thus, a good starting place is to look at stock circuits that utilize a photoresistor. Then, use a solderless breadboard to create a mock-up of the circuit.

On the software side, you will need to consider how to best monitor an input such as a switch or photoresistor. You will also develop the program logic that determines how the Arduino will respond to such input. For example, the sketch might output sound at a frequency corresponding to the amount of light that is reaching the photoresistor. In general, additional tweaks will be required to fix and improve the software and hardware in a process that is referred to as *debugging*. An optional final phase of the development cycle is to finalize a project by soldering components to *perfboard*, *stripboard*, or some other permanent solution as described in Chapter 11. Figure 1.5 provides a conceptual overview of the process:

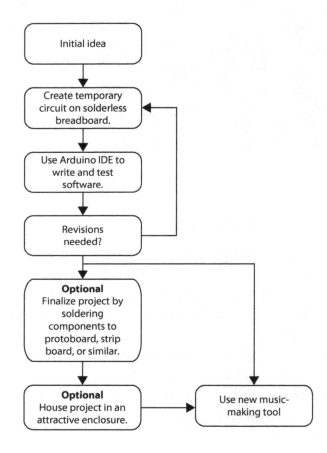

FIGURE 1.5

Conceptual overview of Arduino project development.

Organization of the Book

Arduino for Musicians is organized into three broad sections consisting of building blocks, intermediate concepts, and practical application. Readers with no previous experience with programming or circuitry are encouraged to read the chapters in sequence in order to learn the basics of programming and to understand how various electronic components can be connected to the Arduino. These core concepts will provide a foundation for the more advanced projects that are presented in the third section. The intermediate and advanced chapters are fairly self-contained, so readers with previous experience may find it useful to explore those chapters out of order. The following chapter snapshots will help you to gauge which chapters will be most relevant for your particular background:

Chapter 2: "Introduction to Programming" covers the basics of computer programming including variables, data types, operands, loops, logic, and related concepts. Hands-on coding examples provide an opportunity for mastery through exploration. The chapter concludes with a minimalistic Arduino game, called the "Tempo Guessing Game," that demonstrates many of the concepts in the chapter.

Chapter 3: "Introduction to Electronics" provides a gentle introduction to electronic concepts such as reading a circuit schematic, using a breadboard, conceptualizing voltage and current, and using primary components including resistors, LEDs, capacitors, and diodes. The chapter concludes with three musician-friendly projects: an emergency music stand light, a cigar-box amplifier, and a simple Theremin.

Chapter 4: "Interfacing with Arduino" shows how circuitry and code can be combined to create a useful prototype. The chapter uses an iterative process to develop a working metronome project. Along the way, additional electronic components including switches and variable resistors are used to expand the capabilities of the metronome.

Chapter 5: "Musical Instrument Digital Interface (MIDI) I/O" provides a detailed discussion of the bits, bytes, and protocols associated with the Music Instrument Digital Interface. The chapter concludes with a discussion of MIDI input and output circuits for Arduino as well as how to implement USB MIDI I/O with a Teensy microcontroller.

Chapter 6: "Real-Time Input" explores a number of interesting components such as a force-sensitive resistor, Nintendo DS touchscreen, pressure sensor, and joystick that can be used to provide unique ways to interact with an Arduino.

Chapter 7: "Music-Making Shields" provides an overview of several shields including the Music Instrument Shield, Adafruit Wave Shield, GinSing, and Gameduino that will be of interest to many musicians.

Chapter 8: "Introduction to C++ Programming" explores concepts such as C++ classes, constructors, destructors, and other concepts that will enhance logic flow and enable readers to write programs that are more robust and easier to maintain.

Chapter 9: "Audio Output and Sound Synthesis" focuses on developing classes and algorithms to facilitate *direct digital synthesis*. The chapter details the logic and math behind virtual voltage-controlled oscillators (VCOs) and low-frequency oscillators (LFOs). The chapter also explores methods for outputting sound, including R2R ladders, digital-to-analog conversion ICs, and pulse-width modulation, and introduces readers to Mozzi, a powerful sound-synthesis library.

Chapter 10: "Audio Input" explores techniques for digitizing and responding to audio signals. Two hybrid programs, a waveform viewer and spectrum analyzer, will be created with Arduino and the Processing language. The chapter also provides information about using the Fast Fourier Transform as well as circular buffers and other concepts relating to real-time analysis and signal processing.

Chapter 11: "Finalizing Projects" provides an overview of the process of creating finished Arduino projects. Relevant concepts include soldering, making or using project boxes, and creating overlays.

Chapter 12: "Standalone Arduino" details the process of using an ATmega chip sans an Arduino. The standalone option will be of interest to readers who wish to create multiple projects without the expense of purchasing additional Arduino microcontrollers.

Chapters 13–16: The final four chapters provide an overview of several Arduino and Teensy projects including a touch-sensitive hand drum, digital-analog synthesizer, step sequencer, and MIDI breath controller.

Things You Will Need to Get Started

It can be daunting to determine a shopping list when first exploring the world of electronics. On the most basic level, all that is really needed is an Arduino. You can learn to program the unit, blink the built-in LED, and even interact with the Arduino via a serial interface. However, the real joy (and creative potential) comes when you interact with an Arduino using knobs, buttons, and other components. The following lists detail components that you may want to purchase (or borrow) as you progress from novice to the more advanced stages of Arduino development. Note that these are "general" suggestions that will be used in most projects. There are many *specific* components such as diodes, integrated circuits, jacks, and so on that are listed in conjunction with projects throughout the book.

Beginner

- Arduino UNO microcontroller
- Solderless breadboard
- Hookup wire
- Hookup wire with alligator clips on each end
- Wire snips
- Wire stripper
- Safety glasses

- Resistor pack such as the "Resistor Kit" available from Sparkfun Electronics
- Capacitor pack such as the Joe Knows Electronics 33 Value 645 Piece Capacitor Kit (good value, but a smaller pack might be more appropriate for new users)
- LED pack such as the microtivity IL 188 LED pack with resistors
- Assortment of thru-hole momentary pushbuttons or "breadboard-friendly" pushbuttons
- Assortment of potentiometers (10K and 1M are generally a good choice)
- Several photoresistors for experiments involving light
- Multimeter (used to troubleshoot circuits, read voltage, check for shorts, etc.)

Intermediate

- Items from the beginner kit plus …
- Teensy 3.1 (or similar) microcontroller for USB MIDI or audio projects
- Force-sensing resistors and other sensors of interest such as proximity sensor or pressure sensors
- Joystick such as the Thumb Joystick kit available from SparkFun Electronics
- Shields such as the audio Codec Shield, Music Instrument Shield, etc. (depending on interests)
- Soldering iron
- Bulk hookup wire
- Solder: 60/40 rosin-core solder (1/32 and 1/16)
- Perfboard, stripboard, or similar for finalizing projects
- "Helping Hands"–style clamp for soldering
- Electric drill and bits
- IC Removal tool

Advanced

- Items from the beginning and intermediate kits plus…
- Components for standalone Arduino (see Chapter 12)
- Audio taper potentiometers
- Audio jacks
- Hand miter saw and miter box for making boxes, standoffs, etc.
- Hacksaw for cutting metal, standoffs, etc.
- Various enclosures (commercial, homemade, cigar box, etc.)
- Nibbler for cutting squares in metal

- Optional: analog oscilloscope for viewing waveforms (analog oscilloscopes are available for a modest price on eBay)
- Optional: touch-sensitive screen such as the 4D Systems 32PTU-AR
- Small files
- Vise and/or clamps

Purchasing Parts

It is probably no surprise that prices tend to be significantly higher at typical neighborhood national-chain electronics parts stores. For that reason, I advise purchasing from reputable online dealers when you need to order parts in bulk. Some of my favorite vendors include Adafruit, Digikey, Jameco, Newark, and SparkFun Electronics.

Conclusion

Even if you are new to Arduino, you should now have a good sense of what an Arduino is and what it can do. If you are like me, you are probably pretty excited to realize that the Arduino platform can help you to realize an astounding array of interesting musical control systems, virtual synthesizers, and the like. To quote Nicolas Collins, author of the wonderful book *Handmade Electronic Music: The Art of Hardware Hacking*, "Computers are wonderful, don't get me wrong, but the usual interface—an ASCII keyboard and a mouse—is awkward, and makes the act of *performing* a pretty indirect activity, like trying to hug a baby in an incubator."[3] Although the learning curve to custom-controller nirvana can be steep, the effort will pay big dividends in the form of an expanded palette of creative tools. And the process isn't that much more difficult than learning to use Max, Live, Logic, or the plethora of complex tools that are used by electronic musicians every day.

Introduction to Programming

Programming is at the heart of the Arduino creative process. Although the process of learning to program is somewhat akin to learning a new language, rest assured that the basics are not unduly difficult to learn. Unlike a foreign language, programming involves a relatively small vocabulary, so most of the challenge relates to developing a feel for syntax, structure, and logic.

In my experience, the process of learning a programming language has been beneficial on many levels. First, computer programming provides a palette with a virtually unlimited potential for creative expression; the thrill of bringing a useful program to life rivals the thrill of hearing a new composition being performed for the first time. Second, a knowledge of computer programming will open doors to many new aspects of music making; from the creation of custom electronic instruments, to deeper utilization of music-making tools like Max and Logic, to the incorporation of algorithmic techniques in the compositional process. Third (and perhaps most important), I have been aware of some subtle changes in my creative process as I have developed a deeper understanding of computer and microcontroller programming. Although the impact is subtle, the thought process that is necessary to envision complex programming projects has translated into a perceivable difference in my ability to organize compositional resources on a large scale.

This chapter will provide a gentle (yet thorough) introduction to Arduino microcontroller programming. The first section is devoted to an overview of tools and conceptual processes. The second section will provide a hands-on introduction to the C language with musical examples that will help readers with a musical background to internalize the concepts. The final section is devoted to demonstration programs that will help to introduce large-scale concepts relating to code execution and organization. Note that a later chapter (Chapter 8: Introduction to C++ Programming) will introduce more advanced concepts including classes and callback functions.

Don't worry if you don't internalize each concept on the first pass. As with learning music or another language, repetition and exploration will foster fluency. To that end, code "improvisation" activities are provided after each section to provide an opportunity for comprehension through exploration.

What Is a Programming Language?

In a general sense, a programming language allows a programmer to use special commands to control a computer or microcontroller. In most cases, an Integrated Development Environment (IDE) provides windows in which the programmer can type instructions, organize code, and trace and debug the flow of execution of the program. A *compiler* or *interpreter* is used to translate the instructions into the low-level machine code that the computer executes when a program is run on a given platform.

Programmers typically interact with the compiler or interpreter by typing instructions in a text-editing window. For example, a programmer might use an *operator* such as a plus or minus sign to perform a mathematical calculation:

```
int myVariable = 1 + 1;
```

Although syntactic details will be presented later in the chapter, this example is fairly self-explanatory and unsurprising: The computer assigns the sum of 1 + 1 to a variable (a number that can change) called *myVariable*, and the keyword *int* indicates that *myVariable* is an integer—a number that is not fractional like 3.14. For the most part, the name of the variable is unimportant. The variable could just as well have been named *result*, *sum*, or even *Susan*. The value that is stored in *myVariable* (or *Susan* or some other name) can now be used in another calculation:

```
int myVariable = 1 + 1;
int result = myVariable * 2; //result is now equal to
                             //myVariable × 2
```

Keep in mind as you work through the chapter that, as amazing as computers are as computational and creative tools, these types of simple instructions are at the heart of every program.

Why the C Language?

As with spoken languages, there are many varieties of programming languages. Some of the most common languages include various dialects of Basic, C, C++,

C#, Objective-C, Java, and Python, among others. At the lowest level, *assembly* programmers write code that is only one level up from the sets of instructions that are executed by a computer or microcontroller. On the other end of the programming spectrum, interpreted languages like Basic can, to an extent, shield a programmer from some low-level details such as memory management and pointers. Somewhere in the middle (or perhaps closer to the assembly level) is C, the language that is used to program an Arduino. (If you already have a background in programming you may notice some differences between stand-ard C and what might be called "Arduino C." However, for the purposes of this book the differences are largely inconsequential.)

There are many benefits to learning the C language: The language is "lean and mean" in that a relatively small number of native commands and data types can form the basis of programs that are incredibly powerful. In literary terms, C might be compared to the terse power of an e.e. cummings poem or a Hemingway novel.

Although there are a few aspects of C programming that can be chal-lenging to neophytes, the language is beautiful in its simplicity and power, which is probably one of the reasons that C and C++ seem to be at the core of most college programming curricula. In a word, C is relatively easy to learn, will open the door to a virtually limitless creative potential, and provides a useful founda-tion for learning other programming languages.

Getting Started

A necessary first step is to download and install the Arduino programming en-vironment from www.arduino.cc. Downloads are available for PC, Mac, and Linux. Although the process is similar for each platform, be sure to read and follow the most up-to-date instructions at the Arduino website. Also note that PC users will need to install drivers so that the development computer will be able to communicate with the Arduino. Although a computer is required to pro-gram an Arduino, a computer is *not* required once you have programmed the unit. Any programs that are uploaded to an Arduino will run autonomously when an appropriate power supply or batteries are connected to the unit.

After downloading and installing the Arduino development environment and drivers, connect your Arduino to the host computer via a USB cable and run the Arduino software. You will be greeted with the screen shown in Figure 2.1. It will be helpful to familiarize yourself with the development environment prior to writing a first program: the leftmost button, the checkmark, is used to verify if a given program (or *sketch* as they are called in Arduino parlance) is free of errors. Should an error be found, an error message and explanatory text will be provided in the bottom two panels of the development environment as shown in Figure 2.2. Once you have verified that a sketch is free of errors, use the upload button (the right-facing arrow) to upload the sketch to the Arduino.

16

FIGURE 2.1

Arduino home screen.

FIGURE 2.2

Error message in Arduino environment.

The other three buttons are used to create a new sketch or to save and load sketches.

You will frequently use the rightmost button (an icon of a looking glass) to monitor the serial output of an Arduino during the development process. Given that the Arduino has no visual interface, the Serial Monitor provides a convenient way to communicate with the unit while it is running. Most of the sample programs in this chapter use the Serial Monitor window to provide such feedback.

Writing Your First Sketch

Traditions can be a good thing, and there is no shortage of tradition and convention in the field of computer science. When learning a new computer language or setting up a new development environment, it is customary to begin with what is known as a "Hello, world!" application. The goal is to write a mini-malistic application that outputs the words "Hello, world!"

Enter the text in Listing 2.1 into the main area of the Arduino program-ming environment and save the file with the name *hello_world* (or something similar). The series of instructions will be compiled into an executable program that will run on the Arduino. At this point, don't worry about what all of the instructions mean. Simply connect your Arduino via a USB cable, enter the code, and click the *verify* button to ensure that your program is free of errors. Note that the compiler is not picky about whitespace: in most cases, tabs, spaces, and carriage returns are ignored by the compiler, but the compiler *will* complain if you enter unexpected characters.

Listing 2.1 "Hello, world!" sketch

```
void setup()
{
    Serial.begin(9600);
    Serial.println("Hello, world!");
}
void loop()
{
    //Nothing to do here
}
```

Error Messages

One of two things should happen after clicking the verify button: 1. You will see a "Done compiling" message at the bottom of the screen. 2. You will see an error message such as the following:

```
hello_world.ino: In function 'void setup()':
hello_world:5: error: expected ';' before '}' token
```

One of the most challenging aspects of C programming is learning to translate cryptic compiler error messages into something meaningful. Don't despair, a terse error message does provide some useful information: First, it is evident that there is some sort of error in the function named *setup* (this is the chunk of code between braces after the word setup()). Second, the compiler noticed the error on line five of a sketch titled "hello_world." Last, the compiler expected a semicolon but found a closing brace. This is enough information to identify that there is a missing semicolon after the closing parenthesis in line four. Although the com-piler complained about line five, the problem was actually caused by an error on the previous line. This is common in C and C++ programming—it is often helpful to look at the line *just prior* to the line of code indicated by an error message.

Assuming you entered the sketch without error, it would be helpful to pur-posely enter a few errors to get a sense of how syntactic errors translate into compiler messages. For example, omit the closing parenthesis on the third line and note the similar message that is generated:

```
hello_world.ino: In function 'void setup()':
hello_world:3: error: expected ')' before ';' token
```

With practice and experience you will be able to quickly identify and correct most errors.

Uploading a Program

Correct any syntactical errors and click the *verify* button to ensure that the program is free of errors. A final step is to click the *upload* button to upload the compiled sketch to the Arduino. As with verifying a sketch, you should see a message titled "Done uploading" if the sketch uploaded to the Arduino board without any errors. Alternatively, an error message such as one of the following indicates a problem with the serial port or Arduino board respectively:

```
Serial port name_of_port already in use. Try quitting any programs
that may be using it.
Problem uploading to board. avrdude: stk500_recv(): programmer
is not responding
```

You will need to check that the correct Arduino board and serial port are selected if you receive such a message. (Also make sure that you have installed the appropriate serial driver, if necessary, for your platform.) Arduino Uno should be selected in the Tools→Board menu (assuming you are using an Uno). On my system, the serial port shown in Figure 2.3 is used to upload sketches to Arduino. Note that your settings will likely look different.

Once your sketch has been uploaded to Arduino, click the Serial Monitor icon (or click the Tools→Serial Monitor menu) to view the output of the sketch. Assuming the Serial Monitor is set to a baud rate of 9600, you should be greeted with the text "Hello, world!" Although this sketch is mundane, it represents an incredible potential: an autonomous microcontroller that, with appropriate programming and circuitry, can form the basis of a virtually limitless number of performance controllers, real-time synthesizers, algorithmic composers, and the like. To quote author Chris Anderson: "We are all designers now. It's time to get good at it."[1]

The remainder of the chapter is devoted to a discussion of the primary commands and syntax associated with the C language. As with learning an instrument, work through the basics slowly until you master them, and take time

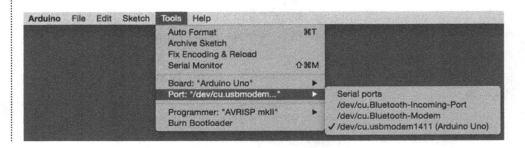

FIGURE 2.3

Serial port.

to explore and experiment with each concept. This book is all about the creative application of technology, so you will get the most out of the book if you strive to use new concepts in creative ways. Exploration will also help to foster ownership and retention of the material. To use another musical analogy: there has been some great music written with just three chords—don't hesitate to get creative after you have learned a few of the "chords" in this chapter.

"Hello, world!" in Detail

Let's work through the "Hello, world!" sketch line by line. Although the sketch is rudimentary, it will provide a useful vehicle to explore a number of fundamental programming concepts. The first thing to notice is that the sketch comprises two *functions*. We will look at functions in detail later in the chapter, but for now, understand that a function represents a useful block of code. All Arduino sketches have the two functions listed below, and the following boilerplate will form a foundation for all of your Arduino sketches:

```
void setup()
{
}
void loop()
{
}
```

Figure 2.4 illustrates the name and function of each symbol in the sketch.

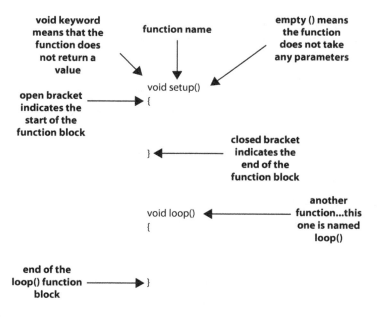

FIGURE 2.4

Code description.

Functions

Note how an opening and closing brace forms the *body* of each function and that the name of the function is followed by parentheses. Although it is common to provide additional information to a function in the form of *parameters*, numbers or characters that are sent to the function between the parentheses, empty parentheses indicate that the function does not accept such parameters. Also, some functions perform calculations and return a number, text, or some other value but, in this case the *void* keyword indicates that a function does not return anything.

There is some behind-the-scenes magic associated the *setup()* and *loop()* functions in Arduino. The first is that the *setup()* function is called as soon as the program starts running. As the name implies, *setup()* is typically used to initialize variables or other housekeeping chores when a sketch first runs. Where *setup()* is called once and only once when a program first runs, the *loop()* function is called repeatedly for as long as the Arduino is running. As is probably obvious, the *loop()* function is typically used to poll the state of buttons, output Music Instrument Digital Interface data, or perform any number of real-time activities. Although you can use creative names for your own functions, it is important to note that the *setup()* and *loop()* functions must be spelled *exactly* as in the previous example because the compiler looks for those specific function names. Also note that C is case sensitive: the functions *setUp()* and *setup()* are different as far as the complier is concerned.

The interesting part of the "Hello, world!" application occurs in the body of the *setup()* function. The first thing to note is that the body contains two lines, each of which are followed by a semicolon:

```
void setup()
{
    Serial.begin(9600);
    Serial.println("Hello, world!");
}
```

Semicolons follow all *statements* in C. In contrast, code that involves program structure and logic does not require a semicolon. For example, a semicolon is not used after the name or braces that denote a function block.

Serial Output

A second thing to note is that both lines use the word *Serial* followed by a dot. One of the great things about *object oriented* programming is that useful chunks of code and logic can be stored as *objects* that can be used again and again in other sketches. In this case, the Serial keyword represents a *class* that encapsulates all of the details of establishing, maintaining, and polling a serial connection. This will become more clear in the chapter titled "Programming Part II," but, for now, it is fine to use the *Serial* object without a deep understanding of its inner workings. In fact, that is the beauty of object oriented programming. In this case we can rely on the work of some really clever programmers to handle the details associated with establishing a serial connection.

Note that the "dot" following the class name indicates a class method—a function that is associated with a particular class. The first line calls a method named *begin()* that takes a number representing the *baud* rate or speed of the serial connection.

This would be a good time to point out that the implementation details of classes like Serial (and many others) can be found by selecting *Reference* from the Arduino Help menu. For example, open the reference page, select Serial in the bottom right, and click the *begin()* method to view the following description:

> Sets the data rate in bits per second (baud) for serial data transmission. For communicating with the computer, use one of these rates: 300, 1200, 2400, 4800, 9600, 14400, 19200, 28800, 38400, 57600, or 115200. You can, however, specify other rates - for example, to communicate over pins 0 and 1 with a component that requires a particular baud rate.[2]

Moving back to the *setup()* function, the second line calls the *Serial.println()* method. The *println()* method takes text (referred to as a *string* or *character array* in the C language) and prints it to the Serial Monitor. Note that the method automatically advances to the next line in the Serial Monitor. A related method, *print()*, also accepts a string but does not advance after printing to the Serial Monitor. For example, you might combine the Serial print methods as follows:

```
Serial.print("This text is ");
Serial.println("on the same line");
Serial.print("I'm on a new line!");
```

Again, don't worry about the underlying details at this point. All that is really important is that a serial connection is established by calling *Serial.begin(9600)*, and text strings can be printed to the Serial Monitor window with the *Serial.println()* or *Serial.print()* methods. Such visual feedback will be very useful as you begin to explore the C language.

One final note: The *loop()* function doesn't actually do anything yet, but it does contain some important text called a *comment*. I can't overstress the importance of adding liberal comments to your code. Comments can be used to provide a play-by-play of the structure of a program, and they can alert other programmers to important details in your source code. Most importantly, comments will save you hours of head-scratching when you inevitably revisit a project weeks, months, or years later. In fact, I like comments so much that I often program in "pseudo-code." With pseudo-code, a programmer describes all of the steps of a program in human readable shorthand prior to writing code. For example, the logic for a sound-sensitive LED might be described this way:

```
//Read a sample from the analog port
//If the value is greater than 500 turn on an LED
//otherwise, turn off an LED
```

Adding Comments

There are two ways to add comments to your sketches. The first is to use two forward slashes followed by the comment as in the following example. Such comments are limited to a single line.

```
//This is a one-line comment
```

An alternative method is to use a single forward slash followed by an asterisk and one or more lines of text followed by an asterisk and another forward slash:

```
/*
    This is a multi-line comment.
    Programmers often use this style of comment at the top
    of their source files to indicate the name of the pro-
    grammer, dates, copyright, and other relevant information.
*/
```

Code Improvisation

Before moving on, take some time to experiment with the *Serial.print()* and *Serial.println()* methods and see if you can program an Arduino to output the following haiku by Lois Edstrom:

```
Creativity
Wild currents of circuitry
Mastery is yours.
```

Variables, Data Types, and Operators

Most Arduino programs involve the use of numbers for counting, data processing and manipulation, or to track the status of buttons or other hardware components. Such numbers are generally categorized as *variables* or *constants*. As the name implies, the value of a variable can change over the life of a program. In contrast, a constant is guaranteed to stay the same throughout the life of the program. Let's look at the syntax for creating a variable integer:

```
int a = 2;
```

In the C language, the *int* keyword is used to indicate that the variable is an integer type (i.e., a whole number, not a fractional value such as 1.5), and the letter "a" that follows the type keyword is the name of the variable. As I mentioned previously, you can select almost any name (such as *my_number* or *someRandomNumber*) as long as the name is not the same as a language keyword or a variable already in use in the program. For example, you can't have an integer with the name "int" because that would conflict with the language keyword. Of course, the equals sign is used to *assign* a value of 2 to the integer named *a*.

Listing 2.2 shows how several variables could be initialized and used to perform a simple calculation:

Listing 2.2 Variable exploration

```
void setup()
{
    Serial.begin(9600);

    //Initialize a few variables:
    int a = 2;
    int b = 3;
    int c = a + b;     //c equals a + b

    //Note difference between print() and println()
    Serial.print("a + b = ");
    Serial.println(c);
}
void loop()
{
    //Nothing to do here
}
```

Initializing Variables

In the preceding example, all of the variables were assigned to a specific value. Unlike some languages, variables in C do *not* default to zero, so their value is *undefined* unless an assignment is made. In C parlance, undefined behavior is a polite way of saying a "bug waiting to happen." So, it is usually best to set variables to a known value when you instantiate them:

```
int a;      //value of a is undefined...may (or may not) be zero
int b = 0;  //value of b is known
```

Operators

Unsurprisingly, variables can be used for any arithmetic operation. The following table (from the Arduino reference)[3] lists the possible options:

- = (assignment operator)
- + (addition)
- − (subtraction)
- * (multiplication)
- / (division)
- % (modulo)

With the exception of the modulus operator, the other operators are all self-explanatory. Although the modulus operator is not as common, it is very useful in certain situations. The modulo operator "produces the remainder from integer division. Integer division truncates the result (it doesn't round)."[4] In musical terms, you might use the operator to determine if a timestamp represents a beat, division, or subdivision of a beat.

24

Note that arithmetic operators can be combined with parenthesis to force the program to evaluate an expression in any arbitrary order. For example, consider the nested parenthesis in the following expression:

```
result = ((a * b)/(c + d)) / 2;
```

In this example, *a* times *b* is divided by *c* plus *d* prior to the division by 2.

Tip: To decipher complex expressions involving parentheses it is helpful to start with the innermost parentheses and work your way out. For example, it is possible to use the parentheses to visualize substitutions for a * b and c + d in the preceding example (let's call them X and Y) to yield the following simplification:

```
result = (X / Y) / 2;
```

Code Improvisation

Explore integer math by changing operators or adding additional variables to the code in Listing 2.2. For example, what happens if you subtract b from a? Can you teach Arduino how to square one of the numbers and assign the product to a variable named *mySquare* or something similar? Also consider adding additional variables and using parentheses to force the Arduino to evaluate the mathematical expression in an unexpected way.

Data Types

In addition to integers, there are several other data types available to Arduino programmers. This would be a good time to point out that Arduino microcontrollers have a limited amount of memory space available for storing variables. Thus, it is important to be resourceful in selecting data types that are big enough to hold a given number but not unduly large. Phrased in laymen's terms, big numbers require more memory than small numbers, so don't use a big data type if a small data type will do.

Bits

In order to understand how variables are stored in memory, it is necessary to explore the concept of a *bit* (which stands for *binary digit*).[5] While bit-level manipulation is rarely needed in Arduino programming, a conceptual understanding of bits will help you to visualize the data types in this section. A more thorough discussion is provided in later chapters of the book as well as in Appendix C, "Introduction to Bit Twiddling."

One of the easiest ways to explore the concept of bits is to run a software calculator (such as the calculators available in Windows and OS X) in programmer mode. Enter the number 255 (decimal) in the calculator and then switch to programmer mode to view a bitwise representation of the value. You will see that eight bits are required to represent the number 255. Similarly, only four bits are required to represent the number 15. As you can see in Table 2.1, a whopping 32 bits are required to store numbers in the range of a billion. Using the programmer mode of a calculator in this way will provide a good conceptual framework for understanding why multiple data types are necessary and why large data types require more memory:

TABLE 2.1 Bitwise Representation of Decimal Values

Decimal value	Bitwise representation
1	1
3	11
7	111
15	1111
255	11111111
65,535	1111111111111111
4,294,967,295	11111111111111111111111111111111

Signed and Unsigned Data Types

As is evident in Table 2.1, a larger range of numbers can be stored if additional bits are used, but how is it possible to determine if a number is positive or negative? With a *signed* number such as an *int*, the first bit determines the sign and the remaining bits store the number (reducing the numeric range by one bit). The *unsigned* keyword is used to tell the compiler that a data type such as an *int* has no sign and, thus, is always positive. This effectively doubles the positive

TABLE 2.2 Arduino Data Types

Keyword(s)	Bits	Description	Example
boolean	8	Logical true and false.	boolean on = false;
byte	8	Unsigned number (0–255).	byte data = 75;
char	8	Signed number (–128 to 127). Typically used for text characters.	char keystroke = 'a';
unsigned char	8	Same as a *byte*. In most cases it is best to use *byte* instead of unsigned char.	unsigned char v = 100;
word	16	Unsigned number (0–65535).	word value = 30000;
unsigned int	16	Same as a *word*.	unsigned int a = 30000;
int	16	Signed number (–32768 to 32767).	int myNumber = –50;
unsigned long	32	Unsigned number (0– 4,294,967,295).	unsigned long milliseconds = 0;
long	32	Signed number (–2,147,483,648 to 2,147,483,647)	long value = –2000000;
float	32	Signed fractional number such as 3.14. "Floats" are slow on the Arduino (see Chapter 9).	float pi = 3.14159

range of values that can be stored by the variable. Data types such as *int* default to *signed* (capable of storing positive and negative numbers) if the *unsigned* keyword is absent. Here are two examples to illustrate the concept:

```
int a = -1;          //Signed integer: positive and negative
                     //numbers possible
unsigned int b = 1; //Unsigned integer—only positive numbers
                     //possible
```

As is evident in Table 2.2, there are a number of keywords that can be used to create variables for different purposes. On the small end, a *byte* requires only eight bits but can only store numbers in the range of 0 to 255. On the other end of the spectrum, an *unsigned long* requires 32 bits and can store numbers over 4 billion. All of the data-type keywords are used in the same fashion as the integer type that was presented in a previous section.

Universal Data Types

You will sometimes see data types such as *uint_8t* or *uint_16t* in Arduino sketches. These data types are helpful in explicitly showing the "size" of the given number (unsigned 8-bit or unsigned 16-bit in this case) and thus offer better portability to other systems in which a different number of bits may be used to represent some data types. Although not required, I typically utilize this form any time I manipulate bits directly.

Here are several examples that will serve to illustrate how various data types might be declared and initialized:

```
//Signed integer: positive and negative numbers possible
int a = -1;

//Unsigned long would be a good choice for a timestamp or
//other variable that might grow very large:

unsigned long timestamp = 0;

//A char is typically used when dealing with letters of the
//alphabet or other characters:

char c = 'A';

//Behind the scenes, a byte is like a char. Use bytes for data
//such as MIDI data in the range of 0-255:

byte dataByte = 100;

//Floats are used for fractional numbers:
float tempo = 150.75;

//uint8_t is an unsigned 8-bit value just like a byte.
//Use this form when you want to explicitly specify
//8-bit numbers:

uint8_t myByte = 50;
```

Constants

Although we have focused on using variables thus far, there are many situations where constants are useful. Use the *const* keyword with a data type such as an *int* when you know a number won't change over the life of the program. This is good programming practice and will help to prevent bugs. Constants can also be defined using the *#define* preprocessor directive. For example, *pi* might be defined as a constant in either of the following ways.

```
const float pi = 3.14;
#define pi 3.14
```

Constants can be used in expressions just like variables:

```
#define pi 3.14

float radius = 5.5;
float area = pi * (radius * radius);
```

Although there are some subtle differences between *const* and *define#*, (a *const* can have a local scope that hides its value from other parts of the program, for example), either approach will work fine for an Arduino sketch.

Enumerations

A related keyword, *enum*, can also be useful in clarifying code. Use an enumeration when you want the compiler to establish default values for a group of related constants. By default, the compiler will assign a value of zero to the first item, one to the second, and so on (although this can be changed by assigning one or more of the enumerated items to a specific value).

Notice how the following enumeration is useful in establishing constants associated with the days of the week. Behind the scenes, the compiler assigns a value of 0–7 to the following weekdays:

```
enum days{monday, tuesday, wednesday, thursday, friday, saturday,
sunday};

if(today == saturday)
{
    //Do something fun
}
```

In this context, the enumeration is functionally equivalent to defining a series of constants as follows:

```
const int monday = 0;
const int tuesday = 1;
const int wednesday = 2;
.
.
.
```

Comparison Operators and Control Structures

Comparison operators such as "less than" and "greater than" are combined with control structures such as "if" or "else" to provide the logic behind most computer programs. It will be helpful to consider a real-world application in order to demonstrate the concept: Imagine that you are working on a Music Instrument Digital Interface (MIDI) sketch and want to limit the velocity of incoming note-on messages to some arbitrary level such as 100. Describing the problem in English yields the underlying logic:

If a given velocity is greater than 100, set the velocity to 100.

In the C language, the "greater than" comparison operator can be combined with the "if" control structure to provide such logic. Note that, in the next example, *midiVelocity* is assumed to be a variable that is defined elsewhere in the program.

```
if(midiVelocity > 100)
{
    midiVelocity = 100;
}
```

There are several things to note in this snippet of code: the "if" control structure consists of a comparison operator in parenthesis followed by opening and closing braces. This is true of most control structures and is conceptually similar to a function block. Any code within the braces will execute if the comparison operator is true. In this case, the value of *midiVelocity* is set to 100 anytime the "if" statement determines that the value is greater than 100.

Similarly, imagine you are writing Arduino software that will transpose MIDI messages. In this instance, you only want to apply the transposition to Note-On or Note-Off messages. The "equals" comparison operator can be utilized to perform the necessary logic. In this instance, let's assume a transposition of a minor third (three half-steps). The pseudo-code version could be described as follows:

If the status byte of a given MIDI message is equal to a note-on message, add three half steps to the data byte.

(Note that a thorough discussion of MIDI status and data bytes will be presented in Chapter 5, "Music Instrument Digital Interface I/O.") As with the last example, assume that the following variables are defined elsewhere in the program:

```
if(midiStatusByte == noteOnMessage)
{
    midiDataByte = midiDataByte + 3;
}
```

As you can see, such blocks of logic are very similar to the way we describe problems in the real world. One thing is important to stress in the last example: the "equals" comparison operator consists of *two* equal signs to differentiate the comparison from an assignment operator consisting of a single equal sign. The following logic error is common, so get in the habit of double-checking for two equal signs in any situation where you want to compare two variables for equivalence:

```
if(a = b)    //ERROR! a is now equal to b
{
    //Do something here
}
```

All of the comparison operators function in a similar fashion. The following operators are available:

```
== (equal to)
!= (not equal to)
< (less than)
> (greater than)
<= (less than or equal to)
>= (greater than or equal to)
```

"If" Statements

"If" statements are often combined with "else" statements to form a useful control structure. In the following example, the block of code following the "else" statement executes whenever the "if" statement is not true. It might be helpful to think of an "else" statement as a type of default. In musical terms, a practical example might involve tracking the beats of a metronome such that beat one is always louder than the other beats. Again, pseudo-code is useful in illustrating the underlying logic:

Set the volume to 100 if a given beat is equal to 1; otherwise, set the volume to 50.

```
if(beat == 1)
{
    clickLoudness = 100;
}else{
    clickLoudness = 50;
}
```

"If" and "else" control structures can also be nested. Building on the previous example, the following code snippet might be used to alter the loudness of a metronome to differentiate between beats one and three. Note that this could also be accomplished with a separate "if" statement.

```
if(beat == 1)
{
    clickLoudness = 100;
}else{
```

```
        if(beat == 3)
        {
          clickLoudness = 75;
        }else{
          clickLoudness = 50;
        }
}
```

Boolean Operators

This would be a good time to discuss one other class of operators known as *boolean operators*. The boolean operators "and," "or," and "not" provide an extremely useful form of logic. For example, you might want to transpose any incoming MIDI messages that are note-on *or* note-off messages. In the following example, note how the "||" (OR) symbols separate the two parts of the "if" statement. The statement could be read as:

If the midiMessage is a Note-On message OR the midiMessage is a Note-Off message, transpose dataByte1

```
if(midiMessage == noteOn || midiMessage == noteOff)
{
    dataByte1 = dataByte1 + transposition;
}
```

Where the || symbol represents logical "or," two ampersands represent logical "and." The following example demonstrates how the "and" (&&) operator might be used in an Arduino sketch. Here, Note-On messages are limited to an arbitrary threshold. The expression reads as follows in pseudocode:

If midiMessage is a Note-On message AND the midiVelocity is greater than 100, set the velocity to 100.

```
if(midiMessage == noteOn && midiVelocity > 100)
{
    midiVelocity = 100;
}
```

Note that the logical "not" operator (!) is used in a similar same way. For example, you might use the operator to set the level of a metronome on the weak beats.

If the current beat is NOT beat one, set the click level to 50.

```
if(currentBeat != 1)
{
    clickLevel = 50;
}
```

Switch Statements

It is sometimes necessary to evaluate a given variable against a number of possible conditions. Although multiple "if" statements can be used, the C language offers the "switch case" control structure as an elegant solution. Similar to an "if" control structure, the "switch case" starts with the keyword *switch* followed by parentheses containing a variable or logical expression. One or more "case" statements follow and are functionally equivalent to a number of "if" statements. In the following example, note how each *case* keyword is followed by a colon and then one or more lines of code. A *break* keyword signifies the end of a given case block. Program execution jumps out of the switch block whenever the *break* keyword is encountered, so be sure to add the keyword at the end of each segment. Note the use of the *default* keyword at the end of the code block: the *default* keyword is optional and can be used as a catch-all if none of the case statements evaluate to true. As with the preceding examples, assume that *menuSelection* is a variable that was defined elsewhere in the sketch:

```
switch(menuSelection)
{
    case 1:
        Serial.println("You selected option 1.");
        //Do something meaningful for case 1 here…
        //Note that the break command is required to jump
        //out of the switch control block.
        break;
    case 2:
        Serial.println("You selected option 2.");
        //Do something meaningful for case 2 here…
        break;
    case 3:
        Serial.println("You selected option 3.");
        //Do something meaningful for case 3 here…
        break;
    default:
        // This is the default block.
        // Note that the break keyword is not needed here.
        // Print default error message:
        Serial.println("Error: Please select option 1-3.");
}
```

Switch statements can be awkward for new programmers, so don't hesitate to rely on "if" statements. However, switch statements can clarify menus and other applications that require checking a variable against a number of possible cases.

Code Improvisation

We have covered many of the primary concepts associated with C programming, including "if" and "else" statements, data types, constants, enumerations,

Boolean logic, and sending numbers and text to the Serial Monitor with the *Serial.print()* and *Serial.println()* methods. Listing 2.3 provides an opportunity to explore these concepts. The following sketch provides a foundation for a primitive number translator that allows numbers to be viewed in decimal, hexadecimal, and binary formats. As is evident in the sketch, the output of the *Serial.print()* method can be formatted using the *DEC*, *HEX*, and *BIN* keywords. Alter the sketch by using different data types or, better yet, explore the *Serial.print()* documentation to see some of the other ways that the method can be used to format output.

Listing 2.3 Exploring numbers and bits

```
//Use an enumeration to clarify the logic of the sketch
enum {decimal, hexadecimal, binary};

//Define a constant with desired selection
//(an advanced sketch might get a variable from the serial
//input)

const int format = binary;

void setup()
{
    Serial.begin(9600);

    int myNumber = 255;

    if(format == decimal)
    {
        Serial.print("The decimal value is: ");
        Serial.println(myNumber, DEC);
    }
    if(format == hexadecimal)
    {
        Serial.print("The hexadecimal value is: ");
        Serial.println(myNumber, HEX);
    }
    if(format == binary)
    {
        Serial.print("The binary value is: ");
        Serial.println(myNumber, BIN);
    }

}
void loop()
{
    //Nothing to do here
}
```

Control Loops

One of the great things about computers and microcontrollers is that they are good at doing iterative tasks such as counting or polling the state of a port. Such tasks are typically handled by *control loops*.

While Loop

One such control structure, a "while" loop, is useful when you want to repeatedly check the value of a variable. In Listing 2.4, the code block following the *while()* keyword loops continuously until the user enters a 1 in the text field of the Serial monitor window. Note that this sketch uses two new methods associated with the *Serial* class: *available()* and *parseInt()*. The *available()* method checks to see if data is available via the serial port, and the *parseInt()* method "translates" the incoming data into an integer. As with the *print()* and *println()* methods, we do not need to know the inner workings of the methods to use them. This is another example of the beauty of object-oriented programming.

Listing 2.4 While loop

```
void setup()
{
    Serial.begin(9600);
    Serial.println("Enter a number. Press 1 to exit.");

    int input_byte = 0;

    //This will loop repeatedly until user enters a 1
    while(input_byte != 1)
    {
        if (Serial.available() > 0)
        {
            input_byte = Serial.parseInt();
        }
    }
    Serial.println("You exited the while loop...");
}
void loop()
{
    //Nothing to do here
}
```

Do While Loop

A related control loop, the "do while" loop, is functionally similar, but the evaluation takes place at the end of the loop:

```
do
{
   // statement block
} while (some_condition == true);
```

My experience has been that the "while" form of loop is more common than a "do" loop, but the form you choose will be determined by the underlying logic. Use "while" if you want to check a variable at the start of the loop, and use "do" if it makes more sense to run the loop and evaluate an expression at the end of the loop.

For Loop

Where "while" and "do while" loops might be considered passive—they simply check a given expression until it is true—"for" loops provide a method for counting between arbitrary numbers. Unfortunately, the syntax involving "for" loops is somewhat cumbersome. In the following example, note how there are three things (separated by semicolons) that follow the "for" keyword in parenthesis:

```
for(int index = 0; index <10; index++)
{
    //Do something useful here
}
```

Prior to the first semicolon, an integer named *index* is declared and initialized. Although the integer can be declared prior to the for loop, this is a common way of setting up a loop. Notice the logic expression that follows the first semicolon (*index < 10*). This expression establishes the condition that must be met for the loop to end. Finally, an arithmetic expression is used to increment or decrement the variable that is being evaluated in the for loop. Note the use of a double "+" sign. This is functionally equivalent to saying *index = index + 1*. (A double "−" sign can be used to decrement by one). Also note that the variable need not be incremented or decremented by a value of one—you might, for example, use *index = index + 2* or some other value.

Listing 2.5 demonstrates how a loop could be used to count from 0 to 9:

Listing 2.5 "For" loop

```
void setup()
{
    Serial.begin(9600);
    //Count from 0 to 9
    for(int index = 0; index <10; index++)
    {
        Serial.print("Index: ");
        Serial.println(index);
    }
}

void loop()
{
    //Nothing to do here
}
```

Output:

Index: 0

Index: 1

Index: 2

Index: 3

Index: 4

Index: 5

Index: 6
Index: 7
Index: 8
Index: 9

Endless Loops

Take care when using loops or you can place the Arduino in a state known as an *endless loop*. Such a loop can occur due to a logic error or when an expected input never materializes. If an Arduino project stops responding, double-check the logic involving any loops. The following example demonstrates one such error:

```
int input_byte = 0;
while(input_byte == 0)
{
    //Endless loop No provision to alter the value of the
    //variable named input_byte.
}
```

Practical Application

Thus far we have covered many of the primary features of the C language, which include variables and data types, arithmetic operators, comparison operators, and common control structures. Although the concepts may still feel somewhat abstract, hands-on experimentation will help to solidify and internalize the concepts.

Type the code shown in Listing 2.6 into a new project and save the file as number_exploration (or something similar). Although the source code for this (and all of the projects in the book) is available at the Oxford companion website, I encourage you to type the code into the Arduino IDE in order to get a better feel for the syntax and control structures. (Be sure to set the Serial Monitor window to 9600 in the Arduino IDE so you can view the output of the sketch on your computer monitor.)

Listing 2.6 Number Exploration

```
//Number Exploration
void setup()
{
    Serial.begin(9600);
    Serial.println("Enter a number: ");
}
void loop()
{
    if (Serial.available() > 0)
    {
        //Read the incoming byte.
        long input_byte = Serial.parseInt();

        //Do something interesting with the number…
```

```
//Calculate its square
long square = input_byte * input_byte;
Serial.print("The square of the number is: ");
Serial.println(square);

//Calculate its cube
long cube = input_byte * input_byte * input_byte;
Serial.print("The cube of the number is: ");
Serial.println(cube);

//Use the modulo operator to test if the number is
even or odd:
if(input_byte % 2 == 0)
{
    Serial.println("The number is even.");

}else{

    Serial.println("The number is odd.");

}
}
}
```

Verify and upload the sketch to the Arduino and enter some numbers to get a feel for how the demonstration program works. Some sample output is shown below. Although there aren't very many lines of code, the program actually does some interesting things, including calculating squares and cubes. The program can also determine if a given number is odd or even.

```
Sample output:

Enter a number: 5
The square of the number is: 25
The cube of the number is: 125
The number is odd.
```

Most of the code should be clear, but a few points of clarification are in order. "Long" types are used so that the program is capable of handling larger numbers such as the cube of 111. Change "long" to "int," recompile, and enter a number like 111 to see what happens when integer *overflow* occurs. (You will see unexpected negative numbers that indicate a value that was too large to fit the given data type.) Also note that all of the action occurs in the *loop()* function. This makes it possible for the block of code to continuously monitor the serial port to see if a byte is available.

Before moving on, I encourage you to take the time to experiment with the sketch. Consider adding additional calculations or logic statements, or change the program into a primitive calculator. Although you will likely experience a few frustrations, your effort will be rewarded by a deeper understanding of a fascinating discipline, and these building blocks will provide a foundation for some incredible musical applications when code is combined with some relatively simple circuitry.

Code Improvisation

Before moving into the final section of the chapter, take some time to improvise with control loops, counting, and serial input and output. A few improvisatory suggestions include:

- Use a "for" loop to count to a million. (Hint: Be sure to select an appropriate data type.)
- See if you can program the Arduino to count backwards from 100 to zero.
- Use a "for" loop to count from 1 to 1,000 and add logic to print a special message for any numbers that are divisible by seven. (Hint: Explore the documentation for the modulo operator.)
- Revise Listing 2.3 to accept user input via the serial port (combine elements of Listing 2.3 and Listing 2.4)

Writing a First Function

The demonstration sketches have been relatively simple to this point. However, as programs grow in complexity, it is useful to organize code into discrete blocks. To that end, *functions* provide one of the most useful ways to organize code. We have already used preexisting functions and methods such as *setup()* and *Serial. print()*, but writing custom functions opens the door to the real creative potential of the C language.

As the name implies, a *function* is a block of code that performs some useful functionality. Building on Listing 2.6, functions could be used to clarify the logic of the sketch (and provide an opportunity to reuse code in future projects). One approach would be to write functions to square and cube a number. Notice how the function called *square_number()* takes an integer as a function parameter and returns a long. As with variables, you can name the function almost anything as long as there aren't spaces in the name or the name is not already in use.

```
long square_number(int value)
{
    long square = value * value;
    return square;
}
```

Alternatively, the squared value could also be returned without first assigning it to a variable:

```
long square_number(int value)
{
    return value * value;
}
```

Function Parameters

One way you might visualize the concept of function parameters is to think of a transaction at a convenience store. The money that you hand to a teller is similar to passing a value to a function, and the convenience item or change that is returned by the teller is conceptually similar to the value that is returned by a function. A fanciful function that represents such a transaction is shown below. Notice how this function takes two parameters: *amount_paid* and *cost*. The function takes and returns "floats" since the values are fractional (e.g., 1.55).

```
float getChange(float amount_paid, float cost)
{
    return amount_paid - cost;
}
```

Using a Custom Function

Custom functions can be used just like built-in Arduino functions and methods. For example, the *square_number()* function could be used this way:

```
void setup()
{
    Serial.begin(9600);
    long mySquare = square_number(5);
    Serial.println(mySquare);
}

long square_number(int value)
{
    return value * value;
}

void loop()
{
    //Nothing to do here
}
```

You could even use the output of the function as a function parameter in another function like *Serial.println()* as in the next example:

```
void setup()
{
    Serial.begin(9600);
    //Send the output of square_number() as a parameter to
    //println()
    Serial.println(square_number(5));
}

long square_number(int value)
{
    return value * value;
}

void loop()
{
    //Nothing to do here
}
```

As you can see, functions are useful in organizing code into discrete blocks. Ideally, good functions are generic enough to be utilized in other projects although it will not always practical to do so.

Listing 2.7 demonstrates how functions could be used to create a more robust and useful sketch. This sketch will print the octave and note name associated with a Music Instrument Digital Interface (MIDI) note number. You can interact with the sketch by entering values in the Serial Monitor window. Before looking at source code, consider the logic of the sketch in pseudo-code:

- Ask the user to enter a MIDI note value
- If the user has entered a number:
  - o Determine the octave
  - o Determine the note number (0–11)
  - o Convert the note number to text description
  - o Print the results
  - o Ask the user to enter another number

At the heart of the sketch are two convenience functions. The first functions returns the octave designation of a MIDI note, and the second function returns the note number (a value from 0 to 11) representing the chromatic notes from C to B.

```
int getOctave(int midi_note)
{
    //Calculate the octave of the midi note
    return (midi_note / 12)-1;
}
int getNoteNumber(int midi_note)
{
    //Calculate the midi note value (0-11)
    return midi_note % 12;
}
```

A third function, *getNoteName()* returns a text representation of the note based on its MIDI note number. The function does this by using a switch statement to evaluate the value returned by *getNoteNumber()*. Also note that the function compares the result returned by *getNoteNumber()* to an enumeration that is initialized at the top of the sketch. The values could have been "hard-coded" into this example, but the enumeration makes the logic of the sketch easier to follow and maintain. We will talk about strings and character arrays later in the chapter, but bear in mind that this syntax is a common way to return a *string literal* (a block of text) from a function.

```
char const *getNoteName(int midi_note)
{
    //Get note number (0-11)
    int note = getNoteNumber(midi_note);

    //Use a switch statement to determine note name. This
    //could also be done with if statements.
```

```
    switch(note)
    {
      //Note: each case returns so break keyword is not
      //needed here
      case C:  return "C";
      case Db: return "Db";
      case D:  return "D";
      case Eb: return "Eb";
      case E:  return "E";
      case F:  return "F";
      case Gb: return "Gb";
      case G:  return "G";
      case Ab: return "Ab";
      case A:  return "A";
      case Bb: return "Bb";
      case B:  return "B";
      default: return "Unknown";
    }
}
```

A final function, *printNoteInfo()*, is used to print note information to the Serial Monitor. The function takes the note value, octave, and text description as parameters and formats the output to the Serial Monitor.

```
void printNoteInfo(int value, int octave, char const * note_
name)
{
    //Print information about the note:
    Serial.print("Value: ");   Serial.println(value);
    Serial.print("Octave: ");  Serial.println(octave);
    Serial.print("Note: ");    Serial.println(note_name);
    Serial.println("=========================");
}
```

Although this sketch could have been written without functions, it is easy to see that functions simplify the underlying logic. In fact, only a few lines of code are required in the main *loop()* to complete the sketch:

```
void loop()
{
    if (Serial.available() > 0)
    {
        //Read the incoming byte.
        int value = Serial.parseInt();

        //Print note information.
        printNoteInfo(value, getOctave(value), getNoteName
        (value));

        //Prompt the user to enter another number:
        Serial.println("Enter a MIDI note number: ");
    }
}
```

The sketch is shown in its entirety in Listing 2.7

```
//An enumeration is a convenient way to refer to note numbers.
//In this case, C = 0, Db = 1, and so on
enum{C, Db, D, Eb, E, F, Gb, G, Ab, A, Bb, B};

void setup()
{
    Serial.begin(9600);
    Serial.println("Enter a MIDI note number: ");
}

void loop()
{
    if (Serial.available() > 0)
    {
        //Read the incoming byte.
        int value = Serial.parseInt();

        //Print note information.
        printNoteInfo(value, getOctave(value), getNoteName
        (value));

        //Prompt the user to enter another number:
        Serial.println("Enter a MIDI note number: ");
    }
}

int getOctave(int midi_note)
{
    //Calculate the octave of the midi note
    return (midi_note / 12) -1;
}

int getNoteNumber(int midi_note)
{
    //Calculate the midi note value (0-11)
    return midi_note % 12;
}

char const *getNoteName(int midi_note)
{
    //Get note number (0-11)
    int note = getNoteNumber(midi_note);

    //Use a switch statement to determine note name. This
    //could also be done with a series of "if" statements.
    switch(note)
    {
    //Note: each case returns so break keyword is not
    //needed here
    case C:    return "C";
    case Db:   return "Db";
    case D:    return "D";
    case Eb:   return "Eb";
    case E:    return "E";
    case F:    return "F";
    case Gb:   return "Gb";
```

```
            case G:    return "G";
            case Ab:   return "Ab";
            case A:    return "A";
            case Bb:   return "Bb";
            case B:    return "B";
            default: return "Unknown";
            }
}

void printNoteInfo(int value, int octave, char const * note_
name)
{
      //Print information about the note:
      Serial.print("Value: ");    Serial.println(value);
      Serial.print("Octave: ");   Serial.println(octave);
      Serial.print("Note: ");     Serial.println(note_name);
      Serial.println("=========================");
}
```

Listing 2.7 Midi Note Explorer

Sample output from the sketch is shown below:

```
Enter a MIDI note number:
Value: 60
Octave: 4
Note: C
=========================
Enter a MIDI note number:
Value: 31
Octave: 1
Note: G
=========================
Enter a MIDI note number:
Value: 49
Octave: 3
Note: Db
=========================
```

A First Sketch Involving Hardware

One concept that can be a source of confusion when first learning to program is a concept called *scope*. This section will detail the code for a simple blinking-light metronome as a way to explore the concept of scope.

Stated simply, scope refers to the lifetime and visibility of a variable.[6] Listing 2.8, which can be used as the foundation for a simple blinking-light metronome, uses several variables with varying scope. Note how the constant named *LED_PIN* and the variable named *delay_per_beat* are defined *outside* of any block of code. This is done so that the variables are visible to all of the functions in a program. Constants or variables that are visible in this way are described as having *global scope*.

In contrast, a variable that is defined within a function (such as the variables named *milliseconds_per_minute* and *beats_per_minute* in the *setup()* function) only "live" within that function (between the opening and closing brace where the variable was defined).[7] In this example, the variables go out of score as soon as program execution reaches the closing brace of the *setup()* function. In this context, "going out of scope" means the variables no longer exist. This is a good thing. Without scope, temporary variables would quickly overwhelm the available memory space of the microcontroller.

Although the primary purpose of this example is to demonstrate the concept of scope, the program also utilizes two built-in functions named *pinMode()* and *digitalWrite()*. We will explore these functions in detail in Chapter 4, but, for now, understand that the functions are used to configure and write to a digital port on the Arduino. The Arduino Uno has a built-in light emitting diode on digital pin 13, so the code below blinks the Arduino LED at the specified rate. After verifying and uploading the program, see if you can expand the program to accept variable tempos via the Serial Monitor:

Listing 2.8 Blinking metronome

```
const int LED_PIN = 13;              //This constant has
                                     //global scope
unsigned int delay_per_beat = 0;     //This variable has
                                     //global scope

void setup()
{
    pinMode(LED_PIN, OUTPUT);    // Set the digital pin as
                                 // output

    //Calculate the amount of delay:
    //milliseconds per minute/beats per minute
    //milliseconds_per_minute and beats_per_minute have local
    //scope
    unsigned int milliseconds_per_minute = 1000*60;
    unsigned int beats_per_minute = 60;

    delay_per_beat = milliseconds_per_minute/beats_per_minute;

    //divide by 2 to get half the period
    delay_per_beat = delay_per_beat/2;
}

void loop()
{
    digitalWrite(LED_PIN, HIGH); //Turn LED on
    delay(delay_per_beat);       //Delay = 1/2 period
    digitalWrite(LED_PIN, LOW);  //Turn LED off
    delay(delay_per_beat);       //Delay for the other 1/2
                                 //period
}
```

One last word relating to scope is in order; the *static* keyword can be used to force the compiler to extend the life of local (function level) variables.[8] Although this is different than having global scope, such variables retain their values between function calls. This is a powerful concept as can be seen in Listing 2.9. In this case, the static local variable *number_of_calls* tracks the number of times the *printMessage()* function has been called.

Listing 2.9 Static keyword sketch

```
void setup()
{
    Serial.begin(9600);

    for(int c=0; c<10; c++)
    {
        printMessage("Calling printMessage()");
    }
}
void loop()
{
    //Nothing to do here
}
void printMessage(char* message)
{
    static int number_of_calls = 0;
    number_of_calls++;  //increase each time the function is
    //called

    //Print the message
    Serial.println(message);

    //Print the number of times the function has been called
    Serial.print("printMessage() has been called ");
    Serial.print(number_of_calls);
    Serial.println(" times.");
}
```

Introduction to Arrays

Some Arduino applications utilize dozens of variables, so it is desirable to let the microcontroller bundle variables into useful groups when possible. For example, imagine that you are creating a MIDI sketch to output a variety of chords. Wouldn't it be convenient to group notes into chords instead of trying to keep track of individual notes? This is just the type of programming problem that can be simplified with an *array*. For this reason, an array might be thought of as a "data bag." You could use separate arrays to store the notes of chords, audio samples, or some other type of data.

Array Syntax

Arrays are used just like other variables, but the syntax is slightly different. Compare the following example for instantiating a byte and an array of bytes:

```
byte myByte;            //Single byte
byte myByteArray[10];   //Array of ten bytes
```

The first line creates a single byte named *myByte*, and the second line allocates memory for an array of 10 bytes called *myByteArray*. The only difference in terms of usage is that brackets are used to tell the compiler *which* of the 10 bytes in *myByteArray* are to be used. To *index* the specific element of an array, use a range from zero to one less than the number of items in the array. Thus, the valid index range for an array of ten items would be 0–9.

```
myByte = 64;              //Set the value of myByte to 64

myByteArray[0] = 64;    //Set the value of the first byte to 64
myByteArray[1] = 55;    //Set the value of the second byte to 55
```

Using an element of an array is similarly easy. The following snippet of code demonstrates how the value of an array element could be multiplied by two:

```
//Multiply the value stored in the first element of the array
//by two.
myByteArray[0] = myByteArray[0] * 2;
```

Don't let the wonky syntax throw you. The preceding example is just like multiplying the variable *someNumber* by two, it's just that the variable happens to be the first element in the array.

Array Initialization

There are two common ways to initialize the contents of an array. One approach is to assign values to each of the elements of the array once the array has been instantiated:

```
byte majorChord[3];       //Create an array with three
                          //elements

//Assign a MIDI note value to each element (0-2)
majorChord[0] = 60;       //Middle C
majorChord[1] = 64;       //E
majorChord[2] = 67;       //G
```

Alternatively, the array can be instantiated and the values initialized all at the same time. This is a nice shorthand if you know the values to be used prior to runtime:

```
byte majorChord[]={60, 64, 67};     //Shorthand for the
                                    //preceding example
```

Figure 2.5 provides a conceptualization of the data in the array called *majorChord*. Notice how each element in the array can be accessed using indices in the range of 0 to 2.

Listing 2.10 demonstrates how an array could be used to store the notes of a major triad. The contents of the major triad are printed with a "for" loop, and

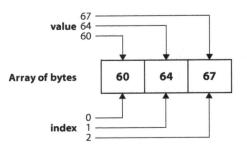

FIGURE 2.5

Array of bytes.

additional loops are used to transpose the loop and print the results of the transposition. Of course this is not an efficient implementation—the goal of this sketch is to demonstrate how the elements of an array could be initialized, modified, and printed.

Listing 2.10 Using loops to access an array

```
byte majorChord[]={60, 64, 67};    //C-E-G
void setup()
{
    Serial.begin(9600);

    //print the chord:
    Serial.println("Chord: ");
    int index;
    for(index = 0; index < 3; index++)
    {
        Serial.println(majorChord[index]);
    }

    //Transpose the chord
    for(index=0; index<3; index++)
    {
        //Notice that +=3 is functionally the same as
        //majorChord[index]=majorChord[index]+3;
        majorChord[index] += 3;
    }

    //Print the transposed array:
    Serial.println("Transposed chord: ");
    for(index = 0; index < 3; index++)
    {
        Serial.println(majorChord[index]);
    }
}
void loop()
{
    //Nothing to do here
}
```

Output:

Chord:

60

64

67

Transposed chord:

63

67

70

It is sometimes useful to create an uninitialized array that can be used to store values at runtime. Such an array might be used to store incoming MIDI bytes or used as an audio *circular buffer*, an array in which the index repeatedly wraps around the end of the array to the beginning. Listing 2.11 demonstrates how an uninitialized array could be used to store incoming bytes from the Serial Monitor. In this case, an array of characters is used to store the incoming bytes, and the variable named *current_index* is used to index the elements of the array. The tilde (~) character signals that the contents of the array should be printed and the *current_index* reset. In this example, also notice how a constant (*BUFFER_SIZE*) is used to establish the size of the array and as a range check in the *for* loops. This is a good example of how constants can help you to avoid bugs. I speak from experience when I say that hard-coded array indices often lead to trouble.

Although there is a lot to take in in this example, no new concepts have been added, so it should be possible to follow the logic of the sketch by working your way through the comments a line at a time. As with the other sketches in this chapter, the source code is available at the OUP.

Listing 2.11 Storing characters in a buffer

```
//Use a constant to define the size of an array
const int BUFFER_SIZE = 20;

//Create an uninitialized array to store characters
char buffer[BUFFER_SIZE];

//Create a variable to track the current array index
int current_index = 0;

void setup()
{
    Serial.begin(9600);
    Serial.println("Enter text and press ~: ");
}

void loop()
{
    if (Serial.available() > 0)
    {
        //Read the incoming byte.
        char character = Serial.read();

        //See if we should print the contents of the buffer
        if(character == '~')
        {
            //Print the contents of the buffer
            for(int i = 0; i < current_index; i++)
            {
                Serial.print(buffer[i]);
            }
            Serial.println("");
            Serial.println("=====END OF BUFFER=====");
            //Reset index
            current_index = 0;

        }else{
        //Store the character if there is room in the buffer
        if(current_index < BUFFER_SIZE - 1)
        {
```

```
                    //Place the character in the array
                    buffer[current_index] = character;
                    //Advance to next index
                    current_index++;
                }
            }
        }
}
```

The Ugly Truth: Working with Text in C

Although we have utilized text in several examples in this chapter, I have purposefully avoided a discussion of the details. Text (usually referred to as *strings* or *character arrays* by C programmers) is an important topic when writing software for computers, but less so when dealing with the memory constraints of a microcontroller. For that reason, I will limit the discussion to the basics.

String Literals

Most of the programs in this book utilize a type of string known as a *string literal*. You have already seen a number of examples. A string literal is "an array of type char".[9] Characters or "chars" are similar to bytes but are typically used when working with text strings. Moving back to the "Hello, world!" application, the text in quotes is an example of a string literal.

```
Serial.println("Hello, world!");
```

Character Arrays

The length of strings can also be variable, in which case they are handled just like other arrays. In this case, the array contains a list of characters instead of numbers. Listing 2.11 utilized this approach.

```
char text[] = "Hello, world!";
char letter=text[1];      //letter equals e--the 2nd index
```

However, there is one subtle difference between variable arrays of characters and integers. In the preceding example, a "hidden" element is appended to the array. The hidden element is a *null value* ("\0") that is used to indicate the end of the string.[10] This will be handled behind the scenes in the code in this book, but it is something to be aware of should you find yourself manipulating strings as part of an Arduino sketch.

Also note that the following statements are functionally equivalent. The second example uses a *pointer* to indicate the first element in an array. Pointers are really useful in programming, but they will not be necessary in the projects in this portion of the book. Further, pointers are often a source of confusion for new programmers. For this reason, I will not cover them at this point.

```
char text[]="Hello, world!";
char *text2="Hello, world!";
```

An Easier Way: Using the String Class

Where traditional strings are the best choice when you want to keep your programs lean and mean, a String class is available to handle many of the tricky details of working with character arrays. The String class makes it possible to concatenate or add strings together, convert numbers to strings, trim whitespace, convert to upper or lower case, and a number of other useful functions you can read about at http://arduino.cc/en/Reference/StringObject.[11]

To use the String class, simply create an instance of the class and assign it to a string literal or call one of its member functions as shown in Listing 2.12:

Listing 2.12 String demonstration 1

```
void setup()
{
    Serial.begin(9600);

    //Create two strings
    String aString = "This is a string. ";
    String bString = " This is another string.";

    //Combine the strings into a new string
    String cString = aString + bString;
    Serial.println(cString);

    //Change all characters to upper case
    cString.toUpperCase();
    Serial.println(cString);

    //Get a substring from first element (0) through fourth
    //element
    String subString = cString.substring(0, 4);
    Serial.println(subString);
}
void loop()
{
    //nothing to do here
}
```

Output:

This is a string.   This is another string.

THIS IS A STRING.   THIS IS ANOTHER STRING.

THIS

Tip: Be sure to check out the Standard Template Library if you ever program on full-fledged computers. The STL provides helpful container classes and a string class that is powerful and easy to use.

String Class Example

Listing 2.13 shows the power of the String class. This example will output any and all bytes that are sent to the Arduino via the Serial connection. This example, which was adapted from an example at Stackoverflow.com, could form the basis for any number of interactive Arduino applications where the micro-controller is configured to respond to text commands:

Listing 2.13 String class

```
int count = 0;

void setup()
{
    //Establish 9600 baud serial connection
    Serial.begin(9600);
}

void loop()
{
    //Read the serial port and output incoming data…
    //Based on an example from stackoverflow.com

    //The String variable msg acts like a buffer to store
    //characters
    String msg;

    if(Serial.available() > 0)
    {
        while(Serial.available() > 0)
        {
          msg += char(Serial.read());
          delay(3);
        }

        //Print the message
        Serial.println(msg);

        //Print the message length
        int length = msg.length();
        String new_message = "The string is " +
            String(length) + " characters long.";
        Serial.println(new_message);
    }
}
```

A Complete Demonstration Program

We have covered the primary concepts associated with the C language in this chapter: variables, data types, arithmetic operators, comparison operators, control structures, constants and enumerations, functions, scope, arrays, and strings. Now it is time to do something creative in the form of a tempo guessing game.

I once had a student who had absolute pitch *and* tempo, and I marveled at his ability to detect the exact tempo of a piece of music, oscillating fans, and other devices. This tempo game will allow you to practice the skill of detecting tempos. A variable called *precision* can be altered so guesses are evaluated with more (or less) precision.

Playing the Tempo Game

The tempo game sketch blinks an LED at a random tempo and the user guesses the tempo by entering numbers in the Serial Monitor window. The program provides feedback on each guess and tracks the number of tries it takes to guess the tempo. Although the listing is fairly long, the flow of the program should be relatively easy to understand after reading the discussion that follows. Don't be discouraged if any parts of the sketch are unclear. As I have mentioned previously, hands-on experimentation will help you to make the jump from abstract code to practical application.

Given the length of the sketch, we will explore the code in sections in the following paragraphs.

Setup

The "prelude" (see Listing 2.14) is similar to other sketches in this chapter: a global constant and several variables are initialized, and a Serial connection is established in the *setup()* function. Two lines of the *setup()* method are unfamiliar: *randomSeed()* and *newGame()*. *randomSeed()* is a built-in function that seeds a random number generator with a unique value. Without this step, the random number generator would always return the same pattern of numbers. In this case, a random value is read from an analog port (more on this in Chapter 3) to seed the generator.

Listing 2.14

```
const int LED_PIN = 13;

int tempo;                     //Tempo in BPM
long delay_MS;                 //Delay in milliseconds
boolean blink_status = true;   //true == LED on, false == LED
                               //off
int tries;                     //Tracks the number of tries to
                               //guess the tempo
int precision= 3;              //Determines accuracy of guess
                               //(within +/- 3 BPM)

void setup()
{
    //Establish 9600 baud serial connection
    Serial.begin(9600);

    //Set up digital pin as an output:
    pinMode(LED_PIN, OUTPUT);

    //Initialize (seed) the random number generator
    randomSeed(analogRead(0));

    //Set up a new game:
    newGame();
}
```

newGame() Function

newGame() is a custom function that is called at the start of each game. As is evident in Listing 2.15, its job is to select a new random tempo, reset the variable that corresponds to the number of tries, and calculate the number of milliseconds per beat:

Listing 2.15

```
void newGame()
{
    //Reset the number of tries
    tries = 1;

    //select a random tempo between 30 and 150 BPM
    tempo = random(30, 150);

    //Calculate the amount of delay:
    //milliseconds per minute/beats per minute
    unsigned int milliseconds_per_minute = 1000 * 60;
    delay_MS = milliseconds_per_minute/tempo;

    //divide by 2 to get half the period
    delay_MS = delay_MS/2;

    //Print a message:
    Serial.println("Enter the tempo in BPM (e.g. 120): ");
}
```

Helper Functions

Three helper functions—*blinkLED()*, *updateLED()*, and *showCorrectAnswer()*—simplify the logic in the main loop. Although this code could have been placed in the main loop, it would make for a long and unwieldy function. Breaking the code into smaller chunks of code clarifies the logic and provides an opportunity to reuse code in other sketches.

The *blinkLED()* function uses a static variable, *last_time*, to track the number of milliseconds between calls. As mentioned previously, the *static* keyword means that the value of the variable is stored between calls to the function (even though the variable does not have global scope). As you can see from the comments in Listing 2.16, *blinkLED()* toggles the status of the LED each time *current_time – last_time* is greater than or equal to *delay_MS*. The following line:

```
blink_status = !blink_status;
```

is a handy way to toggle boolean (true/false) variables between states. Another helper function, *updateLED()*, is called each time the state of the LED changes. This function simply turns the LED on or off depending on the value of the variable, *blink_status*.

Listing 2.16

```
void blinkLED()
{
```

```
    static long last_time = 0; //Used to track milliseconds
                                //between blinks

    //Get the current time in milliseconds
    long current_time = millis();

    //If the current time - last time is greater than the
    //delay time
    if(current_time - last_time >= delay_MS)
    {
        //Toggle blink status (false = true or true = false
        blink_status = !blink_status;
        last_time = current_time; //reset last_time
        updateLED();
    }
}

void updateLED()
{
     //Toggle the LED
    if(blink_status == true)
    {
        digitalWrite(LED_PIN, HIGH);
    }else{
        digitalWrite(LED_PIN, LOW);
    }
}
```

A final helper function, *showCorrectAnswer()*, is called whenever the user enters a correct response. You might want to add additional feedback such as snarky comments when responses exceed a certain number of tries.

```
void showCorrectAnswer()
{
    Serial.print("Congratulations! You selected the correct
    tempo in ");
    Serial.print(tries);
    Serial.println(" tries!");
    Serial.print("The exact tempo is: ");
    Serial.println(tempo);
}
```

Main loop()

The main *loop()* function (Listing 2.17) is the heart of the tempo_game program. Its job is to call the *blinkLED()* method and to evaluate user responses. A pseudo-code version might look like this:

- Call *blinkLED()*
- Read data from the serial port (if available)
- Increment the *tries* variable and provide feedback for an incorrect response
- Call *showCorrectAnswer()* and *newGame()* if user enters a correct response.

The complete *loop()* function is shown below.

Listing 2.17

```
void loop()
{
    blinkLED();

    //Check responses
    if (Serial.available() > 0)
    {
        //Read the incoming byte.
        long input = Serial.parseInt();

        //Check responses:
        if(input > tempo + precision)
        {
            Serial.println("Sorry, your guess is too high.
            Try again.");
            tries++;
        }

        if(input < tempo - precision)
        {
            Serial.println("Sorry, your guess is too low. Try
            again.");
            tries++;
        }

        //See if guess is within the range of the current
        //tempo + precision and current tempo - precision
        if(input <= tempo + precision && input >= tempo
        - precision)
        {
            //Correct answer
            showCorrectAnswer();

            //Start a new game:
            newGame();
        }
    }
}
```

Conclusion

I encourage you to spend time following the flow of the Tempo Game sketch and changing and improving the application. Ideally, you will feel relatively comfortable with the concepts, and your burgeoning skills in the C language will lead to some wonderful Arduino projects. If, on the other hand, the concepts and flow of the application still seem unclear, take some time to play with the examples presented earlier in the chapter. Just as it is sometimes necessary to slow down a passage of music or work on a single measure in order to master a section of a composition, it may be useful to experiment with each building-block concept in order to develop fluency with the C language.

Introduction to Electronics

The last chapter focused on the use of the C language to program an Arduino microcontroller. This chapter is devoted to an exploration of concepts that will enable you to create electronic circuits that can interact with an Arduino. The powerful combination of custom software and circuitry will enable the creation of any number of expressive musical controllers and instruments.

Overview

The first half of the chapter is devoted to a discussion of the primary components and tools that are used to create circuits. A building-block LED project provides an introduction to many fundamental concepts including the flow of electrons, primary electronic components, and the logic and conventions involving circuit diagrams. The chapter concludes with three full-fledged electronic projects; an emergency music stand light that is activated by darkness, a $10 "Cigar Box" amplifier, and a simple Theremin.

Pep Talk

A few words about my background might be helpful in providing some encouragement for the somewhat arduous learning curve associated with Arduino programming and circuit design: I am, first and foremost, a performing musician who happens to be an avid programmer, music theorist, and technologist. I became aware of Arduino several years ago and recognized the potential of the platform as a component of my music-making endeavors. The thought of designing custom hardware and software as an aid in the studio or new controllers to utilize in the performance hall was incredibly exciting. Since that time, my enthusiasm hasn't waned at all. If anything, I am even more excited about the musical potential of the platform. With that said, the learning curve can be steep. Not only is it necessary to develop fluency with a programming language, it is also necessary to develop an understanding of the primary concepts and components associated with electronic circuitry. One of the things I noticed as I immersed myself in electronic textbooks and project guides is that I could better understand and internalize the material when I translated concepts to musical terms. Thus, that is the approach I will take throughout most of the tome; nearly all of the concepts and components associated with circuitry will be related in a direct way to a specific musical application. For example, it is one thing to say that a potentiometer is a variable resistor, but it is quite another thing to demonstrate how a potentiometer can be used to control the tempo of a metronome.

After working through these concepts for the past several years, I would share the following suggestions with readers who are new to electronics: 1. Mock up all of the circuits and take the time to explore and experiment. 2. Don't be discouraged if you need to read a section more than once. 3. Take your time: although the concepts aren't unduly hard to comprehend, the number of terms and concepts can be overwhelming at first. Don't worry, the concepts will soon seem as familiar as notes and chords.

By the end of the chapter you should be familiar with many of the primary electronic components including resistors, capacitors, LEDs, diodes, switches, potentiometers, and photoresistors. In addition to understanding the form and function of these components, you will be able to look at a basic circuit schematic and translate the circuit to a working model by utilizing a solderless breadboard.

Safety Warning

Although the projects contained in this book involve low voltages, there are still potential dangers associated with the technology. The most important thing to stress is that **AT NO POINT SHOULD YOU EXPERIMENT WITH THE MAIN (HOUSEHOLD) POWER SOURCE.** Circuits involving "mains" power should be left to professionals with appropriate training and experience. All of the circuits in this book are designed to work with low-voltage battery or USB power supplies. The only exception is that individuals with a sufficient level of experience may elect to utilize an appropriate adapter to supply low-voltage power for some projects.

It is also important to note that the potential exists for fires or flying fragments, even with low-voltage batteries. A simple reversal of the connections of a capacitor or an inadvertent short can cause a component to burst or catch fire. Thus, you should **ALWAYS** disconnect the battery or USB connection after you have finished experimenting with a circuit. Also, it is important to wear appropriate eye protection for the same reason. Not only can a part burst, but flying bits of solder are not uncommon. **ALWAYS** protect your eyes.

Finally, it should be understood that a short or other circuit flaw can cause an Arduino or connected device to fail. Avoid attaching devices like expensive microphones, headphones, iPods, amplifiers, or keyboards unless you have an appropriate amount of training and experience with electronics. A great deal of time and effort went into the research for this book, and the entire project was peer-reviewed by experts in this field, but it should be understood that there is an inherent risk with any such experimental project. Mistakes in the illustrations or underlying logic are still possible. With that said, I have been avidly using and exploring the world of Arduino for several years without a single mishap. The process of designing, creating, and using Arduino projects is exciting and satisfying on many levels, and you will enjoy the incredible creative potential that Arduino provides.

Tools and Process

Although you might want to finalize some of the projects in this chapter by soldering components to solderboards, my intent is for readers to create temporary mock-ups of the circuits using a solderless breadboard (more on this in a moment). Hands-on experimentation will enable you to internalize and master the concepts and will foster a more creative approach to using and altering electronic circuits. This book is not a "project book"; ideally, the sample projects will provide a jumping-off point for your own creative endeavors. Thus, don't be in a hurry to start soldering. Work through some (or all) of the examples in the book before you decide to finalize or adapt projects to your own needs.

One of the great things about exploring Arduino is that most of the tools and components are relatively inexpensive, and just a handful of items are required to get started with the projects in this first section of the book:

Parts required to create temporary (solderless) mock-ups of the projects in the first section of the book

- Arduino Uno.
- Solderless breadboard. The breadboard will be used as a sort of electronic sketch pad to connect and explore the circuits in the book.
- Hookup wire: 22-gauge solid-conductor.[1]
- Wire cutter/stripper.

- Patch cords (test leads).
- 9 volt battery and snap connector.
- An assortment of resistors, capacitors, potentiometers, LEDs, diodes, miniature loudspeaker, and switches.
- Digital multimeter. Digital multimeters are inexpensive and are very useful in exploring and troubleshooting circuits.
- Optional: Precut hookup wire that can help to keep your breadboard projects tidy.
- Optional: Teensy microcontroller (particularly useful for MIDI projects).

The Arduino Uno is the most expensive item of the components listed above, so you might be wondering about the economics of purchasing Arduinos for multiple projects. As you will see in Chapter 12, it is possible to purchase separate components and create your own bare-bones Arduino for about $10.

A First Circuit

Chapter 2 started with a "Hello, world!" software application. This chapter begins with an electronic equivalent: a "Hello, world!" LED project. Although this project does not have a direct relationship to music, a second iteration of the project, "Emergency Music Stand Light," will be useful for some musicians.

Let's jump in feet first with a first circuit schematic—a switchable LED light. Look at the circuit in Figure 3.1 and familiarize yourself with the symbols associated with the various components in the circuit. Each of the components has a specific function which will be detailed in the paragraphs that follow. For comparison, a solderless breadboard version of the circuit is shown in Figure 3.2.

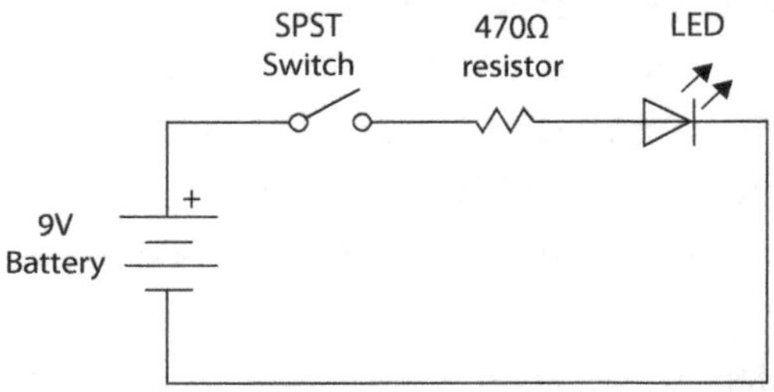

FIGURE 3.1

Basic LED light circuit.

FIGURE 3.2

Basic LED light circuit: solderless breadboard version.

9V Battery

The battery provides *direct current* to power the circuit. Author Charles Platt describes DC current as being "like the flow of water from a faucet, it is a steady stream, in one direction."[2] When the terminals of the battery are connected to the circuit, electrons flow from negative to positive in what is unsurprisingly known as *electron flow*. However, the term *conventional flow* "describes current as the flow of charge from positive to negative."[3] These seemingly contradicting terms have their basis in a historic misunderstanding about the flow of electrons. We now know that electrons flow from negative to positive, but circuits are still drawn in a way that implies "conventional" flow—positive to negative (see Figure 3.3). For our purposes the direction of flow is relatively unimportant. The important thing to understand is that, for a circuit to work, the components and connections in the circuit must form a *closed* circuit.

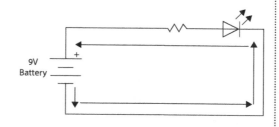

FIGURE 3.3

Flow of electrons through a circuit from negative to positive.

59

SPST Switch

The battery is connected through a *single-pole, single-throw* (SPST) switch. As is evident in the symbol representing the switch, the switch can be "thrown" to complete the circuit connecting the terminals of the battery. The term *pole* refers to the common center terminal of the switch. In a single-pole, single-throw switch, the connection is either open or closed. In contrast, a *single-pole, double-throw (SPDT)* switch can make two possible connections (see Figure 3.4).

SPST   **SPDT**

FIGURE 3.4

Single-pole, single-throw (SPST) and single-pole, double-throw (SPDT) switches.

Resistor

Resistors are used to limit current (the flow of charge) in a circuit. We will discuss this concept in more detail later in the chapter. For now, it might be helpful to think of the water analogy from earlier in this chapter: A resistor is somewhat akin to a faucet in that the faucet can be used to limit the flow of current. (As you will see, a faucet is more like a potentiometer—a variable resistor.) Without a resistor, too much current would flow through the LED, likely destroying it.

LED

A light-emitting diode (LED) "converts an electrical current *directly* into light."[4] We will explore LEDs in some detail later in the book, but it is important to understand a few characteristics about these components. One thing to note is that an LED will happily gobble up current to the point that the LED fries itself. (This is the reason a resistor is used to limit current.) Second, the LED must be connected with the correct orientation or *polarity*: the *anode* is connected to positive and the *cathode* to negative. In most cases a shorter leg and/or flat side of the LED indicates the cathode or negative lead.

Using a Breadboard

A solderless breadboard can be used to bring the circuit to life. A breadboard, like the one shown in the Figure 3.5, consists of a number of holes into which components and hookup wires can be plugged.

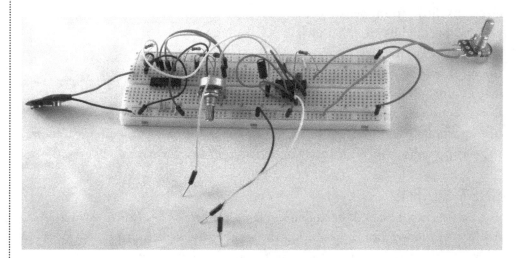

FIGURE 3.5

Solderless breadboard.

In most cases, a horizontal set of *rails* are provided on the top and bottom of the breadboard. The holes in a rail are connected to one another and are typically attached to the positive and negative terminals of a battery (or to the +5V and ground pins on an Arduino). In musical terms, the rails are functionally similar to a *bus* on a mixing console. Note that it is common to connect the positive terminal to the top rail and the negative terminal to the bottom rail.

The holes in the center of the breadboard are connected vertically. This is the area where most of the components of a circuit will be placed. The breadboard is broken by a horizontal blank space in the center of the board. It is important to note that the columns are *not* connected across this space. Integrated circuits (ICs) and some other components are placed so they straddle the two sections of rows to avoid shorting the pins—the small projections on the underside of the IC that are used to make electrical connections with the component.

A First Breadboard Project

Start by plugging the components of the LED circuit to the breadboard as shown in the Figure 3.6. Note how the switch is used to connect the power rail to the resistor and the resistor is connected to the anode of the LED. Also note how the resistor is placed in a horizontal configuration. Although it is tempting to place the resistor between two vertically adjacent holes, the current will simply bypass the resistor since a path of least resistance is available between the two vertical holes. This is a common mistake, so it is helpful to remember that components are generally positioned so the ends straddle *adjacent* columns.

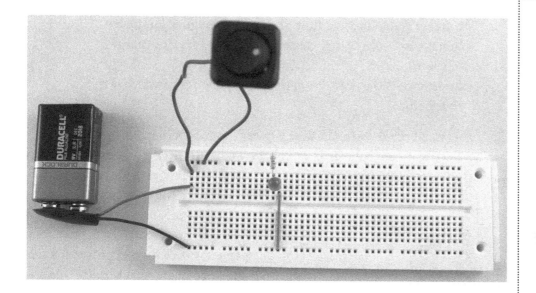

FIGURE 3.6

Breadboard version of the LED circuit.

The cathode side of the LED is connected to the ground rail via a length of hookup wire, thus completing the circuit.

Attach a battery to the circuit and use the switch to toggle the LED on and off. If the LED does not light, check each connection to ensure that the components are connected (it is easy to plug a wire into the wrong hole) and check that the battery has a charge.

Ohm's Law

This would be a good time to explore some of the fundamental concepts associated with electronic circuitry. Although it will not be necessary to delve deeply into math and circuit analysis in this book, it will be helpful to understand several primary concepts associated with the flow of electrons in order to fully utilize building-block electronic components such as resistors, LEDs, capacitors, and diodes. To use a musical analogy, theory and technique can provide artists with a greater range of expression. In a similar way, a knowledge of fundamental theoretical concepts associated with electronics can help you to better utilize the concepts for your own creative endeavors. With that said, don't hesitate to jump ahead to the projects at the end of this chapter if you are anxious to experiment with other circuits. You can always fill in the basics of voltage, current, resistance, and related concepts once you have had additional hands-on experience building the circuits at the end of the chapter.

Conceptualizing Voltage, Current, and Resistance

The three fundamental properties of electricity are current, voltage, and resistance. Robert T. Paynter and B. J. Toby Boydell provide a concise definition in *Electronics Technology Fundamentals*:

- Current is the directed flow of charge through a conductor.
- Voltage is the force that causes the directed flow of charge (current).
- Resistance is the opposition to current that is provided by the conductor.[5]

As I mentioned earlier in the chapter, a water analogy is often used to describe electrical concepts such as voltage and current. Although the analogy doesn't always "hold water," I find that a water analogy provides a useful way to visualize the concepts. One of my favorite analogies for describing the relationship of voltage, current, and power, involves a pail of water, a tap, and a rotating turbine. In this example (see Figure 3.7), the level of water in a pail relates to *voltage*. More force is directed to the flow of water when the pail is full.

In this example it is easy to see that water pressure relates to the stream or *current* that flows out of the tap. This is conceptually similar to the way that voltage and resistance are related.

This illustration is also useful in conceptualizing resistance: a tap that is wide open obviously creates less resistance to the flow of current than one that is partially closed.

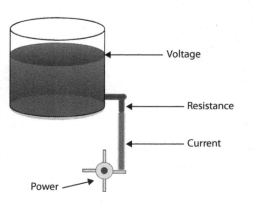

FIGURE 3.7

Conceptualization of voltage, current, resistance, and power. (Adapted from an illustration in *Getting Started in Electronics*, Forrest M. Mims III.)

Using Ohm's Law

Current, voltage, and resistance are related to one another and can be described mathematically using Ohm's law, which is often referred to as a *Very Important Rule*:

$$V = IR$$

Ohm's law states that voltage equals current times resistance. (In this equation, the letter I denotes current.)

Using some basic algebra it is easy to see two other relationships: (1) that resistance is equal to voltage divided by current:

$$R = \frac{V}{I}$$

and (2) that current is equal to voltage divided by resistance:

$$I = \frac{V}{R}$$

This would be a good time to visualize one other related concept: in the water bucket analogy, the term *power* refers to the amount of work done by the turbine. As the following equation shows, power is the product of voltage and current:

$$P = IV$$

Given that voltage is equal to current times resistance (V = IR), it is possible to substitute current and resistance for voltage as follows:

$$P = IV = I^2R$$

Units of Measurement

Before moving on to some hands-on experiments, it is necessary to discuss units of measurement and engineering notation. Although Arduino circuitry does not require a lot of deep math, some simple calculations will be necessary on occasion, so a basic familiarity with units and engineering conventions is useful.

The units of measurement for voltage, current, and resistance are *volts* (V), *amperes* (A), and *ohms* (Ω), respectively. This would be a good time to mention the *farad* (F), the unit of measurement for capacitance. Capacitors oppose changes in voltage and are often combined with resistors in a circuit. As you will learn, capacitors are often used to "smooth" a voltage source or in conjunction with a resistor to form a passive filter.

Electronic measurements often yield very small or very large numbers, and scientists have developed a notation system to help prevent the errors that would inevitably occur when working with a number like. 000000355. *Scientific notation* is "a method of expressing numbers where a value is represented as the product of a number and a whole-number power of 10."[6] With this system, numbers are written to conform to a range of 1 and 9.999 and multiplied by 10 with an exponent to specify the number of places. The process is very simple: for positive exponents, move the decimal to the right the number of spaces given by the exponent. For negative exponents, move the decimal the decimal to the left the number of spaces indicated by the exponent. If the exponent is zero, the decimal does not move. See Table 3.1 for several examples:

TABLE 3.1 Examples of Units of Measurement

Value	Scientific notation equivalent
2300	2.3×10^3
47,500	4.75×10^4
.0683	6.83×10^{-2}
.000000355	3.55×10^{-7}
1.45	1.45×10^0

TABLE 3.2 Prefix Notation

Range	Prefix	Symbol
(1 to 999) × 10^{12}	tera-	T
(1 to 999) × 10^{9}	giga-	G
(1 to 999) × 10^{6}	mega-	M
(1 to 999) × 10^{3}	kilo-	k
(1 to 999) × 10^{0}	(none)	(none)
(1 to 999) × 10^{-3}	milli-	m
(1 to 999) × 10^{-6}	micro-	μ
(1 to 999) × 10^{-9}	nano-	n
(1 to 999) × 10^{-12}	pico-	p

Source: *Electronics Technology Fundamentals* by Robert T. Paynter and B. J. Toby Boydell.

In the field of electronics, practitioners use a variation of scientific notation called *engineering notation*. Instead of using exponents, standard prefixes are used to specify the magnitude of a number. Table 3.2 lists the common prefixes. Figure 3.8, adapted from an illustration in *Electronics Technology Fundamentals*, will help to clarify the relationship of terms such as *tera* and *giga* to a decimal point.

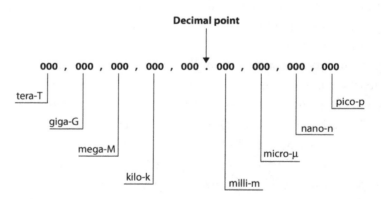

FIGURE 3.8

Engineering notation. (Adapted from an illustration in *Electronics Technology Fundamentals*.)

To use a number specified in engineering notation in an equation, visualize the prefix as ten to the specified power and move the decimal point the necessary number of places. For example, a 1kΩ resistor can also be visualized as 1,000Ω (1×10^3), and a 1MΩ resistor translates to 1,000,000Ω (1×10^6).

Practical Example of Ohm's Law

Moving back to Ohm's law, the concepts of units of measure and magnitude provide the information necessary to perform calculations with the equation. For example, a common formula that is used to calculate an appropriate resistor value for a circuit containing an LED is shown below. In this equation, the forward voltage is subtracted from available voltage and divided by the current (in amps) to yield the resistance—Ohm's law at work:

(Available voltage-forward voltage) / amount of current that should flow through LED

However, the current requirement is likely listed in milliamps (mA) on the *data sheet*—an informational guide provided by the manufacturer. To successfully apply the formula, the current must be rewritten in amps. Thus, for an available voltage of 5V, forward voltage of 1.8V, and required current of 15mA, the equation would be written as follows:

$$\frac{5V - 1.8V}{0.015A} = \frac{3.2V}{0.015A} = 220\Omega$$

The important thing to note is that the current, which was listed as 15mA, must be converted to amps to prior to being used in the equation:

$$15mA = 15 \times 10^{-3} = 0.015A$$

Using a Digital Multimeter

A digital multimeter (DMM) is a tool that can help you to develop a deeper understanding of concepts like current, voltage, and resistance. In fact, the function of the multimeter is to measure those basic electrical properties. If you have access to a meter, use it to measure the following properties in the circuit you just constructed.

Measuring Voltage

We will begin the exploration of the circuit by exploring the *potential difference* or *voltage drops* that occur in the circuit. There are two primary points to keep in mind. One is that such measurements are *relative* to a given point on the circuit. I've heard this concept described in terms of distance. You wouldn't, for example, ask someone how "far" they are because such a question only makes sense if you ask how far that person is from a known point. Similarly, when measuring voltage drops in a circuit, it only makes sense to reference the voltage in terms of a known reference. The second point to keep in mind is that the sum of the voltage drops in a circuit should equal the voltage supplied by the battery.[7]

A Few Words About Ground

This brings up an important point about the term *ground*. When talking about "mains" power (which is dangerous and will not be utilized in this book), *earth ground* refers to a physical connection between a circuit and an earth ground rod that is driven deep into the earth to take advantage of its "infinite charge neutrality."[8] For our purposes, the term ground can be thought of as the point of reference for a circuit. For example, the negative terminal of a 9V battery is used as the ground or point of reference for all of the circuits in this chapter. In this case, the positive terminal is at 9V relative to the 0V ground reference. However, in the case of two 1.5V batteries in series, the point of reference can be placed at the negative terminal of the first battery *or* between the batteries. In the first case, the voltage of the first and second battery are 1.5V and 3V with respect to ground. In contrast, when the ground reference is moved between the batteries, the negative terminal of the first battery is −1.5V relative to ground, and the positive lead of the second battery is +1.5V with respect to ground—termed a *common return* in this instance.[9]

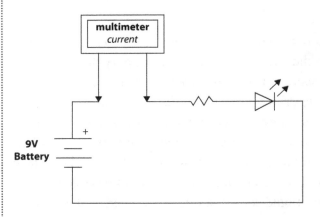

Moving back to the multimeter, to measure potential difference, set your digital multimeter to the volts DC setting and touch the leads to each side of a component as in Figure 3.9. Explore the concept of potential difference in the circuit and see if the readings add up to something close to the expected voltage of the battery.

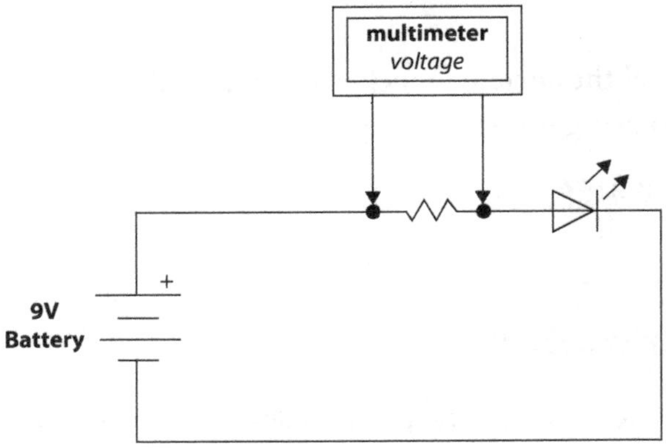

FIGURE 3.9

Multimeter: reading potential difference.

Measuring Current

Where voltage drops can be measured "passively" by connecting leads of the multimeter to components, the meter must be inserted directly into the circuit in order to measure current. Interestingly, current will be the same at all points in the circuit. Set your multimeter to an appropriate mA setting (e.g., a setting that is higher than the current to be read) and insert the leads into the circuit as in Figure 3.10. After taking the first reading, insert another resistor in series (i.e., daisy chained) and take a second reading. Such experimentation will help to solidify the concept that resistors limit current and that the same current is available to all the parts of the circuit.

FIGURE 3.10

Using a multimeter to measure current.

Measuring Resistance

Change the dial on your meter to the ohms (Ω) setting prior to measuring resistance. Resistance can't be measured with power applied to the circuit, so the best strategy, according to Paynter and Boydell, is often to "remove a resistor and test across the component."[10] They suggest the approach shown in Figure 3.11.

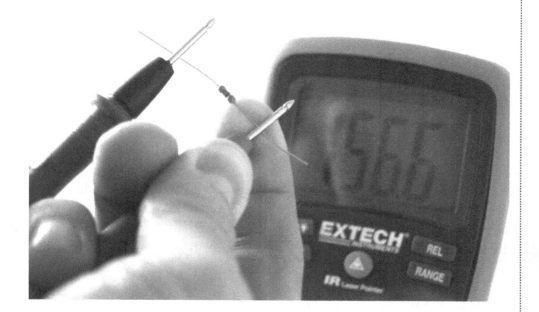

FIGURE 3.11

Using a multimeter to measure resistance.

Note how one hand holds the resistor to one of the test leads, but the other hand does not touch a lead. The built-in resistance of the body will change the results of the reading, so this strategy will provide the most accurate result. (You can avoid holding the resistor by attaching alligator clip probes.) Also note that in a series circuit (all of the components are connected end-to-end), you can calculate the total resistance in a circuit by summing all of the individual resistors.

Series Circuit

Total resistance $= R_1 + R_2 + R_3 \ldots$

Take a reading of the resistor and compare the reading to the expected value. You will likely notice a small discrepancy. Resistors are manufactured to perform within a specified tolerance such as 5 or 10 percent, so slight variations are to be expected. For critical application like digital audio converters, purchase resistors with lower tolerance.

68

Parallel Circuit

Although a detailed discussion of analyzing parallel circuits is beyond the scope of this book, it is helpful to understand that the total resistance in a parallel circuit will be *less* than the least resistive component. In a two-branch parallel circuit, the following formula can be used to determine total resistance:

$$\text{Total resistance} = \frac{R_1 R_2}{R_1 + R_2}$$

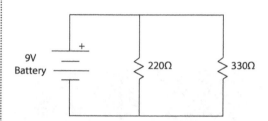

FIGURE 3.12

Parallel circuit with two resistors.

By way of example, consider a parallel circuit containing two resistors of 220Ω and 330Ω, respectively (see Figure 3.12).

Plugging the values into the formula for parallel resistance yields the following:

$$\text{Total resistance} = \frac{220 \times 330}{220 + 330} = \frac{72{,}600}{550} = 132\Omega$$

At this point in the chapter, you should have a good understanding of the relationship of voltage, current, and resistance, and you should be able to use a digital multimeter to explore voltage drops, current, and resistance. These theoretical concepts will provide a useful foundation for understanding and exploring circuits throughout the rest of the book.

A Word About Resistor Color Codes

For *standard precision* resistors, four color bands are used to encode the *nominal value* of the resistor and its *tolerance*.[11] Use the number column of Table 3.5 to determine the value of the resistor as follows:

First color

- Corresponds to the first digit of the resistor value.

Second color

- Corresponds to the second digit of the resistor value.

Third color

- If the third color is *not* gold or silver: color indicates the number of zeros
- If the third color is gold: multiply first two digits by. 1
- If the third color is silver: multiply first two digits by. 01

Let's look at two unknown resistors from my junk box to clarify the concept. The color sequence on the first resistor is orange, black, brown, and red. Plugging in values from Table 3.3 yields the following:

TABLE 3.3 Resistor Code: Example 1

Color	Number	Description
Orange	3	First digit
Black	0	Second digit
Brown	1	Number of zeros
Red	+/− 2%	Tolerance

TABLE 3.4 Resistor Code: Example 2

Color	Number	Description
Orange	3	First digit
Orange	3	Second digit
Yellow	4	Number of zeros
Gold	+/− 5%	Tolerance

TABLE 3.5 Resistor Color Codes

Color	Number	Tolerance
Black	0	+/− 20%
Brown	1	+/− 1%
Red	2	+/− 2%
Orange	3	+/− 3%
Yellow	4	+/− 4
Green	5	n/a
Blue	6	n/a
Violet	7	n/a
Gray	8	n/a
White	9	n/a
Gold	.1	+/− 5%
Silver	.01	+/− 10%

n/a = not applicable.

Value: $300\Omega\,(+/-2\%)$
Multimeter reading: 299.9Ω

As shown in Table 3.4, a second resistor has the color code of orange, orange, yellow, and gold, which translates to:

Value: $300,000\Omega$ $(330k)(+/-5\%)$
Multimeter reading: $332k\Omega$

Tip: For most hobbyists, it may be faster to use a multimeter to determine the value of an unknown resistor (as shown in Figure 3.11). Although a multimeter will not help you to determine the tolerance or "accuracy" of the resistor, it is the method I typically use unless I am concerned with tolerance.

Safety Diode and Potentiometer

Although the LED project works fine as is, there are a few modifications that could make it better. One is the addition of a component to adjust the brightness of the light. Imagine that you could somehow change the resistance of the resistor to allow more or less current to flow to the LED. This would have the effect of making the LED more or less bright. Fortunately there is such a component, known as a *variable resistor*, or, more commonly, a *potentiometer* or "*pot*."

Potentiometers have three prongs or connections. Although we will look at examples that utilize all three prongs later in this book, at this point only two prongs (the middle prong and one of the outer prongs) will be used in the circuit. I encourage you to use your multimeter to experiment with a potentiometer prior to using it in a circuit. Connect the leads of the multimeter to the center prong and one of the outer prongs and view the resistance using the ohms (Ω) setting on the multimeter. You will note that as you turn the shaft of the potentiometer, the resistance will vary from zero (or close to zero) to a resistance that is close to the amount of resistance listed on the potentiometer. Now, connect the leads to the other outer pin and center pin and note how adjustments to the shaft have the opposite effect (high to low resistance instead of low to high, for example).

Connect a 1MΩ (or 10kΩ or similar) potentiometer in series with the resistor as in Figure 3.13. The potentiometer can now be used to adjust the LED from off (or low depending on the value of the pot) to full brightness. (The fixed resistor is still required because when the potentiometer is adjusted so that it has no resistance, only the fixed resistor prevents the current from destroying the LED.) Figure 3.14 illustrates one way that the switch, resistor, potentiometer, and LED could be connected on a solderless breadboard.

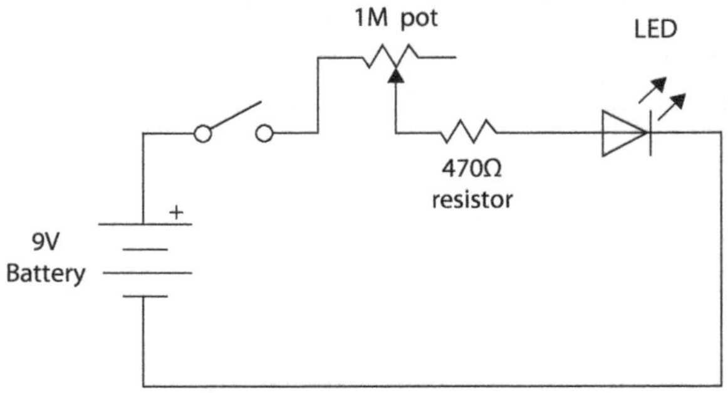

One other component, a safety diode, could be added to make a "perfect" LED flashlight. A diode is an electronic component that is similar to a one-way valve. Given that an LED can be damaged if current is applied to the wrong lead of the LED, a safety diode can be useful in preventing this problem. The diode is attached between the positive terminal of the battery and the power rail, and it will prevent current from flowing in the wrong direction should you inadvertently touch the wrong terminals of the battery to the snap connector. For clarity, I have

FIGURE 3.13

Adding a potentiometer to the LED circuit.

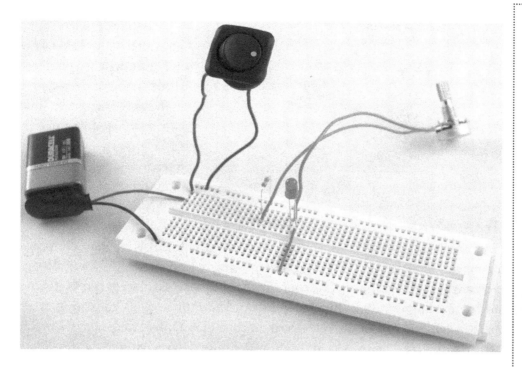

FIGURE 3.14

Photo of LED circuit with potentiometer.

elected not to use safety diodes in most of the circuits in the book, but you might want to consider leaving one plugged into your breadboard as you explore electronic circuits. The completed LED circuit is shown in Figure 3.15.

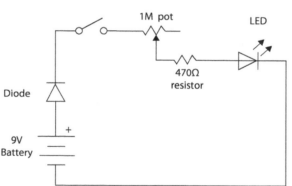

FIGURE 3.15

LED circuit with safety diode.

Emergency Music Stand Light

Although it was fun to work through a first electronics circuit, a few additional components could be added to make a truly useful project. In the last section we learned that resistors are used to limit current and that a variable resistor can provide a varying amount of current. A *photoresistor* is a unique component that provides a varying amount of resistance based on the amount of light. Resistance decreases when more light hits the surface of the photoresistor. In contrast, resistance increases in darker environments. We will use the photoresistor as the basis for an emergency music stand light. After completing this circuit you will have a small stand light that will turn on *automatically* if the lights suddenly dim or turn off. Add the photoresistor in lieu of the potentiometer that was used in the last iteration of the circuit. Connect the components as shown Figure 3.16, apply power, and try the circuit in a variety of light environments.

photoresistor

LED

470Ω
resistor

9V
Battery

+

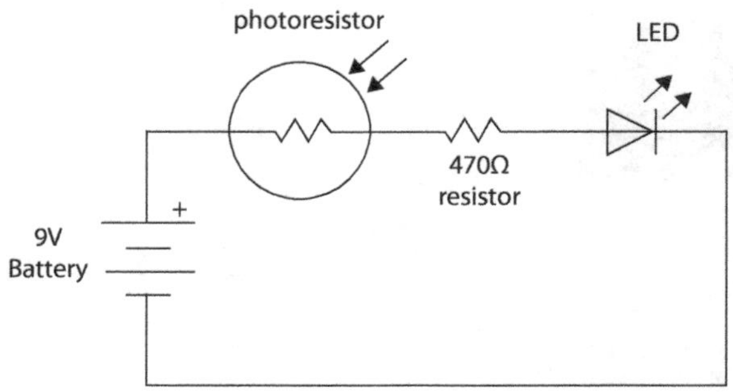

Astute readers may have already noticed a flaw in Figure 3.16. If a photoresistor has more resistance in dark environments, how can it be used to turn an LED on? To answer this question we will turn our attention to *transistors*.

FIGURE 3.16

Adding a photoresistor in lieu of a potentiometer.

Transistors

There are many flavors of transistors, but I will limit the discussion to the basics of *bipolar* transistors. NPN (negative/positive/negative) and PNP (positive/negative/positive) bipolar transistors are used for two primary tasks: switching and signal amplification. Bipolar transistors have three leads consisting of an *emitter*, *base*, and *collector*. When a small current is applied to the base, a much larger emitter-collector current is allowed to flow. In the context of the emergency stand light project, we will use varying current provided by the photoresistor to turn the LED on and off in response to changing light levels.

Before exploring transistors, it is important to understand that too much current or voltage can damage a transistor. (Transistors are similar to LEDs in that you should protect them with a resistor.) Also, it is important to avoid connecting the transistor backwards.

FIGURE 3.17

Circuit symbols for NPN and PNP transistors.

C

B

E

NPN

E

B

C

PNP

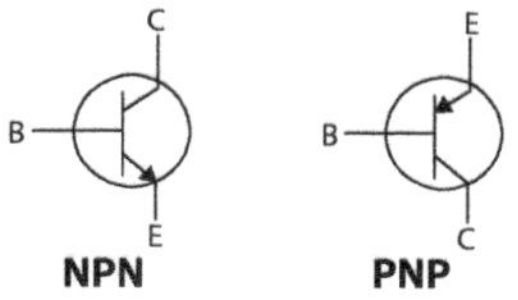

The symbols in Figure 3.17 are used to indicate NPN and PNP transistors in a circuit diagram. Note how the arrow points from the base to the emitter in an NPN transistor and the arrow points from the emitter to the base in a PNP transistor.

Both NPN and PNP transistors "block the flow of electricity between the collector and emitter"[12] in their passive state (although transistors do allow a small amount current to flow in the form of "leakage"). The primary difference between NPN and PNP transistors is the way the base reacts. In an NPN transistor, relatively positive voltage to the base causes current to flow from the collector to the emitter. In a PNP transistor, a relatively negative voltage to the base causes current to flow from the emitter to the collector. Figure 3.18, based on an illustration from Charles Platt's *Make: Electronics*, will help to illustrate the point:

FIGURE 3.18

NPN and PNP transistors.

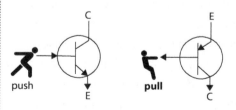

C

E

push

E

pull

C

Although there is a lot more to learn about transistors than can be covered in this necessarily short introduction, the primary concept to remember is that transistors can function like a switch or an amplifier. A small voltage or current applied to the base can cause a larger current to flow through the emitter and collector.

Incorporating a Photoresistor and Transistor

As you can see in Figure 3.19, an illustration based on a diagram in *Hacking Electronics*,[13] an NPN transistor functions something like a potentiometer that is controlled by light. In this example, the photoresistor and 10k resistor form a light-sensitive voltage divider. In light, the resistance of the photoresistor decreases, causing a decrease in the voltage applied to the base of the transistor. In darkness, the resistance of the photoresistor increases, causing an increase in voltage to the base of the transistor. *Note*: It might be helpful to experiment with different LED and resistor combinations (using the formula from the section titled Practical Example of Ohm's Law) to tailor the project to your needs. For example, the more diffuse light produced by a "straw hat" LED may be more helpful than a more directional LED. It may also be helpful to place the LED in front of a reflector (or inside a quilted jelly jar) for additional distribution of light.

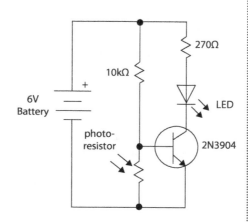

One version of the finished emergency music stand light is shown in Figure 3.20. You may want to read the chapter on soldering at this point if you are anxious to finalize a first project, or you might want to wait to see what other things can be done with a photoresistor. Ideas might include a light-activated filter or light-controlled "mood sound machine."

Cigar Box Amplifier

We will look at two more circuits prior to learning how to integrate circuits and code with an Arduino in Chapter 4. In this section you will learn how to breadboard a "Cigar Box Amplifier," a battery-powered amplifier and speaker that will can be used to amplify many of the projects in this book (see Figure 3.21).

73

FIGURE 3.19

Emergency stand light circuit.

FIGURE 3.20

Photo of completed emergency stand light.

3.1 EMERGENCY STAND LIGHT

74

FIGURE 3.21

Photo of Cigar Box "Screamer" Amplifier.

Not only is the project fun to build, it will provide a vehicle to talk about capacitors and operational amplifiers, two of the most useful and prevalent electronic components. Although the project will be constructed on a solderless breadboard, more experienced readers may want to create a finished version in an appropriate enclosure. (See Chapter 11 for more information regarding soldering and project construction.)

Operational Amplifier

The heart of the amplifier is a useful component called an *operational amplifier* or "*op-amp*" for short. Op-amps "amplify the *difference* between voltages or signals (AC or DC) applied to their two inputs. The voltage applied to only one input will be amplified if the second input is grounded or maintained at some voltage level."[14]

In a circuit diagram, op-amps are usually shown as a triangle with two inputs and a single output. In actuality, additional connections will be required to power the circuit. As you will learn in other projects throughout the book, some op-amps require a dual (+/−) power source, while others are designed to work with a single positive supply. In terms of output, some op-amps are "*rail to rail*," that is, the output can swing close to the positive and negative values of the supply voltage.

The Cigar Box Amp will utilize an LM386 amplifier. Although the LM386 is not an op-amp in the traditional sense (it is designed to be a power amplifier), its form and function is similar to some of the op-amps featured in other places in the book. While the LM386 isn't the most pristine amplifier in the world (the output is actually fairly noisy), it is inexpensive, easy to use, and will be a good choice for a first power amplifier project.

Look at Figure 3.22 and familiarize yourself with the numbering scheme that is used to identify pins on the device. When using op-amps and integrated circuits, it is important to remember that the pins are counted starting from the lower left (assuming the notch is on the left side) and moving counterclockwise

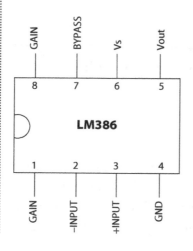

FIGURE 3.22

Pin layout of LM386 including notch on left side.

around the component. Further, some kind of notch or indentation will indicate the left side or lower-left side of the component. Unfortunately, the pin assignments on the device rarely match the layout of pins in a circuit diagram— the goal of a circuit diagram is to present the information in the clearest possible way, but it is im-

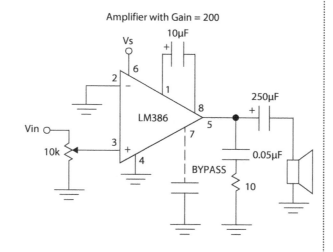

FIGURE 3.23

LM386 circuit (note different order of pins in circuit schematic).

portant to remember to connect pins according to their physical layout on the device—not the arbitrary ordering of pins you will likely see in a circuit diagram (see Figure 3.23).

Let's unpack the amplifier circuit diagram shown in Figure 3.23. As with many circuit schematics used in audio, signals flow from left to right (input to output) while power is generally shown on the top and ground connections are shown on the bottom of the schematic. In this case, the input signal runs through a 10kΩ potentiometer into pin three, thus, the potentiometer can be used to adjust the level of the signal. Although any 10kΩ potentiometer will work, a *logarithmic* pot is preferred over a *linear* pot in this application. Our ears respond logarithmically to sound levels, so a logarithmic pot will feel the most natural as you turn the level of the signal up and down. As is also evident in the diagram, pins 2 and 4 connect to ground, and the positive terminal of the battery (denoted by the voltage supply symbol) connects to pin 6. It is also helpful to note that individual ground connections are shown in this example. Many schematics show ground connections in this way for clarity, but understand that the individual symbols all refer to the *same* ground rail on your solderless breadboard.

Capacitors

One of the symbols, the figure representing a *capacitor*, may look unfamiliar to some readers. Capacitors store electrons and are often used in conjunction with resistors to filter signals, or to "smooth" a power supply. It might be helpful to visualize the function of a capacitor almost like a temporary battery in that capacitors "fill up" with electrons. Capacitors also have the unique property of blocking DC current when they are full.

There are a number of categories of capacitors, including ceramic, polystyrene, mica, and electrolytic. We will primarily use *ceramic* and *electrolytic* capacitors in the projects in this book. Ceramic capacitors are not polarized—they don't have a positive or negative side. In this way they are similar to resistors and

FIGURE 3.24

Nonpolarized capacitor symbols.

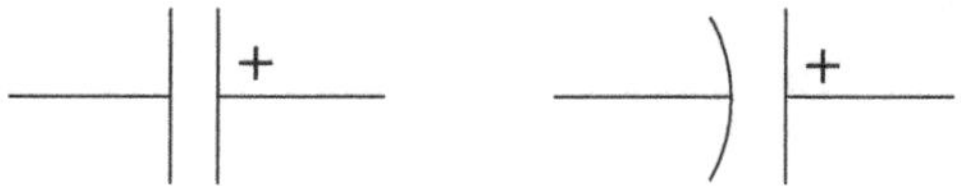

FIGURE 3.25

Two common polarized capacitor symbols.

can be connected in either orientation. Common symbols for non-polarized capacitors are shown in Figure 3.24.

In contrast, electrolytic capacitors are polarized and, thus, must be connected in the proper orientation to prevent damaging the capacitor or other components in the circuit.[15] The positive (+) lead of an electrolytic capacitor should be more positive than the negative (−) lead. (There is usually a symbol to indicate the positive or negative wire on an electrolytic capacitor.) The symbols shown in Figure 3.25 are commonly used to indicate polarized capacitors.

Calculating Capacitance

The formulas for calculating capacitance in a circuit might be described as "similar but opposite" to the formulas for calculating resistance. The total capacitance of a parallel circuit can be found by adding the values or all the capacitors:

Parallel Circuit

$$\text{Total capacitance} = C_1 + C_2$$

However, the total capacitance in a series circuit is found as follows:

Series Circuit

$$\text{Total capacitance} = \frac{C_1 \times C_2}{C_1 + C_2}$$

Although the analysis of complex circuits is beyond the scope of this book, the total capacitance for multiple series capacitors can be found with the following formula:

$$\text{Total capacitance} = \frac{1}{\dfrac{1}{C_1} + \dfrac{1}{C_2} + \dfrac{1}{C_3} \cdots}$$

Capacitors are used for three different applications in the "Cigar Box" amplifier circuit. A relatively large electrolytic capacitor (at least 100μF) helps to smooth the power supply from the battery. A way to visualize this process is to think of the way the stream of water from a faucet may slow down when a toilet is flushed. The power-smoothing capacitor is functionally similar to the idea of adding a small reservoir of water just prior to a tap to prevent a large draw of water (e.g., a flushing toilet) from temporarily affecting the supply of water to the tap.

A second application of a capacitor in the amplifier circuit is to (optionally) connect pins 1 and 8. When a 10μF capacitor is added, the gain of the amplifier is increased from 20 to 200. One option, which I used in the Cigar Amplifier project, is to add a switch to toggle between low and high gain as needed. Although a gain selection switch is not shown in the diagram, simply add a SPST switch between the first pin and the bridging capacitor.

Finally, one or more capacitors are used between the output of pin 5 and the speaker. The. 1μF capacitor and 10Ω resistor form a *Boucherot cell* (also called a *Zobel network*) that is used to "dampen out high frequency oscillations."[16] The 250μF capacitor blocks the *DC component*—which might be thought of as a sort of base that the signal rides on—from reaching (and potentially damaging) the speaker (more information is provided later in the book).

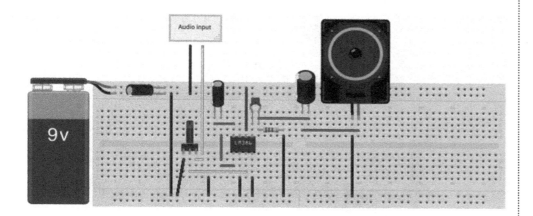

FIGURE 3.26

Breadboard version of Cigar Box Amplifier.

The breadboard version of the amplifier can be seen in the Figure 3.26. I encourage you to explore the circuit by trying different combinations of components (e.g., power-smoothing capacitor but no Boucherot cell, or no power-smoothing capacitor with a high-gain capacitor). It is interesting and informative to hear the effect of the various components on an audio signal.

Connecting an Audio Signal to the Amplifier

Test leads can be used to connect a 1/4" or 1/8" plug to the test circuit as shown in Figure 3.27, and an audio jack can be utilized in a finished version of the project.

Completed Project

One approach to a finished version of the project is shown in Figure 3.28. Readers might want to skip ahead to Chapter 11, Finalizing Projects, to learn how to solder and construct projects similar to the one in the photo.

3.2 CIGAR BOX AMPLIFIER

78

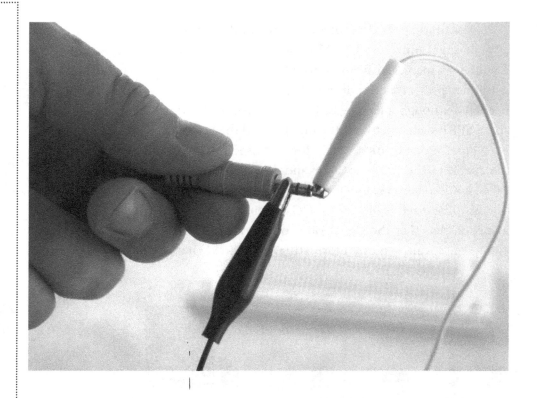

FIGURE 3.27

Using test leads to connect an audio plug to the breadboard.

FIGURE 3.28

Completed Cigar Box Amplifier.

Simple Theremin

A final demonstration project that will be of interest to many readers is the "Simple Theremin." Leon Theremin (1896–1993) was a Russian physicist who developed an innovative electronic instrument in which the pitch and amplitude of the instrument is controlled by the proximity of a performer's hands to

the circuit. The Simple Theremin is a simplified version of the original instrument.

The project, which was adapted from a circuit at http://loublett .blogspot.com/, features many of the components in this chapter, including resistors, capacitors, and potentiometers. The project also utilizes two inexpensive integrated circuits: a 4069 Hex Inverter and 4046 Phase-Locked Loop.

Hex Inverter

We won't go into the details of the function of each component other than to summarize the basics. The Hex Inverter shown in Figure 3.29 contains six digital inverter gates. The output of pin 15 is a steady square wave when the IC is configured as shown in the illustration. The square wave signal is routed to pin 14 of the 4046 Phase-Locked Loop integrated circuit.

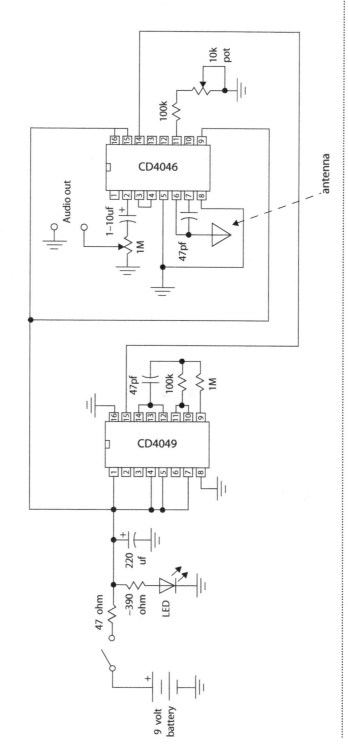

3.3 SIMPLE THEREMIN

FIGURE 3.29

Simple Theremin circuit.

Phase-Locked Loop IC

The Phase-Locked Loop integrated circuit contains a voltage-controlled oscillator and three phase comparators. Comparator 1 is an XOR gate that produces a fluctuating voltage on pin 2 based on the signal input and comparator input as shown in Figure 3.30.

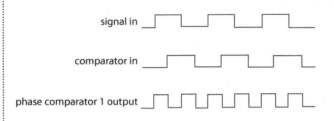

FIGURE 3.30

Typical phase comparator 1 waveforms.

The resistor and potentiometer connected between pin 11 and ground work in conjunction with the antenna and capacitor connected to pins 6 and 7 to determine the frequency range. Interestingly, the capacitance changes as a hand or other object is placed in proximity to the antenna, so changes in hand position result in changes in frequency.

Mocking Up the Simple Theremin

Although the circuit in Figure 3.29 might seem complicated at first glance, it is not unduly difficult to connect the components on a solderless breadboard. For example, many of the connections are between a pin and the 9V power supply or through one or more components to ground. Start on the left side of the schematic and work your way to the right routing each pin or component as necessary. Figure 3.31 demonstrates one approach to mocking up the circuit on a breadboard.

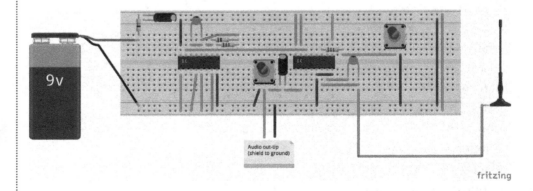

FIGURE 3.31

Simple Theremin breadboard.

Note that it is not necessary to connect a "real" antenna. A length of rigid copper wire or other metal object can be connected to the circuit with alligator clips. Also note that an optional LED is not shown in the illustration.

Conclusion

We have covered much ground in this chapter, but the concepts provide a necessary foundation for getting the most out of Arduino microcontrollers. I have noticed in my own work that, often, the simple act of breadboarding a circuit like the Cigar Box amplifier or Simple Theremin multiple times can help me to more quickly internalize and master the underlying concepts. In a way, the process of connecting components with hookup wire is similar to the process of rewriting notes after listening to a lecture. The process provides a proactive, hands-on affirmation of the function and logic associated with the given circuit and can facilitate learning. Also keep in mind that though there are many new terms and concepts in this chapter, there are only a few primary electronic components that form the backbone of most circuits. Bringing the discussion back to music, these concepts are the notes, chords, and rhythms that can help you to "compose" some interesting electronic devices. In the next chapter we begin to apply these concepts to the Arduino platform, where software and hardware are combined to form an ensemble of functionality.

4

Interfacing with Arduino

Chapters 2 and 3 were devoted to the core concepts of the C-language and electronic fundamentals. In this chapter, programming and circuitry are combined in the form of a first full-fledged project, an Arduino metronome. Although a metronome is not necessarily the most flashy device, it will be a good project from a pedagogic standpoint: metronomes are frequently used by musicians, so a metronome project provides an opportunity to relate programming and electronic concepts to something that will be familiar to most readers. For example, it is one thing to describe the use of a potentiometer to vary current, but it much more intuitive to show how a potentiometer or rotary encoder can be used to alter tempo. For this reason, the metronome will provide a good vehicle to explore a variety of components including potentiometers, momentary switches, LEDs, and rotary encoders. By the end of the chapter you will have a good understanding of how software and hardware work together in a useful Arduino project, and the concepts will form another layer of knowledge for the more complex projects that are presented later in the book.

Some readers may wonder about the cost of using an Arduino to build something that can be purchased for less than $10 at a music store. That is a good question, and it was a question that crossed my mind several times when I started working with the Arduino. The good news is that the core components of an Arduino (ATMega chip, voltage regulator, clock crystal, various resistors and capacitors) can be purchased for less than $10. Thus, it is economically feasible to build an inexpensive metronome. In fact, an entire chapter (Chapter 12,

Standalone Arduino) is devoted to the process of creating inexpensive Arduino projects. For now, use a breadboard to mock up the various iterations of the metronome, and give some thought to the features that your final version might include. Also keep in mind that, by doing the work yourself, you will have the opportunity to add unique features such as a metronome that emphasizes strong beats and has memory locations to store frequently used tempos or other useful features.

Overview of Arduino UNO

Before we look at interfacing a first circuit with the Arduino, it will be helpful to look at the various pins that are found on an Arduino UNO board and to discuss a few cautions that can help to prevent damage to your Arduino.

Hold the Arduino Uno with the USB connector facing to the left and look for the pins shown in Figure 4.1. Near the bottom of the board you will see a row of pins with markings including Reset, 3.3V, 5V, and so on. The pins (under the word POWER) are used to power the circuits you will connect to the Arduino. Most circuits in this book will use 5V and ground (GND). (In this context, ground simply means zero volts.) "It is the

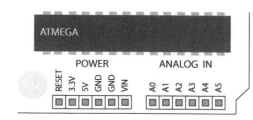

FIGURE 4.1

Power and analog section.

reference voltage to which all other voltages on the board are relative."[1] Use hookup wire to connect 5V and ground to the appropriate rails on your breadboard. Some electronic components require 3.3 volts, so the 3.3V jack can be used, if necessary, to power those circuits. The reset pin can be used to "reboot" the Arduino by momentarily connecting the pin to 0V.

In the same region of the board, you will also see six pins labeled A0–A5. These are the analog pins and are used to measure components such as potentiometers and photoresistors that provide varying voltage (as opposed to digital on/off values). (Incidentally, the analog pins can also be configured to function as regular digital pins.)

Now, look at the headers at the top of the Arduino (see Figure 4.2). The digital pins (0–13), can be configured to function as digital inputs or outputs. When used as an output, you can configure the pin (via software) to output either HIGH (5V) or LOW (0V). Digital pins are typically used to track the status of a switch (on or off), light an LED, or interface with digital integrated circuits. As you

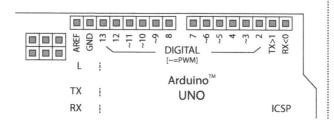

FIGURE 4.2

Digital section.

will see in Chapter 9 (Audio Output and Sound Synthesis), the digital pins can also be used to output a variety of waveforms.

Some digital pins have a tilde (~) mark. Pins with such a mark are capable of *pulse- width-modulation (PWM)*, a technique that can be used to modulate the output of the pins. A common application involves changing the perceived brightness of an LED connected to one of the PWM digital pins. The LED will be perceived as being fully bright if the output of the pin is 5V (and the LED is connected to an appropriate current-limiting resistor). Now, imagine that the pin alternates at a fast rate such that half the time it is at 5V and the other half at 0V. If the pin alternates at a fast enough rate the eye will not perceive any flicker, but the LED will appear to dim by 50 percent. You will learn more about pulse width modulation later in the book.

A Caution

As Dale Wheat notes on his book *Arduino Internals*, "each of the I/O pins on the Atmel AVR can sink or source up to 40mA at 5.0V. That's perfect for driving LEDs! However, you can't drive two 20mA LEDs from every pin of the chip (at least not at the same time) because of the 200mA overall device limitation."[2] What this means is that you need to be careful to avoid trying to drive certain devices directly from the pins: motors and speakers, for example, *cannot* be directly driven because they will draw too much current and may damage the Arduino. Although the digital pins can drive an LED, you have to be careful not to exceed the overall 200mA device limitation.

Overview of the Metronome Project

The following pages are devoted to several versions of a metronome project. Each iteration will provide an opportunity to learn about a new component, so it will be helpful to mock up (and experiment with) all of the examples in order to internalize the concepts.

Metronome with Speaker

The first iteration of the metronome project builds on the flashing light sketch from Chapter 2, Introduction to Programming. In order to make an audible clicking sound, connect a small 8 ohm speaker through a 100 ohm resistor to one of the digital pins as in Figure 4.3. Don't worry if the sound level is low, an amplifier subcircuit will be added to a later iteration of the project.

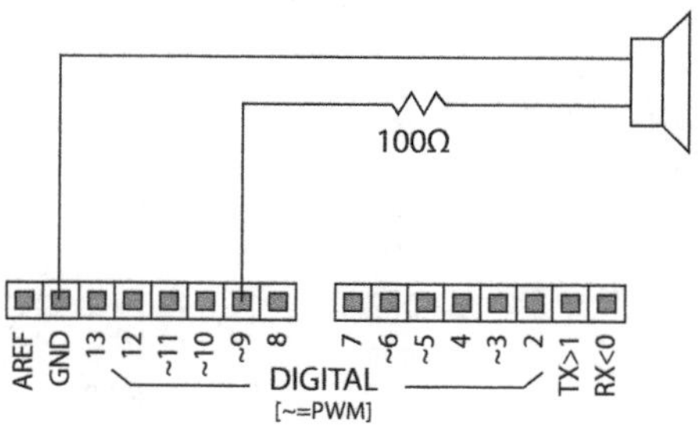

The software for a basic metronome is relatively simple (see Listing 4.1). In the main *loop()*, the sketch calls a built-in function called *tone()*,

FIGURE 4.3

Metronome with speaker and 100Ω resistor.

100Ω

AREF GND 13 ~12 ~11 ~10 ~9 8   7 ~6 ~5 4 ~3 2 TX>1 RX<0

DIGITAL [~=PWM]

which outputs a tone at with the specified frequency and duration. To my ear, a value of 880 Hz and a duration of 50 ms worked well, so I defined constants to represent those values. Another constant, *speakerPin*, is set to the same pin that is connected to the speaker (pin 9 in this case). A variable, *delay_per_beat*, is used to store the amount of time to delay between clicks. Although *delay_per_beat* is essentially a constant in this sketch, other iterations of the metronome will change the value as the sketch runs.

The *setup()* method requires some explanation. Musicians are obviously accustomed to working with beats per minute instead of milliseconds per beat, so it made sense to calculate an appropriate delay in milliseconds based on a given tempo such as 60 beats per minute. Although this version of the program does not accept a variable tempo as input, that functionality will be developed in other versions of the program. The calculation is simple: 60/BPM yields the duration of a beat in seconds (e.g., 60 BPM equals a 1-second beat, 120 BPM equals a half-second beat, and so on). The product of the duration in seconds times 1000 yields the amount of delay in milliseconds (thousandths of a second). The complete listing is shown in Listing 4.1:

Listing 4.1

```
//Arduino for Musicians
//Listing 4.1: Metronome 1

//Constants for output of tone to speaker
const int speakerPin = 9;
const int frequency = 880;
const int duration = 50;

//Variable to track time delay
unsigned int MS_per_beat = 0;

void setup()
{
    //Calculate the amount of delay:
    //milliseconds per minute/beats per minute
    unsigned int milliseconds_per_minute = 1000 * 60;
    unsigned int beats_per_minute = 60;
    MS_per_beat = milliseconds_per_minute/beats_per_minute;
}

void loop()
{
    //Output the tone
    tone(speakerPin, frequency, duration);

    //Delay loop for specified amount of time
    delay(MS_per_beat);
}
```

Metronome with Potentiometer

A metronome with a hard-coded tempo is obviously not very helpful, but there are a number of electronic components that can be utilized to allow a user to

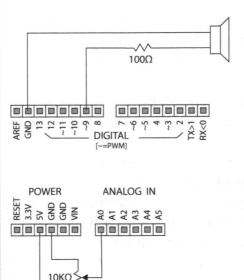

FIGURE 4.4

Metronome with 10K pot.

interact with the program. One approach is to use a potentiometer. As you may recall from Chapter 3, a potentiometer or "pot" is component that can function as a variable resistor. When a potentiometer is connected to the Arduino as in Figure 4.4, it functions as a voltage divider. Be sure to connect the center wiper to A0 and the outer pins to 5V and ground respectively to avoid a short across the pins.

The *analogRead()* method is used to take readings from the wiper or center post of the potentiometer. The readings will be in the range of 0 to 1,023, which represents a voltage range of 0V to 5 V. Though a range of 0 to 1,023 is not very useful for a metronome, the *map()* function can be used to scale or "map" the values to a more useful range. The *map()* function takes a given value (the value returned by *analogRead()* in this instance), the expected range (0–1,023), and the ideal range (the tempo range in this case) as parameters.

```
int map(value, fromLow, fromHigh, toLow, toHigh)
```

The function will return a number that has been scaled to the ideal range. An example will help to clarify the concept: A useful range of tempos for a metronome is in the range of about 30 to 350 BPM. If the user adjusts the potentiometer to the midpoint of its range, the *analogRead()* method will return a value of 511 (half the expected range of 0–1,023). Given a tempo range of 30 to 350 BPM, the map() function would return a value of 160 (halfway between the tempo range of 30–350) for the value returned by *analogRead()*.

There are a few additional adjustments to the first version of the source code (see Listing 4.2). One change is to move the local variable, *beats_per_minute*, from the *setup()* function so that it has global scope. Although users still won't be able to visualize tempos when selecting values with a potentiometer, that functionality will be added in later versions of the program. Another change is that a constant, *potPin*, is assigned to the value of analog pin 0 (A0). One other change is that a new variable, *potValue*, is used to track the value of the potentiometer. The value of the pot is read with *analogRead()* during each iteration of the loop and assigned to the local variable, *value*. If *value* and *potValue* are not equal, it indicates that the potentiometer has changed. (Note that this value may fluctuate slightly on its own depending on the position of the pot.

You might want to add a "fudge" factor to control such fluctuations. For example, you could check to see if *value* is greater than *potValue* plus 2 or less than *potValue* minus 2.)

Listing 4.2

```
//Arduino for Musicians
//Listing 4.2: Metronome with potentiometer

//Constants for output of tone to speaker
const int speakerPin = 9;
const int frequency = 880;
const int duration = 50;

//Potentiometer pin:
const int potPin = 0;

//Variable to track the value of the pot
int potValue;

//Variables to track tempo and time delay
unsigned int beats_per_minute = 60;
unsigned int MS_per_beat = 0;

void setup()
{
    //Calculate MS_per_beat based on tempo in BPM
    unsigned int milliseconds_per_minute = 1000 * 60;
    MS_per_beat = milliseconds_per_minute/beats_per_minute;

}

void loop()
{
    //Check the status of the potentiometer:
    int value = analogRead(potPin);

    //Recalculate the tempo if the value has changed.
    if(value != potValue)
    {
        //Map the value to a reasonable metronome range of
        //30 BPM to 350 BPM
        beats_per_minute = map(value, 0, 1023, 30, 350);

        //Recalculate the delay time
        unsigned int milliseconds_per_minute = 1000 * 60;
        MS_per_beat = milliseconds_per_minute/beats_per_
        minute;

        //Update potValue
        potValue = value;

    }

    //Output the tone
    tone(speakerPin, frequency, duration);

    //Delay loop for specified amount of time
    delay(MS_per_beat);
}
```

Metronome with Pushbutton Switch

It is fairly annoying to have a metronome running nonstop. A momentary switch (pushbutton) can be incorporated to allow a user to turn the metronome on and off.

Switch with Resistor

There are two common ways of approaching the use of a momentary switch on the Arduino. One approach is to use the circuit shown in Figure 4.5. In this

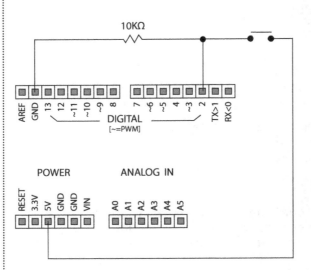

example, one pin of a momentary pushbutton switch is connected to a digital pin on the Arduino through a 10kΩ resistor connected to ground. The other pin connects to 5V. The button is connected to digital pin 2, and the status of the button is read using the *digitalRead()* function. Listing 4.3 shows the relevant changes. Note how the function *pinMode()* is called in *setup()* to establish that the pin will be used for input.

FIGURE 4.5

Switch circuit with 10kΩ resistor.

Listing 4.3 Reading the value of a switch (external 10k resistor)

```
//Arduino for Musicians
//Listing 4.3: Switch with 10k external pullup resistor

const int buttonPin = 2;      // pushbutton pin

int last_state      = 0;      //Stores the last state of the
                              //pushbutton

void setup()
{
    Serial.begin(9600);
    // initialize pushbutton pin as an input
    pinMode(buttonPin, INPUT);
}

void loop()
{
    // check the pubshbutton state
    int state = digitalRead(buttonPin);

    //Print the state if it has changed
    if(state != last_state)
    {
        Serial.println(state);
        last_state = state;    //Update the button state
    }
}
```

Switch with Pullup Resistor

Another approach is to use an internal *pullup* resistor. As Paul Scherz and Simon Monk note in their wonderful book, *Practical Electronics for Inventors*, "…a pullup resistor is used to keep an input high that would otherwise float if left unconnected. If you want to set the 'pulled up' input low, you can ground the pin, say, via a switch."[3] As is evident in Figure 4.6, the legs of the switch are connected to a digital input and ground, respectively, and an internal pullup resistor is activated in software.

When an internal pullup resistor is used, a value of HIGH (5V) is read when the button is open, and a value of LOW (0V) is read when the button causes the connection to ground to be completed. An excerpt of code for using a switch with a pullup resistor is shown in Listing 4.4. Take special note of how the pullup resistor is activated in the *setup()* function:

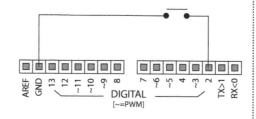

FIGURE 4.6

Switch connected to digital pin and ground. (Pullup resistor activated in software.)

89

Listing 4.4 Activating a pullup resistor and reading the value of a switch

```
//Arduino for Musicians
//Listing 4.4: Switch internal pullup resistor

const int buttonPin = 2;      // pushbutton pin

int last_state      = 0;      //Stores the last state of the
                              //pushbutton

void setup()
{
    Serial.begin(9600);
    //set up the internal pullup resistor on digital pin 2
    pinMode(buttonPin, INPUT_PULLUP);
}

void loop()
{
    // check the pubshbutton state
    int state = digitalRead(buttonPin);

    //Print the state if it has changed
    //NOTE: Button press == LOW
    if(state != last_state)
    {
        Serial.println(state);
        last_state = state;     //Update the button state
    }
}
```

Debouncing

One of the problems with most momentary switches is that the transition between states is often "dirty." The symptom is a button that seems to behave erratically. For example, the button may cause the metronome to run and immediately turn off, or it might take several presses to trigger an event. In order to avoid such problems, switches must usually be *debounced*. Debouncing can be accomplished by adding additional logic in software, or additional circuitry can be added to stabilize the switch. I will use the software approach throughout the book since software debouncing can be easily handled by the Arduino.

One somewhat kludgy method of debouncing a switch is to add a delay statement to allow the button to stabilize after noting a change in the status of the switch (see Listing 4.5).

Listing 4.5 Kludgy button debounce

```
//Check for button press
if(button_state == LOW && button_state != pushButtonStatus)
{
    //update button status;
    pushButtonStatus = button_state;
    //Use delay for a kludgy form of debouncing
    delay(20);
}
```

Although this approach will work fine for a metronome where precise stops and starts are not required, the delay method is generally a bad idea since it actually stops the execution of the program and other events, such as another button press, might be missed. As you will see in later chapters, a more elegant solution is to use a special *EasyButton* class that utilizes its own internal counting mechanism.

The next iteration of the metronome has several new features (see Listing 4.6). One change is that a new constant and two variables are added to track the status of the button and whether the metronome is on or off (tracked by the global boolean variable, *on*).

Listing 4.6 Global variables and constants

```
//Switch pin:
const int pushButtonPin = 2;

//Variable to track pushbutton status
int pushButtonStatus = HIGH;

//A boolean variable to track if metronome is on or off:
boolean on = false;
```

A new function, *checkPushButton()*, is added to track the state of the on/off switch. The function checks to see if the button state is currently low (indicating a button press) and that the button status is not already low. If those conditions are met, the current "on" state is swapped from true to false (or vice versa) using the following line of code. Although the logic might seem unclear, you could read the statement as "the status of *on* equals the opposite of on":

```
on =! on;
```

The *checkPushButton()* function also checks for the button to be released (button_state is high) and resets *pushButtonStatus* to the new status:

Listing 4.7 checkPushButton() function

```
void checkPushButton()
{
    //Check digital pin 2 for a button press
    int button_state = digitalRead(pushButtonPin);

    //Check for button press
    if(button_state == LOW && button_state !=
    pushButtonStatus)
    {
        //Swap on/off states
        on =! on;
        //update buttonStatus;
        pushButtonStatus = button_state;
        //Use delay for a kludgy form of debouncing
        delay(20);
    }
    //Check for button release
    if(button_state == HIGH && button_state !=
    pushButtonStatus)
    {
        //Updtate the pushbutton status to off
        pushButtonStatus = button_state;
        delay(20);
    }
}
```

Checking the Value of the Potentiometer

Yet another change is that the code for checking the potentiometer is moved to a new function named *checkPot()*. Although the new function is not the best since it is overly program specific (it's always best to strive to write functions that can be used in other sketches), it does clean up the code considerably. The pushbutton and pot can be checked from within the main loop as follows:

```
void loop()
{
    checkPushButton();
    checkPot();
    .
    .
    .
}
```

Improving Tone-Generation Logic

In the first two iterations of the program, the *delay()* function was used to pause the metronome between clicks. As was mentioned previously, it is generally a bad idea to use the *delay()* function in your code because the program might become unresponsive to button presses and other events. The *delay()* function also precludes some of the most interesting things you can do with audio such as Direct Digital Synthesis. For this reason, a more "noninvasive" approach is required to produce metronome clicks. The new loop() method checks the current time (in milliseconds) by calling the *millis()* function—a function that returns the number of milliseconds that have elapsed since the start of the program—at the start of each loop. Next, the program checks the value of *current_time* against a new global long integer, *last_time*, to see if the given amount of delay time has elapsed. When an appropriate amount of delay has elapsed and the variable *on* is "true," a tone is emitted and the variable *last_time* is updated to the current time. The relevant code is shown in Listing 4.8:

Listing 4.8 Tracking time using the *millis()* function

```
//Play a tone if the metronome is on.
 long current_time = millis();
 if((current_time - last_time >= MS_per_beat) && on ==
 true)
 {
     //Output the tone
     tone(speakerPin, frequency, duration);
     last_time = current_time;
 }
```

Complete Source Code

The entire sketch is shown in Listing 4.9. I encourage you to spend time following the flow of the program. The new functions clarify the logic, and the new approach to tracking time makes the program much more responsive to button presses and changes in the state of the potentiometer. Also consider other possible enhancements: for example, it might be nice to track strong and weak beats and adjust the tone() function accordingly, or it could be useful to add another potentiometer to set the number of beats.

Listing 4.9 Complete metronome source code

```
//Arduino for Musicians
//Listing 4.9: Metronome 3 (Complete Metronome)

//Constants for output of tone to speaker
const int speakerPin = 9;
const int frequency = 880;
const int duration = 50;

//Potentiometer pin:
const int potPin = 0;

//Variable to track the value of the pot
int potValue;

//Switch pin:
const int pushButtonPin = 2 ;
```

```
//Variable to track pushbutton status
int pushButtonStatus = HIGH;

//A boolean variable to track if metronome is on or off:
boolean on = false;

//Variables to track tempo and time delay
unsigned int beats_per_minute = 60;
unsigned int MS_per_beat = 0;

//Variable to track time
long last_time = 0;

void setup()
{
    //Set the digital pin for input and pullup resistor:
    pinMode(pushButtonPin, INPUT_PULLUP);

    //Calculate MS_per_beat based on tempo in BPM
    unsigned int milliseconds_per_minute = 1000 * 60;
    MS_per_beat = milliseconds_per_minute/beats_per_minute;
}

void loop()
{
    checkPushButton();
    checkPot();

    //Play a tone if the metronome is on.
    long current_time = millis();
    if((current_time - last_time >= MS_per_beat) && on ==
    true)
    {
        //Output the tone
        tone(speakerPin, frequency, duration);
        last_time = current_time;
    }
}

void checkPot()
{
    //Check the status of the potentiometer:
    int value = analogRead(potPin);

    //Re-calculate the tempo if the value has changed.
    if(value != potValue)
    {
        //Map the value to a reasonable metronome range of
        //30 BPM to 350 BPM
        beats_per_minute = map(value, 0, 1023, 30, 350);

        //Recalculate the delay time
        unsigned int milliseconds_per_minute = 1000 * 60;
        MS_per_beat = milliseconds_per_minute/beats_per_
        minute;

        //Update potValue
        potValue = value;
    }
}
```

```
void checkPushButton()
{
    //Check digital pin 2 for a button press
    int button_state = digitalRead(pushButtonPin);

    //Check for button press
    if(button_state == LOW && button_state !=
    pushButtonStatus)
    {
        //Swap on/off states
        on =! on;

        //update buttonStatus;
        pushButtonStatus = button_state;
        //Use delay for a kludgy form of debouncing
        delay(20);
    }
    //Check for button release
    if(button_state == HIGH && button_state !=
    pushButtonStatus)
    {
        //Updtate the pushbutton status to off
        pushButtonStatus = button_state;
        delay(20);
    }
}
```

Metronome with Quadrature Rotary Encoder

A fourth iteration of the metronome will incorporate a *quadrature rotary encoder*. Where a potentiometer is an analog component, rotary encoders are devices that produce a digital output in response to clockwise or counterclockwise movement of a shaft. Although a rotary encoder is not necessarily a better choice for tempo control in this context, the component does have the potential of providing more precise input. Rotary encoders are also useful since there are no stops—they can make an unlimited number of turns in either direction. Given that encoders are useful for many types of input, we will look at the circuits and code that are necessary to incorporate these useful components.

Rotary Encoder

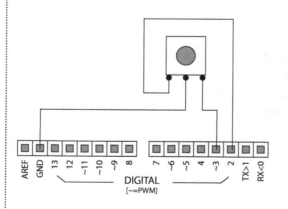

FIGURE 4.7

Connecting a rotary encoder to an Arduino (use internal pullup resistors).

A quadrature encoder has a pair of tracks that act like switches—they output HIGH or LOW depending on the rotation of the encoder. In this sense, tracking the state of an encoder is similar to tracking a pushbutton, and the circuitry is akin to connecting a pair of switches. As can be seen in Figure 4.7, the

94

outer pins connect to digital inputs on the Arduino, and the center pin connects to ground.[4]

As with other momentary switches, the pins corresponding to the two "switches" of the encoder are initialized with an internal pullup in the *setup()* function:

```
pinMode(encoderPinA, INPUT_PULLUP);
pinMode(encoderPinB, INPUT_PULLUP);
```

As the shaft rotates, the outer pins on the encoder produce a series high and low states that can be used to determine the direction of rotation (see Figure 4.8). The high and low states for clockwise and counterclockwise rotation are as follows:[5]

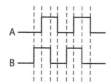

FIGURE 4.8

Low and high states of a rotary encoder.

```
Clockwise (AB): LH HL HH HL
Counterclockwise (AB): HL HH LH LL
```

Figure 4.9 may help to clarify how encoder tracking occurs. When the A track "falls" from 1-0 in clockwise motion, the B track is always low. However, when the A track "falls" from 1-0 going counterclockwise, the B track is always high.

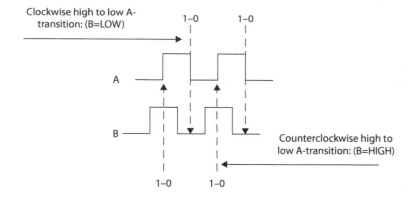

FIGURE 4.9

Tracking pulses on a rotary encoder.

Tracking these movements in software is a two-stage process. First, the algorithm looks for a transition from high (1) to low (0) on the A track. This transition or "edge" represents either clockwise or counterclockwise movement. Next, the value of the B track is evaluated. A low value (0) indicates clockwise rotation, and a high value (1) indicates counterclockwise rotation. Also note how the variable *beats_per_minute* is incremented or decremented according to the value returned by the encoder and, if the value changes, the variable *MS_per_beat* is recalculated. The code shown in Listing 4.10 is based on an example by Michael Margolis.[6]

Listing 4.10 Reading the state of a rotary encoder (based on an example by Michael Margolis)

```
void checkEncoder()
{
    boolean encoderA = digitalRead(encoderPinA);
    if((encoderALast == HIGH) && (encoderA == LOW))
    {
        if(digitalRead(encoderPinB) == LOW)
        {
            beats_per_minute = beats_per_minute + 1.0;
        }else
        {
            beats_per_minute = beats_per_minute - 1.0;
        }
        //Recalculate the delay time
        unsigned int milliseconds_per_minute = 1000 * 60;
        MS_per_beat = milliseconds_per_minute/
        beats_per_minute;
    }
    //Update encoder status and tempo
    encoderALast = encoderA;
}
```

4.1 DEMON-
STRATION
METRONOME

Conclusion

At this point, you should have a fully functional metronome and a good understanding of how to interface a number of electronic components with an Arduino. We will look at several additional enhancements such as adding an amplifier to increase loudness and a seven-segment display to show the tempo in Chapter 12 (Standalone Arduino). By the time you reach that chapter you will likely have many other ideas for creating the perfect personal metronome.

Although an Arduino metronome is a relatively humble project, the many concepts we have explored in this chapter should open the door to your own creative explorations. As stated earlier, I encourage you to experiment and explore. Just as practice is an essential part of the development of a musician, experimenting with circuits and code will allow you to apply these concepts in a creative way to your own Arduino projects.

Music Instrument Digital Interface I/O

What Is MIDI?

The Music Instrument Digital Interface (MIDI) is a communications protocol and hardware specification that was established in the early 1980s and was developed to provide a "standardized and efficient means of conveying musical performance information as electronic data."[1] It is astounding to consider that modern music production relies, to an extent, on a technology that was introduced nearly 30 years ago. The longevity and pervasiveness of MIDI in modern music production is a testament to the elegance and extensibility of the technology.

Unlike streams of audio data, it is interesting to note that MIDI is used to transfer a digital representation of a performance, *not* the actual sound of the performance. For example, when a MIDI keyboard is connected to a computer via a MIDI interface, the keyboard may transmit information about which keys have been pressed and released, the status of the damper pedal, the position of modulation and pitch bending controllers, and so on. It is up to the receiving instrument or computer to respond by utilizing the performance data to trigger sounds or for some other purpose.

MIDI is not just used to transmit performance data from a keyboard; the protocol can also be used to transmit automation data representing the settings on a virtual mixing board, timing information for system synchronization, streams of data used to control a light show, and performance data from many types of musical instruments including digital drum sets, guitars, and violins. To quote MIDI Manufacturers Association (MMA) president Tom White in a 1996 interview for *MusikkPraxis* magazine, "MIDI has been an extremely successful technology. It has been applied far beyond the original concept of connecting keyboards, to connect computers, tape recorders, lighting, and even the rides and events at major theme parks and attractions around the world."[2] Given its many uses in music production, MIDI technology will form a necessary foundation for many of the projects in this book.

This chapter is devoted to a discussion of MIDI networks, messages, and circuitry. The first section provides an overview of MIDI ports and connections. The second section looks at the structure and function of MIDI *packets* (the data comprising a complete MIDI message). The final section of the chapter is devoted to MIDI input and output circuits that can interface with an Arduino or *Teensy*, a relatively inexpensive microcontroller that can function as a driverless USB MIDI interface. Readers with a background in MIDI may wish to skip ahead to the sections involving MIDI circuitry and programming.

Although "the MIDI protocol has grown to encompass such additional concepts as: standardized MIDI song files…; new connection mechanisms such as USB, FireWire, and wi-fi,"[3] this chapter will focus on the transmission of MIDI data via five-pin DIN ports. As you will see in the last part of the chapter, the concepts are readily applicable to the Teensy range of USB microcontrollers.

MIDI Ports

There are three types of MIDI ports (IN, OUT, and THRU) commonly found on keyboards, sound modules, and other types of MIDI hardware.

MIDI OUT Port

As the name implies, the MIDI OUT port is used to transmit data *to* another MIDI device (see Figure 5.1). This is an important distinction: MIDI that is transmitted via a MIDI cable travels in one direction. It is also important to note that the connection is a *serial* connection—data flows one byte at a time at a rate of 31,250 baud.[4]

MIDI IN Port

A MIDI IN port is used to establish a connection *from* a MIDI device as in Figure 5.2. MIDI messages arrive at the input port and the receiving hardware uses the information to do something meaningful such as triggering a sound or moving a motorized fader.

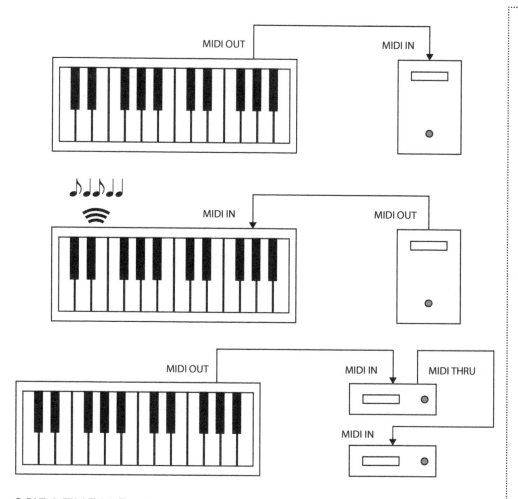

FIGURE 5.1

Connecting a MIDI keyboard to a computer via a MIDI OUT port.

FIGURE 5.2

MIDI IN port triggering a sound on a keyboard.

FIGURE 5.3

Keyboard connected to two MIDI sound modules.

MIDI THRU Port

MIDI THRU is primarily used to daisy chain MIDI devices. The THRU port simply passes along any messages that are received at the MIDI IN port. For example, Figure 5.3 illustrates how a single MIDI keyboard could be configured to send MIDI messages to two sound modules.

MIDI Messages

Status Byte

Chapter 2 covered, among other things, data types including *int*, *char*, and *byte*. Interestingly, 8-bit bytes are at the heart of the MIDI protocol. MIDI messages start with a *status byte* that specifies the type of event such as a Note-On or Note-Off event. Depending on the type of message, the status byte may be followed by data bytes that provide additional information such as a number corresponding to a particular MIDI note and the velocity with which a key was pressed.

Status bytes fall within the decimal range of 128 to 255. While this might seem like an arbitrary number, the numbers correspond to a range of possible

8-bit values in which the first bit has been set. In fact, MIDI status bytes can always be identified by checking to see if the first bit is equal to one.

Decimal	Binary
128	**1**0000000
255	**1**1111111

Data Byte

In contrast, the first bit of a *data byte* is always zero, thus, data bytes range in value from 0 to 127 (decimal):

Decimal	Binary
0	**0**0000000
127	**0**11111111

Although a binary representation of MIDI messages is useful in clarifying the function of status and data bytes, it is not usually necessary to utilize binary numbers when working with MIDI devices on the Arduino platform. Decimal equivalents for all MIDI messages can be found in the text that follows as well as at the MMA website (www.midi.org).

Channel Messages and System Messages

MIDI messages are organized in two broad categories: *Channel Messages* and *System Messages*. Channel Messages are used to transmit data that is intended for one of the 16 channels provided by the MIDI specification (more on this in a moment). System Messages are system-wide messages that are primarily used to transmit timing information.

Channel Messages are divided into two smaller categories consisting of *Channel Voice* messages and *Channel Mode* messages, which are detailed in the next several paragraphs.

Channel Voice Messages

A MIDI Channel number from 1 to 16 is encoded in each Channel Message. This makes it possible to use a single serial MIDI cable to transmit performance data that is intended for up to 16 different sound sources on a single device. For example, a MIDI sound module or Digital Audio Workstation (DAW) might be configured with a bass sound on MIDI Channel one, electric piano on Channel two, B3 organ on Channel three, and so on. When the receiving hardware or software receives a Channel Voice message such as a Note-On message, it plays the sound that is associated with the given MIDI Channel. In a Channel Voice status message, the first four bits are used to indicate the type of message (e.g., Note-On or Note-Off), and the second grouping of four bits specifies the MIDI Channel:

Status Byte	Decimal Value	Message Type	Channel
10010000	144	1001 = Note-On	0000 = Channel 1
10000000	128	1000 = Note-Off	0000 = Channel 1
10010001	145	1001 = Note-On	0001 = Channel 2
10000001	129	1000 = Note-Off	0001 = Channel 2

We will look in some detail at one of the most common Channel Voice messages, the Note-On message. All of the other Channel Messages are handled similarly, so the concepts will be readily applicable to the other Channel Voice Messages listed in this section.

Note-On Message

The first four bits of the message (1001 binary) indicate the type of message—a Note-On message. The second series of four bits indicate the MIDI Channel (0000 through 1111 binary). Note that, behind the scenes, MIDI uses a range of 0 to 15 to indicate channels 1 to 16). Thus, Note-On messages for MIDI Channels 1 to 16 always fall within the range of 144 to 159 decimal.

Note-On status byte (binary range)

Message	MIDI Channel
1001	nnnn (0000 through 1111)

Note-on status byte (decimal range)

Message	MIDI Channel
144-159	1–16

A Note-On message requires two data bytes in addition to the status byte. The first byte (0kkkkkkk) is the key or note number, and the second byte (0vvvvvvv) is the velocity of the key press.

Data Bytes

Byte	Description
0kkkkkkk	Key/note number (0–127)
0vvvvvvv	Velocity (0–127)

Although some Channel Voice messages require two data bytes and others require one, all of the messages are handled in a way that is conceptually similar: the status byte encodes the message type and MIDI Channel, and one or two data bytes provide the specified data (see Figure 5.4).

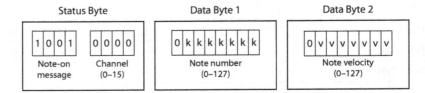

FIGURE 5.4

Note-On message with
two data bytes.

102

Later in the chapter you will learn how to create hardware ports for MIDI input and output on an Arduino, but this would be a good time to preview that process by seeing a practical example of how MIDI messages are transmitted in software. In this example, three bytes are initialized to represent a status byte (Note-On message), Data Byte 1 (note number), and Data Byte 2 (velocity). Outputting a MIDI note via an attached MIDI transmitter circuit is as simple as establishing the appropriate baud rate (more on this later in the chapter) and sending the notes via the Serial port. Note that, behind the scenes, a start and stop bit are automatically added to the eight bits that are transmitted via the serial connection.[5]

Listing 5.1 Sending a Note-On message

```
//Arduino for Musicians
//Listing 5_1: Note-on message

void setup()
{
    //Establish standard MIDI baud rate
    Serial.begin(31250);

    byte noteOnStatus = 144;        //Note-On message ch. 1
                                    //(Hexadecimal = 0x90)
    byte noteNumber = 60;           //Middle C
    byte velocity = 100;            //Velocity ranges from
                                    //0-127

    //Output a MIDI mote-on message:
    Serial.write(noteOnStatus);         //Send status byte
    Serial.write(noteNumber);           //Send data byte 1
    Serial.write(velocity);             //Send data byte 2
}

void loop()
{
    //Nothing to do here
}
```

Although it is easy to send MIDI notes in this way, later in the chapter you will learn about two MIDI libraries that make it even easier to send and receive messages.

With this preview in mind, let's review some of the other common Channel Voice messages.

Note-Off Message

Note-Off messages are often sent when a note is released, but be aware that some keyboards and *sequencers* (software programs or hardware that record MIDI data) use a Note-On message with a velocity of zero to signify a Note-Off event.

   As with Note-On messages, the status byte specifies the message type and Channel:

Note-Off status byte (binary range)

Message	MIDI Channel
1000	nnnn (0000 through 1111)

Message	MIDI Channel
128-143	1–16

Note-Off status byte (decimal range)

Data Bytes

Two data bytes provide the note number and release velocity.

Byte	Description
0kkkkkkk	Key/note number (0–127)
0vvvvvvv	Release velocity (0–127)

A Note About Running Status

The reason that a Note-On event with a velocity of zero is sometimes used instead of a Note-Off message has to do with a form of data compression called *Running Status*. As long as the status byte doesn't change, it is possible to transmit *just* the data bytes. Given that MIDI transmission is serial (and runs at a fairly slow baud rate), Running Status can be used to optimize streams of data. However, Paul Messick, author of *Maximum MIDI Music Applications in C++*, suggests that the status byte should be refreshed every 16 to 32 events.[6] Note that Running Status is an advanced topic that will not be incorporated into the sketches in this book. You will likely only need to utilize Running Status if you are sending thick streams of MIDI data or responding to Channel Voice Messages from a commercial software or hardware product.

Polyphonic Key Pressure (Aftertouch)

Aftertouch is used to provide an extra element of expression after a key has "bottomed out." For example, additional key pressure might be used to trigger modulation, a change of filter cutoff, or some similar function. As you can see in the text below, two data bytes are required for *Polyphonic Key Pressure* aftertouch.

Polyphonic Key Pressure status byte (binary range)

Message	MIDI Channel
1010	nnnn (0000 through 1111)

Polyphonic Key Pressure byte (decimal range)

Message	MIDI Channel
160-175	1–16

Data Bytes

Byte	Description
0kkkkkkk	Key/note number (0–127)
0vvvvvvv	Key pressure value (0–127)

Channel Pressure (aftertouch)

A more common form of aftertouch, *Channel* Pressure, uses a single data byte to represent the "greatest pressure value (of all the current depressed keys)."[7]

Channel Pressure status byte (binary range)

Message	MIDI Channel
1101	nnnn (0000 through 1111)

Channel Pressure status byte (decimal range)

Message	MIDI Channel
208-223	1–16

Data Byte

Byte	Description
0vvvvvvv	Channel Pressure value (0–127)

Program Change

Program Change messages are used to specify a new sound or "patch." For example, a Program Change with a value of 1 to 8 will call up a piano sound on a given General MIDI instrument, while numbers 25 to 32 are reserved for General MIDI guitar sounds. However, not all keyboards and synthesizers are General MIDI compatible, so a given Program Change may indicate something very different than the standardized General MIDI sound set. Program Changes consist of a status byte and a single data byte indicating the patch number.

Program Change status byte (binary range)

Message	MIDI Channel
1100	nnnn (0000 through 1111)

Program Change status byte (decimal range)

Message	MIDI Channel
192-207	1–16

Data Byte

Byte	Description
0vvvvvvv	Program Change value (0–127)

Pitch Wheel Change

Pitch Wheel Changes require two data bytes. Interestingly, the seven bits of each data byte (0–127 each) form the least and most significant bits of a 14-bit number. This provides a much higher resolution (16,384 discrete values) than would be possible than using only the seven bits available to a single data byte.

Pitch Wheel status byte (binary range)

Message	MIDI Channel
1110	nnnn (0000 through 1111)

Pitch Wheel status byte (decimal range)

Message	MIDI Channel
224-239	1–16

Data Bytes

Byte	Description
0LLLLLLL	Least significant bits (0–127)
0MMMMMMM	Most significant bits (0–127)

Figure 5.5 provides a conceptualization of the way the least and most significant bits are combined to form a 14-bit integer.

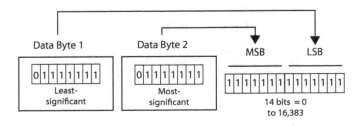

FIGURE 5.5

Conceptualization of pitch wheel data.

Control Change

Control Change messages represent a complex class of messages that might be thought of as a "message within a message." The first data byte of a Control Change message specifies one of 120 possible controller numbers or functions such as 0 (Bank Select), 7 (Channel Volume), 10 (Pan), 11 (Expression), and so on, and the second data byte specifies the Controller value. Controllers in the range of 64 to 69 are *Switch Controllers*: for example, Controller 64 (damper pedal) and 66 (sostenuto) are either on or off. In such cases, a value <=63 is used to specify the Controller is off while values >=64 specify that the Controller is on.

Control Change status byte (binary range)

Message	MIDI Channel
1011	nnnn (0000 through 1111)

Control Change status byte (decimal range)

Message	MIDI Channel
176-191	1–16

Data Bytes

Byte	Description
0ccccccc	Controller number (0–119[*])
0vvvvvvv	Controller value (0–127)

* Continuous Controller numbers 120–127 are reserved for Channel Mode Messages. (See the Channel Mode Messages section below.)

Like a Pitch Wheel Change message, two Control Change messages can be used together to provide a greater range of numbers (16,384 instead of 0–127). For example, a manufacturer might elect to use Control Change 0 (bank select) together with Control Change 32 to specify the most and least significant bytes of a bank-select message.

Listing 5.2 demonstrates a common approach to sending single-byte bank select messages. In this example, which I tested on a Kurzweil K2500, a bank select message selects a bank in the range of 0 to 9. This is followed by a program change message that selects the specific program or patch in the bank.

Listing 5.2 Sending bank select and program select messages

```
//Arduino for Musicians
//Listing 5_2: Control Change Message (Bank Select)

void setup()
{
    //Establish standard MIDI baud rate
    Serial.begin(31250);

    /* Note: multiple control change messages may be required
       depending on the configuration of your MIDI device.
       Some devices use CC0 or CC32 only or a combination of
       the two.
     */

    byte statusCC = 176;   //Control change on channel 1
    byte bankSelect = 32;  //Control change type: bank select
    byte bank = 1;         //Bank 1

    //Send a Control Change message
    Serial.write(statusCC);         //Send status byte
    Serial.write(bankSelect);       //Send data byte 1
    Serial.write(bank);             //Send data byte 2

    //Set up bytes to send a program change
    byte programChange = 192;
    byte program = 5;

    //Send program change message
    Serial.write(programChange);    //Send status byte
    Serial.write(program);          //Send data byte 1
}
void loop()
{
    //Nothing to do here
}
```

Other Control Changes and Mode Changes

Although there are many possible Control Change messages, all of the messages are handled similarly to Listing 5.2 in that the first data byte selects the control function and the second byte determines the value. A complete list of Control Changes and Mode Changes are provided in Appendix A.

Channel Mode Messages

Channel Mode Messages are a subset of *Control Change Messages* in the range of 120 to 127. Some of the Channel Mode Messages are less common, so I will limit the discussion to those messages that would likely be incorporated into an Arduino sketch.

Reset All Controllers

If the first data byte of a Control Change Message is equal to 121, a device should "reset the condition of all its controllers."[8] Some Digital Audio Workstation applications may send a Reset All Controllers when first loading a project to indicate that controller values should be reset.

Control Change status byte (binary range)

Message	MIDI Channel
1011	nnnn (0000 through 1111)

Control Change status byte (decimal range)

Message	MIDI Channel
176-191	1–16

Data Bytes

Byte	Description
0kkkkkkk	121 (Indicates Reset All Controllers)
0vvvvvvv	Usually zero

Local Control

Local Control is used to "interrupt the internal control path between the keyboard and the sound-generating circuitry of a MIDI synthesizer."[9] Local Control is typically turned off when a keyboard is used in a sequencing environment so that notes are not triggered twice—once by the keyboard and a second time as the notes are simultaneously routed from the output of a sequencer. A Control Change data byte value of 122 indicates the Local Control function. If the second data byte is equal to 0, Local Control is Off. A value of 127 will set Local Control to On.

Control Change status byte (binary range)

Message	MIDI Channel
1011	nnnn (0000 through 1111)

Control Change status byte (decimal range)

Message	MIDI Channel
176-191	1–16

Data Bytes

Byte	Description
0kkkkkkk	122 (Indicates Local Control function)
0vvvvvvv	0 = Local Control off, 127 = Local Control on

System Messages

As the name implies, *System Messages* are messages that relate to the entire MIDI system. There are two broad categories of messages: *System Common* and *System Real-Time*.

System Common Messages

Table 5.1 lists the decimal value for the most important System Common messages. Note that, unlike Channel Voice Messages, these messages do not pertain to a particular channel. The first four bits of each of the following messages is equal to 1111 binary, and the second set of four bits specifies the particular message.

System Real-Time Messages

As Paul Messick states in *Maximum MIDI*, "system Real-Time messages indicate that something is happening *right now*. They are all single-byte messages, and they have the unique ability to appear anywhere, even between the status

TABLE 5.1 System Common Messages

Binary Value	Decimal Value	Data byte(s)	Notes
1111 0000	240	Various	System Exclusive (see System Exclusive section)
1111 0001	241	0nnndddd	MIDI Time Code Quarter Frame
		nnn=Message Type	
		dddd=values	
1111 0010	242	0LLLLLLL	Song Position Pointer: 14-bit value representing the number of MIDI beats "since the start of the song" (LSB and MSB)
		0MMMMMMM	
1111 0111	247	NA	End of Exclusive: signals the end of a System Exclusive dump.

TABLE 5.2 Real-Time Messages

Binary Value	Decimal Value	Notes
11111000	248	Timing Clock: 24 Timing Clock messages are sent per quarter note. This message is particularly useful for synchronizing a MIDI arpeggiator or delay when ultra-precise timing is not required.
11111010	250	Start: indicates that a sequence will begin playing when the next timing clock message is received.
11111011	251	Continue: indicates that a sequence will continue playing when the next timing clock message is received.
11111100	252	Stop: stops the sequence. Ignore timing clock messages until a Start or Continue message is received.
11111110	254	Active sensing: some instruments send active sensing messages every 300 ms. These messages are largely ignored in modern studios, but the original intent of the message was to indicate that a device had become disconnected.
11111111	255	Reset: According to the MIDI Manufacturers Association, "Reset all receivers in the system to power-up status. This should be used sparingly, preferably under manual control. In particular, it should not be sent on power-up."[11]

byte and the data bytes of a MIDI message."[10] Table 5.2 lists the relevant real-time messages.

System Exclusive Messages

System Exclusive or "SysEx" messages were originally intended as non–real-time messages that could be used to transfer variable-length data in the form of sample dumps, device settings, and the like. Although SysEx messages are still used for those types of functions, they are also utilized for some real-time applications.

The idea behind System Exclusive messages is that a System Exclusive status byte would be followed by a one- or three-byte number representing a Manufacturer ID. In this way, a unique message could be sent to a device by a particular manufacturer, and ignored by any device with a different Manufacturer ID. An arbitrary number of data bytes follows the initial System Exclusive header, and an End of Exclusive byte signals the end of the transmission. Table 5.3 provides a conceptualization of a typical SysEx message.[12]

TABLE 5.3 Example of a System Exclusive Message

Byte (decimal)	Description
240	System Exclusive status byte
18	E-MU ID byte
04	Product ID byte
dd	Device ID (more than one of the same device may be connected to the same MIDI network)
data	Variable number of data bytes that mean something to this device
247	End of exclusive.

Universal System Exclusive Messages

Universal System Exclusive messages are another category of SysEx messages. Although the name implies that such messages are exclusive to a given manufacturer, these messages can (potentially) be used by any connected MIDI instrument. There are two broad categories of Universal System Exclusive messages: Real Time and Non-Real Time. Some of the many uses of Non-Real Time SysEx messages include initiating a sample dump or turning Downloadable Sounds (DLS) on or off.

MIDI Machine Control

Real Time Universal SysEx messages are particularly useful to Arduino programmers because they provide access to MIDI Machine Control (MMC) commands. MMC provides a framework for an external device to control a Digital Audio Workstation (DAW) or hardware recorder with remote commands. As is evident in Table 5.4, most MMC commands consist of six bytes.

The first two bytes indicate that the message is a Real Time Universal System Exclusive message. The third byte indicates a device ID: depending on the software or hardware you are communicating with, the device might need to be set to a specific number (127 corresponds to "all devices"). The fourth byte corresponds

TABLE 5.4 Structure of a MIDI Machine Control Command

Byte (hexadecimal)	Decimal	Description
F0	240	F0 followed by 7F indicates Universal Real Time SysEx
7F	127	
Device ID	??	Specifies a particular device 7F (127) = all devices
06	6	MIDI Machine Control command
dd	??	Command (see Table 5.2)
F7	247	End of MMC message

TABLE 5.5 Single-byte MMC Commands

Command (hexadecimal)	Decimal	Description
01	1	Stop
02	2	Play
03	3	Deferred Play
04	4	Fast Forward
05	5	Rewind
06	6	Record Strobe (Punch In)
07	7	Record Exit (Punch out)
08	8	Record Pause
09	9	Pause
0A	10	Eject
0B	11	Chase
0C	12	Command Error Reset
0D	13	MMC Reset

Source: Compiled from a list at http://www.somascape.org/midi/tech/spec.html#rusx_mmcc and from *The Complete MIDI 1.0 Detailed Specification* (MMA, 1996).

to Sub-ID #1 that indicates that the message is a MMC command, and the fifth byte specifies the command such as one of the single-byte commands shown in Table 5.5. An End of Exclusive byte signals the end of the message.

Listing 5.3 shows how two MMC commands (play and stop) could be used to control a DAW or other workstation. In most cases it is necessary to configure the receiving device to specifically listen for incoming MMC control commands. This listing makes use of a function named mmcCommand() that wraps the MMC command in the appropriate System Exclusive structure. The sketch initiates playback for five seconds and then sends a stop command. Of course, a real application would initiate playback in response to buttons or other hardware components.

A Note About Hexadecimal Numbers

All of the MIDI commands to this point have been listed in binary and decimal format. Viewing MIDI values in binary is helpful in showing how MIDI messages work (e.g.,visualizing status bytes, data bytes, and Channel numbers) while decimal numbers will be comfortable to nonprogrammers. With that said, MIDI commands (such as the MMC commands) are often shown in the hexadecimal (base 16) format shown in Listing 5.3. To use a hexadecimal value listed on a website or instrument manual, simply prepend the value with *0x* to tell the compiler the number is in base 16:

```
byte decimalByte     = 15;     //Decimal number
byte hexadecimalByte = 0xF;    //Hexadecimal number
```

The complete sketch is shown in Listing 5.3:

Listing 5.3 Simple MMC example

```
//Arduino for Musicians
//Listing 5.3: MIDI Machine Control example

//MMC command constants: Note use of hexadecimal numbers (e.g.,
//0x01, 0x02 etc,)
const byte stopCommand = 0x01;    //Stop command
const byte playCommand = 0x02;    //Play command

void setup()
{
    //Establish standard MIDI baud rate
    Serial.begin(31250);

    //Call mmcCommand() to start playback
    mmcCommand(playCommand);

    //Test: Let device play for 5 seconds
    delay(5000);

    //Call mmcCommand() to stop playback
    mmcCommand(stopCommand);
}

void mmcCommand(byte command)
{
    //Send bytes indicating Universal Real Time SysEx
    Serial.write(0xF0);
    Serial.write(0x7F);

    //Send command bytes
    Serial.write(0x7F);          //All devices
    Serial.write(0x06);          //Denotes this is an MMC
                                 //command
    Serial.write(command);       //Send the command
    Serial.write(0xF7);          //End of MMC command
}

void loop()
{
    //Nothing to do here
}
```

Advanced users may want to use other MMC commands such as Locate/Go To that require additional data bytes. The commands require setting individual bits and, thus, are not appropriate for the scope of this chapter. However, the commands should be easy to follow after reading the section on "bit twiddling" in Appendix C. For convenience, the Locate/Go To commands are provided in Appendix B.

Additional information on Universal System Exclusive messages is available at http://www.midi.org/techspecs/midimessages.php as well as in the *Complete MIDI Specification*, available from the same organization.

113

MIDI Hardware

The first part of this chapter was devoted to providing a conceptual framework of the various messages that form the MIDI protocol. In this section we look at electronic circuits that will enable an Arduino to communicate with MIDI devices. Fortunately, very few components are required, and the circuits are inexpensive to make and relatively easy to build.

MIDI Output

The MIDI out transmitter is a simple circuit to build. A basic version can be found in Michael Margolis's excellent book, *Arduino Cookbook*. In this example, pin 4 of the DIN is connected through a 220Ω resistor to the 5V pin on the Arduino. The middle pin, pin 2, connects to ground. MIDI messages are sent via digital pin 5, which connects to the transmit pin (TX 1) on the Arduino. A more advanced version of the circuit is shown at www.midi.org and in the MIDI 1.0 Detailed Specification and utilizes two inverters in series and a 220Ω resistor between the transmit (UART) and pin 5. Presumably, the extra components function as a buffer (see Figure 5.6). The specification states that "Gates 'A' are IC or transistor; Resistors are 5%."[13]

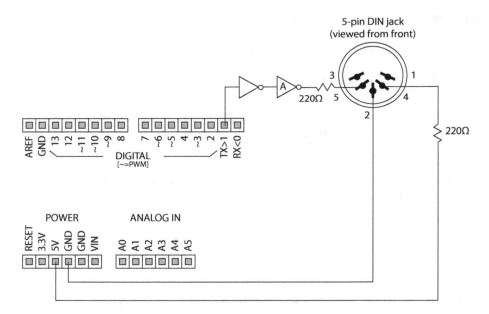

FIGURE 5.6

MIDI Transmitter diagram.

Figure 5.7 illustrates the MIDI transmitter circuit on a solderless breadboard. A 7404 Hex inverter was used between the output of the TX pin and pin 5 on the MIDI jack.

For me, the most confusing part of creating MIDI input and output circuits is ensuring that the connections are made to the correct pins on the five-pin DIN jack. The numbering scheme is "wonky" to begin with, and it can be a challenge to keep track of pins when you view a five-pin DIN jack from various angles. Figure 5.8 shows how the pins are numbered when viewing a MIDI jack from the back (solder side) of the jack—which is how they are shown in *The*

Complete MIDI 1.0 Detailed Specification.

FIGURE 5.7

MIDI Transmitter on solderless breadboard (with 7404 Hex inverter).

Testing the Output Circuit

As you have already seen in some of the preview MIDI sketches, it is surprisingly simple to send MIDI data from an Arduino (see Listing 5.4). After completing the MIDI transmitter circuit and connecting it to an Arduino, simply establish a serial connection at the expected MIDI baud rate of 31,250. MIDI bytes can then be sent using the *Serial.write()* method. In Listing 5.4, a convenience function labeled *playMIDINote()* simplifies the process even more. In this example, which was based on code by Michael Margolis,[14] the function takes three parameters specifying the channel, note, and velocity of the MIDI Note-On message. The function subtracts one from the expected channel range of 1 to 16. (As noted previously, behind the scenes, MIDI Channels are always in the range of 0 to 15.) The complete packet is sent in the expected order of bytes: status byte, data byte 1 (note number), and data byte 2 (velocity). Note that 90 is the hexadecimal value for a MIDI Note-On message on channel 1 (channel 0 in computer terms).

back

FIGURE 5.8

Five-pin DIN jack (viewed from the back).

The *loop()* function sends a series of chromatic notes. A "for" loop is used to increase the value of the note from middle C (60) to the octave above middle C, and each Note-On message is, in turn, followed by another Note-On message with a velocity of zero to turn the note off. A delay function is used to slow down the loop, but note that this is *not* a good way to handle MIDI timing. More sophisticated methods involving timers will be presented in other chapters of the book. The complete listing is shown below. Experiment with the code in order to transmit chords (no delay between notes), nonchromatic scales (use other counting methods), or perhaps add additional functions to transmit program changes or other types of messages.

Listing 5.4 Basic MIDI output

```
//Arduino for Musicians
//Listing 5.4: Basic MIDI output
```

```
void setup()
{
    Serial.begin(31250); //Set up serial output with standard
    //MIDI baud rate
}
void loop()
{
    //Play a chromatic scale starting on middle C (60)
    for(int note = 60; note < 60 + 12; note++)
    {
        //Play a note
        playMIDINote(1, note, 100);
        //Pause
        delay(60);

        //Turn note off (velocity = 0)
        playMIDINote(1, note, 0);
        //Pause
        delay(60);
    }
}
void playMIDINote(byte channel, byte note, byte velocity)
{
    byte noteOnStatus=0x90 + (channel-1);  //MIDI channels
    //1-16 are really 0-15

    //Send notes to MIDI output:
    Serial.write(noteOnStatus);
    Serial.write(note);
    Serial.write(velocity);
}
```

Aleatoric Music Generator

An interesting variation on the preceding code involves adding an element of randomness to create an aleatoric music generator (see Listing 5.5). This code is very similar to Listing 5.4, but random numbers are used to generate notes, durations, and velocities. Many interesting variations can be created by altering the range of possible random values in the first part of the *loop()* function and potentiometers or other components could be utilized to provide real-time control over some or all of the parameters:

Listing 5.5 Aleatoric music generator

```
//Arduino for Musicians
//Listing 5.5: Aleatoric music generator
void setup()
{
    Serial.begin(31250); //Set up serial output with standard
                         //MIDI baud rate
    //Use Analog 0 to seed the random number generator:
    randomSeed(analogRead(0));
}
```

```
void loop()
{
    //Select random parameters:
    byte note=random(20, 100);
    int duration=random(10, 1000);
    byte velocity=random(40, 127);

    //Play the note with the given parameters:
    playMIDINote(1, note, velocity);
    //Delay for the given duration
    delay(duration);

    //Turn the note off
    playMIDINote(1, note, 0);
    delay(10);
}

void playMIDINote(byte channel, byte note, byte velocity)
{
    byte noteOnStatus=0x90 + (channel-1); //MIDI channels
    //1-16 are really 0-15

    //Send notes to MIDI output:
    Serial.write(noteOnStatus);
    Serial.write(note);
    Serial.write(velocity);
}
```

Using a MIDI Library for Output

Although it is simple to use the *Serial.write()* method to output MIDI data, some users may want to explore a ready-made library such as the one written by Francois Best. Source code and documentation are available at: https://github .com/FortySevenEffects/arduino_midi_library.

Use the Add Library menu option (available from the Sketch…Import Library…menu in the Arduino IDE) after downloading the library to make it available in the Arduino IDE.

Description

Best's MIDI library is built around a class, MidiInterface, that provides many methods that simplify the process of outputting (and especially inputting) MIDI data. (Note that a thorough discussion of classes and methods will be presented in Chapter 8, Introduction to C++ Programming.) To use the library, simply include it in a project by using the "include" keyword and instantiate an instance of the class using the MIDI_CREATE_DEFAULT_INSTANCE() macro:

```
#include <MIDI.h>
MIDI_CREATE_DEFAULT_INSTANCE();
```

It is important to note that the include statement will fail if the library has not been installed in the Arduino environment (see above). A multitude of methods

117

5.1 ALEATORIC
MUSIC GENERATOR

(class-specific functions) will now be available. As is evident in Listing 5.6, the *begin()* method is used to establish a channel for input. Behind the scenes, the *begin()* method also initializes a number of variables that will be used to facilitate MIDI input and output. Note the slightly different syntax for outputting MIDI notes in the following listing. Here, instead of sending bytes via the *Serial.write()* method, Note-On messages are sent using the *sendNoteOn()* method of the MIDI class. By way of example, this sketch outputs augmented triads in the pattern of an ascending whole-tone scale. This is achieved by increasing the counter (*i*) by two on each iteration and sending Note-On messages for *i*, *i+4*, and *i+8*.

Listing 5.6 Using a MIDI library for output

```
//Arduino for Musicians
//Listing 5.6: MIDI Library output

#include <MIDI.h>

MIDI_CREATE_DEFAULT_INSTANCE();

const int velocity = 100;
const int channel = 1;

void setup()
{
    // Launch MIDI with default options. Input channel = 1
    MIDI.begin(1);
}

void loop()
{
    for(int i = 50; i< 70; i +=2)
    {
        //Output an augmented triad
        MIDI.sendNoteOn(i, velocity, channel);
        MIDI.sendNoteOn(i + 4, velocity, channel);
        MIDI.sendNoteOn(i + 8, velocity, channel);

        //Wait for 1/4 second:
        delay(125);

        //Send note-off messages
        MIDI.sendNoteOff(i, 0, channel);
        MIDI.sendNoteOff(i + 4, 0, channel);
        MIDI.sendNoteOff(i + 8, 0, channel);
    }
}
```

The following link provides detailed documentation for the class: http://arduinomidilib.fortyseveneffects.com/a00024.html. Of particular import for this portion of the book are the numerous methods for sending various types of MIDI data. Table 5.6 lists the methods that are documented at the website.

TABLE 5.6 Arduino MIDI Library Output Functions

void	send (MidiType inType, DataByte inData1, DataByte inData2, Channel inChannel)
	Generate and send a MIDI message from the values given.
void	**sendNoteOn** (DataByte inNoteNumber, DataByte inVelocity, Channel inChannel)
	Send a Note-On message.
void	**sendNoteOff** (DataByte inNoteNumber, DataByte inVelocity, Channel inChannel)
	Send a Note-Off message.
void	**sendProgramChange** (DataByte inProgramNumber, Channel inChannel)
	Send a Program Change message.
void	**sendControlChange** (DataByte inControlNumber, DataByte inControlValue, Channel inChannel)
	Send a Control Change message.
void	**sendPolyPressure** (DataByte inNoteNumber, DataByte inPressure, Channel inChannel)
	Send a Polyphonic AfterTouch message (applies to a specified note)
void	**sendAfterTouch** (DataByte inPressure, Channel inChannel)
	Send a MonoPhonic AfterTouch message (applies to all notes)
void	**sendPitchBend** (int inPitchValue, Channel inChannel)
	Send a Pitch Bend message using a signed integer value.
void	**sendPitchBend** (double inPitchValue, Channel inChannel)
	Send a Pitch Bend message using a floating point value.
void	**sendSysEx** (unsigned inLength, const byte *inArray, bool inArrayContainsBoundaries=false)
	Generate and send a System Exclusive frame.
void	**sendTuneRequest** ()
	Send a Tune Request message.
void	**sendTimeCodeQuarterFrame** (DataByte inTypeNibble, DataByte inValuesNibble)
	Send a MIDI Time Code Quarter Frame.
void	**sendTimeCodeQuarterFrame** (DataByte inData)
	Send a MIDI Time Code Quarter Frame.
void	**sendSongPosition** (unsigned inBeats)
	Send a Song Position Pointer message.
void	**sendSongSelect** (DataByte inSongNumber)
	Send a Song Select message.
void	**sendRealTime** (MidiType inType)
	Send a Real Time (one byte) message.

119

MIDI Receiver Circuit

MIDI input circuits are somewhat more complex than those used for output. The circuit shown in Figure 5.9, which was adapted from an example in the October 2012 issue *Nuts and Volts* magazine, as well as a samples at http://www .tigoe.com/pcomp/code/communication/midi/ and www.midi.org, utilizes a 6N138 opto-isolator and 1N4148 diode. It is important to note that you may need to temporarily disconnect the RX lead when uploading sketches to an Arduino that is connected to a MIDI receiver circuit because the connection may interfere with the upload process. One solution, which I use in my workshop, was to create a permanent version of the circuit on solderboard and provide a SPST switch to connect or disconnect the RX lead as needed.

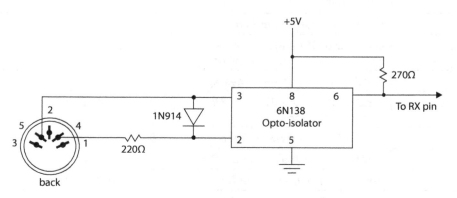

FIGURE 5.9

MIDI input circuit.

The diode prevents current from flowing the wrong way through the circuit should a miswired cable be connected to the unit, and the opto-isolator electrically isolates the sending device from the receiving device—an Arduino in this instance—to prevent ground loops. Documentation at www.midi.org expressly states that a chassis ground connection should *not* be connected to pin two of the MIDI input port.[15] A solderless breadboard version of the circuit is shown in Figure 5.10.

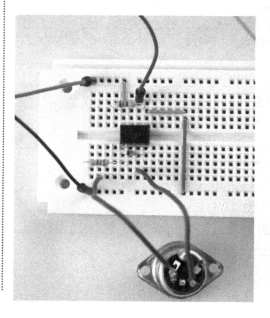

FIGURE 5.10

MIDI input circuit: solderless breadboard version.

MIDI THRU

MIDI THRU ports are used to transmit an exact copy of any data that is received at the input. Figure 5.11 shows one approach to adding MIDI THRU capability to a MIDI input circuit.

Creating Permanent MIDI Circuits

There are several options for creating permanent versions of the circuits shown in this chapter. One option is to purchase an interface

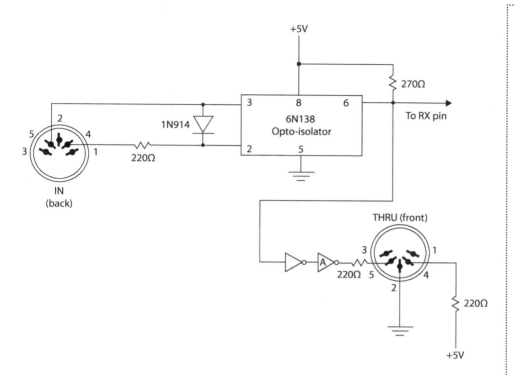

FIGURE 5.11

MIDI input with THRU circuit.

or kit designed for Arduino, but it is typically more economical to solder components to inexpensive solderboard. Yet another option is to purchase custom PCBs from of the many online PCB manufacturing companies that specialize in manufacturing circuits from circuit CAD designs. This is a good option if you intend to create several MIDI devices, and Eagle MIDI circuit files based on the circuits in this chapter are available for download from the OUP website.

Reading MIDI Data

As with the MIDI transmitter circuit, MIDI data can be read directly from the Serial port. However, it doesn't make sense to reinvent the wheel unless there is a particularly compelling reason to do so. Francois Best's Arduino MIDI Library provides a number of helpful features that make it easy to handle incoming MIDI messages on an Arduino.

As was mentioned in the previous section, be sure to include the MIDI library, use the *MIDI_CREATE_DEFAULT_INSTANCE()* macro, and call the *MIDI.begin()* method in the *setup()* function. The library can handle incoming messages in two ways: one option is to call the *MIDI.read()* method repeatedly in the main loop of the sketch and use the *getType()* method to parse incoming messages as in Listing 5.7. This example uses the *getData1()* and *getData2()* methods associated with Note-On and Note-Off messages and transposes the note by the value of the constant *transposition*:

Listing 5.7 MIDI input: simple transposition

```
//Arduino for Musicians
//Listing 5.7: MIDI Library input
```

```
#include <MIDI.h>
MIDI_CREATE_DEFAULT_INSTANCE();

const byte transposition = 3; //transpose up 3 semitones
const byte channel = 1;

byte note = 0;
byte velocity = 0;

void setup()
{
    MIDI.begin();    // Launch MIDI with default options
                     // (input channel is default set to 1)
}

void loop()
{
    //Look for message
    if (MIDI.read())
    {
        //Get message type
        switch(MIDI.getType())
        {
          // Get the message type
          case midi::NoteOn:
            //Transpose note (data byte 1) and send to
            //channel 1
            note = MIDI.getData1();
            velocity = MIDI.getData2();
            MIDI.sendNoteOn(note + transposition, velocity,
            channel);
            break;
          case midi::NoteOff:
            //Transpose note-off and send to channel 1
            note = MIDI.getData1();
            velocity = MIDI.getData2();
            MIDI.sendNoteOff(note + transposition, velocity,
            channel);
            break;
          default:
            break;
        }
    }
}
```

Callback Functions

Another approach, which I find to be more elegant, is to utilize *callback* functions. A callback function is a function that is automatically called from another class or library in response to a certain event. In the case of the MIDI Library, callback functions can automate the process of responding to incoming messages. All that is required is to provide a function with an appropriate name, parameters, and return type (*void*) and to let the library know that the callback function is available. The callback function will then be *automatically* called in response to incoming MIDI data. Listing 5.8 demonstrates how the simple transposition sketch from Listing 5.7 could be rewritten to utilize the callback mechanism provided by the MIDI library.

Listing 5.8 MIDI input callback

```
//Arduino for Musicians
//Listing 5.8: MIDI Library input callback
#include <MIDI.h>

MIDI_CREATE_DEFAULT_INSTANCE();

const byte transposition = 3; //transpose up 3 semitones
//Define the callback functions. Parameters and return value
//must match the values listed in the MIDI library:
void myHandleNoteOn(byte channel, byte note, byte velocity)
{
    MIDI.sendNoteOn(note + transposition, velocity, channel);
}

void myHandleNoteOff(byte channel, byte note, byte velocity)
{
    MIDI.sendNoteOff(note + transposition, velocity, channel);
}

void setup()
{
    //Connect the callback functions to the MIDI library
    MIDI.setHandleNoteOn(myHandleNoteOn);
    MIDI.setHandleNoteOff(myHandleNoteOff);

    MIDI.begin(MIDI_CHANNEL_OMNI); // Listen on all channels
}

void loop()
{
    //Call MIDI.read(). MIDI class will automatically call
    //callback functions as needed.
    MIDI.read();
}
```

Note the use of the methods called *setHandleNoteOn()* and *setHandleNoteOff()* in the *setup()* function. This is where the sketch lets the library know about the callback function. The name of the callback function is given as a parameter and provides a *pointer*—a memory address—to the function. It is not necessary to use a particular naming convention when writing callback functions. In Listing 5.8, the callback could have just as well been called *noteOnHandler* or something similar. All that is important is that the parameters and return type are *exactly* the same as the related function prototype in the library. As noted in the documentation, the following callback functions can be created for use with the library (see Table 5.7).

5.2 MIDI transposition

123

TABLE 5.7 MIDI Callback Functions

void	setHandleNoteOff (void(*fptr)(byte channel, byte note, byte velocity))
void	setHandleNoteOn (void(*fptr)(byte channel, byte note, byte velocity))
void	setHandleAfterTouchPoly (void(*fptr)(byte channel, byte note, byte pressure))
void	setHandleControlChange (void(*fptr)(byte channel, byte number, byte value))
void	setHandleProgramChange (void(*fptr)(byte channel, byte number))
void	setHandleAfterTouchChannel (void(*fptr)(byte channel, byte pressure))
void	setHandlePitchBend (void(*fptr)(byte channel, int bend))
void	setHandleSystemExclusive (void(*fptr)(byte *array, unsigned size))
void	setHandleTimeCodeQuarterFrame (void(*fptr)(byte data))
void	setHandleSongPosition (void(*fptr)(unsigned beats))
void	setHandleSongSelect (void(*fptr)(byte songnumber))
void	setHandleTuneRequest (void(*fptr)(void))
void	setHandleClock (void(*fptr)(void))
void	setHandleStart (void(*fptr)(void))
void	setHandleContinue (void(*fptr)(void))
void	setHandleStop (void(*fptr)(void))
void	setHandleActiveSensing (void(*fptr)(void))
void	setHandleSystemReset (void(*fptr)(void))
void	disconnectCallbackFromType (MidiType inType)

As you can see, the MIDI Library takes care of many of the challenging details of working with incoming MIDI messages. Although we have just scratched the surface of the library, further explanation will be provided, as appropriate, throughout the book.

USB MIDI with Teensy

The Teensy microcontroller is a unique option that will be of interest to many Arduino programmers. Several different flavors of the microcontroller are available for a modest cost at http://www.pjrc.com/store/teensy.html. The microcontroller is particularly useful for musicians since it can implement a "class-compliant" USB MIDI interface. This means that you can use the device as the basis for a MIDI project and the project will work, "out of the box," as a USB MIDI device with all of the major operating systems. I have used the device in a number of projects, and it has worked flawlessly. Prices start at around $16, which is a nominal cost for such a useful device.

124

Configuring Teensy

There are a few things to note before using the Arduino IDE to program a Teensy microcontroller for use as a MIDI device. First, special add-on software must be installed to program the device from within the Arduino development environment. The installer is available at: http://www.pjrc.com/teensy/td_download .html. Second, a class called *usbMIDI* is used instead of the MIDI library that was described in the last section. Third, use the Tools…Board menu in the Arduino IDE to select the Teensy microcontroller and set its type to MIDI via the Tools…USB Type menu. You will receive compiler errors if you attempt to use the *usbMIDI* class without first selecting the appropriate microcontroller type.

The following sketch (Listing 5.9), a demo that is provided as part of the Teensy installation, shows how the Teensy could be used as a MIDI monitoring utility. (Note that the code was slightly modified to fix a casting error.) As with the Arduino MIDI library, callback functions make it easy to visualize the flow of the sketch. The *usbMIDI* class will automatically call the appropriate callback as long as one has been provided and connected to the library via the appropriate *setHandle* method.

Listing 5.9 Teensy MIDI monitor

```
//Arduino for Musicians
//Listing 5.9: Teensy MIDI Monitor
//Modified by author

void setup()
{
    Serial.begin(115200);
    usbMIDI.setHandleNoteOff(OnNoteOff);
    usbMIDI.setHandleNoteOn(OnNoteOn);
    usbMIDI.setHandleVelocityChange(OnVelocityChange);
    usbMIDI.setHandleControlChange(OnControlChange);
    usbMIDI.setHandleProgramChange(OnProgramChange);
    usbMIDI.setHandleAfterTouch(OnAfterTouch);
    usbMIDI.setHandlePitchChange(OnPitchChange);
}

void loop()
{
    usbMIDI.read(); // USB MIDI receive
}

void OnNoteOn(byte channel, byte note, byte velocity)
{
    Serial.print("Note On, ch=");
    Serial.print(channel, DEC);
    Serial.print(", note=");
    Serial.print(note, DEC);
    Serial.print(", velocity=");
    Serial.print(velocity, DEC);
    Serial.println();
}
```

126

```
void OnNoteOff(byte channel, byte note, byte velocity)
{
    Serial.print("Note Off, ch=");
    Serial.print(channel, DEC);
    Serial.print(", note=");
    Serial.print(note, DEC);
    Serial.print(", velocity=");
    Serial.print(velocity, DEC);
    Serial.println();
}
void OnVelocityChange(byte channel, byte note, byte velocity)
{
    Serial.print("Velocity Change, ch=");
    Serial.print(channel, DEC);
    Serial.print(", note=");
    Serial.print(note, DEC);
    Serial.print(", velocity=");
    Serial.print(velocity, DEC);
    Serial.println();
}
void OnControlChange(byte channel, byte control, byte value)
{
    Serial.print("Control Change, ch=");
    Serial.print(channel, DEC);
    Serial.print(", control=");
    Serial.print(control, DEC);
    Serial.print(", value=");
    Serial.print(value, DEC);
    Serial.println();
}
void OnProgramChange(byte channel, byte program)
{
    Serial.print("Program Change, ch=");
    Serial.print(channel, DEC);
    Serial.print(", program=");
    Serial.print(program, DEC);
    Serial.println();
}
void OnAfterTouch(byte channel, byte pressure)
{
    Serial.print("After Touch, ch=");
    Serial.print(channel, DEC);
    Serial.print(", pressure=");
    Serial.print(pressure, DEC);
    Serial.println();
}
void OnPitchChange(uint8_t channel, uint16_t pitch) {
    Serial.print("Pitch Change, ch=");
    Serial.print(channel, DEC);
    Serial.print(", pitch=");
    Serial.print(pitch, DEC);
    Serial.println();
}
```

Conclusion

This chapter has covered a lot of ground. The first section provided an overview of the MIDI protocol, its use, and function in modern music making. The chapter also provided an overview of the messages that form the basis for MIDI's digital representation of performance data. In the second section we looked at the transmitter and receiver circuits that allow MIDI messages to be sent to and from an Arduino. Several sample sketches provide a basis for further exploration. Finally, we looked at the Teensy microcontroller, a device that is capable of implementing a "class-compliant" USB interface.

Although the information in this chapter will provide a solid foundation for most MIDI projects, an entire book could be written on MIDI circuitry and software. More detail will be provided in other chapters of the book, and there are obviously many sources of information available online. One of the best places to start is www.midi.org. There, you will find many useful tables, diagrams, and explanatory text covering many aspects of MIDI. Serious developers may want to purchase a copy of the *Complete MIDI 1.0 Detailed Specification*, also available from the MIDI Manufacturers Association.

There are a number of useful books on MIDI (including coverage in my own *Musicianship in the Digital Age*), but one of my favorites is Paul Messick's *Maximum MIDI*. Although the book is geared toward older operating systems, Messick provides excellent behind-the-scenes details relating to MIDI programming on PCs, and he provides code and detailed descriptions of many useful topics such as handling System Exclusive information, establishing a stable clock using integer math, and reading and writing Standard MIDI Files.

Real-Time Input
Musical Expression

In my estimation, one of the most compelling aspects of the Arduino platform is the rich potential for new forms of expressive control of synthetic instruments. Custom control systems featuring multi-input capability that combine breath, pressure, and proximity sensing are just a few of the many possible approaches. And control systems need not be limited to the realm of electronic music; Arduino microcontrollers can also be used to control servos, motors, and other devices that have the potential of interacting with instruments in the acoustic realm. To quote Jeff Pressing, author of *Synthesizer Performance and Real-Time Techniques*, "Part of music's indescribability lies in the integrated quality of the musical statement, the 'rightness' of it, its 'authenticity', the difference between a mechanical and an inspired performance. These are the nuances that bring the music to life. Such success comes not only from the performer's musical sensitivity but from concern for detail, sympathy with the musical goals that are implied by the material in question, and appropriate hard work. Much of this lies in the correct use of microstructure in performance..."[1] A good controller will open the door to some of the nuances that can contribute to good "microstructure in performance," and this chapter should open the door to your own unique adaptations.

This chapter explores a number of components that can be utilized for expressive real-time control of electronic instruments. Points of discussion include a force-sensing resistor, touch screen, joystick, Wii nunchuck, and pressure (e.g., breath) sensor.

Force-Sensitive Resistor

A force-sensitive resistor (FSR) is a "device which exhibits a decrease in resistance with an increase in the force applied to the active surface."[2] FSRs, like the one shown in Figure 6.1, are useful to musicians because they respond quickly to touch and, thus, can be used for many types of expressive control ranging from triggering percussive sounds to controlling modulation or other forms of continuous control.

Wiring an FSR

One approach to wiring an FSR is detailed in an Adafruit tutorial.[3] A lead of the FSR is connected to 5V, and the other lead is connected to a 10kΩ pulldown resister to ground. The point between the FSR and 10k Ohm resistor is connected to an Arduino analog input as in Figure 6.2.

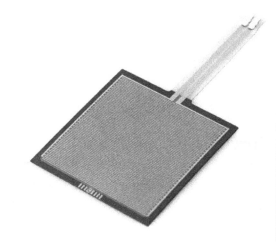

129

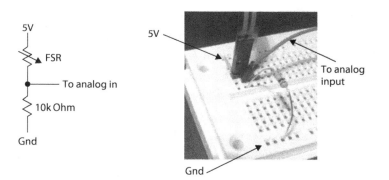

As resistance decreases, the current increases causing an increase in voltage across the resistor. The voltage level can be read from an analog input and mapped to an appropriate range (e.g., for MIDI continuous control). Values from the FSR can be read with the sketch shown in Listing 6.1:

Listing 6.1 Reading an FSR

```
//Arduino for Musicians
//Listing 6.1: FSR Input
const int fsrAnalogPin = 0;
int lastValue = 0;
```

```
void setup()
{
    Serial.begin(9600);
    pinMode(fsrAnalogPin, INPUT);
}
void loop()
{
    int value = analogRead(fsrAnalogPin);

    //Print the value if it has changed since the last
    //reading
    if(value != lastValue)
    {
        Serial.println(value);
        lastValue = value;
    }
}
```

130

Force-Sensitive Drum Pad

One useful application of an FSR is a velocity-sensitive drum-pad trigger. This approach will be fully developed in the "Mongo" hand drum project in the final section of the book. The following sketch outputs velocity-sensitive MIDI Note-On messages in response to force that is applied to the sensor. This sketch was written for the Teensy microcontroller but can be easily modified to work with an Arduino with serial MIDI output (see Chapter 5).

The sketch takes a reading of an analog input and maps the value to a MIDI velocity range of 0 to 127. If the velocity is greater than the threshold constant, *THRESHOLD*, and a note is not currently on, the program enters a *while* loop to give the FSR a chance to stabilize so that the "spike" of the attack can be read. This happens virtually instantaneously and does not contribute to any noticeable latency.

A Note-Off message is generated if the FSR returns a value of zero and a note is currently sounding. Note how the sketch also checks for an existing Note-On or Note-Off message to prevent sending multiple notes after an initial attack. The output is surprisingly subtle and responsive, and this approach can be used for other types of MIDI messages such as pitch bend, expression, or modulation. The sketch is shown in its entirety in Listing 6.2.

Listing 6.2 FSR drum trigger sketch (Teensy USB MIDI version)

```
//Arduino for Musicians
//Listing 6.2: FSR drum trigger (Teensy USB MIDI version)

//Arduino for Musicians
//FSR_drum_trigger

//Definitions:
const int fsrAnalogPin = A0;
const int SNARE = 40;
const int THRESHOLD = 15;
```

```
//Note status and velocity default values
boolean note_on = false;
int last_value = 0;
int midi_velocity = 0;

void setup()
{
    //No setup needed
}

void loop()
{
    //Get the value of the analog pin
    int value = analogRead(fsrAnalogPin);

    //Map the value to a valid MIDI range (0 - 127)
    midi_velocity = map(value, 0, 1023, 0, 127);

    //Play a note if the level is greater than the threshold
    //and we are not already playing a note.
    if(midi_velocity > THRESHOLD && note_on == false)
    {
        last_value = 0;

        //Continue to take readings until value stabilizes or
        //decreases.
        //We are looking for the "spike" of the attack.
        while (analogRead(fsrAnalogPin) != last_value)
        {
            last_value = analogRead(fsrAnalogPin);
        }

        midi_velocity = map(last_value, 0, 1023, 0, 127);

        //send a single note on for value greater than 0
        usbMIDI.sendNoteOn(SNARE, midi_velocity, 1);
        note_on = true;
    }

    //Send a note-off if the velocity is zero and a note is
    //currently sounding
    if(midi_velocity == 0 && note_on == true)
    {
        //send a single note off for velocity of 0
        usbMIDI.sendNoteOff(SNARE, 0, 1);
        note_on = false;
    }
}
```

6.1 DRUM PAD

FSR Caution

One caution regarding FSRs: The leads are fragile and will likely be destroyed when applying heat with a soldering iron. For this reason, I prefer to solder hookup wire to a two-space (.1") female header (or male pins depending on the configuration of the FSR) and plug the FSR as in Figure 6.3.

131

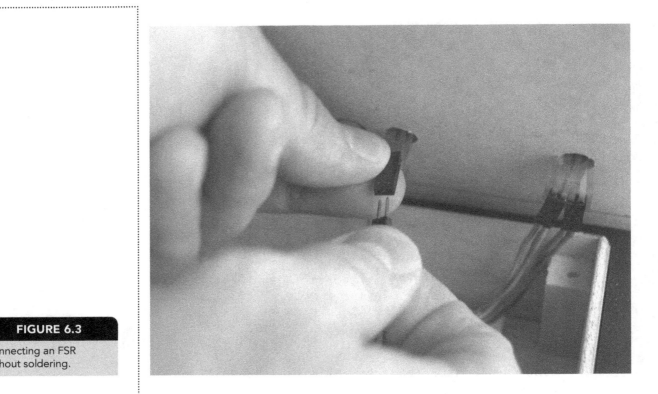

FIGURE 6.3

Connecting an FSR without soldering.

Nintendo DS Touch Screen

A Nintendo DS Touch Screen provides relatively precise readings of the X and Y position of a finger or stylus. As with the other components in this chapter, there are many potential musical applications of this technology. The X and Y position could be used for simultaneous control of two virtual synthesizer parameters such as filter cutoff and resonance, or the touch screen could form the foundation for a virtual mixer or DAW controller (with an appropriate graphic underlay). The touch screen, screen connector, and connector breakout are available for about $15 from SparkFun Electronics.

FIGURE 6.4

Connecting a Nintendo DS touch screen to the analog pins on an Arduino (with 10K pulldown resistors).

Wiring

The connections on the touch screen are *very* fragile so a connector breakout is essential. The pins, labeled Y1, X2, Y2, and X1, are connected to the analog pins of the Arduino as shown in Figure 6.4. It is important to note that a connection should *not* be made where lines cross in this illustration. A dot indicates where one or more electrical connections should be made in this and other illustrations in the book.

The function of the four pins is somewhat confusing at first glance but becomes more clear after you understand how the touch screen works. The screen contains two layers of resistive coating with a pair of buss bars that connect to the data pins. The buss bars are located on the sides of the top layer and the top and bottom of the lower layer (see Figure 6.5).

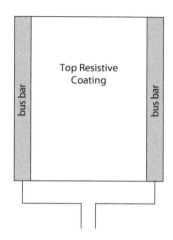 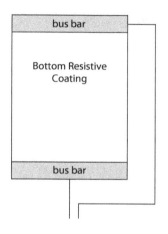

FIGURE 6.5

Construction detail. (Based on a drawing by HantouchUSA.)

Reading the X and Y Positions

To read the X position of a touch, the X1 pin is set to HIGH and X2 is set to LOW. The Y1 pin is then used to read the voltage representing the X-position of the touch (Figure 6.6).

The Y position is handled in a similar fashion, but this time pin Y2 is set to HIGH and Y1 to LOW. Pin X4 is used to read the voltage representing the Y-position of the touch (Figure 6.7).

Thus, to read the X and Y positions of a touch-screen, it is necessary for the Arduino to frequently switch the analog pins from input to output in order to check both axes of the touchscreen. The following functions, which are based on an excellent tutorial at bildr.org,[4] illustrate how the X and Y values are read. Using these values in a sketch is as simple as calling the appropriate function and using the *map()* function to scale the values for use as a MIDI continuous controller (or for some other purpose). The example is shown in its entirety in Listing 6.3.

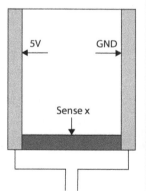

FIGURE 6.6

Sensing the X position of a touch. (Based on a drawing by HantouchUSA.)

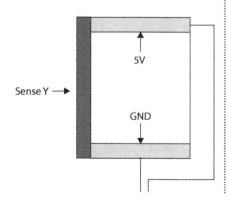

FIGURE 6.7

Sensing the Y position of a touch. (Based on a drawing by HantouchUSA.)

Listing 6.3 Reading X and Y position of a touchscreen

```
//Arduino for Musicians
//Listing 6.3: Touchscreen input

//Constants representing the analog pins
//that will be used for input AND output
const int x1 = A0;
const int y2 = A1;
const int x2 = A2;
const int y1 = A3;

void setup()
{
    Serial.begin(9600);
}

int readX()
{
    pinMode(y1, INPUT);
    pinMode(x2, OUTPUT);
    pinMode(y2, INPUT);
    pinMode(x1, OUTPUT);

    digitalWrite(x2, LOW);
    digitalWrite(x1, HIGH);

    delay(5); //pause to allow lines to power up

    return analogRead(y1);
}

int readY()
{
    pinMode(y1, OUTPUT);
    pinMode(x2, INPUT);
    pinMode(y2, OUTPUT);
    pinMode(x1, INPUT);

    digitalWrite(y1, LOW);
    digitalWrite(y2, HIGH);

    delay(5); //pause to allow lines to power up

    return analogRead(x2);
}

void loop()
{
    int y = readY();
    int x = readX();

    if(x !=0 || y != 0)
    {
        Serial.print("X: "); Serial.print(x);
        Serial.print(" Y: "); Serial.println(y);
    }
}
```

6.2 X-Y MIDI
CONTROLLER

Pressure Sensor

As a pianist, I envy woodwind and brass players' ability to control their instruments with breath. For this reason, I was keenly interested to see if air pressure could be utilized as a form of real-time control. The idea is not new. I purchased a breath controller in the early 1990s, but the unit was awkward to use and not particularly expressive. Fortunately, it is possible to make an expressive breath controller for about $35 dollars (*including* the price of a Teensy microcontroller).

Pressure Sensor Unit

There are many pressure sensors on the market that are geared to industrial applications, and I settled on the Freescale Semiconductor MPX 5050GP Pressure Sensor. The unit runs on a supply voltage ranging from 4.75 to 5.25V and responds to pressure in the range of 0 to 50kPa. Although the pressure range is greater than is needed to respond to breath control, the unit could potentially be connected to other sources of air pressure such as a turkey baster for a unique form of MIDI control.

Wiring the Pressure Sensor

The first three pins are connected to the Arduino's analog pin 0, ground, and 5V, respectively (see Figure 6.8). (Note that pin 1 is marked by a notch near the body of the pressure sensor.) Pins 4 through 6 are not connected.

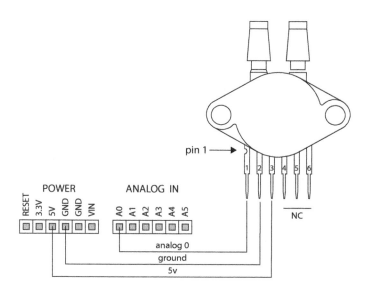

FIGURE 6.8

MPX 5050GP pinout. (Based on an illustration in a Freescale Semiconductor datasheet and an illustration by Gordon McComb.)

Reading Values from the Pressure Sensor

It is surprisingly easy to read values from the pressure sensor and convert them to useful MIDI data. Listing 6.4, which is one of my favorite sketches in the book for its brevity and utility, was written to take advantage of the Teensy microcontroller's built-in MIDI capability. With just a few lines of code and three wires, it is possible to use breath pressure to control a virtual synthesizer in a DAW or iPad. Note that in the case of an iPad, it is necessary to connect the Teensy via a Camera Connection Kit (see Figure 6.9).

Listing 6.4 Pressure sensor to expression controller

```
//Arduino For Musicians
//Listing 6.4: Pressure sensor to expression controller
//              Teensy USB MIDI version

// Pin 1 (notch) - Analog output
// Pin 2 - Gnd
// Pin 3 - 5V

int sensorPin = A0;     //Input pin for the pressure sensor
int lastValue = 0;      //Stores the last value read from the
                        //sensor
int sensitivity = 3;    //Prevents slight variations in
                        //readings
int ambientLevel = 0;   //The "ambient" pressure level
int max_level = 150;    //User preference: the max
                        //comfortable pressure

//NOTE: Readings range from around 33 to 150 without
//excessive pressure

//Constants for MIDI:
const int expression = 11;  //Expression continuous
                            //controller
const int channel = 1;      //MIDI channel 1

void setup()
{
    delay(1000);  //let circuitry stabilize
    //get "ambient" pressure
    ambientLevel = analogRead(sensorPin);
}

void loop()
{
    int sensorValue = analogRead(sensorPin);  // Read sensor
    if(sensorValue < lastValue - sensitivity ||
      sensorValue > lastValue + sensitivity)
    {
      //Map the value to a MIDI range of 0 to 127
      int midi_value = map(sensorValue, ambientLevel, max_
      level, 1, 127);

      //Output the value as an expression controller
      usbMIDI.sendControlChange(expression, midi_value,
      channel);
      lastValue = sensorValue;
    }
}
```

136

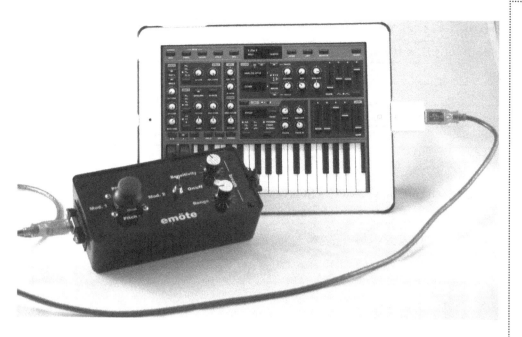

FIGURE 6.9

Connecting a pressure sensor to an iPad via a Teensy microcontroller and Camera Connection Kit.

137

6.3 BREATH CONTROLLER

Joystick

Joysticks are often used to control MIDI pitch bend and modulation and can be very expressive. Unfortunately, not all MIDI instruments come with pitch and modulation controllers. The simple circuits and code in this section provide the necessary foundation to create an expressive joystick controller that can be used with almost any MIDI setup. Also note that a joystick can have many other creative applications such as controlling fast-forward and rewind of a DAW, or as part of a menu system in a custom Arduino project.

The joystick shown in Figure 6.10, along with a joystick breakout board, was purchased for about $6 from SparkFun Electronics.

Wiring a Joystick

The SparkFun Thumb Joystick can be used to track movement on the X and Y axes, and the joystick can also be pressed to engage a momentary switch.[5] Pins from the breakout board are connected to the Arduino as shown in Table 6.1.

Reading Values from a Joystick

Listing 6.5 demonstrates how the X and Y values of the joystick can be read via the analog ports A0 and A1 on an Arduino. The *map()* function (discussed in Chapter 4)

FIGURE 6.10

Thumb joystick. (Image by Juan Pena courtesy SparkFun Electronics.)

TABLE 6.1 Joystick Connections

Breakout Board Pin	Arduino Connection
VCC	Connect to Arduino 5V or 3.3V
VERT	Connect to analog input
HORIZ	Connect to analog input
SEL	Connect to digital input pin (turn on internal pullup).
GND	Connect to Arduino GND

can be used to map the values to an appropriate range such as 0–127 for a MIDI controller.

Listing 6.5 Joystick sketch

```
//Arduino for Musicians
//Listing 6.5: Joystick Input

const int joystick_xPin = A0;
const int joystick_yPin = A1;

//Use a sensitivity value to prevent slight fluctuations
//when the joystick is at rest.
const int sensitivity = 2;

//Variables to store the X and Y position
int oldX = 0;
int oldY = 0;

void setup()
{
    Serial.begin(9600);
}

void loop()
{
    //Read the joystick values
    int joystick_x = analogRead(joystick_xPin);
    int joystick_y = analogRead(joystick_yPin);

    //Print X position if it has changed
    if(joystick_x <= oldX - sensitivity ||
       joystick_x >= oldX + sensitivity)
    {
        Serial.print("X: ");
        Serial.println(joystick_x, DEC);
        //Store the X position
        oldX = joystick_x;
    }

    //Print Y position if it has changed
    if(joystick_y <= oldY - sensitivity ||
       joystick_y >= oldY + sensitivity)
    {
        Serial.print("Y: ");
        Serial.println(joystick_y, DEC);
        //Store the Y position
        oldY = joystick_y;
    }
}
```

Joystick Sensitivity

In this example, the vertical and horizontal pins of the breakout board are connected to analog inputs A0 and A1 on the Arduino. Variables are established to store the last reading from the analog input, and a sensitivity constant is used to prevent the sketch from responding to slight fluctuations of the analog inputs. The following line compares the value of one joystick axis with the previous value and outputs the current position if the value is greater than the old value plus the sensitivity constant or lower than the old value minus the sensitivity constant:

```
if(joystick_x <= oldX - sensitivity ||
    joystick_x >=oldX + sensitivity)
{
    //Joystick has moved
}
```

Wii Nunchuck

A Wii nunchuck is a fun and interesting device to use for real-time control. A number of nunchuck breakout adaptors are available from vendors including Sparkfun and Adafruit for about $2. The version from Sparkfun, shown in Figure 6.11, is inserted into the nunchuck cable and pins in the adapter are used to provide power and to establish serial communication with the device via the I2C protocol.

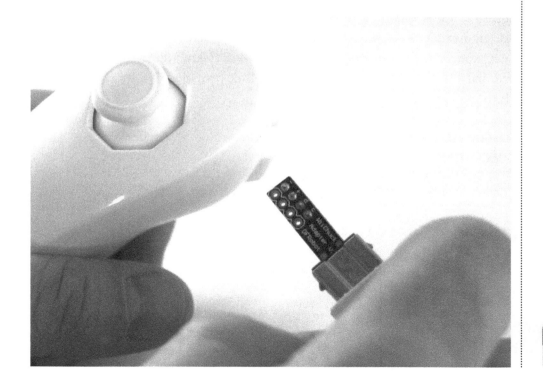

FIGURE 6.11

WiiChuck adapter.

139

Nunchuck Library

Tod E. Kurt wrote an Arduino library that simplifies the process of using a nunchuck with an Arduino. The library and a helpful tutorial is available at http://todbot.com/blog/2008/02/18/wiichuck-wii-nunchuck-adapter-available/.

Nunchuck Code

One thing to be aware of is that the library requires the Nunchuck to be attached via specific analog pins and two of the pins are used to power the device. In general, it is best to avoid powering devices from the pins in this way, but it is appropriate in this instance because the Nunchuck will draw an appropriately small amount of current. The nunchuck pins are connected to the analog pins on the Arduino as shown in Table 6.2.

TABLE 6.2 Nunchuck Pin Assignments

Nunchuck pin	Arduino analog pin	Function
-	A2	GND
+	A3	+5V
d	A4	I2C data
c	A5	I2C clock

Listing 6.6 demonstrates how to take readings of the Nunchuck accelerometer and buttons using the nunchuck library. Unlike most Arduino libraries, all of the functionality of the nunchuck library is contained in a single header file named *nunchuck_funcs.h*. For this test I simply created a new source file tab in the test project, named the tab *nunchuck_funcs.h*, and copied the functions from the GitHub link provided at Mr. Kurt's website into the new tab.

Listing 6.6 Reading accelerometer and buttons on a Wii nunchuck

```
//Arduino for Musicians
//Listing 6.6: Nunchuck demo
//Based on an example by Tod E. Kurt

#include <Wire.h>
#include "nunchuck_funcs.h"

byte accel_x;
byte accel_y;
byte z_button;
byte c_button;

//Constant to establish refresh rate
const int refreshRate = 50;
```

140

```
//Used to track amount of milliseconds between readings
long lastTime = 0;

void setup()
{
    //Note: Using faster baud rate.
    //Be sure to set the same rate in the Serial Monitor
    //window.
    Serial.begin(19200);

    //Initialize the nunchuck
    nunchuck_setpowerpins();
    nunchuck_init();
}

void loop()
{
    //Take a reading at given refresh rate
    if(millis() - lastTime > refreshRate)
    {
        //Update the time
        lastTime = millis();

        //Ask nunchuck to update data
        nunchuck_get_data();

        // new values from nunchuck

        accel_x = nunchuck_accelx(); //range ~ 70 - 182
        accel_y = nunchuck_accely(); //range ~ 65 - 173

        z_button = nunchuck_zbutton();
        c_button = nunchuck_cbutton();

        //Print values:
        Serial.print("accx: "); Serial.print((byte) accel_x,
        DEC);
        Serial.print("\taccy: "); Serial.print((byte)
        accel_y, DEC);
        Serial.print("\tzbut: "); Serial.print((byte)
        z_button, DEC);
        Serial.print("\tcbut: "); Serial.println((byte)
        c_button, DEC);
    }
}
```

6.4 NUNCHUCK CONTROLLER

Conclusion

It is surprisingly simple to create an expressive real-time controller. The components listed in this chapter are relatively inexpensive and can be combined to create any number of interesting and expressive control systems. From my perspective, it is exciting to be able to design and build MIDI controllers that are uniquely tailored to my needs. Not only can the devices contribute to a new level of musicality, they might even inspire new compositional

141

or performance directions. Author Paul Griffiths describes the stimulating potential of the electronic medium when he states that "these devices can also, in the hands of a sensitive musician, give rise to the wonder which is not an insignificant part of our experience of electronic music. The wonder of new discovery, of having one's preconceptions overturned, is part of the excitement of the art."[6]

Music-Making Shields

Overview

A shield is a board that can be plugged into an Arduino to expand its capabilities, and there are a number of music-making shields available for the Arduino platform. Although it is not necessary to purchase a shield to create music and sound with an Arduino, shields can be an attractive option for some users. Most music shields provide functionality that would be difficult to create from scratch such as streaming .wav files from an SD card or voice synthesis. This chapter provides an overview of several music-making Arduino shields that can be used for a number of interesting applications including General MIDI playback, voice synthesis, additive synthesis, audio file streaming, and high-end audio playback and processing. The intent is not to provide a detailed description of the inner workings of each module or to cover all of the available shields, but rather to provide an overview of the function and use of several useful music shields. The overview will help you to decide if a given shield is a good fit for your needs and will provide a starting point as you explore the functions and price of other commercial shields. Demonstration videos of all of the shields can be viewed at the OUP website.

Music Instrument Shield (SparkFun Electronics)

The SparkFun Music Instrument Shield (see Figure 7.1) is a good choice if you want a convenient way to utilize *General MIDI* instruments in a project. The General

FIGURE 7.1

144

Music Instrument Shield.
(Image by Juan Pena
courtesy SparkFun
Electronics.)

MIDI sound set consists of 128 sounds that are available via standardized program changes. For example, Acoustic Grand Piano is always associated with program change 1 in General MIDI, and Acoustic Bass is always program change 33.

The sounds of the *Music Instrument Shield* (based on a VS1053b chip) are not particularly impressive: the chip evidently utilizes a small amount of sample memory, and some noise is evident in the output. However, I have found the unit to be very helpful for prototyping algorithmic composition projects. In particular, it is convenient to be able to stack the unit on an Arduino and produce notes with just a few lines of code. In addition to algorithmic composition, the Music Instrument Shield could be useful as the heart of an ear training kiosk or other type of interactive application.

Using the Shield

Outputting notes on the Music Instrument Shield is surprisingly simple. Listing 7.1, an example that is based on a tutorial by Marc "Trench" Tschudin, illustrates the primary steps.[1] Where the TX and RX pins are typically used to communicate with external devices, a helpful library named *SoftwareSerial* can be used in situations where other pins are used for communication. In this example, an instance of *SoftwareSerial* is created and configured to receive and transmit on pins 2 and 3.

Listing 7.1 Music Instrument Shield demo

```
#include <SoftwareSerial.h>
SoftwareSerial mySerial(2, 3); // RX, TX
byte resetMIDI = 4;              //Tied to VS1053 Reset line
```

Next, the VS1053 chip is reset in the *setup()* function:

```
Serial.begin(57600);

//Setup soft serial for MIDI control
mySerial.begin(31250);

//Reset the VS1053
pinMode(resetMIDI, OUTPUT);
digitalWrite(resetMIDI, LOW);
delay(100);
digitalWrite(resetMIDI, HIGH);
delay(100);
```

At this point, the shield is ready to receive MIDI commands which can be sent by transmitting command and data bytes via the SoftwareSerial object created in step one:

```
mySerial.write(cmd);
mySerial.write(data1);
```

Although it is easy to transmit MIDI data in this way, a few helper functions can simplify the process even more. The following functions are based on the Tschudin example at SparkFun Electronics, but I used a slightly different approach: instead of combining the code for MIDI messages requiring one or two bytes into a single function, the single- and multi-byte messages are handled by separate functions.

Note how the *talkMIDI()* functions simplify the process of sending data and how the *noteOn()* and *noteOff()* functions provide a friendly interface for handling raw MIDI data in Listing 2.

Listing 7.2 Helper functions

```
void noteOn(byte channel, byte note, byte attack_velocity)
{
    talkMIDI( (0x90 | channel), note, attack_velocity);
}

void noteOff(byte channel, byte note, byte release_velocity)
{
    talkMIDI( (0x80 | channel), note, release_velocity);
}

//Sends a MIDI command
void talkMIDI(byte cmd, byte data1, byte data2)
{
    digitalWrite(ledPin, HIGH);
    mySerial.write(cmd);
    mySerial.write(data1);
    mySerial.write(data2);
    digitalWrite(ledPin, LOW);
}

void talkMIDI(byte cmd, byte data1)
{
    digitalWrite(ledPin, HIGH);
    mySerial.write(cmd);
```

```
        mySerial.write(data1);
        digitalWrite(ledPin, LOW);
}
```

The sketch in Listing 7.3, shown in its entirety, repeatedly plays a whole-tone scale. Note how the *talkMIDI()* function is called from within the *setup()* function to establish channel volume, the GM1 bank, and instrument sound (via a program change). Also note that a pin is assigned to the LED, which flashes in response to MIDI messages.

Listing 7.3 Whole-tone sketch

```
//Arduino for Musicians
//Listing 7.3: Music Instrument Shield-Whole Tone
#include <SoftwareSerial.h>

SoftwareSerial mySerial(2, 3); // RX, TX

byte resetMIDI = 4;              //Tied to VS1053 Reset line
byte ledPin = 13;               //MIDI traffic inidicator
void setup()
{
    Serial.begin(57600);

    //Setup soft serial for MIDI control
    mySerial.begin(31250);

    //Reset the VS1053
    pinMode(resetMIDI, OUTPUT);
    digitalWrite(resetMIDI, LOW);
    delay(100);

    digitalWrite(resetMIDI, HIGH);
    delay(100);

    //Set up MIDI: 0xB0 is channel message
    //set channel volume to near max (127)
    talkMIDI(0xB0, 0x07, 120);

    //Default bank GM1
    talkMIDI(0xB0, 0, 0x00);
    //Set instrument with program change (0 = GM piano)
    talkMIDI(0xC0, 0, 0);
}
void loop()
{
    int note = 60; //Middle C
    for(int c = 0; c < 7; c++)
    {
        noteOn(0, note, 120);
        delay(125); //delay for 1/8 second
        noteOff(0, note, 0);

        //Ascending whole-steps = whole-tone scale
        note +=2;
    }
}
```

```
void noteOn(byte channel, byte note, byte attack_velocity)
{
    talkMIDI( (0x90 | channel), note, attack_velocity);
}

void noteOff(byte channel, byte note, byte release_velocity)
{
    talkMIDI( (0x80 | channel), note, release_velocity);
}

/* Some MIDI commands have only one data byte so two
functions are provided to handle messages with one
or two data bytes. */
void talkMIDI(byte cmd, byte data1, byte data2)
{
    digitalWrite(ledPin, HIGH);
    mySerial.write(cmd);
    mySerial.write(data1);
    mySerial.write(data2);
    digitalWrite(ledPin, LOW);
}

void talkMIDI(byte cmd, byte data1)
{
    digitalWrite(ledPin, HIGH);
    mySerial.write(cmd);
    mySerial.write(data1);
    digitalWrite(ledPin, LOW);
}
```

7.1 MUSIC INSTRUMENT SHIELD: SCALE

"Steve Reich" Sketch

A slightly more advanced sketch will illustrate one way that the Music Instrument Shield could be used for an interactive application. In this sketch, two sounds (on different MIDI channels) are panned hard left and right. The sounds are used to play an arpeggiated pattern at a rate determined by one of two potentiometers. Changes to either or both of the potentiometers create musical interactions that are somewhat reminiscent of some of Steve Reich's work, such as "Violin Phase." Of course, there are many interesting enhancements that could be made, such as adding additional potentiometers to control transposition or range. Another enhancement would be to use an array to store notes and durations of a musical phrase. The primary differences with the "Steve Reich" sketch and the basic note output example are shown below, and the entire sketch, along with all of the other examples in this chapter, is available from the OUP website.

Panning

In addition to setting channel volume, the *setup()* function sends a program change on two channels and pans the sounds hard left and right. Note that hexadecimal or decimal notation can be used for any of the parameters in the *talkMIDI()* function—it's just a matter of personal preference. In this example I used decimal notation for the commands (e.g., program change on channel 1 = 192 and program change on channel 2 = 193), but many MIDI tables list those values in "hex," in which case you would simply use the hexadecimal notation *0xC0* and *0xC1*:

```
//0xB0 is channel message, set channel volume to 85
talkMIDI(176, 0x07, 85);
talkMIDI(177, 0x07, 85);
talkMIDI(176, 0, 0x00);        //Default bank GM1
talkMIDI(177, 0, 0x00);

//Set instruments with program change on the given channel
talkMIDI(192, sound1, 0);
talkMIDI(193, sound2, 0);

//Pan the sounds hard left and right
talkMIDI(176, 10, 0);          //Control change on Ch. 1 (pan
                               //= 10)
talkMIDI(177, 10, 127);        //Control change on Ch. 2 (pan
                               //= 10)
```

trackLoop()

The other point of interest in this sketch is a function called *trackLoop()*. Its job is to check the value of a potentiometer and to alter the delay between events by scaling or mapping the value returned by *analogRead()*. The function also outputs MIDI Note-On and Note-Off events depending on the function parameter *last_time*. The function is particularly interesting because the last two parameters are sent by *reference* as is indicated by the ampersand prior to the name of the parameter:

```
unsigned long int &last_time
```

In most cases, parameters are sent by *value*, which means that the parameter can be read (but not altered) by a function. When a parameter is sent by *reference*, the function *can* change the value of a variable and the change "sticks" when the function returns. This can be an incredibly powerful feature (and also a source of hard-to-detect bugs). In the context of the *trackLoop()* function, a *single* function can be used to track and alter the variables associated with multiple patterns. This prevents a great deal of cumbersome and redundant coding that would be necessary to work with separate variables in separate functions. The end result is that the main *loop()* function is very simple:

```
void loop()
{
    trackLoop(channel1, delay1_pin, delay1, last_time1,
            current_pitch1);
    trackLoop(channel2, delay2_pin, delay2, last_time2,
            current_pitch2);
}
```

As shown in Listing 7.4, the *trackLoop()* function reads the pin associated with one of the potentiometers and scales the delay from 20 to 2000 ms. The function checks the current time against the variable, *last_time,* and sends

Note-On and Note-Off messages if the amount of time is greater than the variable named *theDelay*. The variable *current_pitch* (a reference) is transposed by the constant named transposition, and the variable *last_time* (also a reference) is updated to reflect the current time.

Listing 7.4 trackLoop() function

```
void trackLoop(int channel, int delay_pin, int theDelay,
unsigned long int &last_time, int &current_pitch)
{
    theDelay = analogRead(delay_pin);
    theDelay = map(theDelay, 0, 1023, 20, 2000);

    //Pseudo arpeggiator
    unsigned long current_time = millis();
    if(current_time - last_time >= theDelay)
    {
        //Turn off last note
        noteOff(channel, current_pitch, 0);
        current_pitch += transposition;
        if(current_pitch > highestNote)
        {
            current_pitch = lowestNote;
        }
        noteOn(channel, current_pitch, noteVelocity);
        last_time = current_time;
    }
}
```

149

7.2 MUSIC INSTRUMENT SHIELD: "STEVE REICH" SKETCH

Adafruit Wave Shield

Adafruit's *Wave Shield* is a popular shield for audio playback. The shield (see Figure 7.2) provides support for playing low-resolution mono .wav files from an SD card. Although the *Wave Shield* won't replace an iPod, it is a relatively inexpensive way to add wave file playback and could be a good choice for an interactive kiosk or to trigger music or sound effects in a theater production. Note that it is *not* possible to simultaneously play back multiple audio files. Some (more expensive) shields like SparkFun Electronics' *WAV Trigger* do offer polyphonic playback should you want to create an interactive drum machine or other polyphonic device.

Wave Shield Library

As with most shields, a special library is provided by the manufacturer and can be downloaded at: https://learn.adafruit.com/adafruit-wave-shield-audio-shield-for-arduino. The library is built around four primary classes—*SdReader, FatVolume, FatReader, and WaveHC*—that do a great job of hiding the low-level tasks of reading data from an SD card.

FIGURE 7.2

Adafruit Wave Shield.
(Photo by Adafruit. Used
by permission.)

Pin Assignments

Pins 11, 12, and 13 are configured for communication with the SD and can't be changed. The Wave Shield documentation suggests the pin assignments shown in Table 7.1 for the other pins (see Figure 7.3 for a close-up view of the pins).

TABLE 7.1 Wave Shield Pin Assignments

Pin	Function
2	LCS
3	CLK
4	DI
5	LAT
10	CCS

Preparing Audio Files for Use with the Wave Shield

One downside of the Wave Shield is that audio files are limited to 22kHz, 16-bit, mono PCM for playback on the device. Although this is reasonable for playback of music or sound effects on stage, it does preclude the device for high-resolution applications.

For most users, the free open-source application named Audiacity will be a good choice as an audio editor to edit and convert files for use with the Wave Shield. Audacity is available for download at http://audacity.sourceforge.net.

FIGURE 7.3

Close-up view of pin assignments. (Photo adapted from one by Adafruit. Used by permission.)

To prepare a file for use, load a monophonic audio file and ensure that the sample rate is set to 16 bits via the Set Sample Format menu. Then, select 22050Hz (or lower) from the Project rate button. Finally, ensure that WAV (Microsoft 16 bit PCM) is selected from the File Formats tab of the Preferences menu. The file can then be exported as a WAV from the File menu and stored or copied to the SD card you intend to use with the Wave Shield. Be sure to name the file in 8.3 format (e.g., FILENAME.WAV) or the files will not be visible to the Wave Shield library.

Note that stereo files can be converted to mono by selecting the Split Stereo Track option, setting both tracks to Mono, and reducing gain as necessary. The separate mono tracks can then be mixed in mono via the Quick Mix menu option.

Loading a File

It is surprisingly easy to initiate playback of a .wav file using the Wave Shield. A first step is to import the WaveHC header files and instantiate instances of the four primary classes as seen in Listing 7.5.[2]

Listing 7.5 Header files and instantiation

```
//Include libary header files
#include <WaveHC.h>
#include <WaveUtil.h>

SdReader card;          //Holds card information
FatVolume fatVolume;    //Holds partition information
FatReader root;         //Holds root directory information
FatReader file;         //Represents the .WAV file
WaveHC wave;            //Wave audio object
```

Next, the objects representing the card, fat volume, and root directory are initialized as shown in Listing 7.6. (Note that error checks are shown in a later example.)

Listing 7.6 Initializing the card, volume and root directory (error checking shown in a later example)

```
card.init();
fatVolume.init(card);
root.openRoot(fatVolume);
```

Assuming no errors were reported in the previous initialization, it is now possible to open a file with a call to *file.open()* and to associate it with a wave object with a call to *wave.create()* as shown in Listing 7.7.

Listing 7.7 Opening a file and associating the file with a wave object

```
file.open(root, "MYFILE.WAV")
wave.create(file);
```

WaveHC Member Functions and Data Members

As shown in Table 7.2, a number of methods are available once a file has been created for use by the WaveHC class.

TABLE 7.2 WaveHC Methods

Return Value	Method
uint32_t	getSize(void)
uint8_t	isPaused(void)
void	pause()
void	play()
int16_t	readWaveData(uint8_t *buff, uint16_t len)
void	resume(void)
void	seek(uint32_t pos)
void	setSampleRate(uint32_t samplerate)
void	stop()

In addition to the methods listed in Table 7.2, several public data members provide additional information about the given WaveHC object:

```
uint8_t           channels;
uint32_t          dwSamplesPerSec;
uint8_t           bitsPerSample;
uint32_t          remainingBytesInChunk;
volatile uint8_t  isplaying;
uint32_t          errors;
```

For example, the number of samples per second can be determined by reading the value of the data member, *dwSamplesPerSec*, as follows:

```
uint32_t samplesPerSecond = wave.dwSamplesPerSec;
```

Playing a Wave File

Once a file has been loaded and the WaveHC object created, member functions can be used to play the file, stop, resume, or seek to a specific location. For example, toggling play and stop (e.g., via a switch or serial input) could be handled as follows:

```
if(wave.isplaying)
{
      wave.stop();
}else{
      wave.play();
}
```

Demonstration Sketch

The concepts from the preceding section are combined in the form of a demonstration sketch. Listing 7.8, which is available at the OUP website, demonstrates how a file can be loaded from an SD card. Playback and rewind is initiated via the Serial interface, and, in an interesting twist, the playback speed can be set to normal or slow (suitable for transcribing fast melodic passages). This is accomplished by setting the sample rate to half its normal speed:

```
wave.setSampleRate(wave.dwSamplesPerSec/2);
```

Listing 7.8 Interactive playback

```
//Arduino for Musicians
//Listing 7.8: Wave Shield Interactive Playback
//Based on examples distributed with the WaveHC library

//Include libary header files
#include <WaveHC.h>
#include <WaveUtil.h>

SdReader card;         //Holds card information
FatVolume fatVolume;   //Holds partition information
FatReader root;        //Holds root directory information
FatReader file;        //Represents the .WAV file
WaveHC wave;           //Wave audio object

boolean SLOW_SPEED = false;   //Tracks the current speed

void setup()
{
    Serial.begin(9600);
    Serial.println("Wave Shield Test");

    //Attempt to initialize the card
    if(!card.init())
    {
        Serial.println("Card init. failed.");
    }

    //Enable optimized read. Some cards may time out
    card.partialBlockRead(true);
```

153

```
            if(!fatVolume.init(card))
            {
              Serial.println("FAT volume initialization failed.");
            }

            if(!root.openRoot(fatVolume))
            {
                Serial.println("Problem opening root.");
            }

            /*Open a file by name:
            See openByIndex sketch for a more efficient approach.
            Also see daphc sketch for an example of reading
            files from a directory. */

            if(!file.open(root, "MYFILE.WAV"))
            {
                Serial.println("Problem opening file.");
            }

            //Create wave
            if(!wave.create(file))
            {
                Serial.println("ER: Wave create.");
            }
        }

        void loop()
        {
             //Check for command
            if (Serial.available() > 0)
            {
                char command = Serial.read();

                //Use spacebar to toggle play vs. stop
                if(command == ' ')
                {
                    if(wave.isplaying)
                    {
                        wave.stop();
                    }else{
                     wave.play();
                    }
                }

                //Toggle slow speed
                if(command == 's')
                {
                    if(SLOW_SPEED)
                    {
                        //Resume normal speed
                        wave.setSampleRate(wave.dwSamplesPerSec);
                        SLOW_SPEED = false;
                    }else{
                        wave.setSampleRate(wave.dwSamplesPerSec/2);
                        SLOW_SPEED = true;
                    }
                }
```

```
         //Rewind to begining (position 0)
         if(command == 'r')
         {
            //Rewind to beginning
            wave.seek(0L);
         }
      }
}
```

GinSing

GinSing is a unique synthesis shield based on the *Babblebot IC* (see Figure 7.4). The shield is available at http://www.ginsingsound.com and is capable of outputting speech and a variety of synthesized waveforms.

7.3 ADAFRUIT
WAVE SHIELD

FIGURE 7.4

GinSing. (Photo courtesy GinSing.)

Four operational modes are available via the GinSing library:[3]

Preset Mode: A simple mode that is used to access on-board presets.

Poly Mode: Polyphonic mode provides the capability of producing six simultaneous tones.

Voice Mode: Used to create artificial speech via speech fragments called allophones. The pitch of speech playback can also be controlled.

Synth Mode: Provides access to two banks of three digitally controlled oscillators (DCOs) that are functionally similar to an analog synthesizer. The DCOs can be modulated for many interesting synthetic effects.

We will look at two of the modes in this section: *voice mode* and *synth mode*. Once you get a feel for the function of the library, it will be relatively easy to follow the technical information provided in the *GinSing Reference Guide* and *GinSing Programmers Guide*.

Voice Mode

After installing the GinSing library, a first step in writing a GinSing sketch is to import the GinSing library and create an instance of the GinSing class. As is also evident in the following code snippet, pins are defined and passed to the GinSing object via its *begin()* method in the *setup()* function:[4]

```
//Include header files from GinSing library
#include <GinSing.h>

//Create an instance of the GinSing class
GinSing GS;

//Define standard pins for receive, send, and overflow
#define rcvPin 4
#define sndPin 3
#define ovfPin 2

void setup()
{
    //Initialize the GinSing library
    GS.begin( rcvPin , sndPin , ovfPin );
}
```

Pointers and the Voice Object

The GinSing class provides a method, *getVoice()*, that returns a pointer to a GinSingVoice object. Pointers differ from other variables in that a pointer *points* to a memory location instead of storing a "regular" value such as an integer or character. For purposes of using the GinSing library, the main difference between using a pointer and nonpointer involves the way member functions are called. Thus far, we have always used a "dot" to access a member function of a class. For example, in Listing 7.9 the GinSing *begin()* method is called in this way:

```
GS.begin( rcvPin , sndPin , ovfPin );
```

In contrast, an "arrow" representing a *member selection operator* is used to call a member function when a pointer to a class is used:

```
pointerToSomeClass->someMemberFunction();
```

The GinSing class returns a pointer to *member classes*—classes contained by a the main GinSing class. In Listing 7.9, the *getVoice()* method returns a pointer to a member class named *GinSingVoice* and assigns the memory location to the pointer named *v*. (Note that the asterisk before the variable name indicates that the variable is a pointer instead of a regular variable.) Once the pointer points to a valid memory location, it can be used to call member functions through the use of the member selection "arrow" operator.

Listing 7.9 Getting a pointer to GinSingVoice

```
//Ask the GinSing object (GS) to return a pointer to the
//voice object
GinSingVoice *v = GS.getVoice();

//Use the pointer to call the begin() method
v->begin();
```

Speech

The GinSing library provides a full complement of phonemes that can be used to produce words and phrases. Words are formed by combining phonemes into an array of *GSAllophone* objects and passing the array to the *speak()* method as in Listing 7.11. Incidentally, the array shown in Listing 7.10 forms the word "Arduino." A list of phonemes and their descriptions is provided in the *GinSingDefs.h* file that is installed with the GinSing library.

Source Listing 7.10 Creating an array of GSAllophone phonemes

```
GSAllophone phrase[] = {_AA, _R, _DE, _W, _EE, _BENDDN, _NE,
_OE, _ENDPHRASE};

v->speak ( phrase );
```

Voice Mode Demonstration

A complete demonstration sketch is shown in Listing 7.11. This example, which repeats the phrase "Arduino Rocks" with a low-pitched robotic voice, could be used as the basis for a number or interesting applications such as MIDI to speech module or interactive voice synthesizer. Be sure to experiment by using the *setNote()* method to establish the pitch of the voice and try different phonemes to get a feel for how the voice synthesizer works.

Listing 7.11 GinSing voice test

```
//Arduino for Musicians
//Ginsing Voice Test

//Include header files from GinSing library
#include <GinSing.h>

//Create an instance of the GinSing class
GinSing GS;

//Define standard pins for receive, send, and overflow
#define rcvPin 4
#define sndPin 3
#define ovfPin 2
```

157

```
//Create an array of phonemes representing "Arduino Rocks"
//NOTE: See GinSingDefs.h for phoneme constants
GSAllophone phrase[] = {_AA, _R, _DE, _W, _EE, _BENDDN, _NE,
_OE, _PA1, _R, _AA, _PITCHDN , _PITCHUP, _EK ,
_SO , _PAO , _ENDPHRASE };

void setup()
{
    //Initialize the GinSing library
    GS.begin( rcvPin , sndPin , ovfPin );
}

void loop()
{
    //Ask the GinSing object (GS) to return a pointer to
    //the voice object
    GinSingVoice *v = GS.getVoice();
    //Use the pointer to call the begin() method
    v->begin();
    //Set the vocal pitch
    v->setNote ( C_1 );
    //Speak the phrase
    v->speak ( phrase );
    //Delay 500 ms longer than the length of the phrase
    delay ( v->getMillis ( phrase ) + 500 );
}

void shutdown()
{
    //According to the documentation, calling GS.end() in
    //shutdown() should prevent "stuck" notes
    GS.end();
}
```

7.4 GINSING VOICE SYNTHESIZER DEMO

Synthesizer Mode

The GinSing synthesizer mode is functionally similar to voice mode, but additional methods are provided to select banks and to set patches. The next few paragraphs show one way to configure a synthesizer patch on the shield.

Setting Up the Synthesizer

The setup method shown below initializes an instance of the GinSing object and calls the *getSynth()* method to return a pointer to the synthesizer object. The object is assigned to the global pointer, *pSynth*.

```
void setup()
{
    //Initialize the GinSing library
    GS.begin( rcvPin , sndPin , ovfPin );

    //As GinSing to return a pointer to the synth object:
    pSynth = GS.getSynth();
    //Start the synth
    pSynth->begin();
```

The pointer, *pSynth*, is then used to call the *setBank()* method in order to select bank A. It is also used to call *setPatch()* in order to set the basic patch for the unit. A number of enumerations, which are listed in the *GinSingDefs.h* header file, can be combined using the logical OR operator to create a patch for the instrument. In the following example, oscillator one provides audio output to the mixer while oscillator 3 is configured to modulate the frequency of oscillator 1.

```
//Set up the synth
pSynth->selectBank(BANK_A); //Subsequent calls will refer to
//this bank

pSynth->setPatch( OSC_1_TO_MIXER | OSC_3_FRQMOD_OSC_1 );
```

The *setup()* function concludes with calls to *setWaveform()*, *setFrequency()*, and *setAmplitude()* to establish the waveform, frequency, and amplitude of the digitally controlled oscillator.

```
//Set parameters for OSC_1:
pSynth->setWaveform(OSC_1, RAMP);
pSynth->setFrequency(OSC_1, 440.0f);   //Default frequency
pSynth->setAmplitude(OSC_1, 0.0f);     //Amplitude = 50%
```

Mini Synthesizer Project

A complete "Mini Synthesizer" project is shown in Listing 7.12 and could be used as the basis for a more expansive digital synthesizer. The MIDI receiver circuit from Chapter 5 is used, along with the MIDI library, to provide MIDI input to the synthesizer, and two potentiometers, connected to the A0 and A1 analog pins, provide real-time control of modulation rate and depth. As described in Chapter 5, callback functions are used to process incoming MIDI messages. A final function, *handleLFOPots()*, tracks the position of the potentiometers and updates the rate and depth of modulation. Ideas for expanding the synthesizer include adding switches to select waveforms, adding additional (possibly detuned) oscillators, and using a global floating point variable to create portamento—a gradual sliding between notes.

Listing 7.12 Mini GinSing Synthesizer

```
//Arduino for Musicians
//Listing 7.12: Mini GinSing Synthesizer

//Include header files for GinSing and MIDI libraries
#include <GinSing.h>
#include <MIDI.h>

//Instantiate GinSing and MIDI objects
GinSing GS;
MIDI_CREATE_DEFAULT_INSTANCE();

//Create a pointer to the GinSing synth
GinSingSynth *pSynth = NULL;
```

159

```
//Define standard pins for receive, send, and overflow
#define rcvPin 4
#define sndPin 3
#define ovfPin 2

//Define analog pins for reading low frequency oscillation
//rate and depth
#define lfoRatePot 0
#define lfoDepthPot 1

//LFO sensitivity
#define lfoSensitivity 2

//Variable to track note-on status
byte note_on = 0;

void setup()
{
    //Initialize the GinSing library
    GS.begin( rcvPin , sndPin , ovfPin );

    //As GinSing to return a pointer to the synth object:
    pSynth = GS.getSynth();
    //Start the synth
    pSynth->begin();

    //Set up the synth
    pSynth->selectBank(BANK_A); //Subsequent calls will
                                //refer to this bank

    //Patch OSC1 and OSC2 to the mixer and set OSC_3 to
    //modulate the frequency of OSC_1
    pSynth->setPatch( OSC_1_TO_MIXER | OSC_3_FRQMOD_OSC_1 );

    //Set parameters for OSC_1:
    pSynth->setWaveform(OSC_1, RAMP);
    pSynth->setFrequency(OSC_1, 440.0f);    //Default frequency
    pSynth->setAmplitude(OSC_1, 0.0f);     //Amplitude = 50%

    //Set parameters for OSC_3.
    //Experiment with waveform, frequency, and amplitude
    //settings to hear different LFO effects:
    pSynth->setWaveform(OSC_3, SINE);        //Classic sine

    pSynth->setWavemode(OSC_3, POSITIVE);    //No zero crossing

    //These values will be set via potentiometers--uncomment
    //to "hard code" LFO
    //pSynth->setFrequency(OSC_3, 6.0f);
    //pSynth->setAmplitude(OSC_3, 0.03f);

    //Connect the callback functions to the MIDI library
    MIDI.setHandleNoteOn(myHandleNoteOn);
    MIDI.setHandleNoteOff(myHandleNoteOff);

    MIDI.begin(MIDI_CHANNEL_OMNI);    // Listen on all channels
}

void loop()
{
```

```
      //Call MIDI.read().
      //MIDI class will automatically call callback functions
      as needed.
      MIDI.read();
      handleLFOPots();
}

void shutdown()
{
   //Calling GS.end() in shutdown() should prevent "stuck"
   //notes
   GS.end();
}

void myHandleNoteOn(byte channel, byte note, byte velocity)
{
    //Convert MIDI note to frequency
    float freq = (float) 440.0 * (float) (pow(2, (note - 57)
    /12.0));
    pSynth->setFrequency(OSC_1, freq);

    //Convert MIDI velocity to amplitude (0.0 to 1.0)
    float amp = (float) velocity / 127.0f;
    pSynth->setAmplitude(OSC_1, amp);

    //Store the current note
    note_on = note;
}

void myHandleNoteOff(byte channel, byte note, byte velocity)
{
    //Avoid turning off sound if another note is playing
    if(note == note_on)
    {
        pSynth->setAmplitude(OSC_1, 0.0);
    }
}

void handleLFOPots()
{
   //Use two static variables to store most recent
   //potentiometer reading
   static int lastRate = 0;
   static int lastDepth = 0;

   //Read the LFO rate potentiometer and update LFO if
   //necessary
   int rate = analogRead(lfoRatePot);
   if(rate < lastRate - lfoSensitivity || rate > lastRate +
   lfoSensitivity)
   {
       lastRate = rate;
       //This line turns the rate into a percentage and
       //multiplies the theresult by 50
       pSynth->setFrequency(OSC_3, ((float) rate / 1023.0f) *
       50.0f);
   }
```

161

```
//Read the LFO depth potentiometer and update LFO if
necessary
int depth = analogRead(lfoDepthPot);
if(depth < lastDepth - lfoSensitivity || depth >
lastDepth + lfoSensitivity)
{
    lastDepth = depth;
    //This line turns the depth into a percentage and
    //multiplies theresult by 50
    pSynth->setAmplitude(OSC_3, ((float) depth / 1023.0f)
            * 50.0f);
}
}
```

**7.5 GINSING
MINI SYNTH**

162

Gameduino

The Gameduino (see Figure 7.5) is an interesting shield in that it provides primitive audio *and* VGA graphic capabilities. The functionality in terms of audio output is limited: the unit can produce sine waves, noise, or output sample data, but the unit *can* produce 64 simultaneous sine waves, making it a good platform for *additive synthesis* (more on this in a moment). Gameduino could also be a good choice for individuals who want to explore the intersection of audio and visual elements for music synthesis. For example, pixel position could be used to indicate pitch and time, and pixel color could indicate the intensity of a waveform in a way that is reminiscent of the visual/audio software synthesizer, *MetaSynth*.

FIGURE 7.5

Gameduino.

Using the Gameduino

The Gameduino library, which is available for download at http://excamera
.com/sphinx/gameduino/GD/index.html, provides a header file (GD.h) that
contains a C++ class named GDClass. As with other libraries in this chapter, the
GD class hides most of the challenging details of working with the Serial
Peripheral Interface (SPI) and the hardware layer.

A Gameduino project begins by including SPI.h and GD.h. SPI.h is a
header file that contains functions and data for the *Serial Peripheral* Interface,
a protocol used to quickly communicate with peripheral devices over short
distances.[5] In contrast, GD.h contains the software underpinnings of the
Gameduino system.[6]

The *setup()* function calls *GD.begin()*, which handles all of the details of
initializing the Gameduino board and setting up SPI. In Listing 7.13, two constants are also defined (SINE = 0, and NOISE = 1).

Listing 7.13 Gameduino setup

```
//Arduino for Musicians
//Listing 7.13: Gameduino LFO

#include <SPI.h>
#include <GD.h>

const int SINE = 0;
const int NOISE = 1;   //Not used in this sketch

float freq = 100.0;

void setup()
{
    GD.begin();
}
```

The main loop outputs a sine wave via the *voice()* method, which takes the
following parameters: the voice number (0 to 63), type of waveform (0 = sine or
1 = noise), frequency in Hertz, left amplitude, and right amplitude. In the following example, a variable named *freq* is slightly increased on every iteration of
the loop. The variable is used to change the frequency of voice 0 in much the
same way that an analog *low-frequency oscillator* functions as a source of voltage
control for a voltage-controlled oscillator.

```
void loop()
{
    GD.voice(0, SINE, freq, 100, 100);

    //Pseudo low-frequency oscillator
    freq += 0.2;
    if(freq > 4000)
    {
        //reset frequency
        freq = 100;
    }
}
```

Additive Synthesis

The concept of additive synthesis is related to Fourier's theorem, which states that "any signal may be broken down into a sum of sine waves of various amplitudes and phases."[7] The reverse is also true, so any complex waveform can be created by combining sine waves of various amplitudes and phases. A simple example of this concept comes from the excamera website. In the following function, the second, third, and fourth partials are added to the fundamental waveform (voice 0). In this example, each partial is fractionally smaller than the previous partial which results in an approximation of a sawtooth waveform:

```
void sawtooth_wave(int f0)
{
    GD.voice(0, SINE, f0,     100,   100);
    GD.voice(1, SINE, 2 * f0, 100/2, 100/2);
    GD.voice(2, SINE, 3 * f0, 100/3, 100/3);
    GD.voice(3, SINE, 4 * f0, 100/4, 100/4);
}
```

A square wave can also be formed by combining sine waves of various frequencies and amplitudes. In this example, note how odd partials (3, 5, and 7 times the fundamental) approximate a square wave:

```
void squarewave(int f0)
{
    GD.voice(0, SINE, f0,     100,   100);
    GD.voice(1, SINE, 3 * f0, 100/3, 100/3);
    GD.voice(2, SINE, 5 * f0, 100/5, 100/5);
    GD.voice(3, SINE, 7 * f0, 100/7, 100/7);
}
```

Additive Gameduino Synthesizer

More complex waveforms can be created by altering the amplitude and frequency of the overtones in real time. The final demonstration project, an interactive additive synthesizer, demonstrates one such approach. In this example, six sine waves are configured to produce an initial sawtooth waveform, and a bank of potentiometers function like the rate control on a low-frequency oscillator to modulate the amplitude of each of the overtones, thus providing a way to "morph" the timbre of the tone in real time. The potentiometers are wired as in Figure 7.6, but take care when making connections: it is all too easy to connect the wrong terminals on the potentiometer, which can create a component-damaging short when the potentiometer is set to zero resistance.

Using a Structure and an Array

As with most sketches, the additive synthesizer sketch establishes several variables and constants. However, the *struct* keyword used in this section of the sketch is new and requires some explanation. Given that the sketch will track

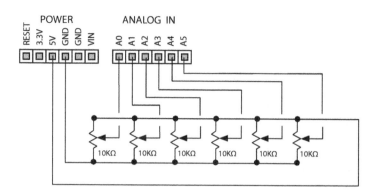

FIGURE 7.6

Potentiometer wiring.

several oscillators and associated parameters such as frequency, amplitude, and modulation rate, it would be convenient to bundle the parameters into a single unit. The *struct* keyword provides one way to accomplish the task. A structure can contain any number of *data members* that can be used to define a given object. In this example, we will use a structure to group the parameters relating to a sine wave into a convenient "bundle:"

```
struct SineParameters{
  long last_time;  //Updated at the end of each wait_time
                   //cycle
  long wait_time;  //Amount of time to wait before altering
                   //amplitude
  int amplitude;   //The current amplitude or level of the
                   //sine wave
  boolean add;     //True if amplitude is currently being
                   //incremented
  float frequency; //The frequency of the sine wave
};
```

Next, an array of objects of the type SineParameters (the structure that was defined in the last step) are created:

```
//Create an array of structs
SineParameters sine_wave[NUM_POTS];
```

Use braces and an index number to read or set the values of one of the objects in the array. For example, the frequency of the first (zero) element in the array could be set as follows:

```
sine_wave[0].frequency = 440;
```

Initializing a Sawtooth Waveform

Using arrays makes it easy to read or alter the values of each sine wave parameter without using lots of redundant code. For example, a helper function named *initSawtooth()* (Listing 7.14) makes quick work of setting up the fundamental and each overtone based on an arbitrary frequency and amplitude.

Listing 7.14 Initializing a sawtooth waveform

```
//Use this function to initialize the sine array as a
//sawtooth
void initSawtooth(int f0, int amplitude)
{
    //initialize overtones
    for(int i = 0; i < NUM_POTS; i++)
    {
        //Handle the fundamental differently than the
        //overtones
        if(i == 0)
        {
            sine_wave[i].frequency = f0;
            sine_wave[i].amplitude = amplitude;
        }else{
            //Initialize overtones
            sine_wave[i].frequency = f0 * (i+1);
            sine_wave[i].amplitude = amplitude/ (i + 1);
        }
        //These defaults are the same for the fundamental
        //and overtones:
        sine_wave[i].last_time = 0;
        sine_wave[i].add = true;
    }
}
```

Updating the Fundamental Frequency

Similarly, updating the frequency of the waveform is easy using a loop to index each element in the array. The helper function named *updateFrequency()* (Listing 7.15) accomplishes the task.

Listing 7.15 Updating frequency

```
void updateFrequency(int f0)
{
    for(int i = 0; i < NUM_POTS; i++)
    {
        if(i == 0) //Handle the fundamental differently than
                   //overtones
        {
            sine_wave[0].frequency = f0;
        }else{
            sine_wave[i].frequency = f0 * (i+1);
        }
    }
}
```

Main Loop()

All of the fun happens in the main loop (Listing 7.16). Here, the current time is compared to the "last time" parameter of each sine wave to see if the amplitude should be incremented or decremented. The function also reads the values of each pot and uses the value to update the *wait_time* parameter associated with each sine wave. Bigger values slow the rate of amplitude modulation. Finally, the function calls *GD.voice()* to update sine wave parameters each time *current_time – last_time >= wait_time*.

Listing 7.16 Main *loop()*

```
void loop()
{
    //Get the current time
    long current_time = millis();

    //Update the wait time of each sine wave based on the
    //value of pots 1-6
    for(int i = 0; i< NUM_POTS; i++)
    {
        //Comment the following line to experiment sans
        //potentiometers
        sine_wave[i].wait_time = analogRead(i);
        if(current_time - sine_wave[i].last_time >= sine_
        wave[i].wait_time)
        {
            updateSineParams(i);
            sine_wave[i].last_time = current_time;
        }
        GD.voice(i, SINE, sine_wave[i].frequency, sine_
        wave[i].amplitude,
                  sine_wave[i].amplitude);
    }
    //Call updateFrequency(freq) to update the frequency in
    //response to user input, algorithm, etc.
}
```

The entire sketch is shown in Listing 7.17. Although the sketch is not unduly long, it is a bit awkward to follow given its "pure C" underpinnings. As you will see in the next chapter, C++ can often be used to simplify and clarify the logic of more complex sketches.

Listing 7.17 Complete additive synthesizer sketch

```
//Arduino for Musicians
//Listing 7.17: Gameduino Additive Synthesizer

#include <SPI.h>
#include <GD.h>

const int SINE = 0;
const int NUM_POTS = 6;
const int STEP = 2;

//Define a struct to hold sinewave paramters
struct SineParameters{
  long last_time;   //Updated at the end of each wait_time
                    //cycle
  long wait_time;   //Amount of time to wait before altering
                    //amplitude
  int amplitude;    //The current amplitude or level of the
                    //sine wave
```

167

```
    boolean add;        //True if amplitude is currently being
                        //incremented.
    float frequency; //The frequency of the sine wave
};
//Create an array of structs
SineParameters sine_wave[NUM_POTS];

void setup()
{
    //Initialize a sawtooth wave
    initSawtooth(400, 100);

    //Initialize the Gameduino
    GD.begin();

    /* TEST: Uncomment and change values to experiment sans
    potentiometers (also comment out the analogRead()
    line in the main loop()) */
//    sine_wave[0].wait_time = 1000;
//    sine_wave[1].wait_time = 800;
//    sine_wave[2].wait_time = 600;
//    sine_wave[3].wait_time = 300;
//    sine_wave[4].wait_time = 200;
//    sine_wave[5].wait_time = 100;
}

void loop()
{
    //Get the current time
    long current_time = millis();

    //Update the wait time of each sine wave based on the
    //value of pots 1-6
    for(int i = 0; i< NUM_POTS; i++)
    {
        //Comment the following line to experiment sans
        //potentiometers
        sine_wave[i].wait_time = analogRead(i);
        if(current_time - sine_wave[i].last_time >= sine_
        wave[i].wait_time)
        {
            updateSineParams(i);
            sine_wave[i].last_time = current_time;
        }

        GD.voice(i, SINE, sine_wave[i].frequency, sine_
        wave[i].amplitude,
                    sine_wave[i].amplitude);
    }

    //Call updateFrequency(freq) to update the frequency in
    //response to user input, algorithm, etc.
}

void updateSineParams(int i)
{
    if(sine_wave[i].add == true)
```

```
    {
        sine_wave[i].amplitude += STEP;
        if(sine_wave[i].amplitude > 100)
        {
            sine_wave[i].amplitude = 100;
            sine_wave[i].add = false;
        }
    }else{
        sine_wave[i].amplitude -= STEP;
        if(sine_wave[i].amplitude < 0)
        {
            sine_wave[i].amplitude = 0;
            sine_wave[i].add = true;
        }
    }

}
//Use this function to initialize the sine array as a
//sawtooth
void initSawtooth(int f0, int amplitude)
{
    //initialize overtones
    for(int i = 0; i < NUM_POTS; i++)
    {
        //Handle the fundamental differently than the overtones
        if(i == 0)
        {
            sine_wave[i].frequency = f0;
            sine_wave[i].amplitude = amplitude;
        }else{
            //Initialize overtones
            sine_wave[i].frequency = f0 * (i+1);
            sine_wave[i].amplitude = amplitude/ (i + 1);
        }

        //These defaults are the same for the fundamental and
        //overtones:
        sine_wave[i].last_time = 0;
        sine_wave[i].add = true;
    }
}

//Use this function to update the frequency in real-time
void updateFrequency(int f0)
{
    for(int i = 0; i < NUM_POTS; i++)
    {
        if(i == 0) //Handle the fundamental differently than
        //overtones
        {
            sine_wave[0].frequency = f0;
        }else{
            sine_wave[i].frequency = f0 * (i+1);
        }
    }
}
```

Codec Shield

Open Music Labs Codec Shield is a good choice for musicians who want a convenient shield for high-resolution audio input and output. The shield provides 24-bit ADCs and DACs, microphone input, line input and output, and headphone output. Two built-in potentiometers provide a convenient way to update parameters such as modulation rate or depth.

Using the Codec Shield

As with the other shields in this chapter, a first step is to download the Codec Shield library, which is available at: http://wiki.openmusiclabs.com/wiki/ AudioCodecShield.

Once the library is installed and the shield is attached to an Arduino Uno, the library can be included in a sketch with the following statement:

```
#include <AudioCodec.h>
```

However, it is important to note that several constants must be specified before including the file. For example, the following lines specify that both ADCs will be used and a sample rate of 44.1kHz is established:

```
#define SAMPLE_RATE 44 // 44.1kHz sample rate
#define ADCS 2 // use both ADCs

#include <AudioCodec.h>
```

Listing 7.18, which is provided as part of the Codec Shield installation, demonstrates how samples representing the microphone input can be passed through to the audio output. A timer interrupt is automatically called at the specified sample rate, and the samples are read and passed to the output buffer in the ISR function. Although this example doesn't do anything useful other than to show how the unit can be configured for audio input and output, the real power of the Codec Shield will be evident after reading Chapters 9 and 10, which demonstrate direct digital synthesis, audio input, and the basics of real-time signal processing. Several additional sketches involving real-time signal processing and direct digital synthesis are also provided with the Codec Shield library.

Listing 7.18 Codec Shield: microphone input to output

```
/*
microphone.pde
guest openmusiclabs 8.17.11
this program takes input from the MIC pins on the
codecshield.
NOTE: you will have to do a few solder joints to connect
your microphone, a description of this is on the wiki:
http://wiki.openmusiclabs.com/wiki/CodecShieldMicMod
this can also be used with low level instruments, like
guitars,
```

```
to boost the volume on the input.
*/

// setup codec parameters
// must be done before #includes
// see readme file in libraries folder for explanations
#define SAMPLE_RATE 44 // 44.1kHz
#define ADCS 0 // no ADCs are being used
#define MUTEMIC 0 // turn off the mute on the microphone
#define INSEL 1 // select the microphone input
#define MICBOOST 1 // enables the microphone +10dB amp
                   // set this to 0 if its too loud

// include necessary libraries
#include <Wire.h>
#include <SPI.h>
#include <AudioCodec.h>

// create data variables for audio transfer
int left_in = 0x0000;
int left_out = 0x0000;
int right_in = 0x0000;
int right_out = 0x0000;

void setup() {
  AudioCodec_init(); // setup codec registers
  // call this last if setting up other parts
}

void loop() {
  while (1); // reduces clock jitter
}
// timer1 interrupt routine - all data processed here
ISR(TIMER1_COMPA_vect, ISR_NAKED) { // dont store any
//registers

  // &'s are necessary on data_in variables
  AudioCodec_data(&left_in, &right_in, left_out, right_out);

  // pass data through
  left_out = left_in;
  right_out = right_in;

  // dont forget to return from interrupt
  reti();
}
```

Although the sketch utilizes several concepts such as timer callbacks that will be explained in later chapters, the brief sketch is useful in showing how easy it is to establish high-resolution audio input and output using the Codec Shield.

Conclusion

While it is fun and informative to create Arduino projects from scratch, shields can be a good choice for many users. In some many cases, shields are attractive from the perspective of time *and* cost saving. For example, the many components such as a microSD card reader, Digital Audio Converter, connectors, potentiometer, and related parts in the Adafruit Wave Shield would likely cost as much as (or more than) the premade commercial product if purchased separately. Similarly, the Gameduino and GinSing shields feature unique functionality that would be challenging to develop from scratch. It goes without saying that the Web is the best source to learn about new and interesting shields, and advanced readers may even want to consider *crowdsourcing* a shield if you feel there is a need for a new product. One of the real joys of Arduino development is participating in a vibrant ecosystem and having access to the innovative designs and concepts that emerge from other users and commercial developers.

Introduction to C++ Programming

Overview: Moving Away from a Procedural Approach

C is a great language. It's lean and mean and understood by programmers around the world. C provides everything you need to create some wonderful projects with an Arduino. But there is something better; something that can simplify your work and clarify your thought process. I am referring to C++, an extension of the C language that provides a framework for utilizing an *object-oriented* approach to design. Although there is an additional learning curve associated with C++, rest assured that it is not hard to learn once you understand the basics of C, and the extra effort is worth it in terms of a new programming paradigm that will help to simplify and clarify your work. Even if you decide not to embrace C++ in your own work, be sure to skim through the chapter. C++ classes like *EasyButton* and *RotaryEncoder* will make your life easier, so it is a good idea to learn how to utilize preexisting classes in your own projects.

Using Objects

What is object-oriented programming anyway? An object-oriented approach is a way of organizing code so that it more closely resembles the way we organize things in the real world. For example, most people don't look out a window and see tires, glass, chrome, and metal; they see a *car* when those materials are combined in the form of an automobile. Similarly, a *day* represents a unit of time that nicely encapsulates concepts like *ante meridiem* and *post meridiem* as well as hours, minutes, and seconds. C++ is all about helping programmers organize their work in a way that more closely resembles how we already think about objects in the real world. Author Bruce Eckel sums up the benefits of C++ this way: "Like any human language, C++ provides a way to express concepts. If successful, this medium of expression will be significantly easier and more flexible than the alternatives as problems grow larger and more complex."[1]

This chapter explores the basics of the C++ language with a special focus on *classes*, objects that can help you to organize your code and simplify the design process. The section on classes will conclude with a discussion of two demonstration classes, *EasyButton* and *RotaryEncoder*, that will simplify the process of working with momentary switches and rotary encoders. A final class, *TwelveToneMatrix*, will make it easy to write Arduino sketches that incorporate 12-tone matrices and algorithmic functions.

Moving to C++

In pure C, functions or "procedures" form the underlying logic of a program. Although functions often manipulate data, such functions have no real understanding of or relationship to data. To use a modern metaphor, pure C is akin to using an automated voice system to solve a technical problem: the system may help you to eventually solve the problem, but a technical support person will likely be able to help you in a more nuanced way.

Classes

At the heart of C++ is an object-oriented structure called a *class*. Classes are "types that group data and functionality together into encapsulated, cohesive units."[2] One way to visualize the concept of a class is to think of built-in data types like an integer or byte. In C or C++ it is trivial to use an integer in an equation like x = a + b; it just *works* because that logic is built into the language. In the same way, a class can be designed to function just as easily. Once you start thinking in C++, you will likely want to encapsulate everything in a class, and that is not a bad thing.

The classes that you write in C++ will usually consist of two files, a .h *header* file, and a related .cpp *source* file. In essence, the header file provides an "at a glance" overview of the data and methods contained in the class, and the source file provides the code that implements or *defines* the functions declared in the header. (In actuality, programmers sometimes write the body of functions in the header. To keep things simple, I will usually *declare* functions in the header file and *define* them in the .cpp file.)

To make a class in the Arduino environment, click "New Tab" from the drop-down menu on the far right of the IDE and create two files with the name of your class. One file should be named *NameOfClass.h* and the other should be

NameOfClass.cpp. Once you perfect your class, it is easy to make the class available to other sketches by copying the header and implementation files to the Arduino\libraries folder.

Anatomy of a Class

One of the things I find to be tiresome when creating Arduino projects is writing code to track the status of push buttons. The code is always similar: select a pin assignment, set the pin to HIGH in the *setup()* method, turn on an internal pullup resister, poll the input to see if the button has been pressed, and so on. Instead of cutting, pasting, and editing the same code over and over again, a C++ class can be used to encapsulate this useful functionality.

In terms of design, I want the class to hide the tiresome details of handling pushbuttons (including debouncing), but I also want the class to be flexible enough to be easily adapted for use in any program and with a variety of switches. To solve the problem, I created a class called *EasyButton* that contains three variables and three methods. The header (.h) file for *EasyButton* is shown in its entirety in Listing 8.1. Each line of the class will be detailed in the paragraphs that follow.

Listing 8.1 EasyButton.h header file

```
#ifndeif_EASY_BUTTON
#define_EASY_BUTTON

#include "Arduino.h" //Include header file that defines INPUT
//and HIGH

class EasyButton
{
private:
    int m_pin;                      //Digital pin the button
                                    //is connected to
    int m_debounceMS;               //Number of milliseconds
                                    //for debouncing
    unsigned long m_lastEventTime;  //Timestamp of the last
                                    //event
    boolean m_currentState;         //The current state of
                                    //the button
public:
    //Constructor
    EasyButton();

    //Helper method to set pin and number of milliseconds
    //for debounce.
    //Also sets up pullup register.
    void init(int pin, int debounce_milliseconds);

    //Call this to see if the button is being pressed
    bool checkButtonPressed();

    //Use this method when the millis() function is
    //disabled. For example, use increment a counter
    //in the main loop to generate "pseudo" time.
```

```
        bool checkButtonPressed(unsigned long ticks);
};
#endif
```

Preprocessor Directives

The most awkward-looking part of the class is likely the keywords that start with a pound sign. These are known as *preprocessor directives* and are used to prevent compilation errors if a header file is included by more than one source file in a project. These preprocessor directives really function like a big "if" statement that surrounds the class. If the class has not yet been included in a source file in the project, the token following *#ifndef* is defined. If the token has already been defined, the compiler skips to the *#endif* and ignores the code between *#define* and *#endif*. You can name the token anything you want. I usually use a token that relates to the class name.

The keyword *class* is a *declaration* that indicates that a class name is to follow. Its use is similar to declaring a built-in data type, but the class name is followed by opening and closing brackets that contain additional information about the class:

```
class EasyButton
{
    //This is an empty class named EasyButton.
    //Class data and function declarations go here.
};
```

Member Variables

One of the great things about classes is that a class can contain variables and member functions that pertain solely to the class. This marriage of data and functionality is a powerful aspect of the language. In this case, the class contains four *member variables* (variables that are only known to the class). As the names of the variables imply, they are used to store the pin number, debounce time (in milliseconds), current state of the button, and the time (in milliseconds) of the last button press.

```
private:
  int m_pin;                      //Digital pin the button is
                                  //connected to
  int m_debounceMS;               //Number of milliseconds for
                                  //debouncing
  unsigned long m_lastEventTime;  //Timestamp of the last event
  boolean m_currentState;         //The current state of the
                                  //button
```

Similarly, a Vehicle class might include variables to store the number of wheels, minimum and maximum speed, and so on. As with variables in C, you can name member variables almost anything, but I like to prefix *data members* with the letter "m" and an underscore so it is easy to see that the variable is a member of a class.

Public and Private Keywords

C++ allows programmers to control the *access level* of member variables and functions. The *public*, *private*, and *protected* keywords are used for this purpose. As you might guess, the *public* keyword means that data or functions are available to everyone, and the *private* keyword limits visibility to the class itself. The *protected* keyword is a subtle variation on *private* access: protected members are available to the class *and* derived classes—classes that *inherit* from a parent class. Inheritance and polymorphism is one of the most interesting aspects of C++, but the concept is beyond the scope of this chapter. However, inheritance is used and described in Chapter 9, where the technique forms the basis for a number of oscillator classes.

In general, it is a good idea to make data members *protected* or *private* and write class functions called "getters and setters" to provide access to the data. The main reason for doing this is to prevent logic errors that can occur when other classes and code can arbitrarily change the values of class member variables. Arduino programs are necessarily small due to memory constraints, so it's likely not a big deal if you want to make the data in member variables public. On the other hand, getters and setters fit better with an object-oriented paradigm, and you may find that they help you to write sketches that are easier to debug and maintain.

Note that the *public*, *private*, and *protected* keywords apply to all of the member data or functions that follow until the next *public*, *private*, or *protected* keyword. In the *EasyButton* class, all of the member variables are private, and all of the member functions are public.

```
class EasyButton
{
private:
    //Anything after this keyword is private.
public:
    //Anything after this keyword is public.
private:
    //You can use the public, protected, and private keywords
    //multiple times and in any order...
};
```

Constructors and Destructors

The *EasyButton* class makes three *member functions* (also called *methods*) publicly available. The first member function is known as a *constructor*. A constructor is automatically called whenever a class is instantiated and is a good

177

place to initialize variables or perform other "first time" tasks. For example, the *EasyButton* constructor is automatically called in the following line:

```
EasyButton myButton;      //Create an instance of EasyButton.
                          //Default constructor is
                          //automatically called.
```

Constructors must follow a few specific rules:

1. Constructors *must* have the same name as the class name.
2. Constructors *cannot* have a return type, not even *void*.
3. Constructors *must* be public.
4. A class *can* provide more than one constructor as long as the parameters are different (more on this in a moment).

Source File

The source file (EasyButton.cpp) provides the body of the constructor that was declared in the class header file. In this case there is not much for the constructor to do—it simply initializes the member variables to default values. As you will see in a moment, two data members can also be set in a "setter" function. In general, it's best to establish default values for all data members in a constructor; however, there are lots of cases where it makes better sense to use a "setter" function. For example, the *Serial.begin()* function is an example of a method that is meant to be called from within the main *setup()* function of a sketch. The *EasyButton* class uses a similar approach—the variables and functions involving digital pins will be set from within *setup()*.

```
EasyButton::EasyButton()
{
    //Set default values
    m_lastEventTime = 0;
    m_pin = 0;
    m_debounceMS = 200;
    m_currentState = false;
};
```

The syntax for the constructor looks unusual at first glance, but it is actually very simple: the name of *any* class function (or constructor/destructor) is *always* preceded by the name of the class and two colons. This is the way the C++ compiler determines that a function or constructor belongs to a particular class (e.g., that it is a *member function*):

```
void className::someFunction()
{
}
```

Note that the .cpp implementation file starts with an include statement indicating the name of the header file:

```
#include "EasyButton.h"
```

This is necessary so that the .cpp file will know about the declarations that were made in the header file. Always include the header file in this way or you will receive lots of link errors. (I've been programming for a long time and I still forget to do this on occasion.)

Constructors (and methods) can also be *overloaded*. This means that more than one constructor or method can be implemented as long as the parameters are different. For example, I used a default constructor (no parameters) in *EasyButton* because I knew that I would typically use the class in the context of an array (the default constructor is always used when initializing an array of class objects). However, it might make sense to provide more than one constructor. Listing 8.2 shows definitions of two constructors: the default constructor and a constructor that takes the number of a digital pin and debounce time as parameters.

Listing 8.2 Multiple constructors

```
//Overloaded constructor in EasyButton.h file
EasyButton ();
EasyButton (int pin, int debounce_milliseconds);
//Implementation of two constructors in EasyButton.cpp file
EasyButton:: EasyButton ()
{
    m_lastEventTime = 0;

    m_pin = 0;
    m_debounceMS = 200;
    m_currentState = false;
}
void EasyButton:: EasyButton (int pin, int debounce_
milliseconds)
{
    m_pin = pin;
    m_debounceMS = debounce_milliseconds;
    m_lastEventTime = 0;
    m_currentState = false;
}
```

Destructor

Although the EasyButton class does not implement a destructor, destructors can be a powerful tool. The destructor is automatically called when an instance of a class goes out of scope. In C++, destructors are often used to clean up memory that was allocated with the *new* keyword, but a destructor might also be used to shut down hardware, blink an LED, or some other action that might make sense at the end of the life of an instance of a class. Destructors *must* have the same name as the class but are preceded by a tilde (~). Destructors *cannot* have parameters. Here is how a destructor could be declared and implemented in the *EasyButton* class:

Destructor declaration in the EasyButton.h file:

```
//Destructor:
public:
    ~EasyButton();
```

Destructor implementation in the EasyButton.cpp file:

```
//Destructor implementation:
EasyButton::~EasyButton()
{
    //Do something useful here when class goes out of scope.
}
```

Class Methods

The *EasyButton* class provides two public member functions that are used to set the pin and debounce time and to track the status of the pushbutton:

```
//EasyButton.h
void init(int pin, int debounce_milliseconds);

bool checkButtonPressed();
```

The first method, *init()* takes two parameters and assigns those values to the member variables *m_pin* and *m_debounceMS*. The method also takes care of setting the pin mode and turning on an internal pullup resistor (the .cpp implementation is shown in Listing 8.3).

Listing 8.3 setParameters() method

```
void EasyButton::init(int pin, int debounce_milliseconds)
{
    m_pin = pin;
    m_debounceMS = debounce_milliseconds;
    pinMode(m_pin, INPUT_PULLUP); //turn on internal pullup
}
```

The second method, *checkButtonPressed()*, returns true if the associated switch is pressed and false if no press has been detected (see .cpp implementation in Listing 8.4). The method assigns the state of the digital pin to a local variable named *state*. If the state of the pin is different than the last state (stored in the data member named *m_currentState*), the function checks to see if enough milliseconds have elapsed to switch states. Debounce time is calculated by subtracting the value of *m_lastEventTime* from the value returned from the *millis()* function. In this way, the class is able to passively debouce the switch without halting the sketch with a call to *delay()*.

Listing 8.4 checkButtonPressed() method

```
//Call this to see if the button is being pressed
bool EasyButton::checkButtonPressed()
```

180

```
{
    boolean state;
    if(digitalRead(m_pin) == LOW)
    {
        state = true;
    }else{
        state = false;
    }

    //See if the state has changed
    if(state != m_currentState)
    {
        //See if enough time has passed to change the state
        if((millis() - m_lastEventTime) > m_debounceMS)
        {
            //Okay to change state:
            m_currentState = state;
            //Reset time count
            m_lastEventTime = millis();
        }
    }

    return m_currentState;
}
```

One potential issue with the *EasyButton* class has to do with the fact that the *millis()* function may be unavailable depending on the way that timers are used in a sketch. A workaround is to provide an overloaded *checkButtonPressed()* method that takes a *long* integer representing the passage of time. For example, the calling sketch could implement a simple counting mechanism in the main loop that would be sufficient for providing timing data for button debouncing. The overloaded function is shown in Listing 8.5.

Listing 8.5 Overloaded checkButtonPressed() method

```
bool EasyButton::checkButtonPressed(unsigned long ticks)
{
    boolean state;
    if(digitalRead(m_pin) == LOW)
    {
        state = true;
    }else{
        state = false;
    }

    //See if the state has changed
    if(state != m_currentState)
    {
        //See if enough time has passed to change the state
        if((ticks - m_lastEventTime) > m_debounceMS)
        {
            //Okay to change state:
            m_currentState = state;
            //Reset time count
            m_lastEventTime = ticks;
        }
```

```
        }
        return m_currentState;
}
```

One of the reasons I like C++ so much is that the header files are almost a form of pseudo-code shorthand. I usually mock up the basic functionality of a class (the member variables and functions) in the header file and move to the implementation file once I am happy with the logic. For example, pseudo-code for the EasyButton class might look like the following:

- The class will include variables to store the pin, debounce time, current state, and amount of time that has passed since the last button press.
- A function named setParameters provides a way to set the values of the pin number and debounce time. The function will also initialize a digital pin and turn on the pullup resistor.
- A function named checkButtonPressed will determine if a push-button has been pressed by polling the appropriate digital input. State changes are only allowed if the number of milliseconds since the last state change is greater than the value stored in *m_debounceMS*.

Note how clearly the header file provides a birds-eye view of the functionality of the class in Listing 8.6.

Listing 8.6 *EasyButton* **header file**

```
class EasyButton
{
private:
    int m_pin;                          //Digital pin the button
                                        //is connected to
    int m_debounceMS;                   //Number of milliseconds
                                        //for debouncing
    unsigned long m_lastEventTime;      //Timestamp of the last
                                        //event
    boolean m_currentState;             //The current state of
                                        //the button

public:
    //Constructor
    EasyButton();

    //Helper method to set pin and number of milliseconds
    //for debounce.
    //Also sets up pullup register.
    void init(int pin, int debounce_milliseconds);

    //Call this to see if the button is being pressed
    bool checkButtonPressed();
```

```
        /* Use this method when the millis() function is
        disabled. For example, use to increment a
        counter in the main loop to generate
        "pseudo" time. */
        bool checkButtonPressed(unsigned long ticks);
};
```

As you develop classes, consider using the pseudo-code to header file approach in working out the underlying logic of the class. It is usually relatively easy to fill in the details in the .cpp file once the overall logic has been established. As you get more comfortable with the language, you will likely find that the header file itself will become a form of logical pseudo-code.

Using a Class

Classes can be used just like built-in data types in a sketch. You can instantiate them one at a time or create an array of objects (see Listing 8.7).

Listing 8.7 Instantiating a button

```
//Instantiate a button
EasyButton button; //Default constructor automatically called

//Instantiate an array of five buttons
EasyButton myButtonArray[5];
```

To call a class member function, simply use the "dot" (.) operator as in Listing 8.8. Note how the dot operator can also be used with an array of objects.

Listing 8.8

```
//Call the member function checkButtonPressed() for an
//object named myButton
boolean press = myButton.checkButtonPressed();

//The syntax doesn't change when an array is used.
//Call checkButtonPressed() for the third element in an
//array called myButtonArray[].

boolean button_press = myButtonArray[2].checkButtonPressed();
```

More on Overriding Methods

It is often useful to provide multiple versions of the same method. For example, it might be convenient to offer multiple versions of a function to set the parameters of a hypothetical class called MidiMessage. In Listing 8.9, three versions of a single function named setParams are provided to set the status byte and two data bytes, just the two data bytes, or the first data byte.

Listing 8.9 Overriding methods

```
void setParams(byte status_byte, byte data1, byte data1);
void setParams(byte data1, byte data2);
void setParams(byte data1);
```

183

This could be very convenient when using the class as in the following example:

```
myMidiMessage.setParams(144, 60, 100);
//Do things with the message
.
.
.

//Change the note and velocity (data bytes 1 & 2)
myMidiMessage.setParams(64, 120);
//Do more things with the message
.
.
.

//Change just the note (data byte 1)
myMidiMessage.setParams(60);
```

Other Topics

Thus far, we have looked at a number of primary concepts associated with C++ classes in Arduino. Concepts such as member variables and functions will help you to use an object-oriented approach that will simplify the design process and make your code more reusable.

The downside of any introduction to a complex topic is that the discussion is necessarily incomplete. There are a number of additional C++ topics that readers may want to explore. In particular, C++ inheritance is a powerful (but sometimes complex) aspect of the language. Memory allocation and deallocation is another concept that could be useful for some projects but is beyond the scope of this discussion. (The projects in this book use global variables to allocate a fixed amount of memory for the sake of simplicity, but variable allocations are possible using the *new* keyword.) There are also lots of nuances to the language such as *pointers* (variables that "point" to a memory location) that may be useful once a fluency with the primary aspects of the language has been attained.

Developing a Rotary Encoder Class

Before moving on to some musical applications of C++ classes, it will be helpful to look at one more "helper" class to solidify the concepts that were presented in the first part of the chapter. The class, *RotaryEncoder*, was designed to make it easier to work with rotary encoders.

As is evident in Listing 8.10, the class declares a number of data members. The variables are well commented so no additional explanation is required. As with the *EasyButton* class, *RotaryEncoder* also provides several methods: a default constructor, "setter" methods to initialize the values of the data members, and a function that returns an integer representing the current position of the shaft. The class automatically increments or decrements this value based on the position of the encoder shaft, and it also ensures that the value stays within the range established by the *m_encoderMin* and *m_encoderMax* data members.

184

Listing 8.10 RotaryEncoder class

```cpp
#ifndef _ROTARYENCODER
#define _ROTARYENCODER

#include "Arduino.h" //Include header file that defines INPUT
                     //and HIGH

class RotaryEncoder
{
private:
    int m_pinA;              //Digital pin encoder A
    int m_encoderALast;
    int m_pinB;              //Digital pin encoder B
    int m_debounceMS;        //Number of milliseconds for
                             //debouncing.
    unsigned long m_lastEventTime;  //Timestamp
    int m_encoderPosition;  //Current position of the encoder:
    int m_encoderMax;        //Sets the maximum value
    int m_encoderMin;         //Sets the minimum value
public:
    //Constructor
    RotaryEncoder();

    void init(int pinA, int pinB, int debounce_milliseconds,
              int start_position = 0, int min_position = 0,
              int max_position = 100);

    //"Setters" and "getters"
    void setShaftPosition(int position);
    void setMinValue(int min);
    void setMaxValue(int max);

    //Returns value of m_encoderPosition--use trackShaftPosition()
    //to track changes
    int shaftPosition();

    //Call this in main loop() to track the position

    int trackShaftPosition();

    //Call this in main loop() to track the position

    //if the millis() function is disabled. For example,
    //increment a counter in the main loop() to generate
    //"pseudo" time.
    int trackShaftPosition(unsigned long ticks);
};
#endif
```

Again, the beauty of a header file is that it provides a "CliffsNotes" view of the functionality of the class. The only unfamiliar concept is that *default values*

185

are provided for the last three parameters in the *init()* method. As the name implies, default parameters can be used to provide reasonable default values. The only syntax requirements are that, once you assign a default value, all the remaining parameters in the function must also be assigned a default value. Also note that the defaults are only assigned in the function prototype of the header file, *not* in the .cpp implementation file. The *init()* method can be used as follows:

```
//Pins 4 & 5, 20ms debounce, default position = 50,
//min = 0, max = 200
myEncoder.init(4, 5, 20, 50, 0, 200);

//Pins 4 and 5, debounce of 50ms, default starting position
myEncoder.init(4, 5, 50);
```

trackShaftPosition()

The *trackShaftPosition()* is the primary point of interest in the implementation file. The function encapsulates the encoder tracking routine that was described in Chapter 4. The function, which was based on an example by Michael Margolis,[3] evaluates the binary output of the two tracks of the encoder and updates the *m_encoderPosition* variable accordingly. As with the *EasyButton* class, the function also debounces the encoder by comparing the change in state against the number of milliseconds since the last event (see Listing 8.11). Also note that *trackShaftPosition()* is overloaded so the class can be used even if the *millis()* function is disabled by a timer.

Listing 8.11 Tracking the shaft position of a rotary encoder

```
int RotaryEncoder::trackShaftPosition()
{
    boolean pinAValue = digitalRead(m_pinA);
    unsigned long current_time = millis();
    unsigned long time_between_events = current_time - m_
    lastEventTime;

    //Based on an example from Arduino Cookbook p. 191
    if((m_encoderALast==HIGH) && (pinAValue==LOW) &&
            time_between_events >m_debounceMS)
    {
        if(digitalRead(m_pinB)==LOW)
        {
            if(m_encoderPosition>m_encoderMin)
                m_encoderPosition--;
        }else{
            if(m_encoderPosition<m_encoderMax)
                m_encoderPosition++;
        }
        m_lastEventTime=current_time;
    }

    m_encoderALast=pinAValue;
    return m_encoderPosition;
}
```

186

Using RotaryEncoder

The extra work of creating a class will pay big dividends in your next project. Note how easy it is to incorporate a rotary encoder in a project now that a useful class is available to take care of the details (Listing 8.12).

Listing 8.12 Using the RotaryEncoder class

```
#include "RotaryEncoder.h"

//Constants for digital pins and encoder parameters
const int pinA = 3;
const int pinB = 4;
const int debounceTime = 40;

//Variable to track the position of the shaft
int lastShaftPosition = 0;

//Create an instance of the RotaryEncoder class
RotaryEncoder encoder;

void setup()
{
    //Initialize the encoder with pin numbers and a debounce
    //time. Starting position = 50, range 1-100
    encoder.init(pinA, pinB, debounceTime, 50, 1, 100);

    Serial.begin(9600);
}

void loop()
{
    //Read the position of the encoder
    int pos = encoder.trackShaftPosition();

    //Print the position if it has changed
    if(pos != lastShaftPosition)
    {
        Serial.println(pos);
        lastShaftPosition = pos;
    }
}
```

Making Your Own Library

Once you have developed a useful class, it is time to make it available to other sketches. The mechanism for making this happen in Arduino is as follows:

1. Navigate to the folder that contains the project where you created the class.
2. Copy the .h and .cpp files associated with the class.
3. Navigate to the libraries subfolder in your Arduino folder (e.g., Arduino\libraries).
4. Create a folder with the same name as your new class library.
5. Copy the .h and .cpp class files to the new folder.
6. Exit the Arduino environment if it is currently running.

7. Load the Arduino IDE and create a new sketch.

8. Select Sketch→Import Library…and select your class in the drop-down menu.

Your new class can now be used just like other Arduino libraries.

Developing a 12-Tone Matrix Class

This chapter concludes with a music class that will be of interest to composers and theorists. Twelve-tone matrices are used by some composers and are particularly useful for composers who write *atonal* music. Although 12-tone matrices developed out of a desire to "equalize" the 12 tones of western European music, matrices need not be limited to composing abstract atonal music. I occasionally use matrices to write music that might be described as *freely tonal*—where a tonal center is evident but the music is highly chromatic. Given the frequent use of 12-tone (also known as *dodecaphonic*) process, a matrix class could be a useful foundation for an algorithmic music generator.

Tone Row

A matrix starts with a *tone row* referred to as *prime-0* in 12-tone parlance. The row is a set of all 12 chromatic tones that are carefully ordered by the composer. Often, the composer will select notes such that no clear tonal center is evident when the notes are played in succession (see Figure 8.1).

Next, the tone row is inverted and the notes are placed in the leftmost column of the matrix (see Figure 8.2).

The inversion is labeled as *I-0* (for *inversion-0*), and the bottom of the column is labeled *RI-0* (for *retrograde of inversion-0*). Also note that the left and right sides of the original row are labeled *P-0* (*prime-0*) and *R-0* (*retrograde-0*). At this point, the matrix can be completed by transposing the prime row using the ordering shown in Figure 8.3.

Although it is not particularly difficult to create a 12-tone matrix, the process is tedious and better suited to a computer. Thus, a 12-tone class could be useful in taking out the drudgery of the task while providing all of the potential of matrices as a creative tool.

A brief discussion of a tone row class follows. Readers who are new to programming may want to skip to the final section that shows how the class can be used in a sketch, while more advanced programmers may be interested to read about the design of the class.

FIGURE 8.1

Twelve-tone row from Webern's *Variations, Op. 30.*

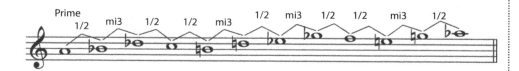

Prime

Inversion

	Inversion											
Prime	A	Bb	Db	C	B	D	Eb	Gb	F	E	G	Ab
Ab												
F												
Gb												
G												
E												
Eb												
C												
Db												
D												
B												
Bb												

FIGURE 8.2

Inverting a tone row (leftmost column).

	Inv 0												
Prime 0	A	Bb	Db	C	B	D	Eb	Gb	F	E	G	Ab	Retrograde 0
	Ab												
	F												
	Gb												
	G												
	E												
	Eb												
Prime 3	C	Db	E	Eb	D	F	Gb	A	Ab	G	Bb	B	Retrograde 3
	Db												
	D												
Prime 2	B	C	Eb	D	Db	E	F	Ab	G	Gb	A	Bb	Retrograde 2
Prime 1	Bb	B	D	Db	C	Eb	E	G	Gb	F	Ab	A	Retrograde 1
	RI0												

FIGURE 8.3

Completing a matrix by transposing the prime row.

Overview of Design

One design goal for the class is to create a minimal memory footprint. Although it is tempting to create a 12×12 matrix of bytes, that might limit the usefulness of the class since it would take up so much of the Arduino's precious memory space. Arduino has a fast processor, so it makes better sense to write a class that can calculate permutations of a row "on the fly" with several accessor functions. With this approach, only 12 bytes are required to store the prime version row.

One other goal is that the class should provide the logical underpinnings of a 12-tone matrix—no more and no less. Or, to quote Scott Meyers, "strive for class interfaces that are complete and minimal."[4] When I was first developing my programming chops, my classes tended to lose focus as I made them "tricky" by adding extra features such as a user interface or formatted output. With object-oriented design, the goal is to provide specific objects for specific data and functionality. In the context of a 12-tone class, a function to handle formatted output to the Serial port is an example of code that is likely going astray from the object-oriented ideal. This type of application-specific functionality is better handled in the main part of a sketch (or with inheritance or a "friend" class).

Pseudo-code Logic

As mentioned previously, it is often helpful to start a class or complex function by describing the function in pseudo-code. If you can describe the steps using a spoken language, it is usually easier to translate these concepts to computer code. A description of the 12-tone class might be codified as follows:

Pseudo-code logic for initializing the matrix:

- Allocate memory to store a 12-tone row.
- Provide a method (or constructor) to set the values of the row.
- Provide a public method named *resetMatrix()* that can be called once note values have been established for the prime row (see below).

Provide accessor methods to retrieve values from the row:

```
byte getRow(int row, int index);
byte getInversion(int inv, int index);
byte getRetrograde(int ret, int index);
byte getRetrogradeOfInversion(int ri, int index);
```

Pseudo-code logic for accessor methods:

- Validate input parameters (0–11).
- Accessors will take two parameters (transposition and index).
- Find the *n*th index of the given permutation (row, retrograde, inversion, or retrograde of inversion).

- The first parameter represents the transposition (e.g., getRow(1, 3) would find the 4th note of P1 and getRetrograde(2, 2) would return the third value of R2.
- Adjust the value indicated by the index parameter by the transposition indicated by the first parameter.
- Check for octave "wrap around" and return.

Header File

The header file for the *ToneRow* class is shown in its entirety in Listing 8.13.

Listing 8.13 ToneRow header file

```
#ifndef _TONEROW
#define _TONEROW

#include <Arduino.h>

class ToneRow{

    private:
    //Trick: in-class enumeration functions like a constant.
    //The enumeration is used to avoid "hard coding" the
    //index bounds
    enum{m_arraySize = 12};

    //Private array to store the row (prime-0)
    byte m_row[m_arraySize];

    //Private helper function:
    //Returns true if array index is valid.
    boolean validIndex(int i);

    public:
    //Constructor
    ToneRow();

    //Call this method to add a note to the prime
    //row at the nth position
    void addNote(byte note, int n);

    //Call this method to zero the matrix after all
    //the notes of the row have been added
    void resetMatrix();

    /* Accessor methods: Call these to get the nth
    value (0-11) of the given permutation of the row.
    For example, getRetrograde(2, 3) returns the
    fourth note of R2. These functions return -1
    for invalid range. */
    byte getRow(int row, int n);
    byte getRetrograde(int ret, int n);
    byte getInversion(int inv, int n);
    byte getRetrogradeOfInversion(int ri, int n);
};

#endif
```

As is evident in the header file, the class contains a private data array, *m_row*, that stores the value of the row. There is also a private helper function that is used internally by the class to check that indexes are in a valid range. Interestingly, an in-class enumeration is used to establish a constant whose scope is limited to the class.

The public portion of the class consists of a constructor, two methods for working with variables, and four functions that return a specified note from the given permutation of the row.

Source File

As is usual in source files, the first line of ToneRow.cpp is an "include" statement that is used to import the header file:

```
#include "ToneRow.h"
```

Although a constructor is not really required for this class, I wrote a default constructor that initializes the row to a chromatic scale. This is a useful feature for debugging and testing the output of the class (Listing 8.14).

Listing 8.14 Constructor

```
ToneRow::ToneRow()
{
    //Initialize a chromatic scale for testing
    for(int i = 0; i < m_arraySize; i++)
    {
        m_row[i] = i;
    }
}
```

Bounds Checking

You will experience problems if you attempt to use an index to access a variable beyond the bounds of an array. For this reason, I'm in the habit of checking ranges whenever I write a function that accepts an index to an array as a parameter. All of the functions in the class check bounds in this way, so it made sense to write a simple function to handle the task (Listing 8.15).

Listing 8.15 Bounds checking

```
//Returns true if array index is valid.
boolean ToneRow::validIndex(int i)
{
    if(i >= 0 && i < m_arraySize)
    {
        return true;
    }
    return false; //must not be a valid range.
}
```

The function simply looks at the index and compares it against the known range of the matrix (0 to m_arraySize -1).

addNote()

The *addNote()* method takes a note value and desired index as parameters and checks the index to make sure it is in a valid range. The note is assigned to the given index in the array if the index is in a valid range (Listing 8.16).

Listing 8.16 addNote method

```
void ToneRow::addNote(byte note, int n)
{
    //validate range:
    if(!validIndex(n))
    {
        return; //Return. Invalid range.
    }
    //Set the nth note in the row to the value of note
    m_row[n] = note;
}
```

ResetMatrix()

ResetMatrix() is called to zero or normalize the matrix once all of the notes have been added to the row (see Listing 8.17). The algorithm iterates through the row and adjusts notes so that the matrix is zero based. The transposition is based on the first note in the row (*m_row[0]*), and the modulo (remainder) operator handles octave "wrap around" to force values to stay within a valid range.

Listing 8.17

```
void ToneRow::resetMatrix()
{
    //Zero row:
    for(int i = 0; i< m_arraySize; ++i)
    {
        m_row[i] = (m_row[i] + 12 - m_row[0]) %12;
    }
}
```

The accessor functions all share a similar logic to that described in the previous section:

- Check that the index is valid.
- Find the nth note in the array.
- Transpose the note according to the value in the first parameter.
- Handle octave "wrap around."

Again, note how the modulo operator simplifies the process of keeping intervals in a valid range. Note, too, that the range validation has been omitted in these examples to save space and clarify the function of these methods:

```
byte ToneRow::getRow(int row, int n)
{
    return ((12 + m_row[n]) + row) %12;
}
```

193

```
byte ToneRow::getRetrograde(int ret, int n)
{
    return ((12 + m_row[11 - n])) %12;
}

    byte ToneRow::getInversion(int inv, int n)
{
    return ((12 - m_row[n]) + inv) %12;
}

byte ToneRow::getRetrogradeOfInversion(int ri, int n)
{
    return ((12 - m_row[11 - n+ri])) %12;
}
```

Using ToneRow in a Sketch

The *ToneRow* class demonstrates how a fairly complex concept like a 12-tone matrix can be encapsulated in an object-oriented class. Although it is useful to be able to write classes, it is perhaps even more important to be able to understand the mechanisms of classes and to be able to use them in sketches.

Listing 8.18 shows one of the many ways that the *ToneRow* class could be used. In this example, an instance of the class is created and the *addNote()* method is called to fill the tone row with notes.

Listing 8.18 Using ToneRow

```
#include "ToneRow.h"

//Use an enumeration to clarify printing logic:
enum{row, inversion, retrograde, retrograde_inversion};

//Create an instance of the matrix
ToneRow matrix;
void setup()
{
    Serial.begin(9600);

    //Set the notes of the row
    matrix.addNote(0, 0);      //C
    matrix.addNote(5, 1);      //F
    matrix.addNote(7, 2);      //G
    matrix.addNote(1, 3);      //Db
    matrix.addNote(6, 4);      //Gb
    matrix.addNote(3, 5);      //Eb
    matrix.addNote(8, 6);      //Ab
    matrix.addNote(2, 7);      //D
    matrix.addNote(11, 8);     //B
    matrix.addNote(4, 9);      //E
    matrix.addNote(9, 10);     //A
    matrix.addNote(10, 11);    //Bb

    //Calculate the matrix
    matrix.resetMatrix();

    //Print some permutations of the row
    printPermutation("P0:", 0, row);
    printPermutation("I0:", 0, inversion);
```

194

```
    printPermutation("RO:", 0, retrograde);
    printPermutation("RIO:", 0, retrograde_inversion);
}
```

Helper Functions

Two helper functions are provided to facilitate printing of the row. The first function (see Listing 8.19) converts the numeric values returned by the row into note names. Although this functionality could have been incorporated into the class, it is better object-oriented design to separate the user interface and data in this way. Class inheritance could be a particularly elegant way to incorporate this functionality (e.g., create a new class that inherits the functionality of the base class and adds formatted printing capability).

Listing 8.19

```cpp
String getNoteName(int note_value)
{
    String note_name = "unknown";
     switch(note_value)
    {
      case 0:  note_name = "C";  break;
      case 1:  note_name = "Db"; break;
      case 2:  note_name = "D";  break;
      case 3:  note_name = "Eb"; break;
      case 4:  note_name = "E";  break;
      case 5:  note_name = "F";  break;
      case 6:  note_name = "Gb"; break;
      case 7:  note_name = "G";  break;
      case 8:  note_name = "Ab"; break;
      case 9:  note_name = "A";  break;
      case 10: note_name = "Bb"; break;
      case 11: note_name = "B";  break;
    }
    return note_name;
}
```

The second helper function, shown in Listing 8.20, prints permutations of the row based on the transposition (e.g., Prime-3 or Retrograde-5) and type of permutation.

Listing 8.20

```cpp
void printPermutation(String title, int transposition, int type)
{
    Serial.print(title);
    String note_name;

    //Loop through the tone row and print notes based on
    //permutation type
    for(int n = 0; n < 12; n++)
    {
       //Print tab character to advance to next column
       Serial.print("\t");
```

195

```
//Get a string representing the note based on
//permutation type
switch(type)
{
    case row:
        note_name = getNoteName(matrix.
        getRow(transposition, n));
    break;
    case retrograde:
        note_name = getNoteName(matrix.
        getRetrograde(transposition, n));
    break;
    case inversion:
        note_name = getNoteName(matrix.
        getInversion(transposition, n));
    break;
    case retrograde_inversion:
        note_name = getNoteName(matrix.getRetrogradeOf
        Inversion(transposition, n));
    break;
    }
    //Print the note
    Serial.print(note_name);
}
//Print a blank new line
Serial.println(" ");
}
```

Conclusion

C++ can make your life easier, but there is a lot to take in (and more that we could talk about). Don't worry if some of the details are still unclear. Start by writing some simple classes, and use the examples in this chapter as a starting point. Don't forget to describe your given task using pseudo-code and let the idea gel before you start writing code.

It is also helpful to look at other classes, especially the classes that are provided in the Arduino environment. You can learn a lot about program design by reading through the header and implementation files in the Arduino\libraries folder, and, just like a written language, the logic and functionality will become more and more clear as you start to see the connections between terms, syntax, and logic.

Audio Output and Sound Synthesis

This chapter explores concepts relating to digital *sound synthesis*. Along the way, you will learn how to output audio signals and digitally synthesize and modulate waveforms. The chapter concludes with an introduction to Mozzi, a wonderful sound-synthesis library designed by Tim Barrass, and Teensy 3, a powerful microcontroller that can be used for many audio applications. Readers who are anxious to synthesize sounds on an Arduino may want to jump to the sections on pulse-width modulation and fill in the theoretical foundation after exploring some of the Mozzi demonstration sketches. However, the sections relating to waveform synthesis will provide a theoretical foundation for getting the most out of Mozzi and for developing many types of Arduino projects including the *Stella Synth* and *Step Sequencer* synthesizers in the final section of the book.

Analog vs. Digital

In the analog domain, a transducer such as a microphone produces continuously fluctuating voltages that are *analogous* to the alternating high and low pressure that our ears hear as sound. For example, in an analog sound system (see Figure 9.1), the fluctuating voltage produced by a microphone is amplified and reproduced by one or more speakers (another type of transducer).

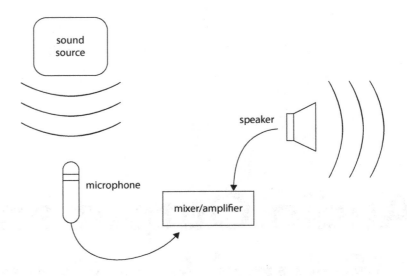

FIGURE 9.1

Microphone signal, amplification, and output of signal.

198

Unlike analog signals, which are *continuous*, digital signals represent waveforms as a series of discrete numbers. Figure 9.2 illustrates how a series of numbers could be used to represent the instantaneous voltages of an analog signal.

FIGURE 9.2

Using numbers to represent the instantaneous voltages of a sine wave.

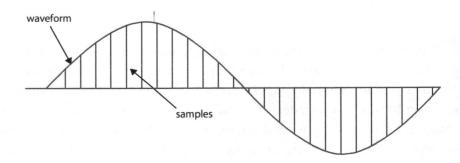

Sample Rate and Resolution

The process of periodically taking a *sample* of a signal and using a number to represent its instantaneous value is called *sampling* or *digitizing*, and the accuracy of the digitized signal is primarily dependent on two factors called the *sample rate* and *resolution* or *bit depth*. If the sample rate is too slow, it will be impossible for the system to accurately reproduce a waveform. This is akin to the *pixelation* that is evident on low-resolution computer monitors. If the pixels are too large, an image may look jagged. In a similar way, a digitized audio signal that has too few steps may sound distorted or unnatural (see Figure 9.3). However, just like a mosaic can be a powerful (if "pixilated") form of visual expression, low sample rates can also provide some unique opportunities for creating new and interesting sounds.

In general, the sample rate should be slightly more than twice the rate of the highest frequency as is expressed by the Nyquist theorem.[1] For example, an

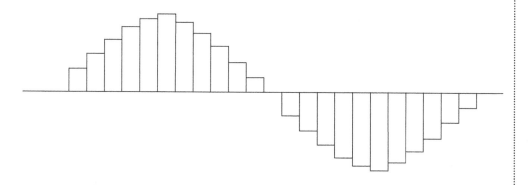

FIGURE 9.3

Pixelated audio signal.

audio CD plays back at a rate of 44.1kHz, which is slightly more than twice the upper range of human hearing (around 20kHz). Fortunately, the Arduino is capable of some fairly high sample rates and can produce convincing waveforms.

Resolution

Bit depth or resolution refers to the number of bits that are used to represent the instantaneous voltage of a given sample. Using the previous analogy of a computer monitor, where sample rate relates to the accuracy of a drawing, bit depth is conceptually similar to the accuracy of a color palette. For example, it is only possible to represent 256 colors with an 8-bit number. While such a palette might be appropriate for a gray-scale image, only a few shades of color could be accurately represented with such a limited range. In a similar way, higher numbers of bits can more accurately represent the instantaneous voltages of a signal. With only 8 bits, each sample in a digital audio signal will be *quantized* to one of 256 voltage gradations. In contrast, a 16-bit number (like a CD recording) can represent the same voltage fluctuations with 65,536 gradations (see Figure 9.4).

199

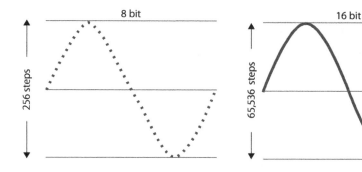

FIGURE 9.4

Using 8 vs. 16 bits to digitize a signal.

Conceptualizing a Digital Audio Converter

The job of a Digital Audio Converter (DAC) is to convert digital samples to fluctuating analog voltage levels. Although the details can be challenging to implement, the basic concept is easy to visualize: the sending device—an Arduino

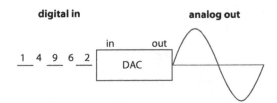

in this case—provides a series of numbers that represent the sample "slices" of a given waveform. The DAC takes the digital numbers at the given sample rate and outputs a continuous voltage stream that is an analog version of the digitized waveform (see Figure 9.5).

Digital Audio Conversion

There are a number of ways to convert digital data to analog on the Arduino platform. Common approaches include using an R2R ladder, dedicated DAC integrated circuit, audio shield, or pulse-width modulation. The first two approaches are covered in the paragraphs that follow, and pulse-width modulation is explored in the final section of the chapter.

R2R Ladder

Although I find electronics to be fascinating, the R2R ladder DAC comes pretty close to being "magical." The name comes from the fact that this DAC is consists entirely of resistors of value X and resistors of value 2X. Given that the total resistance for resistors in series is the sum of the resistors, an R2R ladder can be constructed from resistors of a *single* value. Figure 9.6 illustrates a simple 4-bit R2R ladder. Although a more sophisticated version of the circuit using more bits will be shown in a moment, the 4-bit circuit will provide a good overview of the form and function of R2R circuits. In this circuit, the inputs range from the *most significant bit* (the greatest numeric value) to the *least significant bit* near the bottom of the illustration.

With this circuit, four digital outputs from an Arduino or other microcontroller provide the input to each of the "rungs" on the R2R ladder. In an R2R

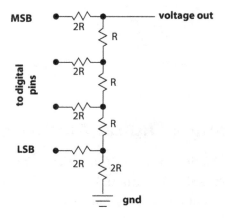

200

TABLE 9.1 4-bit R2R Steps

Digital Inputs	Decimal Equivalent	Output Voltage
A B C D		
0 0 0 0	0	0
0 0 0 1	1	.31
0 0 1 0	2	.62
0 0 1 1	3	.94
0 1 0 0	4	1.25
0 1 0 1	5	1.56
0 1 1 0	6	1.87
0 1 1 1	7	2.19
1 0 0 0	8	2.50
1 0 0 1	9	2.81
1 0 1 0	10	3.12
1 0 1 1	11	3.44
1 1 0 0	12	3.75
1 1 0 1	13	4.06
1 1 1 0	14	4.37
1 1 1 1	15	4.69

ladder, the least significant digit "faces more resistance (and thus voltage drop) than the most significant digit."[3] Essentially, each rung on the R2R ladder produces a fraction of the total current when activated (1/2 I, 1/4 I, 1/8 I, etc.), and the fractional amounts are summed at the output of the DAC. Table 9.1, from *Music Synthesizers: A Manual of Design and Construction*, shows how various combinations of digital inputs produce output voltages that correspond to each of the possible 4-bit steps from 0 to 15.

One of the problems with R2R networks is *loading effect*, which can occur when a load is placed on the output and causes a "decrease in the output voltage amplitude."[4] To combat the problem, the output of the DAC can be connected to the input of an op amp configured as a *buffer follower*. Op amps have a noninverting (+) and inverting (−) input that can, with appropriate circuitry, be configured for an astounding array of applications from signal amplification to filtering and waveform generation. In the case of a buffer, the output of the DAC is routed to the noninverting input of the op amp, and the output of the op amp is routed back to the inverting input (see Figure 9.7), which serves to buffer the circuit from loading. A resistor is optionally added between the output and its return path to the inverting input to prevent offset errors.[5] As mentioned in Chapter 3, op amps typically use a dual (+/−) power source so that signals swing around a virtual

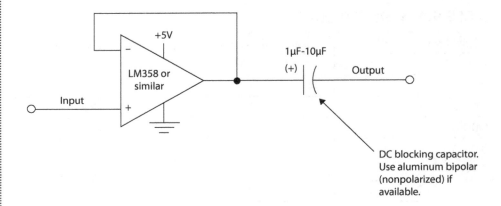

FIGURE 9.7

Op amp buffer.

ground (e.g., –2.5 to +2.5V). However, the op amps such as the LM358 used in this chapter can utilize the single-supply (0–5V) power provided by an Arduino.

DC Component

One thing to be aware of when outputting signals from an Arduino is that the waveforms "ride" on a DC component. Where most audio signals swing positively and negatively around 0V, Arduino signals swing around 2.5V (see Figure 9.8).

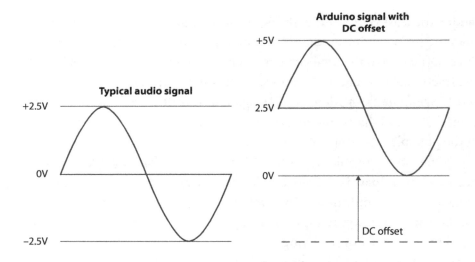

FIGURE 9.8

DC component.

In most cases it is best to remove the DC component—passing DC component to another device is akin to connecting a DC battery to the input of the device. Fortunately, the DC component can be removed with a capacitor. Ray Wilson, author of the excellent book *Make: Analog Synthesizers*, suggests a 10μF aluminum bipolar (nonpolarized) capacitor as the final component of a simple AC-coupled mixer. In my experiments, values in the range of 1 to 10μF work well. The effect of blocking the DC component is illustrated in Figure 9.9.

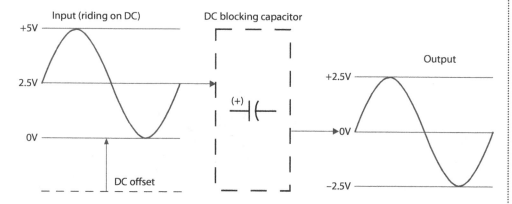

FIGURE 9.9

Removing DC component.

The final version of an 8-bit R2R ladder is illustrated in Figures 9.10 and 9.11. The output of the R2R ladder is connected to an outer pin of a 1M potentiometer and the other outer pin is connected to ground. The middle wiper pin is connected to the noninverting buffer of a single-supply op amp such as the TS922 or LM358 in a *unity gain* buffer configuration. Optionally, the output of the buffer flows through a passive RC filter formed by a resistor and capacitor before running through the unity gain buffer. A DC blocking capacitor removes DC offset prior to connection to the input of another audio device.

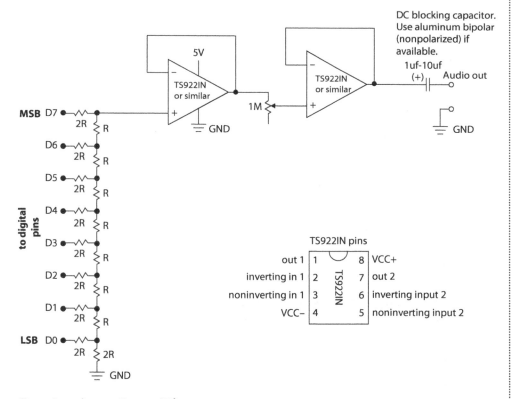

FIGURE 9.10

8-bit R2R ladder with buffer and low-pass filter.

Passive Low-Pass Filter

The 270Ω resistor and .1μF capacitor in Figure 9.10 form a passive low-pass filter, which can be useful in removing some undesirable high-frequency noise from the digital-to-analog converter. To calculate the filter cutoff, use the following formula with the resistance in ohms and capacitance in Farads:

FIGURE 9.11

R2R ladder with op amp buffer and DC-blocking capacitor.

$$\frac{1}{2\pi RC}$$

There are 1,000,000µF in 1F, so the calculation can be worked out as follows:

$$\frac{1}{2\times3.14\times27\times0.0000001} = \frac{1}{0.00016956} = 5897\text{Hz}$$

Figure 9.11 illustrates one approach to finalizing 9.11 illustrates one approach to finalizing the circuit on solderboard from RadioShack. Note that a power-smoothing capacitor, between the power and ground rails, was added to the final circuit and that female headers and ¼" jack provide a convenient way to connect the circuit to an Arduino and audio device.

Setting Up a Timer

In order to use an R2R ladder, the Arduino must be configured to output digital data at a steady sample rate. While it is tempting to output data from within the main *loop()* of a sketch, such an approach is problematic for a number of reasons—the most important of which is that the effective sample rate will vary depending on the complexity of code executed within the loop. Although frequent polling of the time functions can mitigate the problem to a certain extent, a better approach is to use one of the Arduino's built-in timer mechanisms. When properly configured, the timer will fire at a regular interval no matter what code happens to execute in the main *loop()*.

At first glance, the boilerplate code for initializing an Arduino timer is probably the most bewildering code in this book. Fortunately, timers are relatively straightforward once you understand that the bizarre symbols provide access to the inner workings of the Arduino. In this case, *registers* can be thought of as built-in variables that provide access to hardware memory locations, and it's the values assigned to these memory locations that are used to configure an Arduino timer.

The Arduino UNO features three timers labeled as *Timer0*, *Timer1*, and *Timer2*. The timers are simple counters that "count pulses from a time source, called a *timebase*"[6] In many instances, a *prescalar* is used to divide the timebase in order to reduce the frequency of the counter. Listing 9.1 illustrates one approach to setting up a timer.[7] The following paragraphs detail each of the steps.

Listing 9.1 Timer1 initialization

```
//Timer setup boilerplate:
//Set up timer 1 for 16384 Hz sample rate
void InitTimer1()
{
    //SET UP TIMER 1
    cli();          //Disable global interrupts
    TCCR1A = 0;  //Reset Timer 1 Counter Control Register A
    TCCR1B = 0;  //Reset Timer 1 Counter Control Register B

    //Set Timer 1 Output Compare Register A to desired
    //frequency
    //(16,000,000 / 16384) - 1 = 975
    OCR1A = 975;

    //Turn on CTC (clear timer on compare match) mode:
    TCCR1B |= (1 << WGM12);

    TCCR1B |= (1 << CS10);  //Prescalar = 1 (no prescalar used)

    //Enable timer interrupt
    TIMSK1 |= (1 << OCIE1A);

    //Enable interrupts
    sei();
}
```

Disabling and Enabling Interrupts

The timer initialization code begins and ends with the *cli()* and *sei()* functions, which are used to disable and enable interrupts, asynchronous signals that may alter the value of the timer registers while the initialization function is executing. The basic idea is to ensure that the registers involving the timer aren't inadvertently altered before the initialization function has had a chance to establish values for the timer.

Counter Control Registers

In the next section of Listing 9.1, the *Timer1 Counter Control Registers A* and *B* (TCCR1A and TCCR1B) are set to zero. Depending on the state of the Arduino, the registers may already be set to zero or some other value, so this step is necessary to ensure that the appropriate bits will be set. In the next line, the variable OCR1A is another "hidden" system variable that refers to the *Timer1 Output*

205

Compare Register A. Essentially, the timer counts pulses at a rate determined by the timebase and prescalar and calls a timer *callback* function (more on this in a moment) each time the counter reaches the value set in OCR1A. The formula for establishing the value for the timer counter is as follows. (Note that the clock time period will be less than 16,000,000 if a prescalar is used. In this instance, the prescalar is set to 1, so the timer counter fires at the maximum rate.)

$$OCR1A = \frac{\text{Required Delay}}{\text{Clock Time Period}} - 1$$

Clear Timer on Compare Mode and a Brief Overview of Bit Twiddling

If you are new to programming, the following line, *TCCR1B |= (1 << WGM12)*, probably looks like gibberish. While it isn't necessary to understand the nuances of bit manipulation to set up a timer (I typically just use the boilerplate template), a brief overview of the process is presented in the following paragraphs for the sake of completeness. Readers who are relatively new to programming may want to skip to the next section or read Appendix C: Introduction to Bit Twiddling.

The operation, *TCCR1B |= (1 << WGM12)*, isn't too complicated when you understand that the purpose of the line is to set the bits of the variable TCCR1B so the timer functions in *Clear Timer on Compare* (CTC) mode, a mode that causes the timer to call a timer callback function each time the counter reaches the value established for OCR1A. The operation functions like this: On the left side of the equals sign, the bitwise OR operator (|) is used to "merge" the bits from the right side of the equals sign. The *logical inclusive OR* operation does a bitwise comparison of the bits on each side of the equals sign. If either bit (one **OR** the other) is set to 1, the corresponding bit is set in the variable on the left side of the equation (see the example below). Recall that in the first part of the initialization function the value of TCCR1B was set to zero. Using the logical OR operation in this context means that any bits that are set in the variable or constant on the right side of the equals sign will be set in the variable on the left side of the equation:

```
        0010
OR      0111
        ____
=       0111
```

The right side of the equation (1 << WGM12) involves the use of the *left shift* operator (<<). As the name implies, the operator shifts the bits in the number given on the left side of the operator the number of places to the left as indicated by the number on the right side of the operator. In this example, the number one is 00000001 in binary, and the WGM12 constant is 3; thus, all of the bits are shifted three places to the left:

```
00000001     (1 in binary)
00001000     (8 in binary)
```

Combining the left-shift operator with logical OR means that the bits of TCCR1B are set to 00001000 (or 8 in decimal). This would be a good time to consider why the author of this boilerplate code didn't simply use an assignment operator to set the value of TCCR1B to 8? To answer that question, it is helpful to remember that the underlying timer logic is generally looking at individual *bits*, not integral *values*. For this reason, bit shifting and logical operations like AND and OR may be used to set individual bits based on multiple masks. Although bitwise shifting and logical operands admittedly obfuscate this particular example, I elected to use the more complex approach because it will provide a foundation for other timer boilerplate code you are likely to run into in other books and on the Internet.

The remaining lines of code function similarly. The prescalar (TCCR1B) is set to "1," which means that no prescalar is used. The function concludes by enabling the timer interrupt (TIMSK1) and re-enabling global interrupts with the sei() function.

Timer Callback

When initialized with the timer initialization code shown in Listing 9.1, the timer will call the timer callback function shown in Listing 9.2 each time the counter reaches the value in the *Output Compare Register*.

Listing 9.2 Timer callback function

```
ISR(TIMER1_COMPA_vect)
{
    //This function is called automatically by the timer.
}
```

At first glance, the timer callback function may be counterintuitive because it is called independently of any code that executes in the main *loop()*. However, this is the very reason for setting up a timer—we want to establish a function that will be called at a specified rate. Given that the function is called at a high frequency, it is important to keep the code "lean and mean." Complex calculations *will* cause problems at high frequencies, so keep calculations and logic to a minimum and save any heavy lifting for the main loop().

A simple example involves using the timer callback function to produce *white noise* (random frequencies with equal intensities). In Listing 9.3, note how the timer callback writes a random value to the digital pins (0–7) referenced by PORTD. Although the *random()* function can be used as a quick test to see if audio output is working, the function is too slow to keep up with the timer callback, so a more efficient method of random number generation will be provided later in the chapter.

Listing 9.3 Synthesizing white noise

```
ISR(TIMER1_COMPA_vect)
{
    //See text for a faster method of random number
    //generation
    byte random_number = random(255);
    //Write data to digital pins
    PORTD = number;
}
```

PORTD

As with the registers in the timer initialization function, PORTD is a register that allows "for lower-level and faster manipulation of the i/o pins of the microcontroller on an Arduino board."[8] This means that the 8 bits of the variable, *random_ number*, can be written to the corresponding digital pin with a single assignment. As you will recall, the outputs of the digital pins will feed an R2R ladder or 8-bit DAC, so the variables that are assigned to this port directly feed the digital audio converter. Note that the previous function could be simplified by assigning the output of the *random()* function directly to PORTD (see Listing 9.4).

Listing 9.4

```
ISR(TIMER1_COMPA_vect)
{
    //See text for a faster method of random number
    //generation
    //Write data to digital pins
    PORTD = random(255);
}
```

We will revisit the timer callback function later in the chapter.

Establishing a Sampling Rate

Selecting a sample rate is not as easy as it sounds. While the Nyquist frequency would suggest a sample rate of around 40kHz to accommodate frequencies in the range of human hearing up to about 20kHz, and the Arduino can, in fact, output samples at that rate, the 16MHz speed of the Arduino processor doesn't leave much in the way of wiggle room for additional processing. Conversely, a relatively slow rate of 10kHz limits the range of frequencies. With the case of low sampling rates, the problem relates more to the limitation of harmonic content or timbre than fundamental pitch. Initial experiments indicated a rate of around 20kHz to be a good compromise. While the rate is too fast to allow for the calculations required for some types of processing, simple waveforms and wavetable lookups can generally be calculated in real time. As you will see in the section on the Mozzi library at the end of the chapter, a sample rate of 16,384 is perhaps the best balance of speed and accuracy.

DAC Integrated Circuit

A number of integrated DAC circuits can be used in place of an R2R ladder. In this section we will look at the circuits and code that are necessary to output sound from a TLC7226 DAC. The converter is an 8-bit digital-to-analog converter with four latched outputs, meaning that the device can hold or "latch" four simultaneous outputs depending on the status of pins A0 and A1 on the DAC.

TLC7226 Pinout

The TLC7226 is an IC with 20 pins as shown in Figure 9.12.

Connecting the TLC7226 to the Arduino is relatively straightforward. For this application, pins DB0 through DB7 correspond to Arduino digital pins D0 through D7, and Arduino pin D9 is connected to the Write Input (WR) pin 15. On the IC, pins 16 and 17 (A1 and A0) are used to select one of four outputs (OUTA through OUTD). For this example, pins 16 and 17 on the IC are connected to +5V, which selects OUTD as the output. Hence, OUTD (pin 19) is connected, along with ground, to the signal and ground pins on an audio cable or jack. The remaining connections are listed in Table 9.2.

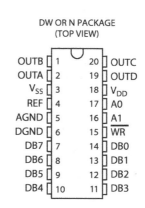

DW OR N PACKAGE
(TOP VIEW)

FIGURE 9.12

TLC7226 pinout.

209

TABLE 9.2 TLC7226 Connections

IC Pin	IC Pin Name	Arduino Pin
1	OUTB	NC
2	OUTA	NC
3	Vss	GND
4	REF	5V
5	AGND	GND
6	DGND	GND
7	DB7	D7
8	DB6	D6
9	DB5	D5
10	DB4	D4
11	DB3	D3
12	DB2	D2
13	DB1	D1
14	DB0	D0
15	WR	D9
16	A1	5V
17	A0	5V
18	Vdd	5V
19	OUTD	Connect to audio tip (also connect GND to audio sleeve)
20	OUTC	NC

Changes to Boilerplate Code

Very few changes are needed to output sound from the DAC. First, enable the digital pins for output in the *setup()* function as in Listing 9.5.

Listing 9.5 Setting up the pin mode

```
pinMode(0, OUTPUT);
pinMode(1, OUTPUT);
pinMode(2, OUTPUT);
pinMode(3, OUTPUT);
pinMode(4, OUTPUT);
pinMode(5, OUTPUT);
pinMode(6, OUTPUT);
pinMode(7, OUTPUT);
pinMode(9, OUTPUT);
```

Next, send a digital HIGH value on digital pin 9 to prepare the IC for a digital to analog conversion. The digital data is transmitted via the PORTD register call (see Listing 9.6) and followed by a digital LOW value on pin 9.

Listing 9.6

```
ISR(TIMER1_COMPA_vect)
{
    //Prepare IC for DAC conversion
    digitalWrite(9, HIGH);

    //Write to DAC
    //See text for a faster method of random number generation
    PORTD = random(255);

    //Finished with conversion
    digitalWrite(9, LOW);
}
```

Note that we will look at one other form of digital-to-analog conversion, *pulse-width modulation*, in the final section of the chapter.

Sound Synthesis

This section of the chapter focuses on strategies for emulating analog waveforms. The information will provide a useful foundation for developing other types of synthesizers such as additive synthesizers or sample playback units. Also, the topic of analog emulation will likely be of interest to many readers given the popularity of "retro" hardware and software synthesizers. Best of all, by the end of the chapter you will be able to construct a fully functional synthesizer like the Stella Synth featured in the final section of the book. The discussion includes an overview of waveforms, sound generation methods, and lookup tables, and a central theme involves the creation of an extensible oscillator class that can be used as the basis for many types of projects. Feel free to jump to the final section of the chapter if you are anxious to start making sounds. The Mozzi and Teensy libraries can handle all of the challenging aspects of direct digital synthesis. However, the synthesis libraries will be easier to use when you get a sense of how waveforms are generated and modified. The oscillators in this section are simple yet powerful and can be used to for additive synthesis, low-frequency oscillation, subtractive synthesis, and sample playback. They are featured in the Step Sequencer project in the final section of the book.

9.1 MUSIC
SYNTHESIS
DEMO

Waveforms

Waveforms are used to visualize the changes in air pressure over time that are associated with a given sound. The Y-axis represents amplitude or "loudness," and the X-axis represents frequency, which generally correlates to "pitch" (see Figure 9.13).

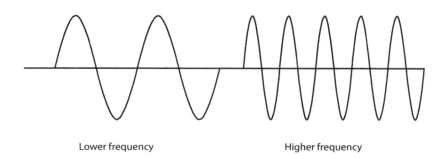

Lower frequency   Higher frequency

211

FIGURE 9.13

Two sine waveforms at different frequencies.

In the early days of analog synthesis, only simple waveforms could be produced due to the limitations of analog oscillators—the sound source of a synthesizer. For example, Figure 9.14 shows some of the most common waveforms associated with early synthesizers including sawtooth/ramp, square, triangle, and sine waves.

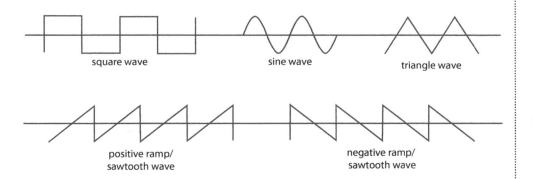

square wave   sine wave   triangle wave

positive ramp/   negative ramp/
sawtooth wave   sawtooth wave

FIGURE 9.14

Common analog waveforms.

These primary waveforms are simple but can be combined to produce more complex timbres. For example, a 220Hz sine wave was combined with a 330Hz triangle wave to produce the waveform shown in Figure 9.15.

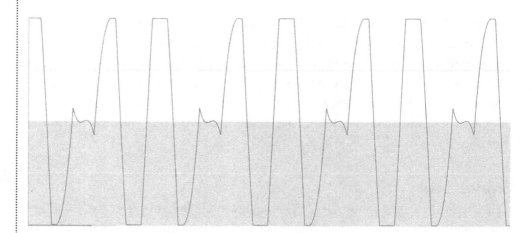

FIGURE 9.15

Combining primary
waveforms.

Generating a Waveform

Although most musicians are comfortable with the concept of *frequency*, the measure of the number of occurrences of a wave in a given unit of time, the concept of *periodicity* is a central concept in developing a waveform generator. In Figure 9.16, note how a repeating wave can be visualized in terms of the number of cycles per second (frequency in Hz) or as the length of time (in seconds) for the wave to complete a cycle:

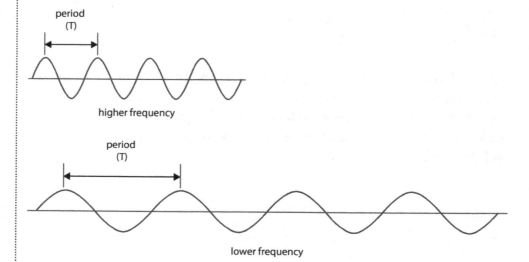

FIGURE 9.16

Visualizing the relationship
of waveform period and
frequency.

Frequency and period are inextricably linked in that higher frequencies decrease the length of a period and lower frequencies increase the length of a period. In fact, the period has a reciprocal relationship to frequency that can be expressed in the following equation:

$$T = \frac{1}{f}$$

Synthesizing a Ramp Waveform

An ascending sawtooth or ramp wave is an ideal starting waveform for a digital sound synthesis system. Computation of the waveform involves simple addition, so the only challenge is to determine how to compute the slices or samples of the waveform for a given frequency. A simple example utilizing the timer may help to illustrate how the waveform is constructed in real time.

To begin, it will be helpful to establish some parameters: as was discussed earlier in the chapter, the sample rate, as determined by the timer, will be 16,384Hz. For the examples in this section we will use a bit depth of 8-bits, which will provide an amplitude range of 0 to 255. Considering the limited amount of available memory, and looking ahead to the possibility of developing a wavetable (sample lookup) oscillator, we will limit the number of steps to represent the waveform to 256 (0–255). In order to produce a sawtooth waveform of, say, 440Hz, it is necessary to increment the variable representing its instantaneous voltage such that the waveform is output 440 times each second. Phrased another way, larger increment values will cause an increase in frequency and smaller increment values will serve to lower the frequency (see Figure 9.17).

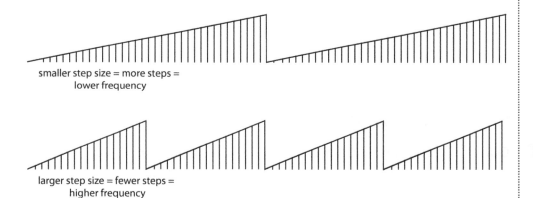

smaller step size = more steps =
lower frequency

larger step size = fewer steps =
higher frequency

FIGURE 9.17

Ramp wave: large vs. small increment values.

The process is as follows: for a given frequency (f), calculate the period (T) by dividing the sample rate by the frequency.

$$T = \frac{\text{sample rate}}{f}$$

Next, determine the increment value by dividing the number of samples per cycle (256) by the period (T):

$$\text{Increment value} = \frac{256}{T}$$

The increment value can then be used to increase the "voltage" of the ramp wave (or index a sample buffer) at a rate that will result in the intended frequency. Running some numbers should serve to illustrate the process. Consider a 400Hz wave at a timer sample rate of 20,000Hz, with 256 possible samples representing one cycle of the waveform:

$$period = 20,000 / 400 = 50Hz = 20ms$$

In this instance, it is not necessary to convert the period to milliseconds, but the formula is shown below since it might be useful as you visualize the logic in this section. To convert Hz to milliseconds, use the formula:

$$period\ in\ milliseconds = \frac{1}{Hz * 1000}$$

To determine the increment value, divide the number of steps representing the waveform by the period (in Hz).

$$Increment\ value = \frac{256}{50} = 5.12$$

Let's flip the numbers around to check the math: if we increment the amplitude of a sawtooth by 5.12 every 50 cycles, we step through one iteration of the waveform (256 steps) each period. Also, 400 repetitions of the waveform with the given period can be completed each second at a sample rate of 20,000: $400 \times 50 = 20,000$.

Fixed-Point Math

One of the problems with the preceding logic is that the increment value is a fractional (floating point) number. Unfortunately, floating-point math is very slow on the Arduino, so it is not possible to maintain an accurate frequency when those numbers are used in a timer callback. The solution is to use *fixed-point math*, as described below.

The trick behind fixed-point math is to scale a small number like 5.12 up to a larger number and visualize an imaginary decimal point.[9] For example, a 16-bit integer could be thought of as a fixed point number with 8 bits for the whole number and 8 bits representing the fractional portion of the number. Such a number is termed an 8.8 number in fixed-point parlance. The first 8 bits represent values in the range of 0 to 255, and the last 8 bits are used for decimal values with 8 bits of precision. However, since the decimal point is imaginary, a 16-bit integer can be used to represent numbers with a greater or lesser amount of precision depending on the needs of the program. With a 4.12 integer, 4 bits provide a range from 0 to 15 for the whole number with 12 digits of precision for the fraction. Similarly, a 12.4 integer would provide a larger range (0–4095) with four digits of precision for the fraction.

An example will help to clarify the concept. Let's use an 8.8 fixed-point integer to represent a floating-point increment value of 5.12. To convert a floating-point number to a fixed-point number, multiply the number by the value representing the number of bits in the whole part of the fixed-point number. For example, to convert 5.12 into an 8.8 integer, multiply 5.12 by 256. This is akin to shifting the number eight places to the left (although it is important to mention that bitwise shifting does *not* work with floating-point numbers).

$$5.12 \times 256 = 1310$$

Simply shift the 8.8 number eight times to the right to retrieve the whole number portion of the 8.8 integer:

$$1310 >> 8 = 5$$

Note that another way to calculate the increment value when 8 bits are used to store the whole number of a fixed-point integer is to multiply the frequency times the maximum value that can be stored in the *entire* integer and divide by the sample rate. For example, the maximum value for a 32-bit integer is 4294967295, so the increment value for an 8.24 fixed-point integer with a frequency of 440Hz and sample rate of 20kHz could be calculated as follows:

$$440Hz * 4294967295 / 20,000 = 94489280$$

As before, getting the whole number is simply a matter of shifting the requisite number of places to the right. In the case of an 8.24 integer, a right-shift of 24 places will yield the whole number:

$$94489280 >> 24 = 5$$

You might wonder why we didn't just round the number in the first place. The problem with that approach is that errors would quickly compound. The beauty of fixed-point math is that it maintains the precision of the original floating-point number because the "gunk" to the right side of the imaginary decimal point is used in mathematical operations. For this reason, precision is only lost when a right-shift is used to retrieve the whole number.

Here are a few examples to demonstrate how fixed-point math works in iterative calculations. The column on the left is the 8.8 version of the floating point number shown in the rightmost column. The middle column shows the running total of the high byte (the whole number portion) of the 8.8 fixed-point number. Although it appears that rounding would work in the first example, the sum of the second example would be off by two after just four iterations!

Example 1

Range of numbers that can be expressed with 8 bits: 256
Frequency for this example: 400
Sample rate for this example: 20,000
Floating point increment = 5.12
Resulting 8.8 increment = 1310 (5.12 × 256 or 400Hz * 65535/20,000)

8.8 increment	Value of high byte	Floating point increment
1310	5	5.12
2620	10	10.24
3930	15	15.36
5240	20	20.48

Example 2

Range of numbers that can be expressed with 8 bits: 256
Frequency for this example 117.19
Sample rate for this example 20,000
Floating point increment = 1.5
Resulting 8.8 increment = 384 (1.5 * 256 or 117.19Hz * 65535/20,000)

8.8 increment	Value of high byte	Floating point increment
384	1	1.5
768	3	3
1152	4	4.5
1536	6	6

Tuning Oscillator

The following sketch illustrates how the concepts above could be used to provide a simple tuning oscillator by utilizing the TLC7226 DAC described in the preceding section. With a few modifications the sketch can also be configured to work with an R2R ladder.

The waveform for this example is a simple sawtooth wave, which is characterized by an ascending ramp. The size of the steps of the ramp are stored in an increment variable called *inc*, and the running total is stored in a variable called an *accumulator*. The accumulator is incremented each time the timer fires the callback function, so the frequency of the waveform is determined by the size of the steps. (As noted earlier, smaller steps result in fewer cycles per second.) To maintain accuracy, a 32-bit 8.24 fixed-point integer is used to store the increment value, and a helper function, *calculateIncrement()*, returns the value for the increment based on the sample rate and given frequency in Hz (see Listing 9.7). Note that two calculations are shown in the listing. The first example, which is commented out, provides a simple increment value based on the frequency and sample rate. The second version, which is documented in a Rugged Audio Shield demo,[10] provides a slightly more accurate increment calculation.

Listing 9.7 Calculating a 24.8 fixed-point increment

```
uint32_t calculateIncrement(float freq)
{
    //Basic increment calculation:
    //return max_32 * freq / sampleRate;
```

216

```
    //Better version: see note in Rugged Audio Shield demo
    return (uint32_t)((freq * max_32 + sampleRate/2)/sampleRate);
}
```

Aside from boilerplate timer initialization code, the only other point of interest is the timer callback function. In this case, the accumulator is incremented and the result is sent to the DAC after a right-shift of 24 places (see Listing 9.8). As was previously noted, the right-shift is necessary to retrieve the whole number portion of the fixed-point number:

Listing 9.8 Timer callback

```
//Timer callback
ISR(TIMER1_COMPA_vect)
{
    accumulator += inc;  //Increment the accumulator

    //Prepare IC for DAC conversion
    digitalWrite(9, HIGH);

    //Output 8-bit portion of the accumulator to the TLC7226 DAC:
    PORTD = accumulator >> 24; //Shift to the right to get
    //8-bit whole number

    //Finished with conversion
    digitalWrite(9, LOW);
}
```

Volatile Variables

The source code for the tuning oscillator is shown in its entirety in Listing 9.9. Aside from the lengthy boilerplate timer initialization, surprisingly few lines of code are required to create an accurate waveform generator. The only other thing to note is that the accumulator is declared as *volatile*. The volatile keyword should be used any time a variable might be altered by a timer callback function in order to prevent the compiler from assuming the variable is in a known state.[11] It might be helpful to think of the volatile keyword as a directive to the compiler to always double check the value of the variable before it is used. This is important because the timer may alter the value *at any time*—even during execution of the main *loop()*.

Listing 9.9 Tuning oscillator (complete listing)

```
//Arduino for Musicians
//Listing 9.9: Tuning Oscillator DAC

//Maximum value that can be stored in 32 bits
const uint32_t max_32 = 4294967295L;

uint16_t sampleRate = 16384;      //Sample rate
volatile uint32_t accumulator;    //32-bit accumulator
uint32_t inc;                     //Used to increment the
                                  //accumulator

void setup()
{
    //Set up pins for use with TLC7226 DAC
    pinMode(0, OUTPUT);
```

```
        pinMode(1, OUTPUT);
        pinMode(2, OUTPUT);
        pinMode(3, OUTPUT);
        pinMode(4, OUTPUT);
        pinMode(5, OUTPUT);
        pinMode(6, OUTPUT);
        pinMode(7, OUTPUT);
        pinMode(9, OUTPUT);

        //Calculate increment for 440.0 Hz tone
        inc = calculateIncrement(440.0);

        //Initialize the timers:
        InitTimer1();
}

void loop()
{
    //Nothing to do...playback is handled in timer callback
}

uint32_t calculateIncrement(float freq)
{
    //Basic increment calculation:
    //return max_32 * freq / sampleRate;

    //Better version: see note in Rugged Audio Shield demo
    return (uint32_t)((freq * max_32 + sampleRate/2)/
    sampleRate);
}

//Timer callback
ISR(TIMER1_COMPA_vect)
{
    accumulator += inc;  //Increment the accumulator

    //Prepare IC for DAC conversion
    digitalWrite(9, HIGH);

    //Output 8-bit portion of the accumulator to the TLC7226 DAC:
    PORTD = accumulator >> 24; //Shift to the right to get
    8-bit whole number

    //Finished with conversion
    digitalWrite(9, LOW);
}

//Timer setup boilerplate:
//Set up Timer 0 for PWM and set up timer 1 for 16384 Hz
sample rate
void InitTimer1()
{
    //SET UP TIMER 1
    cli();      //Disable global interrupts
    TCCR1A=0;   //Reset Timer 1 Counter Control Register A
    TCCR1B=0;   //Reset Timer 1 Counter Control Register B

    //Set Timer 1 Output Compare Register A to desired
    //frequency
    //(16,000,000 / 16384) - 1 = 975
    OCR1A=975;
```

218

```
    //Turn on CTC (clear timer on compare match) mode:
    TCCR1B |= (1 << WGM12);

    TCCR1B |= (1 << CS10);  //Prescalar = 1 (no prescalar used)

    //Enable timer interrupt
    TIMSK1 |= (1 << OCIE1A);

    //Enable interrupts
    sei();
}
```

9.2 TUNING
OSCILLATOR

Developing an Oscillator Class

In this section we will look at an object-oriented approach to encapsulating the functionality of an oscillator such as the tuning oscillator in a C++ class. The source code for the oscillator classes in this section is available at the OUP website, and it will be most convenient to install the classes so they will be available for use in the Arduino IDE. To install the classes, download the folder named AFM_Oscillator and drag it to the *Arduino\libraries* subfolder and provide an include statement (e.g., #include <Oscillator.h>) to use one of the oscillator classes in a sketch. Alternatively, copy one or more Oscillator classes (both the .h and .cpp file) directly into an Arduino project folder (e.g.,*Arduino\MyProjectFolder*).

As mentioned in Chapter 8, one of the wonderful aspects of C++ is the ability to turn a concept into code "objects" that can simplify logic and provide robust and reusable building blocks for future projects. In this instance, we will use *inheritance*, a powerful feature of the language that allows classes to derive functionality from a base class. As you will see in the paragraphs that follow, the inheritance mechanism simplifies the task of creating oscillator objects.

Inheritance

C++ classes are useful because they provide a mechanism for organizing data and functions in a logical way. A class such as an oscillator class might contain data members that store the type of waveform, phase, or frequency, and member functions can be written to manipulate member data. Inheritance provides a way to extend the base functionality to new objects. For example, the counting mechanism of a ramp oscillator could provide the basis for an oscillator that utilizes a sample lookup table. And that is exactly the approach that will be used in this section of the chapter: a base class will provide the data and functionality found in *all* oscillators, and new classes will be derived to expand the base or *parent* class.

A necessary first step when considering inheritance is to determine the function of the parent class. The parent class should provide the essential member variables and functions that will be used by derived classes—no more, no less. The reason I state that so emphatically is that it is easy to get "tricky" when designing a base class by adding data members and functions that may or may not be useful in derived classes. Verbose classes will only serve to complicate logic, so it is best to strive for classes that are clear and concise. A simple class is often a sign of an elegant implementation.

An Oscillator Base Class

The oscillator classes in this section all derive from a base class called *OscillatorBase*. The class contains a number of member variables that are used to calculate samples in real time, and the variables are based on the preceding Tuning Oscillator code example. The *OscillatorBase* member variables (along with comments) are shown in the code snippet in Listing 9.10.

Listing 9.10 Member variables

```
class OscillatorBase
{
    protected:
    //MEMBER VARIABLES:
    uint16_t m_sampleRate;     //The sample rate (e.g.,16384)
    float m_frequency;         //Frequency of the oscillator
    uint16_t m_maxAmplitude;   //Max amplitude 8 bit = 255

    volatile uint32_t m_accumulator;   //32-bit accumulator
    volatile uint32_t m_increment;     //Used to increment
                                       //the accumulator.
```

The variables are used in just the same way as the Tuning Oscillator example, but a key difference is that the variables are not just available to the OscillatorBase class—they will automatically be available to any classes that are derived from OscillatorBase. Not only are member variables available to derived classes, protected and public member functions will be available as well.

The remainder of the base class header file is shown in Listing 9.11 (sans two *inline* function bodies that will be described later in the chapter).

Listing 9.11 Member variables

```
    public:
    //DEFAULT CONSTRUCTOR
    OscillatorBase();

    //GETTERS AND SETTERS
    virtual void setFrequency(float freq);     //Sets current
                                               //frequency
    void setSampleRate(uint16_t sample_rate);  //Sets sample rate

    //HELPER METHODS
    void init();                               //Initializes member
                                               //variables
    void setMIDIFrequency(int note);   //Sets frequency based
                                       //on a midi note
};
```

The following paragraphs detail the various methods that form the oscillator base class.

Default Constructor

The base class provides a default constructor (*OscillatorBase()*), a block of code that is automatically called whenever an object of the class is instantiated. In this case, the default constructor simply calls another helper function to initialize the variables to default values. Although the values could be initialized in the default constructor, an "init()" method is useful because it can be called at any time—not just when the class is instantiated. The constructor and *init()* methods are shown in Listing 9.12.

Listing 9.12

```
#include "OscillatorBase.h"

//Default constructor
OscillatorBase::OscillatorBase()
{
    //Initialize variables to reasonable defaults
    init();
}

//Initialize variables
void OscillatorBase::init()
{
    m_sampleRate = 16384;
    m_frequency = 440;
    m_maxAmplitude = 255;
    m_increment = 1;
    m_accumulator = 0;
}
```

Access Methods

"Accessor" methods (colloquially referred to as *getters* and *setters*) are used to set or retrieve data member values. Although it would be possible to make the data members available through the use of the *public* keyword, that approach can lead to some difficult-to-detect bugs. For example, another class or function might attempt to access the frequency variable as follows:

```
if(myOscillator.m_frequency = 0)
{
    //Error! m_frequency is inadvertently set to zero!
}
```

Unfortunately, the calling code in the previous example did not compare the value of *m_frequency* to zero, it *set the value* of *m_frequency* to zero. This is the type of insidious bug that makes a good case for controlling the access of class data members through accessor methods.

The *setSampleRate()* method is self-explanatory—it takes an unsigned integer as a parameter and uses the number to update the member variable named *m_sampleRate* (see Listing 9.13).

Listing 9.13

```
//Set the sample rate
void OscillatorBase::setSampleRate(uint16_t sample_rate)
{
    m_sampleRate = sample_rate;
}
```

SetFrequency() requires more discussion. The method updates the data member *m_frequency* with the given function parameter, a floating-point number representing the frequency of the waveform. After checking for a zero value (to avoid division by zero), the function updates the *m_period*, and *m_increment* variables based on the sample rate and new frequency. The function also provides a default increment of one to guard against the potential of a value of zero at low frequencies (see Listing 9.14).

Listing 9.14

```
//Set the frequency of the oscillator
void OscillatorBase::setFrequency(float freq)
{
    m_frequency = freq;
    if(m_frequency == 0)
    {
        m_frequency = 1; //Avoid divide by zero
    }

    //Calculate increment
    m_increment = calculateIncrement();
    if(m_increment == 0)
    {
        m_increment = 1;
    }
}
```

MIDI-to-Frequency Conversion

The method *setMIDIFrequency()* is a convenience method that converts a MIDI note in the range of 1 to 127 to a corresponding frequency. The method, which is based on examples by Joe Wolfe,[12] works by taking advantage of the fact that semitones have a frequency ratio of $2^{1/12}$ power, so the frequency can be determined by comparing a given note against a reference note (usually A 440). In the following equation, *n* refers to the number of semitones above or below the reference:

$$f_n = 2^{n/12} * 440H^8$$

In Listing 9.15, all of the values are "upcast" into floats and assigned to the variable *freq*. In this way, the calculation retains floating-point accuracy until it is used by the *setFrequency()* method. As I mentioned earlier in the book, floating-point math is slow on the Arduino. However, this function will not need to be as efficient as the functions called from within the timer callback.

Listing 9.15

```
void OscillatorBase::setMIDIFrequency(int note)
{
    //Convert a MIDI note to frequency
    float freq = (float) 440.0 * (float)(pow(2, (note - 57) / 12.0));
    setFrequency(freq);
}
```

Calculating an Increment Value

As in the tuning oscillator demonstration, a method named *calculateIncrement()* calculates an 8.24 fixed-point increment value based on the frequency and sample rate (see Listing 9.16). Unlike other methods in the class, the function body is defined in the header file and the *inline* keyword is used to let the compiler know that that the method is time-critical.

Listing 9.16

```
inline
uint32_t calculateIncrement()
{
    //Basic version:
    //return max_32 * m_frequency / m_sampleRate;

    //Better version:
    //See note in Rugged Audio demonstration
    return (uint32_t)((m_frequency * max_32 +
            m_sampleRate/2)/m_sampleRate);
}
```

tick() Method

The heart of the base oscillator class is the virtual *tick()* method (see Listing 9.17). Increment values are added to the *accumulator*, a 32-bit integer that keeps a running total of the "slices" of the waveform. The method increments the accumulator and returns an 8-bit sample representing the instantaneous voltage at that given point in time. As with *calculateIncrement()*, the method is time-critical and is defined in the header file with the *inline* keyword. The method will be called from within a timer callback function.

Listing 9.17

```
inline virtual uint8_t tick()
{
    m_accumulator += m_increment;
    return m_accumulator >> 24; //Get 8-bit real number
    //portion of accumulator
}
```

You might be wondering why there isn't any code to check for out-of-range values in Listing 9.17. The good news is that the accumulator will automatically wrap around, so no range checking is required. Here is how it works. Consider a 32-bit value that is almost "full" of digits:

223

Binary value	8-bit	(high-byte) value
111111111111111111111111111111110	255	

Add binary 10 (2 in decimal) to the previous value:

Binary value	8-bit	(high-byte) value
111111111111111111111111111111110	255	
+	10	sum requires 33 bits
000000000000000000000000000000000	0	wraps around to zero

Virtual Methods

A few words about the *virtual* keyword are also in order. The *virtual* keyword provides a mechanism for a derived class to *override* a method in the parent class, which is useful in situations where a pointer or reference is used to call the virtual method. With this approach, a single function could be written to call *any* subclass and, through a process called *late binding*,[13] the appropriate method of the *derived class* is automatically called. The following pseudo-code illustrates the concept. In this case, a pointer to the base class automatically calls the appropriate *tick()* method of the derived class.

```
MyDerivedClass derived_class;
OscillatorBase *ptr =&derived_class; //Point to class
ptr->tick();   //Derived tick method called
```

At this point we have a functional base class that is able to calculate an increment value based on a sample rate and frequency, update an accumulator through a call to a method called *tick()*, and convert MIDI notes into frequency. That is an impressive amount of functionality for just a few lines of code.

Using Inheritance to Create a Ramp Oscillator

Although the base class required some forethought to implement, the extra work will be richly rewarded in this section. Through the power of inheritance, a working subclass can be derived with just a few lines of code (see Listing 9.18). In the following example (from Oscillator.h), the OscillatorBase.h file is included and a new class, *RampOscillator*, is derived from the base class. As is evident in the following example, the syntax for creating a subclass is to provide the name of the new class followed by a colon and then the *public* keyword followed by the name of the base class.

Listing 9.18

```
#include "OscillatorBase.h"
class RampOscillator: public OscillatorBase
{
     public:
     // Override base class version of tick() method
     inline virtual uint8_t tick()
     {
         //Call the base class implementation of tick() to advance
         //the accumulator or use new accumulator logic
         return OscillatorBase::tick();
     }
};
```

Although it would not be necessary to create a derived ramp oscillator class—the base class *is* an ascending ramp/sawtooth oscillator—I am including the class because it shows how to override a virtual method. As you will see in the examples that follow, the primary difference between inherited and base classes is the implementation of the *tick()* method.

9.3 RAMP OSCILLATOR DEMO

225

Sawtooth Oscillator

A descending sawtooth oscillator is functionally similar to an ascending ramp oscillator other than the obvious difference in slope, so the implementation of *SawtoothOscillator* is functionally very similar. The primary difference is that the current sample is calculated by subtracting the maximum amplitude (in 8.24 fixed-point format) from the base-class accumulator (see Listing 9.19):

Listing 9.19

```
class SawtoothOscillator: public OscillatorBase
{
     public:
     // Override base class version of tick() method
     virtual uint8_t tick()
     {
         //Call the base class implementation of tick() to advance
         //the accumulator.
         OscillatorBase::tick();
         /*Determine current sample by subtracting the value
         of the base accumulator from the maximum
         amplitude and returning high 8 bits.*/
         return (max_32 - m_accumulator) >> 24;
     }
};
```

9.4 SAWTOOTH OSCILLATOR DEMO

Pulse-Width Oscillator

Pulse-width modulation is an interesting feature of some analog and digital synthesizers. Pulse-width oscillators provide a mechanism for changing the duty cycle of a pulse, thereby changing the timbre of the waveform and providing some interesting possibilities for waveform modulation.

As with the other classes that are derived from *OscillatorBase*, *PulseWidth Oscillator* overrides the base *tick()* method. The class also includes a member variable, *m_pulseWidth*, that stores the pulse width as it relates to the maximum amplitude of the base accumulator (which counts from 0 to *max_32*). So, a pulse width of 50 percent can be represented by a base-class accumulator value of *max_32/2*. In this case, an accumulator value of < *max_32/2* represents values in the range of the first half of the duty cycle. Similarly, a value of *max_32/4* represents a 25 percent duty cycle.

As is evident in Listing 9.20, a helper function, *setDutyCycle()*, takes a floating point value that represents the duty cycle as a percentage and converts this value to a pulse width based on the maximum accumulator value (*max_32*). Although this approach might seem inefficient, only one floating-point operation is required when the duty cycle is set. Thus, the duty cycle can be tracked with a single "if" statement in the *tick()* method.

Listing 9.20

```
class PulseWidthOscillator: public OscillatorBase
{
        protected:
        uint32_t m_pulseWidth;      //Length of duty cycle in
                                    //proportion to counter
        public:
        //Override default constructor
        PulseWidthOscillator():OscillatorBase()
        {
           m_pulseWidth = max_32/2;  //Default value = 50%
                                     //duty cycle
        }

        void setDutyCycle(float duty)
        {
           //Convert duty percentage to percentage of accumulator
           m_pulseWidth = duty * max_32;
        }

        //Override base class tick() method to handle pulse width
        virtual uint8_t tick()
        {
           //Call base class tick() method
           OscillatorBase::tick();

           if(m_accumulator < m_pulseWidth)
           {
               return max_32>>24;
           }else{
               return 0;
           }
        }
};
```

9.5 PULSE-
WIDTH
OSCILLATOR
DEMO

Triangle Oscillator

Triangle waves are more challenging to produce since the accumulator must be incremented in the first half of the period and decremented in the second half. For this reason, the increment value must be twice that of the other waveforms in this section because the accumulator needs to reach the maximum amplitude halfway through the period. The *TriangleOscillator* class adds a new accumulator data member and overrides the base-class *setFrequency()* method to provide an opportunity to reset the accumulator (see Listing 9.21).

In the *tick()* method, the value of the base-class accumulator is compared to *max_32* with a right-shift, which represents half of the full amplitude in 32 bits. This admittedly awkward instruction is done to avoid a divide operation that would cause the *tick()* method to run too slowly. Similarly, a left-shift is used to multiply *m_triangleAccumulator* by two if the base accumulator is in the upward slope of the waveform. A similar operation is performed if the base waveform is in the downward slope. The end result is that the underlying sawtooth accumulator is converted to a triangle wave without resorting to any time-intensive multiplication or division.

Listing 9.21 Triangle oscillator

```
class TriangleOscillator: public OscillatorBase
{
    protected:
    //Add new member variable to store triangle amplitude
    uint32_t m_triangleAccumulator;

    public:
    //Override setFrequency() to have a chance to calculate
    //triangle accumulator values
    virtual void setFrequency(uint16_t freq)
    {
        //Call the base class to set the internal accumulator
        OscillatorBase::setFrequency(freq);

        //Set up the triangle accumulator (which increments
        //twice as fast as the internal counter).
        m_triangleAccumulator = 0;
    }

    //Override the tick() method to handle triangle accumulator
    virtual uint8_t tick()
    {
        //Call the base class to update the internal accumulator
        OscillatorBase::tick();

        //Use left shift to compare the accumulator against half
        //the full amplitude (in 32 bits)
        if(m_accumulator < max_32 >>1 )
        {
            //Use left shift to multiply the accumulator by two
            //if we are less than 1/2 the maximum amplitude
            m_triangleAccumulator = m_accumulator <<1;
```

227

```
        }else{
            /*If we are over the halfway point, subtract
            the accumulator from maximum amplitude
            and use left shift to multiply by two. */
            m_triangleAccumulator = (max_32 -
            m_accumulator) <<1;
        }
        return m_triangleAccumulator >>24;
    }
};
```

Noise Generator

We will look at one more class, *NoiseGenerator*, before moving to lookup tables. As you might imagine, noise generators produce noise (usually white or pink noise). A virtual version of a noise generator can be easily achieved by using a random number generator and selecting random values from an appropriate range of amplitudes. Unfortunately, I found the *random()* function to be too slow in my tests, so a more efficient method of random number generation is required.

Linear Congruential Random Number Generation

The topic of generating truly random number is an area of research for many computer scientists. Fortunately, the needs of an audio random number generator are less rigorous. The only requirements are that generator is fast and the samples *sound* random. One approach is to use a *linear congruential* method where the current audio sample is used as an input to a function that returns another sample:[14]

$$R_{new} = (A * R_{old} + B) \bmod M$$

Although the method is not truly random—the sequence repeats every 256 samples—it does sound random and is very fast: 100,000 pseudo-random numbers can be generated in just 112ms vs. a whopping 9,530ms for the overhead involved in calling the standard *random()* function!

As Hal Chamberlin notes in *Musical Applications of Microprocessors*, the mod function can be implemented by ignoring overflow, so a randomizing function could be implemented as follows. It is important to note that the function relies on two "magic numbers" (77 and 55) for A and B in the preceding example. These values will yield the maximum sequence length of 256 bytes:

```
byte randomByte(byte last_value)
{
    return (77 * last_value + 55);
}
```

Incorporating the random number function into a noise generator can be easily achieved by adding an unsigned integer data member representing the current sample and overriding the base class *tick()* method to produce a new pseudorandom sample. The class is shown in its entirety in Listing 9.22.

Listing 9.22

```
class NoiseGenerator: public OscillatorBase
{
    protected:
    uint16_t m_randomSample;

    public:
    NoiseGenerator()  {m_randomSample = 1;}

    /* Override base class tick() method to return random values
    Random byte generator based on the Linear Congruential Method:
    Rnew = (A * Rold +B)mod M
    Note that mod is handled by ignoring integer overflow
    */
    virtual uint8_t tick()
    {
        m_randomSample = (77 * m_randomSample) +55;
        //Return most significant bits
        return m_randomSample >>8;
    }
};
```

9.7 NOISE GENERATOR DEMO

229

Using a Lookup Table

The waveforms presented thus far are easily computed "on the fly" by an Arduino. However, one common waveform—the sine wave—is missing. Although the formula for generating sine wave samples is not complex, the calculations are processor intensive and, thus, are too slow for direct digital synthesis on an Arduino. A common workaround is to utilize a *lookup table*. A lookup table is nothing more than an array of samples.[15] In this case, the lookup table represents one complete cycle of a sine wave. Instead of calculating sine wave samples in the *tick()* method, the samples can be looked up from a table of precalculated values (see Figure 9.18). In this case, the base-class accumulator functions as an index—the index will increment faster at high frequencies and slower at lower frequencies.

One thing to remember about lookup tables is that they require lots of memory (256 bytes in this instance), so be judicious in using tables. Given the extra memory

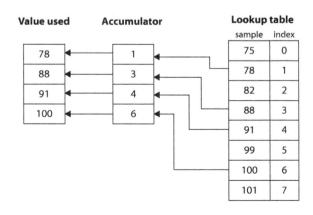

FIGURE 9.18

Retrieving values from a lookup table.

requirements, it made sense to separate the sine wave oscillator from the other oscillators in Oscillator.h. That way, you can easily include the sine wave oscillator (or not) depending on memory constraints of a sketch. The class, *SineWaveOscillator*, is divided into two files: *SineWaveOscillator.h* and *SineWaveTable.cpp*. *SineWave Oscillator.h* contains the class declaration and *tick()* function, and *SineWaveTable.h* contains an array that holds the values of the sine wave.

Since the values of the lookup table do not change while the sketch executes, we are able to take advantage of a trick to minimize the memory impact of using the lookup table. The keyword *PROGMEM* can be used to tell the compiler to store the values in the program memory space instead of RAM. In *SineWaveTable.h*,[9] 256 numbers representing a sine wave are assigned to *sine256*, an array of bytes (see Listing 9.23). Please note that the entire array is not shown in order to save space.

Listing 9.23

```
#ifndef SINEWAVETABLE__
#define SINEWAVETABLE__

PROGMEM const byte sine256[] = {
  127,130,133,136,139,143,146,149,152,155,158,161,
  164,167,170,173,176,178,181,
        .
        .
        .
      108,111,115,118,121,124
};

#endif
```

Creating a Sine Wave Oscillator

Now that a sine wave lookup table is available, it is relatively easy to create the *SineWaveOscillator* class (see Listing 9.24). As with the other oscillator classes, *SineWaveOscillator* inherits from OscillatorBase. The *tick()* method is very similar to the code in *rampOscillator* in that *m_increment* increments the accumulator on each tick. The primary difference is that the accumulator is used to index a lookup table.

The following line requires some explanation:

```
return (uint8_t)pgm_read_byte_near(sine256 + index);
```

Recall that *sine256* represents an array of bytes that can be accessed using an index such as *sine256[index]*. However, *sine256* (sans brackets) is a *pointer* to the first index in the array, thus, sine256 + *n* points to the nth item in the array named *sine256*. Although the pointer syntax looks awkward, it might be helpful to visualize the process by considering how you might ask a store clerk for an item from a shelf: asking for "the fifth item to the right" is somewhat akin to the retrieving the value returned by *sine256 + 5*.

The entire SineOscillator class is shown in Listing 9.24. It is interesting to note how short the listing is—most of the functionality is handled by *OscillatorBase*, the base class. Again, this is an example of the power of the inheritance mechanism in C++.

Listing 9.24 Sine oscillator

```
#ifndef SINEWAVEOSCILLATOR__
#define SINEWAVEOSCILLATOR__

#include "SineWaveTable.h"
#include "OscillatorBase.h"

class SineOscillator: public OscillatorBase
{
    public:
    // Override base class version of tick() method
    uint8_t tick()
    {
        //Call the base class version to update the tick counter.
        uint8_t index = OscillatorBase::tick();

        //Use the accumulator to index the sine256 array
        return (byte)pgm_read_byte_near(sine256 + index);
    }
};

#endif
```

Although the process of using a lookup table is useful in generating a sine wave, keep in mind that you can apply this process to a lookup table containing samples of *any* sound. Although the Arduino Uno has a limited amount of memory to store samples, there are still many exciting applications of this concept such as an interactive PC waveform designer in a language like Processing. Such an application could be used to "draw" any number of arbitrary waveforms for use by an oscillator like the *SineWaveOscillator*. In fact, the only change that would be needed is to add a member variable that points to another lookup table. Similarly, a talking metronome or variable wavetable synthesizer could be easily created using the lookup approach demonstrated in the preceding section.

Preparing Samples for Use with a Lookup Table

One approach to preparing samples for use with Arduino is to use a program like Audacity (available for free at http://audacity.sourceforge.net) to prepare the samples. Audacity can be used to record and edit audio and the data can be exported in a RAW (header-less) 8-bit signed or unsigned format suitable for use in a lookup table. Unfortunately, the raw samples need to be converted to an array (similar to the *sine256* array in Listing 9.23) before they can be used in a sketch. A free conversion application (along with a file-conversion video tutorial) is available at the OUP website. You will also find a sketch named SamplePlayback that demonstrates a simple digital oscillator capable of playing wavetables of varying length.

Using Oscillators

If you are like me, you are probably excited at the prospect of constructing a custom digital/analog synthesizer. In my case, it was thrilling to hear the sounds

9.8 SINE WAVE DEMO

9.9 PREPARING SAMPLES FOR USE WITH A LOOKUP TABLE

231

of a retro synthesizer emanate from a homemade amplifier as I did research for the book, and I sincerely hope that you are similarly inspired as you work through the examples in this chapter. I happen to own an original Korg MS20 analog synthesizer and was pleased to find that the digitally created Arduino waveforms sound similarly charming. This would be a good time to discuss how to use the oscillators described in this section of the book.

The timer boilerplate code that was presented earlier in the chapter will suffice to initialize the timer. The only other detail, as can be seen in Listing 9.25, is to import the appropriate header files and create an instance of the oscillator class. In each case, the *tick()* function of the given oscillator returns the current sample, so all that is required in the timer vector function is to assign this value to *PORTD* to send the data to an R2R ladder or DAC. (Note that the timer initialization function is not shown to save space—it is the same as the one shown previously in this chapter.)

Listing 9.25 Note: Timer initialization function not shown

```
#include "Oscillator.h"
#include "SineOscillator.h"

//SAMPLE RATE
const unsigned long SAMPLE_RATE = 16384;

PulseWidthOscillator pulse_osc;

void setup()
{
    //Initialize an oscillator:
    pulse_osc.setSampleRate(SAMPLE_RATE);
    pulse_osc.setFrequency(440);
    pulse_osc.setDutyCycle(.5);

    //Set up pins for use with TLC7226 DAC
    pinMode(0, OUTPUT);
    pinMode(1, OUTPUT);
    pinMode(2, OUTPUT);
    pinMode(3, OUTPUT);
    pinMode(4, OUTPUT);
    pinMode(5, OUTPUT);
    pinMode(6, OUTPUT);
    pinMode(7, OUTPUT);
    pinMode(9, OUTPUT);

    //Initialize the timer:
    InitTimer1();
}

void loop()
{
    //Add code to respond to pot values, modulation, etc. here
}

//Timer callback
ISR(TIMER1_COMPA_vect)
{
    //Prepare IC for DAC conversion
    digitalWrite(9, HIGH);
```

232

```
    //Get an 8-bit sample from the oscillator
    PORTD = pulse_osc.tick();

    //Finished with conversion
    digitalWrite(9, LOW);
}
```

That's it! Through the wonders of object-oriented programming, all that is required are a few lines of code to produce a stable digital/analog waveform.

Modulation

Now that the primary waveforms are available in the form of some handy C++ classes, it is time to add another layer of fun and consider waveform *modulation*. In electronic music, *low-frequency oscillators* (known as LFOs) are a common source of modulation control. LFOs, which are just slow-moving oscillators, can be used as a control source to modulate parameters including pitch, filter cutoff, filter resonance, or amplitude.

Control Voltage: VCO vs. DCO

The concept of *control voltage* is a key aspect of analog synthesis. In a voltage-controlled synthesizer, a keyboard, low-frequency oscillator, or other component outputs voltage that can be used to control the frequency of a voltage-controlled oscillator (pitch), the cutoff of a filter (timbre), output of an amplifier (volume), or some other parameter. In an Arduino-based synthesizer, the same concept can be applied in the form of *digital control*. Where the oscillator of an analog synthesizer responds to varying voltage, the oscillator in a digital synthesizer can be controlled with streams of numbers.

Modulating a Signal

The concept of pitch modulation can seem awkward if you don't happen to have a background in music synthesis, but the concept is really very simple. In Figure 9.19, the output of a slow-moving waveform on the left (LFO) is used to alter the pitch of the oscillator on the right. The idea here is that the fluctuating amplitudes produced by the LFO are used to control or *modulate* the frequency of the oscillator. Thus, the range of amplitudes produced by the LFO controls the frequency range of the oscillator, and the frequency of the LFO affects the speed of modulation.

The good news is that LFO modulation can be achieved by using the classes that were described in the preceding section. All that is required is to create an instance of one of the oscillator classes and set the frequency to a low value like .5. Call the *tick()* method of the newly created LFO and use its output to set the frequency of another oscillator. The following pseudo-code demonstrates the process:

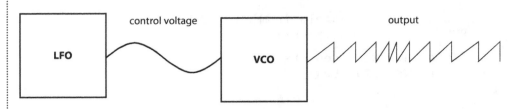

```
//LFO modulation pseudo-code
//Global variables:
SawtoothOscillator saw;
RampOscillator lfo;

//In setup()
saw.setSampleRate(sample_rate)
lfo.setSampleRate(sample_rate)
lfo.setFrequency(0.5);

//In the main loop()
saw.setFrequency(lfo.tick());

//In the timer callback
PORTD = saw.tick();
```

234

9.10 LFO
DEMO

I encourage you to explore the classes by altering values in the *setup()* function, using potentiometers and other components to control the parameters, and deriving new oscillator and LFO classes from their respective base classes. It is thrilling to hear how capable the Arduino is as a sound source, and there are many interesting directions to go with the concepts presented in this section.

Introduction to Mozzi

We have covered much ground in this chapter from fixed-point math to C++ inheritance, accumulators, and low-frequency oscillators. The information will provide a good starting point for your own explorations, and the theoretical concepts will provide a necessary foundation for understanding and utilizing Mozzi, a wonderful synthesis library by Tim Barrass. I can't say enough good things about Mozzi—the code has been highly optimized, is well commented, and provides a rich toolkit of sound-producing resources.

The Mozzi code is fairly "deep" in that it makes use of many advanced concepts including templates, fixed-point math, and the like. However, an understanding of the theoretical concepts presented thus far in the chapter will enable you to explore and understand many of the inner workings of the library.

Pulse-Width Modulation

Before we look at the Mozzi synthesis library, it will be helpful to consider how sound can be produced with pulse-width modulation. Unlike the code in the first part of this chapter, which blasts 8-bits at a time to an R2R ladder or DAC, the Mozzi library is designed to output signals on one or two digital pins through a process called *pulse-width modulation*. One way to visualize pulse-width modulation is to think of a light switch. Imagine that you turn a light on and off at a slow rate of about once every few seconds—aside from periodic flashes of light, a room would appear dark most of the time. Now, imagine that the light is switched on and off twice per second. With a smaller delay between flashes the room would seem brighter. Finally, imagine that it would be possible to switch the light on and off about 60 times per second, creating the illusion that the light is continuously on. (In actuality, this is what happens behind the scenes when alternating current powers a light.) Pulse-width modulation works in a similar way where the proportion of *mark time* (on time) and *space time* (off time) determines the intensity of a signal. Figure 9.20 provides a visualization of this process.

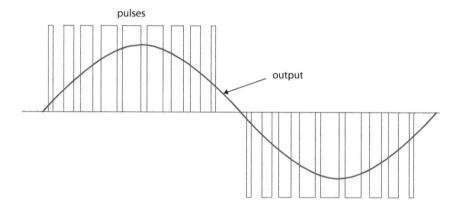

FIGURE 9.20

235

Visualization of pulse-width modulation.

Circuit for PWM Output

A circuit for PWM output requires only two components: a 270Ω (or similar) resistor and .1µF (100n) capacitor to function as a simple RC filter (see Figure 9.21).

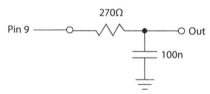

FIGURE 9.21

Circuit for PWM output.

To connect the signal to the input of a battery-powered amp like the Cigar Box Amplifier from Chapter 3, attach the output to the tip of an audio cable and connect the cable's shield to ground. Be sure to read the earlier section about DC offsets if you haven't done so already because it is usually a good idea to remove any DC component from the signal (see Figure 9.22). You can also visit

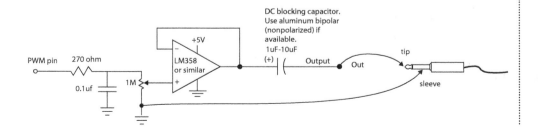

FIGURE 9.22

Connecting PWM output to an audio cable.

the OUP website where you will find a pulse-code modulation version of the direct digital synthesis classes from earlier in the chapter.

A First Mozzi Sketch

As is evident in Listing 9.26, it takes very few lines to output a 440Hz sine wave with the Mozzi library. The paragraphs that follow detail each of the objects and functions in the example—these lines will form a foundation for most Mozzi sketches.

Listing 9.26 Note: Basic Mozzi sketch: 440Hz sine wave (based on an example by Tim Barrass)

```
//Arduino for Musicians
//Listing 9.26: Mozzi Sine Wave
//Based on an example by Tim Barrass

#include <MozziGuts.h>
#include <Oscil.h>                    //Oscillator template
#include <tables/sin2048_int8.h>   //Sine wave table

//Instantiate an oscillator: <table size, update rate> and
                              //wavetable
Oscil <SIN2048_NUM_CELLS, AUDIO_RATE> sineOsc(SIN2048_DATA);

//Use #define for CONTROL_RATE, not a constant
#define CONTROL_RATE 64 //Use powers of 2

void setup()
{
    startMozzi(CONTROL_RATE); //Set a control rate of 64
    sineOsc.setFreq(440);      //Set the frequency
}

void updateControl()
{
   //Place changing controls here
}

int updateAudio()
{
   //Returns an int signal centered around 0
   return sineOsc.next();
}

void loop()
{
   audioHook(); //required here
}
```

Include Statements

Three include statements are used to include the "guts" of the library, an oscillator template, and a sine wave lookup table. (The lookup table functions in a similar way to the SineWaveOscillator class described earlier in the chapter.)

236

Instantiating an Oscillator

The line that that starts with *Oscil <SIN2048_NUM_CELLS* (just after the include statements) will look strange to many readers. The Mozzi oscillator class (class Oscil in the Oscil.h file) utilizes C++ templates. Templates are a powerful feature of the language that make it possible to reuse source code. Where inheritance (such as the inherited oscillator classes described earlier in the chapter) reuses objects, templates reuse the underlying *source code*.[16] The basic idea is that objects can be instantiated with a variety of data types and the *template* keyword makes the appropriate substitution—essentially writing a new class based on the "cookie cutter" template. We will not delve into the details of templates, but it is helpful to know what is going on in the following line:

```
Oscil <SIN2048_NUM_CELLS, AUDIO_RATE> sineOsc(SIN2048_DATA);
```

Here, the opening and closing template symbols < > indicate template parameters. *SIN2048_NUM_CELLS* is a definition for the number 2048 as is defined in the *tables/sin2048_int8.h* header file, and AUDIO_RATE is defined as 16384—the standard Mozzi rate. The last part of the line, *sineOsc(SIN2048_DATA)* instantiates an Oscil object named sineOsc and passes a pointer to the sine wave data that is also defined in the sin2048_int8.h header file.

Control Rate

Mozzi separates program control from sound output calculation using a callback mechanism. A definition named CONTROL_RATE determines the number of times per second that the *updateControl()* function is called. As the author states in the MozziGuts.h header file, "It can be any power of 2 greater than 64, and the largest value where it starts to become impractical is around 1024. 64, 128, 256 and sometimes 512 are all usable values."[17] *updateControl()* doesn't do anything in the program in Listing 9.26, but you will use the method to check switches, pots, and encoders in more complex sketches.

Updating Audio

The *updateAudio()* method is the place where all the audio action happens. For this reason, it is important to keep any code "lean and mean" because the function will be called at a fast rate. In the case of the sine wave demonstration program, the function simply returns the value that is returned by *sineOsc.next()*. The *next()* method is functionally similar to the *tick()* method that was defined in the base oscillator class of the oscillators presented earlier in the chapter. In this case, *next()* returns the next sample generated by the oscillator.

Audio Hook

The *audioHook()* method, called from within the main loop, drives the audio input and output buffers. A buffer is conceptually similar to a holding tank—input or

237

output data can be stored in a buffer and can be read or written as needed by the program. In general, buffers prevent *dropout* and other problems that can occur when a program is temporarily unable to keep up with audio input or output. Fortunately, this is handled automatically by Mozzi so you won't ordinarily need to worry about buffering.

Responding to an Analog Input

Incorporating user input is simply a matter of reading a digital or analog pin in the *updateControl()* function. However, instead of calling *analogRead()*, call the optimized Mozzi version called *mozziAnalogRead()*. As is evident in Listing 9.27, the value that is returned by *mozziAnalogRead()* is used to set the frequency of a sine-wave oscillator. The remainder of the program is the same as the previous Mozzi sketch.

Listing 9.27 Mozzi sketch to respond to a potentiometer attached to A0 (based on an example by Tim Barrass)

```
//Arduino for Musicians
//Listing 9.27: Mozzi Potentiometer
//Based on an example by Tim Barrass

#include <MozziGuts.h>
#include <Oscil.h>                 //Oscillator template
#include <tables/sin2048_int8.h>   //Sine wave table

//Instantiate an oscillator: <table size, update rate> and
//wavetable
Oscil <SIN2048_NUM_CELLS, AUDIO_RATE> sineOsc(SIN2048_DATA);

//Use #define for CONTROL_RATE, not a constant
#define CONTROL_RATE 64 //Use powers of 2

const int pitchPin = A0;

void setup()
{
    //setupFastAnalogRead();   //increases the speed of
                               //reading the analog input
    startMozzi(CONTROL_RATE);  //Set a control rate of 64
}

void updateControl()
{
    int pot_value = mozziAnalogRead(pitchPin);

    //Update the frequency based on the value of the
    //potentiometer
    sineOsc.setFreq(pot_value);
}

int updateAudio()
{
    //Returns an int signal centered around 0
    return sineOsc.next();
}
```

238

```
void loop()
{
    audioHook(); //required here
}
```

Incorporating a Filter

Filters are used to modify timbre, and the Mozzi library provides two types: *low-pass* and *state variable*. The low-pass filter provides two functions, *setCutoffFreq()* and *setResonance()*, that are used to set the filter cutoff and resonance respectively. To use the low-pass filter in a sketch, include "LowPassFilter.h" and create one or more instances of the filter as follows:

```
LowPassFilter lpf1;
LowPassFilter lpf2;
```

Use the "setter" methods to establish a cutoff frequency and resonance in the *setup()* method of your sketch, or, better yet, use potentiometers or other control sources in *updateControl()* to adjust the parameters in real time. Listing 9.28 demonstrates how a pseudo-LFO effect could be achieved by directly altering the cutoff frequency of a low-pass filter.

Listing 9.28 Simple pseudo-LFO example (LFO▽low-pass cutoff)

```
#include <MozziGuts.h>
#include <Oscil.h>
#include <LowPassFilter.h>
#include <tables/sin2048_int8.h>     //Sine wave table

//Instantiate an oscillator: <table size, update rate> and
//wavetable
Oscil <SIN2048_NUM_CELLS, AUDIO_RATE> oscil(SIN2048_DATA);

//Create an instance of a low pass filter
LowPassFilter lpf;

//Use #define for CONTROL_RATE, not a constant
#define CONTROL_RATE 64 //Use powers of 2

void setup()
{
    startMozzi(CONTROL_RATE); //Set a control rate of 64
    oscil.setFreq(440);
    lpf.setResonance(100);
}

void updateControl()
{
    //Create a pseudo LFO
    stat3ic byte cutoff = 50;

    //Update the filter
    lpf.setCutoffFreq(cutoff);

    //Increase cutoff frequency
    cutoff +=10;
```

```
        //Wrap around at 250Hz
        if(cutoff>250)
        {
            cutoff = 50;
        }
}
int updateAudio()
{
    //Pass the output of the oscillator to the LP filter &
    //return the result
    char sample = lpf.next(oscil.next());
    return (int)sample;
}
void loop()
{
    audioHook();   //required here
}
```

Summing Signals and Adjusting Levels

The *updateAudio()* function can be used to sum multiple signals such as the output of two or more oscillators. Many of the Mozzi examples utilize syntax similar to the following:

```
int updateAudio()
{
    return osc1.next() + osc2.next();
}
```

However, multiple signals can quickly overwhelm the output and create distortion, so a right-shift can be used to efficiently attenuate the output.

```
int updateAudio()
{
    return (osc1.next() + osc2.next()) >> 2;
}
```

Depending on your choice of low- or high-resolution output in Mozzi, a right-shift of one or more can provide a quick way to attenuate levels of multiple oscillators. Table 9.3 illustrates the results of a right-shift to an arbitrary level of 255. As is evident in the table, each shift decreases the output level by half.

TABLE 9.3 Right-Shift Attenuation Levels

Value	Shift	Result
255	>> 1	125
255	>> 2	63
255	>> 3	31

Further Exploration

Although this introduction to Mozzi is necessarily short, the information will provide a foundation that will enable you to explore and understand the many demonstration programs included with the library. Mozzi provides a rich toolkit of synthesis tools including filters, envelopes, and effects processors, and the information throughout this chapter should enable you to understand and use the library as the basis for many interesting sound-synthesis applications. You will also have a theoretical framework that will enable you to dig deeper and create your own libraries or enhance existing libraries.

Audio Output with Teensy 3

We conclude the chapter with a look at audio output on a Teensy 3 microcontroller, a powerful yet inexpensive microcontroller from PJRC that can be programmed with the Arduino IDE. The combination of a Teensy 3 microcontroller, Teensy Adapter Board, and related Teensy Audio Library is a powerful combination that facilitates audio projects involving synthesis, recording, or effects processing. PJRC also provides an online tool called the Audio System Design Tool that makes quick work of setting up audio objects and making connections between virtual objects including oscillators, mixer, filters, and the like.

Figure 9.23 shows how the output of two oscillators could be connected to the input of a virtual mixer using the Audio System Design Tool available at https://www.pjrc.com/teensy/gui/. The output of the mixer is, in turn, connected to a filter object and sent to an I2C object which encapsulates the underlying Teensy Audio Adapter.

241

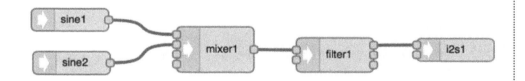

FIGURE 9.23

Teensy Audio Design Tool.

The Audio System Design Tool produces source code which can be pasted into a sketch. Most of the "preamble" shown in Listing 9.29 was generated by the Design Tool. This sketch also demonstrates how an oscillator such as the SineOscillator from earlier in the chapter could be used as a virtual control voltage source, so the SineOscillator.h class is included and a SineOscillator class is instantiated in this segment of code.

Listing 9.29 Teensy "preamble"

```
#include <Audio.h>
#include <Wire.h>
#include <SPI.h>
#include <SD.h>
```

```
//Include SineOscillator class for LFO (this could also be
//handled by the Teensy sweep class)
"SineOscillator.h"

// GUItool: begin automatically generated code
AudioSynthWaveformSine   sine1;        //xy=102,363
AudioSynthWaveformSine   sine2;        //xy=104,420
AudioMixer4              mixer1;       //xy=290,381
AudioFilterStateVariable filter1;      //xy=435,433
AudioOutputI2S           i2s1;         //xy=573,431
AudioConnection          patchCord1(sine1, 0, mixer1, 0);
AudioConnection          patchCord2(sine2, 0, mixer1, 1);
AudioConnection          patchCord3(mixer1, 0, filter1, 0);
AudioConnection          patchCord4(filter1, 0, i2s1, 0);

// GUItool: end automatically generated code
// Create an object to control the audio shield.
AudioControlSGTL5000 audioShield;
float filter_freq = 500;  //Filter cutoff frequency
float filter_Q = 4.0;     //Filter resonance: range is 0.7 to 5.0
SineOscillator sine_osc;
```

Teensy audio classes can be used in a way that is functionally similar to the oscillator classes developed in the first part of this chapter. For example, the sine classes provide methods for adjusting frequency and amplitude, and the virtual mixer provides a *gain()* method that can be used to mixer multiple sources. Similarly, the filter object provides two methods for setting filter cutoff and resonance. It is interesting to note that the filter object provides three possible outputs (which can be selected in the Audio System Design Tool): Low-Pass Output, Band Pass Output, and High-Pass Output, respectively. Listing 9.30 demonstrates how these parameters could be configured in the *setup()* function.

Listing 9.30 Configuring oscillator, mixer, and filter objects

```
void setup()
{
  // Audio connections require memory to work.  For more
  // detailed information, see the MemoryAndCpuUsage example

  AudioMemory(10);
  //Set up sine waves
  sine1.amplitude(1.0);
  sine1.frequency(200);
  sine2.amplitude(1.0);
  sine2.frequency(400);

  //Use a mixer to adjust the gain of each signal
  mixer1.gain(0, .5);
  mixer1.gain(1, .5);

  //Set up the filter:
  filter1.frequency(filter_freq);
  filter1.resonance(filter_Q);

  // turn on the output
  audioShield.enable();
  audioShield.volume(0.8);
```

```
//Set up the LFO:
//Set an arbitrary sample rate since this will be handled
in main loop()
sine_osc.setSampleRate(20000);
sine_osc.setFrequency(2.5);
}
```

As with other sketches, the main *loop()* can be used to alter parameters in real time. For example, Listing 9.31 demonstrates how the output of a SineOscillator could be used to alter cutoff frequency. It goes without saying that other classes from this chapter including the pulse-width oscillator, ramp oscillator, and noise generator could be used in a similar way, and these virtual voltages could be applied to oscillator frequency, filter cutoff, or another parameter. All that is required is to scale the oscillator output (which ranges from 0 to 255) to an appropriate range.

Listing 9.31

```
void loop()
{
  //Call the tick() method of the oscillator class to
  //generate a new virtual voltage level
  filter_freq = sine_osc.tick();

  //Send the voltage level to the filter but offset so range
  //is 0 + 50 to 255 + 50
  filter1.frequency(filter_freq + 50);
}
```

Exploring Teensy 3

The Teensy products and related APIs have undergone considerable revisions since I started writing this book. Not only are the products a good choice for MIDI applications, the Teensy 3 is a terrific tool for many audio applications. The concepts presented in this chapter will provide a good foundation for further exploration, and the many example sketches included with the Teensy Audio library can form the basis for a number of interesting and useful projects.

243

Audio Input

Overview

The last chapter focused on techniques for outputting and synthesizing sounds from an Arduino. This chapter looks at audio data from another angle focusing on analog-to-digital conversion (ADC), the process of digitizing fluctuating voltages. The chapter includes a discussion of circuits that will prepare audio signals to be processed by the Arduino as well as a circuit that will enable you to connect an inexpensive electret microphone to an Arduino. The chapter also explores methods of analyzing a signal and visualizing the data in the time and frequency domains. The last part of the chapter is devoted to an introduction to signal processing techniques.

Analog-to-Digital Conversion

Like digital-to-analog conversion, converting signals from analog to digital requires a steady clock to coordinate the samples that are taken from the analog ports. Analog-to-digital conversion also requires some decisions in terms of allocation of resources. The primary considerations are *sample rate* and *resolution* or *bit depth*. Faster sample rates will allow you to sample higher frequency content, and more bits will enable the range of voltages from 0 to 5V to be more accurately represented. For example, Table 10.1 shows how a 16-bit conversion is exponentially more accurate than ADC conversion utilizing only 8 bits of data.

TABLE 10.1 8-bit vs. 16-bit Conversion

8-bit Conversion	16-bit Conversion
1.25V = 64	1.24V = 16,384
2.5V = 128	2.5V = 32,768
3.75V = 192	3.75V = 49,152
5.0V = 255	5.0V = 65,536

Although it might seem obvious that 16-bit ADC is best, the answer is not quite as clear when you consider the limited amount of memory that is available for variables in Arduino memory. As mentioned in the Chapter 9, the sample rate must be a little more than twice the frequency of the highest frequency you wish to sample. Given that there are only 2K bytes of memory, that leaves room for about 1,000 16-bit integers when you consider that *all program variables* are stored in the same 2K of space. Thus, a 16-bit sample buffer would only be able to store approximately 1/20 of a second of data at a sample rate of 20kHz. On the other hand, while 8-bit samples provide an opportunity for larger sample buffers, they will provide a rather coarse digitization of a source signal.

This points to two observations: while the Arduino is capable of impressive processing tasks including Fourier analysis, the platform is not well suited for real-time tasks like reverb that would require substantial sample buffers. For this reason, we will focus on 8-bit conversion, which will be suitable for spectrum analysis, and some basic real-time effects including tremolo and variable delay. This decision is also informed by the fact that the analog pins on an Arduino scale voltages to a 10-bit range of 0–1,023. Thus, the sampling capabilities of the Arduino is fairly limited without resorting to external converters. Keep in mind that a hybrid approach utilizing digital and analog components can open the door for some other approaches to signal processing. For example, an Arduino could be used to control a digitally controlled potentiometer to make a tremolo effect. In that case, the audio signal would not need to be processed through an Arduino—the Arduino would alter the external audio circuit remotely via the digitally controlled potentiometer. Finally, although an Arduino Uno is not designed for high-end audio, the concepts in this chapter can be readily applied to more robust microcontrollers including Maple, Arduino Due, and Teensy 3, as well as full-fledged prototyping computers including Raspberry Pi and Beaglebone.

Preparing a Signal for Input

An important consideration is that, while most audio signals swing positively and negatively around 0V, the signal must be adjusted or *biased* to a range of 0 to +5V before it can be safely read by the Arduino. Negative voltage (or voltages in excess of +5V) can damage your Arduino, so be sure to avoid connecting such a signal directly to the device. A common solution is to utilize a pair of resistors and a capacitor so that the incoming signal is biased to fluctuate around 2.5 V. Figure 10.1 provides a conceptualization of this process.

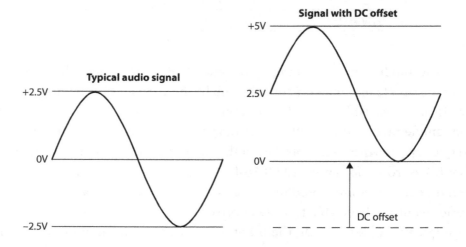

Simple Input Circuit

Figure 10.2 illustrates a common circuit that can be used to bias an analog audio signal to 2.5V so that it can be read by the analog port. In this circuit, resistors R1 and R2 function as a voltage divider[1] to bias the input.

The photo in Figure 10.3 shows one approach to finalizing the circuit on stripboard. For convenience, a mono jack is provided for connection to an audio source.

246

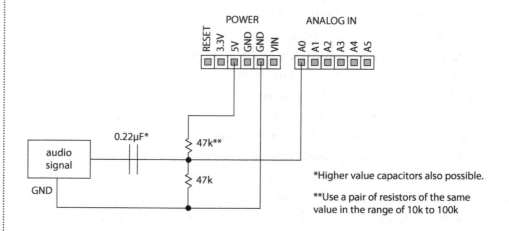

Caution

As Dr. Monk states in *Programming Arduino Next Steps*, using an expensive signal generator such as a cell phone or iPod may void the warranty and could destroy the device.[2] Although I have not had any trouble with my own devices, it is certainly good advice to be cautious. Consider limiting the input to a device

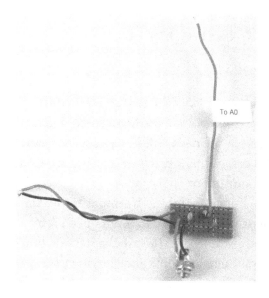

To A0

FIGURE 10.3

Photo of finalized input circuit.

like an inexpensive electret microphone (a circuit is presented later in the chapter) or a signal generator from Chapter 9. Another option is to use a "junker" computer—I picked up a used laptop for $50—for use as a signal source and to program the Arduino.

The code in Listing 10.1 can be used to read the values provided by the Arduino ADC. This simple sketch reads the result returned by the *analogRead()* function and turns on the built-in LED on pin 13 if the input exceeds a predetermined threshold. Although the sketch represents a primitive form of audio input, this approach could provide an easy method for triggering MIDI notes or other types of control data.

Listing 10.1 Using analogRead() to read values from the Arduino ADC

```
Arduino for Musicians
//Listing 10.1: ADC-AnalogRead

#define ANALOG_PIN 0
#define LED_PIN 13
#define THRESHOLD 515

void setup()
{
    //Configure LED pin for output
    pinMode(LED_PIN, OUTPUT);
}
void loop()
{
    //Read a valude from A0
    int value = analogRead(ANALOG_PIN);

    //Turn on LED if value is greater than threshold
    if(value >= THRESHOLD)
    {
        //Turn LED on
        digitalWrite(LED_PIN, HIGH);
```

```
        }else{
            digitalWrite(LED_PIN, LOW);
        }
}
```

Setting Up a Timer for Analog-to-Digital Conversion

While the main loop is fine for simple tasks such as detecting threshold events, a more robust version of the code will be necessary to sample the input at a predictable rate. In this case, a timer provides a way to accurately sample an analog source for signal processing or analysis.

The *initTimer()* function, which is similar to the timer initialization code in Chapter 9, configures the Arduino for high-speed 8-bit analog-to-digital conversion.[3] As with the examples in the last chapter, the boiler-plate initialization method starts by disabling interrupts and clearing the registers that will be used to initialize the ADC:

```
oid initADCTimer()
{
    //Disable interrupts while initializing the timer
    cli();

    //Clear ADCSRA and ADCSRB registers to a known state
    ADCSRA = 0;
    ADCSRB = 0;
    .
    .
    .
```

A *multiway switch*, also called a *multiplexer* or "mux," is used to configure the ADC and to switch the unit between multiple input pins. The next two lines set the ADC Multiplexer Selection Register (ADMUX): bits 7 and 6 of the register (REFS0 and REFS1) are used to set the reference voltage, and setting bit 5 (ADLAR) left-adjusts the results of the ADC conversion. In this example, values are adjusted so the highest eight bits can be read from the ADCH register.

```
ADMUX |= (1 << REFS0); //Reference voltage
ADMUX |= (1 << ADLAR); //Left-adjust to read 8 bits from ADCH
```

The final section of the initialization function disconnects the digital inputs from the ADC channels (see below), sets a prescalar, enables auto trigger and the activate ADC Conversion Complete Interrupt, and enables and starts the analog-to-digital converter. The function concludes by enabling interrupts.

```
    //DIDR (Data Input Disable Register)
    //Disconnect digital inputs from ADC channels[4]
    //See note at: http://www.openmusiclabs.com/learning/
    digital/atmega-adc/
    DIDR0 = 0x01;

    ADCSRA |= (1 << ADPS2) | (1 << ADPS0); //Prescaler = 32:
                                            //16mHz/32 = 500kHz
```

```
ADCSRA |= (1 << ADATE);   //Enable auto trigger
ADCSRA |= (1 << ADIE);    //Enable Conversion Complete
                          //Interrupt
ADCSRA |= (1 << ADEN);    //ADC Enable Bit: set to one to
                          //enable ADC
ADCSRA |= (1 << ADSC);    //ADC Start Conversion Bit: set
                          //to one to start measuring

//Setup complete: enable interrupts
sei();
}
```

Prescalars

The term *prescalar* refers to a divider that is used to reduce the rate that timers count pulses from a *timebase*.[5] The prescalar value is determined by a chart found in the ATmega datasheet (see Table 10.2). Setting ADPS2 and ADPS0 to 1 results in a prescalar of 32, so the timer frequency is 16mHz/32 = 500kHz. Each conversion takes 13 clock cycles,[6] so the actual sample rate is 500kHz/13 = 38.5 kHz.

Listing 10.2 shows one approach to initializing the ADC with a prescalar. Note how the byte named *data* is declared as *volatile* because the value can be altered *at any time* within the timer function. The loop function is admittedly trivial, but it does demonstrate another approach to polling the input of the analog pin to see if a signal has exceeded a threshold. More advanced applications might include keeping a running total of samples to determine root mean square or to perform Fourier analysis. (More information will be provided later in the chapter.)

249

TABLE 10.2 Determining a Prescalar Value

ADPS2	ADPS1	ADPS0	Division Factor
0	0	0	2
0	0	1	2
0	1	0	4
0	1	1	8
1	0	0	16
1	0	1	32
1	1	0	64
1	1	1	128

Listing 10.2 Using a timer for analog-to-digital conversion

```
//Arduino for Musicians
//Listing 10.2: ADCTimer

#define LED_PIN 13
#define THRESHOLD 130

//Byte to store the incoming sample
volatile byte sample = 0;
```

```
void setup()
{
    //Configure LED pin for output
    pinMode(LED_PIN, OUTPUT);

    //Initialize the timer
    initADCTimer();
}

void loop()
{
    //Trigger LED if sample > threshold
    if(sample > THRESHOLD)
    {
        //Turn LED on
        digitalWrite(LED_PIN, HIGH);
    }else{
        digitalWrite(LED_PIN, LOW);
    }
}

//Interrupt automatically called when a sample is ready
ISR(ADC_vect)
{
    sample = ADCH;   //get sample from A0
}

void initADCTimer()
{
    //Disable interrupts while initializing the timer
    cli();

    //Clear ADCSRA and ADCSRB registers to a known state
    ADCSRA = 0;
    ADCSRB = 0;

    ADMUX |= (1 << REFS0);  //Reference voltage
    ADMUX |= (1 << ADLAR);  //Left-adjust to read 8 bits
    //from ADCH

    //DIDR (Data Input Disable Register)
    //Disconnect digital inputs from ADC channels
    //See note at: http://www.openmusiclabs.com/learning/
    digital/atmega-adc/
    DIDR0 = 0x01;

    ADCSRA |= (1 << ADPS2) | (1 << ADPS0); //Prescaler = 32:
                                           //16mHz/32 = 500kHz
    ADCSRA |= (1 << ADATE);  //Enable auto trigger
    ADCSRA |= (1 << ADIE);   //Enable Conversion Complete
                             //Interrupt
    ADCSRA |= (1 << ADEN);   //ADC Enable Bit: set to one to
                             //enable ADC
    ADCSRA |= (1 << ADSC);   //ADC Start Conversion Bit:
                             //set to one to start measuring

    //Setup complete: enable interrupts
    sei();
}
```

Building a Simple Arduino Preamp

Some signals will need additional gain to be useful as an input source to an Arduino. In this section we will look at one solution built around an inexpensive *op amp* (operational amplifier) such as the LM358. Where most op amps use a *dual-supply* (+/− voltage), some op amps can be configured to work with a *single-supply* such as the 0 to 5V provided by an Arduino. While 5V will not be enough to adequately raise the level of some low-level sources, it the approach that is least likely to damage an Arduino pin. As Douglas Self states in *Small Signal Audio Design*, "Bullet-proof protection against input over-voltages is given by running the driving opamp from the same supply rails as the analogue section of the ADC, the opamp saturation voltages ensuring that the input can never reach the supply rails, never mind exceed them."[7] Although this approach will work for low-level sources, it will not prevent damage from sources greater than 5V.

In the following approach, based on an example in *Electronics for Inventors*, the op amp is configured as a noninverting amplifier that is powered by the Arduino.[8] A 10k potentiometer is used to adjust the gain. The incoming audio signal passes through a capacitor (which blocks DC offset), and two resistors provide a voltage divider that is used to bias or offset the signal to swing around 2.5V. As with the circuit in Figure 10.2, use a pair of resistors of the same value in the range of 10 to 100k. The circuit and a close-up of the stripboard version are shown in Figures 10.4 and 10.5.

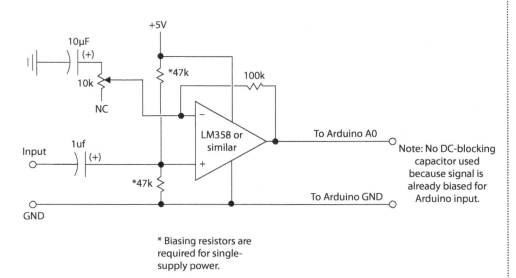

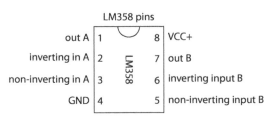

FIGURE 10.4

Noninverting single-supply Arduino preamp.

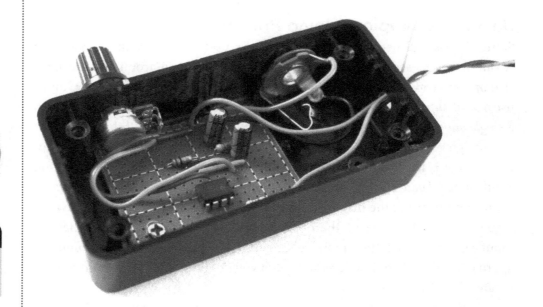

10.1 ARDUINO
PREAMP

FIGURE 10.5

Photo of noninverting
single-supply Arduino
preamp (stripboard).

252

Building an Electret Microphone

Electret microphones are fun and, at about $1–2 per capsule, they are an inexpensive way to add another form of audio input to an Arduino. Although this section will focus on building your own electret microphone, premade versions are available from a number of vendors for a modest cost.

The circuit in Figure 10.6 comes from Scherz and Monk's outstanding tome, *Practical Electronics for Inventors*.[9] There are very few circuits that are this simple: the 5V voltage source of the Arduino is connected to the positive leg of the electret microphone through a 1 to 10k resistor. The positive leg of the microphone is connected to the audio output through a 10µF capacitor, and the other leg of the microphone is connected to ground.

The microphone can be connected to one of the ADC circuits presented earlier in this chapter. A photo of one version of the completed microphone, encased in a length of tubing, is shown in Figure 10.7.

10.2 ELECTRET
MICROPHONE

FIGURE 10.6

Electret microphone
circuit.

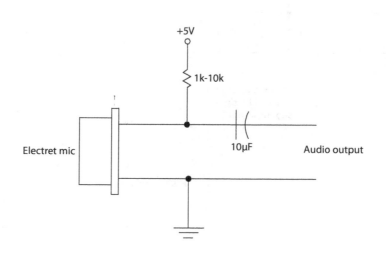

FIGURE 10.7

Electret microphone.

Visualizing Audio Data

Part of the fun of digitizing an analog source is visualizing the data. This section explores several concepts that will make it possible for an Arduino to communicate with a computer over a serial connection. The Processing language, available as a free download from processing.org, will be used to provide a graphical representation of the sample data.

The sketch titled Free-Running ADC (available at the OUP website) demonstrates how a sample can be read by configuring an Arduino for continuous sampling. As is evident in Listing 10.3, an example based on one in Elliot Williams's excellent *Make: AVR Programming* book, a serial connection is established in the *setup()* function, and the ADC is initialized to fire at a fast rate.[10] With this approach, a byte can be read from the ADCL register in the main *loop()*.

253

Listing 10.3 Free-running ADC

```
//Arduino for Musicians
//Listing 10_3: Free-running ADC

//Initialization code based on an example by Elliot Williams in
//Make: AVR Programming

const int delayMS = 20;  //Used to slow things down for
//serial port

void setup()
{
    //Establish fast baud rate
    Serial.begin(115200);

    //Initialize free-running mode
    initFreeRunningADC();
}

void loop()
{
    //Transmit the high byte (ADCH register)
    Serial.write((byte) ADCH);
    delay(delayMS);
}

void initFreeRunningADC()
```

```
{
    ADMUX |= (1 << REFS0);                  //Reference voltage
    ADCSRA |= (1 << ADPS1) | (1 << ADPS0);  //ADC prescaler = /8 =
                                            //2Mhz / 13 clock
                                            //cycles

    ADMUX |= (1 << ADLAR);                  //Left-adjust for 8
                                            //bits

    ADCSRA |= (1 << ADEN);                  //Enable ADC
    ADCSRA |= (1 << ADATE);                 //Enable auto trigger
    ADCSRA |= (1 << ADSC);                  //Start first
                                            //conversion
}
```

Interfacing with Processing

The Processing IDE should feel very comfortable after using Arduino. However, unlike the Arduino version of the C language, Processing provides access to many multimedia tools for working with sound and images. In this example we are interested in reading values from the serial port and using those values to draw a series of lines representing the amplitudes of a waveform (see Figure 10.8). We will look at each function of the Processing sketch in the paragraphs that follow.

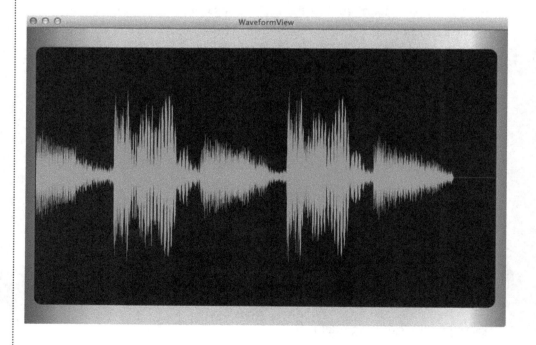

FIGURE 10.8

Waveform View screenshot.

Waveform View Application

The "prelude" of the WaveformView sketch (see Listing 10.4) consists of an *import* statement that provides access to the Processing serial commands. A number of variables are initialized to establish x and y extents of the window, variables used to scale the waveform, and to determine the baseline Y position. (We will look at the *getBaseY()* function in a moment.)

254

Listing 10.4 Waveform View "prelude"

```
import processing.serial.*;

Serial myPort;   // Create object from Serial class

int voltage;     // Voltage level received from the serial port

//Establish variables for screen size, midpoint, background
//image, etc.
int midY = 255;
int lastYp = midY;
int xMargin = 20;
float lastXp = xMargin;
float xIncrement = 3.5;

int screen_width=800;
PImage background_image;
```

Setup()

Like Arduino sketches, Processing sketches also start with a *setup()* function. However, most of the code in the *setup()* method looks unfamiliar and requires an explanation: after establishing the size of the window, a serial object is created using the *new* keyword. This line is "kludgy" in that it uses a string constant to initialize the name of the device—something that is always a "no-no" in serious programming. However, the code to set up a proper menu is beyond the scope of this example and would make it unduly complicated. As is indicated in the comments in the following source code, simply uncomment *println(Serial. list())* to view the list of serial devices on your machine. Type the appropriate name in place of the string constant and you should be able to communicate with the Arduino via a serial connection to a computer.

The *setup()* function also loads a *skeuomorphic*, an image representing an "old-school" oscilloscope. Processing is capable of loading a number of different image types (this one happens to be a .png), and the only requirement is that the size of the image must *exactly match* the size of the window (800 × 500 in this example).

The remainder of the *setup()* function establishes the color scheme and other drawing parameters (see Listing 10.5).

Important: Be sure to set the same baud rate for the Arduino and the Processing sketch (see the initialization of *myPort* below) or you will see strange results on the screen.

Listing 10.5 Waveform View setup()

```
void setup()
{
    //Set size of window
    size(800, 510);

    //Load the background image (dimensions must match the
    //size of the window)
    background_image = loadImage("metal_background.png");

    //Set up serial connection. Port name should match the
    //Tools...Serial
```

255

```
//Port settings in the Arduino environment.
myPort = new Serial(this, "/dev/cu.usbmodem1411", 115200);

//Establish color scheme:
fill(0,0,0);
stroke(0,191, 255); //RGB...sky blue
smooth();
//Set stroke for waveform drawing:
strokeWeight(.5);

//Refresh screen and variables
newScreen();
}
```

draw()

The *draw()* function (see Listing 10.6) forms the heart of the program and is functionally similar to the main *loop()* function in an Arduino sketch. The first two lines are the most important. The statement *while(myPort.available() >0)* checks the value returned by the *Serial.available()* method. The while loop will continue to loop as long as data are available. Within the while loop, the *Serial.read()* method is used to grab a value from the serial port. The given value represents a waveform voltage, which is then "converted" into a Y offset above the base Y-position. The function limits the voltage to the dimensions of the window and draws a line connecting the current X and Y position to the last X and Y position, thus, forming a familiar waveform view of the data. The final section of the function checks the current X-position to see if the screen should be cleared and reset by calling *newScreen()*.

Listing 10.6 Waveform View draw()

```
void draw()
{
    //Check for incoming data:
  while ( myPort.available() > 0) {  // If data is
  //available.

        voltage =  myPort.read();  // read the value
        voltage -= 127;  //Adjust DC offset
        float newXp = lastXp + xIncrement;
        //Do a quick scale of voltage:
        voltage = voltage << 2;

        //Draw amplitude (use + and - voltage to center sample)
        line(newXp, midY - voltage, newXp, midY + voltage);

        //Store the variables for the next iteration
        lastXp = newXp;

        //Clear the screen if we run off the right side
        if(newXp  >screen_width - xMargin)
        {
            newScreen();
        }
    }
}
```

newScreen()

As mentioned previously, the *newScreen()* function (Listing 10.7) clears the screen and resets the variables representing the last X and Y position. The function also draws a line in the center of the screen.

Listing 10.7 Waveform View newScreen()

```
void newScreen()
{
    //Clear the screen:
    background(background_image);

    //Draw center voltage reference:
    line(xMargin, midY, screen_width - xMargin, midY);

    //reset variables
    lastYp = midY;
    lastXp = xMargin;
}
```

Testing Waveform View

In order to test the application, upload the sketch titled Free-Running ADC to the Arduino and run the Waveform View sketch (both available from the OUP website) in Processing. Assuming you have connected a signal using one of the input circuits presented earlier in the chapter, you should see a graphical waveform view of the data. Of course this example is just a basic sketch, so I encourage you to adapt it to your own preferences. For example, it might be interesting to add code to handle adaptive coloring so "louder" voltages are drawn with lighter colors.

Fourier Transform

Not only is it possible to visualize the digital slices that represent digitized audio data, the samples can also be processed and analyzed using a powerful analytical technique called the *Fourier transform*. Where the previous waveform application provided a visualization of data in the *time domain*, the Fourier transform, named after the French mathematician Jean Baptiste Joseph Fourier (1768–1830), can be used to analyze sound in the *frequency domain*. As Fourier was able to demonstrate, a complex signal is composed of sine waves of varying frequency and amplitude. Amazingly, the Fourier transform can be used to extract these sine waves from a complex waveform. The underlying math is well beyond the scope of this book, but some clever individuals[11] have provided an Arduino library that brings the power of FFT—the Fast Fourier Transform—to the Arduino platform.

There are a few versions of FFT and FHT (the Hartley transform) available for download. In this example we will use the FHT library that is available at openmusiclabs.com. Download and install the FHT library before running the sketch in Listing 10.8. The sketch, which also came from openmusiclabs.com, is well commented and shows how to set up the Arduino to do a 256-point FHT analysis.

The heart of the sketch is the main *loop()*, which reads 256 data points from the analog A0 pin. As can be seen in the comments below, the data set is windowed, a process that multiplies the data by a window function and the data is reordered—a necessary step in order for the *fht_run()* function to work its magic.

Listing 10.8 FHT demonstration (from openmusiclabs.com)

```
//Arduino for Musicians
//Listing 10.8:  Fast Hartley Transform
//Demonstration by Open Music Labs:
//http://wiki.openmusiclabs.com/wiki/FHTExample
//Requires FHT2 library available at:
//http://wiki.openmusiclabs.com/wiki/ArduinoFHT?action=Attac
hFile&do=view&target=ArduinoFHT2.zip

#define LOG_OUT 1  //Use the log output function
#define FHT_N 256  //256 point fht

#include <FHT.h>  //Include the FHT library

void setup()
{
    Serial.begin(115200);  //Use serial port at a fast baud rate
    TIMSK0 = 0;            //Turn off timer0 to reduce jitter
    ADCSRA = 0xe5;         //ADC in free funning mode
    ADMUX = 0x40;          //Use acd0
    DIDR0 = 0x01;          //Turn of digital input for adc0
}

void loop()
{
    while(1)  //reduce jitter
    {
        //Get the data
        cli();
        for(int i = 0; i < FHT_N; i++)
        {
            while(!(ADCSRA & 0x10));  //wait for ADC
            ADCSRA = 0xf5;  //restart ADC
            byte m = ADCL;  //fetch adc data
            byte j = ADCH;
            int k = (j << 8) | m;  //form low and high bytes
            into an int
            k -= 0x200;  //form into a signed int
            k <<=6;       //form into 16bit signed int
            fht_input[i] = k;  //put real data into bins
        }

        //Process the data
        fht_window();  //Window data for better frequency
        //response
        fht_reorder();  //Reorder data before doing fht
        fht_run();      //Process data in the fht
        fht_mag_log();  //Take the output of the fht
        sei();
```

258

```
        //Output the data
        Serial.write(255);   //Send start byte
        Serial.write(fht_log_out, FHT_N/2);   //Transmit data
    }
}
```

Using Data from the FHT

After completing the FHT analysis, bins are available which provide the relative magnitude of each "slice" of the frequency spectrum. The number of bins will be half the number of samples that were processed (128 in this example). Further, the frequency-width of each bin is determined dividing the number of bins by the sample rate.

The FHT class provides three output methods than can be called after running *fht_run()*. As described in the class documentation, *fht_mag_log()* "gives the magnitude of each bin in the fht."[12] The values are in sequential order and the output is "essentially in decibels times a scaling factor."[13] In the preceding code, 128 bins of data (FHT_N/2) are sent via the *Serial.write()* method after each iteration of the FHT analysis. As you will see in a moment, these data will form the basis of a Spectrum Analyzer.

```
Serial.write(255); // send a start byte
Serial.write(fht_log_out, FHT_N/2); // send out the data
```

See the fht_read_me.txt document for a description of the other FHT analysis functions, including, *fht_mag_lin()*, and *fht_mag_octave()*, an RMS analysis function.

Spectrum Analyzer

The bins returned by the FHT algorithm can be used to view the harmonic spectrum of a given sound. To bring the visualization to life, the data will be graphed with another Processing application. As with the Waveform View sketch, the Spectrum View sketch receives data via the serial port and translates the data into a visual image. The primary difference between the sketches is that data is drawn as a series of columns representing the relative magnitude of each bin in the FHT (see Figure 10.9).

One challenge with a Spectrum Analyzer is that the microcontroller might start analyzing data before the Processing sketch has had a chance to run. Thus, Processing needs a way to determine which incoming byte corresponds to the first bin. One solution is to send a digital "start" message to indicate the byte representing the first bin. In Listing 10.8, a high byte (255) is sent to signal that the first byte from the FHT analysis will follow. On the receiving end, Processing listens for a value of 255 as a signal to reset the bins. The Processing sketch is shown in its entirety in Listing 10.9.

259

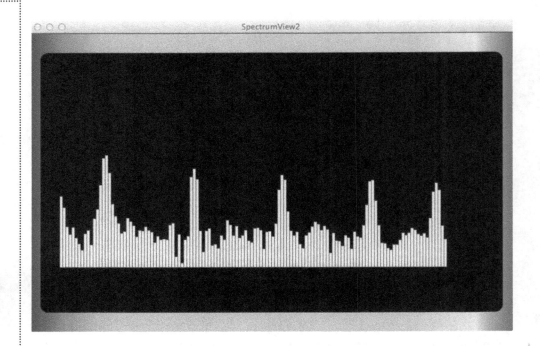

FIGURE 10.9

Spectrum Analyzer screen shot.

Listing 10.9 Processing Spectrum Analyzer sketch

```
/**
 * Arduino for Musicians:
 * Listing 10.9: Spectrum Analyzer
 * Processing sketch
 *
 */

import processing.serial.*;
Serial myPort;  // Create object from Serial class

PImage background_image;

int current_slice = 0;
int[] data = new int[128];

void setup()
{
    //Set size of window
    size(800, 510);
    //Load the background image (dimensions must match the
    //size of the window)
    background_image = loadImage("metal_background.png");

    //Set up serial connection. Port name should match the
    //Tools...Serial

    //Port settings in the Arduino environment.
    myPort = new Serial(this, "COM5", 115200);

    //Establish color scheme:
    fill(255,255,0);
    stroke(0,0, 255);
    smooth();
```

```
    //Set stroke for waveform drawing:
    strokeWeight(.5);
}
void draw()
{
    //Check for incoming data:
  while ( myPort.available() > 0) {  // If data is
  available,
      int sample = myPort.read();
      if(sample == 255)
      {
          //Last FHT complete. Draw it and reset
          //drawData();
          current_slice = 0;
      }else{
        data[current_slice++] = sample;

        if(current_slice >=128)
        {
            current_slice = 0;
            drawData();
        }
      }
    }
}
void drawData()
{
    //Clear the screen:
    background(background_image);

    float x_step = 5.3;
    int xp = 50;
    int yp = 400;

    //Draw the slices
    for(int c = 0; c< 128; c++)
    {
        rect(xp, yp, x_step, -data[c]);
        xp += x_step;
    }
}
```

Other Uses for FFT and FHT

There are innumerable opportunities for exploration with the data returned by a Fourier or Hartley transform. For example, the bin with the highest magnitude could be converted to a MIDI note as a form of rough pitch-to-MIDI conversion, or the values of some of the bins could be translated into MIDI continuous controller data opening the door for interesting voice-to-synthesizer control systems. Yet another idea is to use the data to determine pulse-width-modulation values for LEDs for an interesting performance art installation.

A Brief Introduction to Signal Processing

Now that the basics of audio input and output have been established it is time to explore real-time signal processing. A detailed discussion of digital signal processing (DSP) is beyond the scope of this book, but the basics are not hard to understand and will provide a good foundation for future explorations. In this section we will explore *tremolo* and *delay*, two real-time effects that can be easily achieved on an Arduino UNO. Note that the examples in this section use pulse-width modulation on pin 6, and thus the output requires a passive low-pass filter and unity gain buffer as discussed in Chapter 9.

A Few Words About Buffers

As I have mentioned several times, an Arduino UNO has a limited amount of available memory. However, it is sometimes useful to use some of the memory to store audio samples for additional processing or to guard against audio dropout when outputting samples to a DAC. Conceptually, an audio *buffer* is similar to a small water reservoir in that the water in the reservoir can be supplied to a spigot even if the input source temporarily subsides (see Figure 10.10).

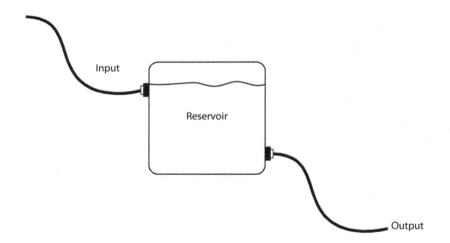

Input

Reservoir

Output

FIGURE 10.10

Conceptulization of an audio buffer as a water reservoir.

Circular Buffers

Where a traditional audio buffer is used to store recorded samples in a linear fashion for playback in a DAW or digital audio device, a small *circular buffer* or *ring buffer* can be used over and over again as a temporary storage location. Not only is this useful for preventing audio dropout in playback, a circular buffer opens up some interesting possibilities for signal processing. Figure 10.11 provides a conceptualization of how a circular buffer works.[14]

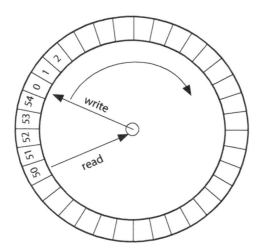

FIGURE 10.11

Conceptulization of a circular buffer.

263

Samples are read from the ADC and written to the buffer starting at the beginning and continuing until the buffer is filled. At this point, incoming samples replace the samples at the start of the buffer and the process continues ad infinitum. As samples are being written to the buffer, they can also be read from a previous location in the buffer. This opens up many possibilities including phase shifting and delay.

Delay

A fixed delay effect can be easily achieved with a circular buffer. Listing 10.10, an excerpt from a sketch available at the OUP website, shows the relevant portions of code. As is evident in this example, an array of bytes, *buffer[bufferSize]* is created to store incoming samples. In this case, the size of the array determines the amount of delay. Next, an incoming sample is read from the ADCH register and a delay sample (that has previously been stored in the buffer) is read from the buffer array. To create the delay effect, the original sample and the delayed sample are combined as the sum of an unsigned integer. The incoming sample is then stored at the location just read by the ADC handler and the buffer index in incremented. A final step, after checking for the buffer to wrap around to zero, is to use a right shift to reduce the level of the combined sample to the 8-bit range of 0 to 255. Once the level has been reduced, the sample is used to establish the desired PWM voltage in the OCR0A register.

Listing 10.10 Fixed delay

```
const int bufferSize = 1600;
byte buffer[bufferSize];
 .
 .
 .
//Interrupt automatically called when a sample is ready
```

```
ISR(ADC_vect)
{
    //Get a sample from A0
    sample = ADCH;

    //Get a sample from the sample buffer
    delay_sample = buffer[buffer_index];

    //Combine the samples to create a delay effect
    combined_sample = sample + delay_sample;

    //Store new sample at the location we just used to read the
    //delayed sample and then increment the index (postfix).
    //The new sample is stored just prior to the current
    buffer index

    //resulting in maximum delay.
    buffer[buffer_index++] = sample;
    //Wrap the buffer index to zero is necessary
    if(buffer_index >= bufferSize)
    {
        buffer_index = 0;
    }
    //Use a shift to quickly reduce the level of the combined
    //sample to a range of 0-255
    combined_sample = (combined_sample >>1);

    //Set timer 0 to do PWM for desired voltage
    OCR0A = (byte)combined_sample;

}
```

264

Variable Delay

Very few changes are required to adapt the previous code to a variable delay. In the next example, variable delay is achieved by comparing the buffer index to a buffer boundary (which can be set with a rotary encoder). In this case, the amount of delay is reduced as the boundary approaches 0, the first index in the array. Larger values (up to *bufferSize -1*) create a longer delay. The entire variable delay effect (including the timer-initialization functions) is shown in Listing 10.11 and should be relatively easy to follow given the many code comments.

Listing 10.11 has one unique special feature to note: a rotary encoder is used to establish the amount of delay, but the rotary encoder classed discussed previously in the book required a modification. The original encoder class relied on the *micros()* function for switch debouncing, but the function is disabled due to the use of timers in this sketch. An easy enhancement was to add an additional method to the rotary encoder class to respond to time "ticks" that are generated in the main loop. Although this is not a good way to generate accurate time slices, such ticks are good enough for switch debouncing.

Listing 10.11 Variable delay

```
Arduino for Musicians
//Variable delay test: Audio input on A0, PWM on pin 6
```

```
#include <RotaryEncoder.h>

//Use bytes to store the incoming sample and delay sample
volatile byte sample = 0;
volatile byte delay_sample = 0;

//Adding samples together will create integers that are too
//large to fit in 8 bits. Use an unsigned int to store the
//combined samples
unsigned int combined_sample = 0;

//bufferSize determines the size of the sample buffer (which
//determines the amount of delay).
//Allocate virtually all of the Uno's memory:
const int bufferSize = 1600;

//Create a buffer to store the samples as well as integers
//that will be used to store the current index and
//buffer boundary
byte buffer[bufferSize];
int buffer_index = 0;
int buffer_boundary = 0;

//Set up a rotary encoder:
RotaryEncoder delayEncoder;
const int encoderDebounceTime  = 5;   //Encoder debounce time

const int delayEncoderA = 10;
const int delayEncoderB = 11;
const int encoderRange = 50;

unsigned long current_time = 0;

const int pwmPin = 6;   //AUDIO OUT ON PIN 6

void setup()
{
    delayEncoder.init(delayEncoderA, delayEncoderB,
    encoderDebounceTime,
      encoderRange, 0, encoderRange);

    //Initialize the timers
    InitPWM0(pwmPin);
    initADCTimer();
}

void loop()
{
    //Increment fake timer for component debouncing. This is
    //not steady but ticks are good enough for
    //debouncing an encoder or switch
    current_time++;

    //Track delay encoder:
    static int last_encoder_value = 0;
    int encoder_value=delayEncoder.
    trackShaftPosition(current_time);
    if(encoder_value!=last_encoder_value)
    {
```

```
                        //Scale encoder value of 0-encoderRange to boundary
                        //value of 0 to bufferSize

                    buffer_boundary = map(encoder_value, 0, encoderRange,
                    0, bufferSize -1);
                }

        }
        //Interrupt automatically called when a sample is ready
        ISR(ADC_vect)
        {

            //Get a sample from A0
            sample = ADCH;

            //Get a sample from the sample buffer
            delay_sample = buffer[buffer_index];

            //Combine the samples to create a delay effect
            combined_sample = sample + delay_sample;

            //Store new sample at the location we just used to read the
            //delayed sample and then increment the index (postfix).
            //The new sample is stored just prior to the current
            //buffer index resulting in maximum delay.
            buffer[buffer_index++] = sample;

            //Wrap the buffer index to zero is necessary
            if(buffer_index >= buffer_boundary)
            {
                buffer_index = 0;
            }

            //Use a shift to quickly reduce the level of the combined
            //sample to a range of 0-255
            combined_sample = (combined_sample >>1);

            //Set timer 0 to do PWM for desired voltage
            OCR0A = (byte)combined_sample;

        }

        void initADCTimer()
        {
            //Disable interrupts while initializing the timer
            cli();

            //Clear ADCSRA and ADCSRB registers to a known state
            ADCSRA = 0;
            ADCSRB = 0;

            ADMUX |= (1 << REFS0);   //Reference voltage
            ADMUX |= (1 << ADLAR);   //Left-adjust to read 8 bits
            from ADCH

            //DIDR (Data Input Disable Register)
            //Disconnect digital inputs from ADC channels
            //See note at: http://www.openmusiclabs.com/learning/
            digital/atmega-adc/
```

```
    DIDR0 = 0x01;

    // 64 prescalar = 19.2 Khz sample rate
    ADCSRA |= (1 << ADPS2) | (1 << ADPS1);
    ADCSRA |= (1 << ADATE);  //Enable auto trigger
    ADCSRA |= (1 << ADIE);  //Enable Conversion Complete
    Interrupt
    ADCSRA |= (1 << ADEN);  //ADC Enable Bit: set to one to
    enable ADC
    ADCSRA |= (1 << ADSC);  //Set ADC Start Conversion Bit

    //Setup complete: enable interrupts
    sei();
}
void InitPWM0(int PWMPin)
{
    //SET UP PWM: Based on an example from www.csulb.edu15
    pinMode(PWMPin, OUTPUT);
    // Set Timer 0 Fast PWM Mode (Section 14.7.3)
    TCCR0A |= _BV(WGM01) | _BV(WGM00);
    TCCR0B &= ~_BV(WGM02);
    TCCR0A = (TCCR0A | _BV(COM0A1)) & ~_BV(COM0A0);
    // COM0B = 0b00, OC0B disconnected (Table 14-6)
    TCCR0A &= ~(_BV(COM0B1) | _BV(COM0B0));

    // No prescaler, CS = 0b001 (Table 14-9)
    TCCR0B = (TCCR0B & ~(_BV(CS02) | _BV(CS01))) | _BV(CS00);
    // Set initial pulse width to the first sample.
    OCR0A = 0;
}
```

Tremolo

A tremolo effect is achieved by slowly modulating the amplitude of an audio signal, and the effect can be easily visualized by thinking of the volume knob of a stereo receiver: a rough form of tremolo can be achieved by slowly (and steadily) rotating the volume knob back and forth.

Fortunately, the oscillator classes developed in Chapter 9 can be used as low-frequency oscillators to modify the amplitude of incoming samples in real time. All that is required is to instantiate an oscillator, set the sample rate and frequency, and multiply the incoming sample by the current sample or "tick" returned by the oscillator. The product of the incoming sample and oscillator sample is placed in an unsigned integer and reduced to an 8-bit range of 0 to 255 for output to the DAC. Although Listing 10.12 illustrates a traditional tremolo effect created by a sine wave LFO, many other interesting effects can be created by using different waveforms (such as triangle or ramp) as the source of amplitude modulation. Note that the entire listing (sans timer initialization code) is shown in Listing 10.12. As with the preceding listing, a rotary encoder is used to alter the rate of the tremolo effect.

267

10.3 VARIABLE DELAY

Listing 10.12 Tremolo

```
//Arduino for Musicians
//Tremolo test: Audio input on A0, PWM on pin 6

#include <RotaryEncoder.h>
#include <Oscillator.h>
#include <SineOscillator.h>

RotaryEncoder rateEncoder;

//Byte to store the incoming sample
volatile byte sample = 0;

//Use an unsigned integer to store the results of amplitude
//modulation
unsigned int processed_sample = 0;

//Sinewave oscillator that will modulate the signal's
//amplitude. Use other oscillators (e.g., triangle,
//pulse, ramp, etc.) for other effects.
SineOscillator sine;

const int encoderDebounceTime  = 5;   //Encoder debounce
time

const int rateEncoderA = 10;
const int rateEncoderB = 11;
const int encoderRange = 20;

 //Use an unsigned long to track time ticks generated
 //in the main loop() function
 unsigned long current_time = 0;

//Pulse Width Modulation will be on pin 6
const int pwmPin = 6;

void setup()
{
    //Set up the rate encoder:
    rateEncoder.init(rateEncoderA, rateEncoderB,
        encoderDebounceTime, 2, 1,
    encoderRange);

    //Sample rate is approximately 19 kHz
    sine.setSampleRate(19200);

    //The frequency of the sine wave determines the tremolo
    //rate
    sine.setFrequency(2);

    //Initialize the timers
    InitPWM0(pwmPin);
    initADCTimer();
}

void loop()
{
    //Increment fake timer for component debouncing. This is
    //not steady
```

```
    //but ticks are good enough for debouncing an encoder or
    //switch
    current_time++;

    //Track rate encoder:
    static int last_encoder_value = 0;
    int encoder_value=rateEncoder.
    trackShaftPosition(current_time);
    if(encoder_value!=last_encoder_value)
    {
        //Set the new tremolo rate based on the encoder
        //change
        sine.setFrequency(encoder_value);
        last_encoder_value = encoder_value;
    }

}

//Interrupt automatically called when a sample is ready
ISR(ADC_vect)
{
    //Get a sample from A0
    sample = ADCH;

    //Process the sample by multiplying it by the value
    //returned by the sine wave oscillator.
    //This produces tremolo

    processed_sample = sample * sine.tick();
    //The processed sample is 16 bits. Use a shift to
    //quickly reduce this back to a range of 0-255.
    processed_sample = (processed_sample >> 8);

    //Set timer 0 to do PWM for desired voltage
    OCR0A = (byte) processed_sample;
}
```

10.4 TREMOLO

High-End Audio Using the Open Music Labs Codec Shield for Real-Time Processing

Although it is fun (and informative) to "roll" your own audio circuits, commercial audio shields can be an attractive option in terms of convenience and fidelity. I have enjoyed using the Open Music Labs Codec Shield (see Figure 10.12) for a number of audio prototypes. The shield, which is based on the Wolfson WM8731 codec, provides audio quality that is difficult to achieve without special integrated circuits.

Fortunately, the shield is very simple to use. Download and install the Arduino library for the shield at http://www.openmusiclabs.com/projects/codec-shield/, attach the shield to your Arduino, and load one of the demonstration sketches to start manipulating high-fidelity samples in real time.

Listing 10.13, which was partly based on an example by Open Music Systems, shows how the Arduino for Musicians oscillators could be utilized with the shield. Note that a high-resolution tremolo example is provided with the Open Music Labs Codec Shield library.

FIGURE 10.12

Open Music Labs Codec
Shield. (Photo courtesy of
Open Music Labs.)

270

Listing 10.13 Tremolo

```
//Arduino for Musicians
//Audio Codec Shield Tremolo test
//Based on an example included with the Audioe Codec Shield

#define SAMPLE_RATE 44 // 44.1kHz sample rate
#define ADCS 2 // use both ADCs

// include necessary libraries
#include <Wire.h>
#include <SPI.h>
#include <AudioCodec.h>

//Include the AFM oscillators
#include <Oscillator.h>
#include <SineOscillator.h>
#include "Oscillator.h"

// create data variables for audio transfer
// even though the function is mono, the codec requires
// stereo data
int left_in = 0; // in from codec (LINE_IN)
int right_in = 0;
int left_out = 0; // out to codec (HP_OUT)
int right_out = 0;

// create variables for ADC results
// it only has positive values -> unsigned
unsigned int mod0_value = 0;
unsigned int mod1_value = 0;

//Create several oscillators to explore different tremolo
//effects.
SineOscillator sine;
SawtoothOscillator saw;
PulseWidthOscillator pulse_osc;
TriangleOscillator triangle;
RampOscillator ramp;
```

```
//Point to the sine oscillator. (Point to other oscillators
//e.g. pOsc = &saw) to explore different effects.
Consider adding a switch to toggle oscillators.

OscillatorBase *pOsc = &sine;

void setup()
{
    sine.setSampleRate(44100);
    saw.setSampleRate(44100);
    ramp.setSampleRate(44100);
    triangle.setSampleRate(44100);
    pulse_osc.setSampleRate(44100);
    pulse_osc.setDutyCycle(.5);   //square wave

  // call this last if you are setting up other things
  AudioCodec_init(); // setup codec and microcontroller
}

void loop() {
  while (1); // reduces clock jitter
}

// timer1 interrupt routine - all data processed here
ISR(TIMER1_COMPA_vect, ISR_NAKED) { // dont store any
registers

    // &'s are necessary on data_in variables
  AudioCodec_data(&left_in, &right_in, left_out, right_out);

    //The Arduino for Musician oscillators are 8-bit so use a
    //shift to quickly multiply to 16-bit output range.
    //See the Audio Codec example for a hi-res way to do
    //amplitude modulation.
    unsigned int sine_sample = (pOsc->tick() << 8);

    // create a tremolo effect by multiplying input signal by
    // sinewave. Turn signed sinewave value into unsigned value
    MultiSU16X16toH16(right_out, left_in, sine_sample);
    // put amplitude modulated data at right output
    // mix modulated and current data at left output
    // divide each by 2 for proper scaling
    left_out = (right_out >> 1) + (left_in >> 1);

    // & is required before adc variables
    AudioCodec_ADC(&mod0_value, &mod1_value);

    //Change the rate if mod0_value pot changes
    static unsigned int last_mod0Value = 0;
    if(mod0_value != last_mod0Value)
    {
        last_mod0Value = mod0_value;
        //Use a shift to quickly reduce the value of mod0_value
        //to a good range for amplitude modulation
        unsigned int new_frequency = (mod0_value>>12);
        pOsc->setFrequency(new_frequency);
    }

    reti(); // dont forget to return from the interrupt
}
```

271

10.5 REAL-TIME
PROCESSING
WITH OPEN
MUSIC AUDIO
CODEC

Using Mozzi for Audio Input and Processing

As mentioned in Chapter 9, the Mozzi library provides many useful tools for sound synthesis and manipulation. Not only is Mozzi capable of outputting sounds, the library supports tools for inputting and processing sound. This chapter concludes with an example of how a signal can be sampled and manipulated with the Mozzi library.

Hardware Setup

As with the other examples in this chapter, an audio input source should be biased prior to being sampled by the Mozzi library (see Figure 10.2). On the output side, the standard audio output configuration utilizes pulse width modulation on digital pin 9. The author of the library suggests the RC filter shown in Figure 10.13—but I also encourage the use of a unity gain buffer and DC blocking capacitor as described in Chapter 9.

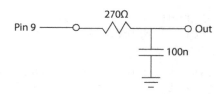

272

Software Setup

The default Mozzi installation disables audio input. To enable sampling capability, navigate to the Arduino\libraries\Mozzi\folder and open the file named *mozzi_config.h* in a plain text editor or IDE and change the following line from false to true:

```
#define USE_AUDIO_INPUT false
```

Setting Up a Low-Pass Filter

Mozzi provides two virtual filters, a low-pass filter and a variable-state filter, that can be used to alter the timbre of a synthesized or sampled signal. In Listing 10.13, a low-pass filter is included in the project and initialized in the *setup()* function. As the *LowPassFilter.h* header file states, the method named *setCutoffFreq()* uses a range of 0 to 255 to represent a 0 to 8192 frequency range (this is half the audio rate). Similarly, a value of 0 to 255 is used to set the amount of filter resonance with a call to *setResonance()* method. This section of the code also defines a constant (*KNOB_PIN*) that will be used to read the value of a potentiometer from the A1 pin.

Listing 10.13 Setting up a low-pass filter in Mozzi

```
#include <MozziGuts.h>
#include <LowPassFilter.h>

#define KNOB_PIN 1

LowPassFilter lpf;
```

```
void setup()
{
  lpf.setCutoffFreq(172);
  lpf.setResonance(220);
  startMozzi();
}
```

updateControl() Mechanism

For optimal playback, Mozzi utilizes a method named *updateControl()* to prevent frequent polling of the analog pins from overwhelming the timing of the synthesis system. As the author notes in the *MozziGuts*.h header file, the constant named *CONTROL_RATE* is used to determine how many times per second the *updateControl()* method is called. It can be "any power of 2 greater than 64." The default is 64, but other rates can be defined and sent via the *startMozzi()* method:

```
#define CONTROL_RATE 128
startMozzi(CONTROL_RATE);
```

Using mozziAnalogRead()

Instead of using *analogRead()* to read the values from potentiometers and other components, Mozzi provides an optimized version called *mozziAnalogRead()*. Listing 10.14 demonstrates how a potentiometer can be read from within the *updateControl()* function. Note that a right-shift is used to quickly scale the input from 0 to 1023 to a range of 0 to 255 for use by the *setCutoffFreq()* method.

Listing 10.14 Setting up a low-pass filter in Mozzi

```
void updateControl()
{
  int knob = mozziAnalogRead(KNOB_PIN);
  unsigned char cutoff_freq = knob>>2; // range 0-255
  lpf.setCutoffFreq(cutoff_freq);
}
```

Scaling Amplitude in *updateAudio()*

Audio input and output is handled in the function called *updateAudio()*. In Listing 10.15, a sample is read via a call to *getAudioInput()* and the sample is adjusted so that it is "0-centered." Next, the sample is sent to an instance of a low-pass filter called *lpf* via the *next()* method, which returns a filtered version if the sample. Finally, the updated sample is returned to the playback system at the end of *updateAudio()*. Note that a right-shift is used to attenuate the level and the amount of attenuation required will depend on the playback mode. The valid range for standard single-pin playback is between -244 to 243 inclusive. Note that, as with all Mozzi sketches, the method called *audioHook()* should be called from within the main *loop()* function.

273

Listing 10.15 Reading and filtering a sample in *updateAudio*()

```
int updateAudio()
{
  // subtracting 512 moves the unsigned audio data into
  // 0-centred, signed range required by all Mozzi units
  int asig = getAudioInput()-512;
  asig = lpf.next(asig>>1);
  return asig;
}

void loop()
{
  audioHook();
}
```

Conclusion

Although many different types of processing can be done within Mozzi or with raw samples using other code in this chapter, this introduction should provide a good foundation for further exploration. To that end, there are many fine books and websites devoted to real-time processing. One of the most helpful sites for filtering can be found at: http://www.schwietering.com/jayduino/filtuino/. There, you will find a helpful filter designer that produces code that can be incorporated into an Arduino sketch. I also learned a lot about filters and direct digital synthesis in Hal Chamberlin's *Musical Applications of Microprocessors*. The book is hard to find but provides a great deal of information on integrating microprocessors and analog circuits. Of course, there are many excellent websites (including the Mozzi website at http://sensorium.github.io/Mozzi/) that will be useful as you incorporate new ideas into your sketches.

Finalizing Projects

Creating a Permanent Project

There are two ways to approach the projects in this book: with the first approach, a solderless breadboard is used to create temporary prototypes that are tested and tweaked to fit individual preferences. While this approach is the best way to learn about programming and circuitry, certain components like R2R ladders and LCDs are cumbersome to wire given the many connections that must be made on a breadboard. At some point it will be advantageous to make permanent versions of a circuit or entire project by soldering components to solderboard and optionally encasing the project in an enclosure or project box.

This chapter provides an overview of the finalizing process including safety tips, tools, options for "proto" boards, transferring ideas from breadboard to solderboard, soldering, and buying and making project boxes and front panels. By the end of the chapter you will be able to solder permanent versions of the circuits and projects in this book, and you will have an understanding of techniques that can help your projects to look more professional.

This would be a good time to review several important safety tips. Although the process of making low-voltage electronic projects is relatively safe, there are a number of ways that injury can occur. The tips in this section come from my own personal experience as well as the experience of numerous authors listed in the bibliography.

Personal Safety

- Do not connect any of the circuits in this book to mains (household) power or use such a power source in any do-it-yourself electronic project. Household power can and does kill and should only be used by professionals with appropriate training and experience. The projects in this book are *experimental* and **intended for low-voltage battery supply only.**

- Always wear eye protection when soldering, drilling, cutting, or using other types of power tools. It is not uncommon for solder to splatter, and molten lead can do serious injury to an unprotected eye.
- Use a sturdy table when soldering and avoid placing the soldering iron near flammable materials.
- Never grab for a soldering iron if you drop it. Pick it up as soon as it settles on the table or floor.
- Never wear loose-fitting garments or jewelry when using power tools as they might get caught in the tool.
- Always use ear protection when using power tools.
- Ensure that any soldering, painting, or gluing is done in a well-ventilated room.

Fire Safety

- Be careful not to short battery terminals. Batteries can cause a fire or even explode if mishandled.
- Always disconnect batteries when you are finished experimenting with any of the circuits or projects in this book.
- Ensure that the soldering workspace is free from flammable material.

Protecting Sensitive Electronic Components

- Keep sensitive components in the antistatic pouch or foam they were shipped in.
- Touch a metal object to discharge static electricity prior to handling sensitive components.
- Consider using an antistatic wrist strap and/or mat when working with sensitive components.
- Double check the orientation of components in a circuit before applying power.

Tools

There are a number of tools that are required to create permanent circuits. The following list is organized into essential items and helpful items. The helpful items are particularly useful when creating custom enclosures.

Essential Tools

- Soldering iron: Approximately 25–30W with adjustable range of 250–450°C (500–850°F).[1] The iron should include a solder pencil holder and cleaning sponge or brass coils.

- Wire stripper
- Miniature wire cutters
- Needle-nose pliers
- Desoldering braid
- Drill
- Drill bits (various)
- Screwdrivers (various)
- "Helping Hands"-style soldering arms with magnifying class such as the one shown in Figure 11.1.

FIGURE 11.1

Soldering arms with magnifying glass. (Photo courtesy Adafruit.)

Helpful Tools

- Small files
- Hand miter saw for making wood enclosures
- Nibbler for cutting sheet metal
- Hacksaw for cutting metal, standoffs, etc.
- Vise and/or clamps
- IC Removal tool

Visualizing a Final Project

Although it might seem obvious, an essential first step in creating a permanent circuit or project is to visualize all aspects of the project including the layout of the parts, size of the enclosure, position of components within the enclosure, and intended use and ergonomics. I speak from experience when I say that a little extra time and thought on the front side of a project can help to prevent problems on the back side. For example, it is all too easy to design an attractive front panel but forget to account for the internal dimensions and proximity of components like potentiometers and switches. I have found the following strategies to be helpful in guarding against these types of problems:

Prototype

Always prototype a project on a solderless breadboard to ensure satisfactory function. In most cases it will be too late to add additional switches, LEDs, or other components once you have committed to a design by drilling holes in an enclosure or face plate. For this reason, I often spend a few days considering potential changes and enhancements before I devote the time and expense of finalizing a project in an enclosure.

Component Connections

Consider how components will be connected electrically. For example, in some cases it may make sense to use hookup wire to connect the ground between

277

components such as potentiometers and switches instead of running a wire from the ground rail to each individual component. It may also be beneficial to keep power and signal runs as short as possible when using audio components such as an LM386 amplifier. It is very easy to create a "rat's nest" of wires inside an enclosure, so some extra forethought can go a long way.

Attaching Components

Consider how you will attach a component to an enclosure or panel. The walls of some enclosures (especially wooden ones) may be too thick to mount pots and switches without using a *countersink* bit. Another common problem is that the thickness of an enclosure may be too thin to allow components such as pressure sensors to be screwed to the walls of the enclosure. Strategies to such problems might include gluing additional material to the inside of the enclosure to provide the necessary screw depth or drilling through the sides and using small bolts and nuts to attach a component.

Consider the Enclosure

A wide range of attractive project boxes is available from companies including Hammond, Serpac, and Bud Industries that can provide a professional look to a project. Be sure to create a mock-up of the project using the steps below before purchasing an enclosure—it is very easy to underestimate the size that is necessary to fit all of the components. In some cases, existing boxes such as a mint tin or cigar box can be repurposed as an enclosure, or a custom enclosure can be constructed (see the section "Project Boxes" later in the chapter).

278

FIGURE 11.2

Placing components on a paper mock-up.

Paper Panel Mock-up

Use software or pencil and paper to create a scale mock-up of the front panel. Place all components such as LCDs, potentiometers, rotary encoders, and switches on the paper mock-up to ensure that there is sufficient room between components (see Figure 11.2).

Print Drilling/Cutting Guides

Use the paper mock-up to create a drilling guide and the guide to transfer drill markings and cutouts to the enclosure or panel. In most cases I tape the paper panel to the front of the enclosure and drill through the paper. It is rarely effective to make drill markings and cutouts by measuring directly on an enclosure.

Test Drill Bits

Before drilling, test each drill bit on a piece of scrap wood or metal to ensure the hole is the correct size for the given shaft, switch, or other component. A better approach is to use a drill gauge—all that is required is to insert the shaft of a switch or potentiometer into the gauge to determine the optimal size of the drill bit. In my experience, it is better to drill holes that are slightly too big because a snug hole may cause potentiometers and encoders to project at an odd angle. With a slightly larger hole, the nut will lock the component into the perfect position.

Moving from a Solderless Breadboard to a Solder Breadboard

Moving a project from a solderless breadboard to *solderboard* can present some unique challenges; the number of connection points on the solderboard will likely be different than a breadboard, and many solderboards do not provide rails for power and ground. Further, the different form factor can be confusing when it comes to transferring an idea from a solderless breadboard to solderboard. One helpful strategy (if you have enough duplicate parts) is to leave the breadboard circuit intact and use it as a model to populate the solderboard. I often create several "dry run" versions of the circuit by placing components on the solderboard before finalizing the position and orientation of the components. Another idea is to use pencil and paper or software like Fritzing as an aid in visualizing the transformation of a solderless circuit to solderboard. Yet another approach is to utilize *stripboard* or *Veroboard*. As the name implies, stripboard provides solder points that are in strips or rows. Many musicians are comfortable with the concept of *bussing* on a mixing console, and the strips or "busses" on stripboard fit nicely with that metaphor.

Staying Neat: Layout and Wires

Another consideration when evaluating the placement of components is the way the components will be connected. Most musicians understand the importance of keeping cable runs neat to guard against noise and other problems that can occur when cables are run "willy-nilly" around power supplies, and this concept also translates to electronics. In general, it is advantageous to minimize the length of connecting wires and to strive for a neat and orderly layout of components. In some cases, this will provide some sonic improvement, and a tidy layout will also be helpful should you need to troubleshoot the circuit or revisit it at some later date.

279

Consistent Layout

When possible, I also find it helpful to use a similar layout for circuits. For example, I usually connect 5V power to the top rail and ground on the bottom rail. This approach is not necessarily standard, but it is part of a personal convention that helps me to avoid some of the many wiring mistakes that can occur when I lose track of the orientation of an IC or the position of the power and ground rails.

IC Sockets

I strongly urge the use of an IC socket (see Figure 11.3) any time your project calls for an integrated circuit. Sockets are relatively inexpensive, particularly when purchased in bulk, and they will protect your ICs from damage during the soldering process. Another benefit is that IC sockets allow you to re-purpose an IC in a different project or use the IC as a stopgap until you have a chance to purchase another part for a new project. Simply solder the IC socket (sans the integrated circuit) and plug the IC into the socket when you finish soldering the complete circuit.

FIGURE 11.3

IC socket on solderboard.

Solder Breadboard Options

There are many types of solderboard to choose from when it comes time to finalize a circuit. Some of the boards feature rails, while others provide discrete holes for connecting components. Some boards are as large as a solderless breadboard, and boards can be purchased that are just big enough to fit a few components. The following paragraphs detail some of the more common options.

Multipurpose Board

One of the best ways to transfer a design from solderless breadboard to solder breadboard is to select a solderboard that has some of the design features of a typical solderless breadboard. For this reason, I recommend the 417-hole Radio Shack Multipurpose board (see Figure 11.4). The board features rails that run down the middle of the board, making it easy to connect power and ground to components, and the close proximity of the rails provides a

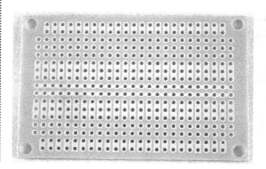

FIGURE 11.4

Radio Shack Multipurpose Board with 417 holes.

convenient way to add a power-smoothing capacitor. Integrated circuits can straddle the center rails, and the grouped hole arrangement is functionally similar to a solderless breadboard.

There are many styles of multipurpose PC board available from Radio Shack and other vendors, so it is likely you will be able to find a style that will work for a given project.

Perforated Board

There are many other breadboard options in addition to the multipurpose PC board mentioned in the last section. Point-to-point *perforated board* (also called "perf board") construction is another option. With the point-to-point approach, components are connected by soldering leads of adjacent components together or using wire to connect components that are not adjacent (see Figure 11.5). It is important to note that some perf boards provide holes but not solder points. Although perf board can be a reasonable option when just a few components need to be soldered, perf board has a tendency to result in "bird's-nest construction."[2]

FIGURE 11.5

Connecting components on perf board (with solder points).

281

Stripboard

Stripboard is similar to perf board but features multiple rows of copper strips. This is a particularly convenient arrangement for connecting 5V power and ground to multiple components. Although the holes in a given row are electrically connected via a copper strip, smaller segments of holes can be used by cutting a portion of the strip with a knife or carefully drilling the copper side of the board to segment the strip. At this time, stipboard is

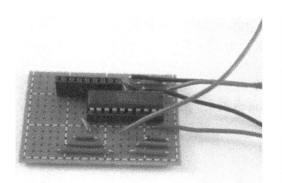
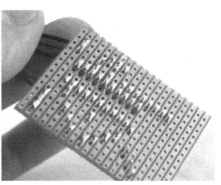

FIGURE 11.6

Stripboard circuit (front and back).

my favorite type of solderboard. It can be purchased in bulk and is easy to cut with a miter saw. I also find that my wiring usually tends to be cleaner when I use stipboard. Figure 11.6 shows an example of front and back of a DAC circuit that was soldered to a small piece of stripboard. (Note the partial-depth drill holes that are used to prevent a short between the pins of the IC.)

Homemade Printed Circuit Boards

Custom PCBs can be manufactured at home if you are willing to devote the time and work with harsh chemicals. It is not unduly difficult to create custom printed circuit boards such as the one shown in the Figure 11.7.

FIGURE 11.7

Custom printed circuit board.

Although a detailed description of the process is beyond the scope of this book, there are many websites and books devoted to the subject, including Jan Axelson's *Making Printed Circuit Boards*.

Ordering Online Printed Circuit Boards

Custom printed circuit boards (see Figure 11.8) can also be manufactured by uploading designs to online services such as Seeed (Fusion PCB Service) and PCB Universe. Pricing can vary widely so it is important to do competitive shopping and read reviews before placing an order. At the time of this writing, ten 2 × 2" custom PCBs can be ordered for about $10—an attractive price when weighed against the time associated with creating PCBs at home. Keep in mind that you can also use online PCB services to manufacture custom solderboards.

FIGURE 11.8

Custom circuit board manufactured by an online service.

Soldering

Before delving into a practice project, it would be prudent to discuss the soldering process and soldering technique. I have noticed that people who are experienced in electronics are often fanatical when it comes to soldering, and there is a good reason for this: ineffective solder technique can cause all sorts of problems such as an intermittent circuit caused by a cold solder, a short circuit caused by too much solder, or a wrecked component caused by too much heat. As with learning an instrument, the basic concepts are not hard to understand, but it takes a lot of practice to be consistent. My son is a good case in point: he started soldering at the age of 12 and had incredible soldering chops by the time he could drive. Rest assured that, with practice, you will be able to make consistently good solders. A quote by acclaimed jazz pianist Kenny Werner in his book, *Effortless Mastery*, will set the stage for this part of the discussion: "A meaningful path is a path of action. The goal is achieved through practice. Without practice, a path is mere philosophy."[3]

Andrew Singmin, author of *Modern Electronics Soldering Techniques*, defines the soldering process thusly: "Soldering is the process of using solder, flux, and heat to effect a reliable mechanical and electrical bond between two metals."[4] The mechanical and electrical bond is made possible by *wetting*, a characteristic of molten solder that allows it to "flow in a smooth, continuous, shiny, unbroken film across the copper surface being soldered to."[5] The next several paragraphs detail the soldering process as well as a number of tips and techniques that can help your solders to be more consistent.

Solder

Solder comes in a number of different thicknesses and a variety of percentages of tin and lead. In general, 60/40 rosin-core solder will be a good choice for most soldering jobs. Thinner 1/32"-thick solder is used for typical solderboard applications, while the thicker 1/16" solder is useful for panel components.[6]

Tinning

A soldering session should start with a process called *tinning*. Once the soldering iron has heated to an appropriate temperature (approximately 670°F),[7] apply a small amount of solder to the tip of the iron and wipe the excess off on cleaning wire or a moist soldering sponge. A small amount of solder will remain on the tip of the "tinned" iron and is necessary to enable the iron to transfer heat to the components that are to be soldered.

Soldering Process

When soldering a connection, it is important to place the iron against *both* of the surfaces that are to be soldered (see Figure 11.9) so that the heat is evenly transferred to the parts. Although it is tempting to touch the iron to one part and apply solder, this will result in an inferior solder.

While the tip of the iron is in contact with the surfaces, apply the solder to the tip *and* surfaces so that it flows around the components to be soldered. The idea is to let the molten solder do its job by flowing freely around surfaces that have been heated. For me, this is the trickiest aspect of soldering, and it takes

284

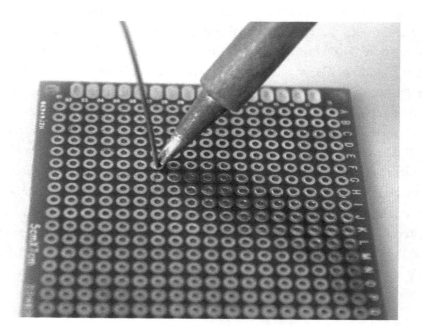

FIGURE 11.9

Placing a soldering iron against both surfaces to be soldered.

some time to get a feel for the amount of heat and solder that is required to make a good joint. Remove the tip as soon as the solder has flowed around the joint, being careful not to disturb the parts that have just been soldered. A good solder joint will not only provide a good electrical connection, the joint will also be mechanically strong (e.g., you should be able to tug on a component once it has cooled and feel no wiggle).

Speed

While it is necessary to apply enough heat to make a good solder joint, too much heat can damage components, particularly those encased in plastic. Some parts such as ICs and LEDs are particularly susceptible to heat damage. For this reason, it is important not to dwell too long on a solder joint. Just heat the components, apply solder, and move on. Randy Sloan, author of *Electricity and Electronics*, suggests that "you should be able to solder a typical connection in well under 5 seconds."[8]

Appearance

A good solder joint will look shiny and smooth and should not have any clumps or bumps (see Figure 11.10). Gray or balled joints indicate improper heating, which may be caused by a failure to periodically tin the tip or a temperature setting that is too low on the iron itself. Larger parts can take more time to heat, so that is another potential cause of improper heating.

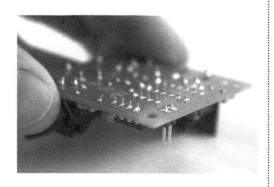

FIGURE 11.10

Good solder joint.

285

Holding Parts in Place

One of the things you will quickly notice when soldering for the first time is that components have a tendency to fall out of their hole when the board is turned over prior to soldering. One strategy is to bend the legs slightly outward so they won't slip out of the hole. Another strategy is to use one hand to hold the component in place (from the bottom while the board is upside down) and use your other hand to hold the soldering pen. A length of solder can be clamped in a "Helping Hands" device and the solderboard, components, and the soldering iron can be moved to make contact with the length of solder. Yet another approach is to use painter's tape to hold components in place while soldering.

Practical Application

As I mentioned in the introduction to this section, soldering is a skill that takes lots of practice. We will now consider a few practical soldering *études* that can

11.1 SOLDERING
VIDEO

help you to hone your skills. If you are new to soldering, be sure to visit the OUP website and watch a soldering tutorial that was created by Evan Edstrom. Evan demonstrates a number of useful techniques, and watching the process in real-time is invaluable for first-time solderers.

Soldering Étude 1

Many Arduino music projects utilize potentiometers, pushbuttons, and LEDs, so a perfect "first project" is to make a simple circuit consisting of components that can be used as a prototyping building block. You might want to add or sub-tract components as desired for your prototyping needs. The layout is shown in the Figure 11.11.

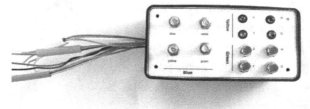

FIGURE 11.11

Layout of prototyping etude. (Multipurpose board with two 10K pots, four momentary pushbuttons, and two LEDs with resistors.)

Although the unit will not save a tremendous amount of time in terms of connecting components on a solderless breadboard, it does make the task of hooking up pots, pushbuttons, and LEDs a bit easier and will be a good practice exercise for readers with minimal soldering experience.

Soldering Étude 2

A minor frustration when using 9V battery clips is that the leads are usually too small to stay in place when connected to a solderless breadboard. (Note that 9V batteries are used to power standalone Arduino projects as presented in Chapter 12.)

Cut two small lengths of solid hookup wire and strip both ends of the wire. (For safety, it is best to cut the wires to different lengths to prevent a dangerous short between the terminals of the battery.) Use alligator clips to hold one battery lead and one of the wires in position as in Figure 11.12. Place the soldering iron below the lowest wire and apply some solder and gently squish the wires together. Ideally, the solder will flow and connect the wires with a sturdy solder joint. (You may need to adjust the wires slightly so they don't spring out of position after removing the soldering iron.) Repeat the process for the other lead, and use heat shrink to cover the solder joints in order to prevent a short.

FIGURE 11.12

Soldering leads to a battery clip.

Project Boxes

A big part of the fun of creating custom electronic instruments is finalizing a project in an attractive (and/or interesting) enclosure. Of course, many commercial products are available, but in this section we will look at a construction techniques that are easy to produce, look good, and don't require much in the way of special tools.

Wood Box

Most home supply stores like Home Depot offer lattice for a reasonable cost, and a piece of 1/4" × 3/4" (or similar) lattice can be used to make an attractive enclosure. First, calculate the dimensions of the box you intend to build, keeping in mind that it is better to have a bit too much room than not enough in terms of the inner dimension of the box. Next, measure the same distance from the blade of a hand- or power-miter saw and clamp a *stop* to the saw fence as in the Figure 11.13.

287

FIGURE 11.13

Clamping a stop board on a saw fence.

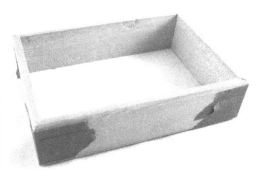

Cut four pieces with a 45° angle so that each side has the same bevel (outside to inside). Of course, you will need to adjust the stop if the box is rectangular. Dry-fit the parts to ensure that the joints make a good fit, and apply wood glue to each of the ends. Flip the wood so that the longest side of the bevel is facing up, and carefully line the pieces up end to end. Apply at least two pieces of painter's tape to each joint as in Figure 11.14, and then close up the pieces to form a box. Check the box for square, and let the glue dry for the length of time indicated on the label.

Preparing the Front and Back

To create a front and back panel, trace the inner outline of the box on a piece of thin plywood or a similar material and use a handsaw, jigsaw, table saw, or other tool to cut the material. Another option is to purchase metal flashing from a home supply store. The flashing can be easily cut with metal shears and painted or covered with a laminated overlay to make an attractive panel. Whatever material you choose, this would also be an ideal time to drill any holes that are required on the sides, front, or back of the enclosure.

Standoffs

Cut lengths of square dowel or similar material to use as standoffs, being sure to subtract the thickness of *both* pieces of material to be used for the front and back of the enclosure. Use wood glue to attach the risers to the corners of the box. (I find it helpful to place the back of the box in position and set the riser on the back to get a uniform position.)

Finishing the Box

The completed box can be sanded and stained for a classic look or painted with glossy paint for a more modern approach. Another idea is to visit a local furniture refinishing store and purchase remnants that can be glued to the box. For example, I found a remnant of the same material that is used to cover amplifiers for about $5 at a local furniture refinisher. Figure 11.15 shows a completed lattice box enclosure.

288

Plexiglas Enclosure

A Plexiglas "sandwich" is one of the easiest enclosures to make. Simply cut two pieces of Plexiglas to the desired size and drill holes in each corner. Use standoffs or spacers with long bolts to form a simple yet modern enclosure (see Figure 11.16).

FIGURE 11.16

Plexiglas "sandwich" enclosure.

289

Front Panels

I love creating panels because they can provide such a distinctive and professional look to a project. While there are many approaches that can yield good results, I favor an approach based on tips by Ray Wilson, author of the delightful book titled *Make: Analog Synthesizers*. The first step is to use graphic design software to create the text and graphics for the panel (see Figure 11.17). The software need not be expensive: the Paint program that comes with Windows will do in a pinch, and there are many options such as Graphic and Inkscape that are available for a modest cost (or as Open Source in the case of Inkscape). Be sure to double-check the dimensions against the material that will be used as the front panel (software programs often scale images when printing, so ensure that the panel is printed at 100 percent).

Print the panel graphics and have the paper laminated at a home office store. Of course you can save money by including several designs on the same paper if there is enough space. Next, place the material that will be used for the front panel over the image and use a knife to cut the laminate forming a perfect cutout. An optional final step is to use contact cement to glue the laminated

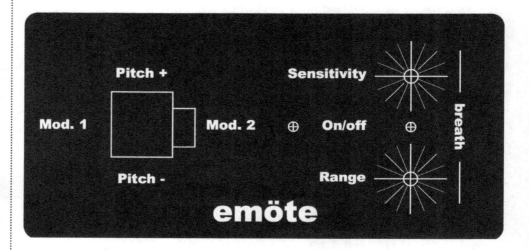

FIGURE 11.17

Graphic for the front panel of the "emote" controller.

graphic to the front of the panel. (Depending on the number and position of through-hole components, glue may be unnecessary.) It's a good idea to use a heavy roller to avoid any bubbles, and be sure to keep some warm water and a sponge handy to clean up any glue that might seep to the front of the panel. The resulting panel can look professional, and the design of the panel is only limited by your imagination. Figure 11.18 shows the completed "emote" project with a laminated front panel.

FIGURE 11.18

Completed "emote" MIDI controller.

Conclusion

The hands-on aspects of creating custom projects takes some practice, but the results are well worth the extra effort. Soldering and related skills like making project boxes and panels can add an entirely new dimension to music making. Now, MIDI controllers, digital synthesizers, and many other types of devices can be designed and manufactured at home for a modest cost and without the need for expensive tools. This freedom opens the door to the world of incredible creative potential. According to Chris Anderson, who discusses how a MakerBot is "thrillingly cool":

> That is the difference between commercial industrial tools and the products of the DIY movement. The Maker gear is as much about its process of creation as it is about the product itself...Buy one and you're not just buying a printer—you're buying a front-row seat to a cultural transformation.[9]

Standalone Arduino

Why Standalone Arduino?

The Arduino Uno is a wonderful device for developing project prototypes. It is relatively inexpensive, provides a reasonable number of digital and analog pins, and can be powered from a USB connection, 9V battery, or an appropriate power adapter. The only downside is cost. While an UNO (or similar device) isn't unduly expensive, the cost becomes prohibitive when you consider building more than one or two projects. Fortunately, it is possible to purchase a handful of parts and make a basic version for about $10.

In this chapter we will look at the primary parts required to build a standalone Arduino. By the end of the chapter you will have an understanding of the function of all of the components and be able to build a bare-bones Arduino on "perfboard," "stripboard," or other permanent solution. The process is surprisingly easy, so there is really no reason to hesitate to finalize projects with this inexpensive approach.

Parts

Table 12.1 lists the primary and optional parts required to build a standalone Arduino based on the ATmega328 microcontroller. The next few paragraphs detail the steps necessary to connect the components on a solderless breadboard. Once the basic function and layout of the parts is understood, it will be easy to move to a soldered version.

TABLE 12.1 Arduino Standalone Parts

Qty.	Description
Various	22 AWG wire
1	7805 voltage regulator
1	10kΩ resistor
1	ATmega328 microcontroller with boot loader
1	28-pin DIP socket
1	16MHz clock crystal
2	10μF electrolytic capacitors
2	22pF ceramic capacitors
1	9V battery with clip
OPTIONAL	
1–2	LEDs with resistors

7805 Voltage Regulator

The job of the voltage regulator is to ensure that voltage does not fluctuate above or below an acceptable range. In the case of the Arduino UNO, we want a steady 5V to power the chip. The 7805 is a type of regulator known as a *linear voltage regulator*. Linear regulators "'step down' voltage from one level to another; the difference in voltage is dissipated as heat."[1] The three prongs on a 7805 are (from left to right when viewed from the front—usually the side with text): Input, Ground, and Output (see Figure 12.1).

As is evident in the Figure 12.2, a pair of 10μF electrolytic capacitors are used to help to stabilize the power supply (either a 9V battery or appropriate power adapter). On the input side, the capacitor is used to minimize periodic fluctuations known as *ripple*. On the output side, the other capacitor is used to "fuel fast-switching circuits, as well as to guard against other transients dips in voltage."[2] Note how the output of the voltage regulator is used to supply power to the power rails on the breadboard. If your breadboard happens to have a pair or rails, use hookup wire to connect the upper power rail to the lower power rail as well as upper ground to lower ground. Although not essential, pairs of 5V and ground rails can help to keep your wires tidy as you make multiple connections to the ATmega328 chip.

293

FIGURE 12.1

Three pins of an 7805 when viewed from the front.

FIGURE 12.2

7805 regulator with smoothing capacitors and connections to power rails.

294

ATmega328

The ATmega328 is the microprocessor or "brains" of an Arduino Uno, and the microprocessor can be purchased with or without a *bootloader*. (A bootloader is a small program that runs on the ATmega chip and facilitates uploading sketches to the board without the need for additional hardware.) Although it is possible to burn the bootloader to a blank ATmega328, extra steps and hardware are required. Chips with preinstalled bootloaders cost $1.50 to $2.00 extra and, in my experience, are worth the small added expense. For this reason, I will limit the discussion to using an ATmega328 with a preloaded bootloader. As discussed later in the chapter, you will also need an existing Arduino UNO with a removable chip to upload sketches to the ATmega chip or an appropriate hardware programmer.

Pins

The pins on the ATmega chip do not correspond to the numbering scheme used by the Arduino. For example, the A5 pin is actually the last (28th) pin on the chip, and the reset is pin 1. If possible, purchase a bootloaded chip that also comes with a sticker showing the Arduino pin mappings. You will find it much easier to follow these steps if you can look at labels on the top of the chips. Figure 12.3,[3] from http://arduino.cc/en/Hacking/PinMapping168, shows the pin layout.

Atmega 168 Pin Mapping

Arduino function			Arduino function
reset	(PCINT14/RESET) PC6 ☐ 1	28 ☐ PC5 (ADC5/SCL/PCINT13)	analog input 5
digital pin 0 (RX)	(PCINT16/RXD) PD0 ☐ 2	27 ☐ PC4 (ADC4/SDA/PCINT12)	analog input 4
digital pin 1 (TX)	(PCINT17/TXD) PD1 ☐ 3	26 ☐ PC3 (ADC3/PCINT11)	analog input 3
digital pin 2	(PCINT18/INT0) PD2 ☐ 4	25 ☐ PC2 (ADC2/PCINT10)	analog input 2
digital pin 3 (PWM)	(PCINT19/OC2B/INT1) PD3 ☐ 5	24 ☐ PC1 (ADC1/PCINT9)	analog input 1
digital pin 4	(PCINT20/XCK/T0) PD4 ☐ 6	23 ☐ PC0 (ADC0/PCINT8)	analog input 0
VCC	VCC ☐ 7	22 ☐ GND	GND
GND	GND ☐ 8	21 ☐ AREF	analog reference
crystal	(PCINT6/XTAL1/TOSC1) PB6 ☐ 9	20 ☐ AVCC	VCC
crystal	(PCINT7/XTAL2/TOSC2) PB7 ☐ 10	19 ☐ PB5 (SCK/PCINT5)	digital pin 13
digital pin 5 (PWM)	(PCINT21/OC0B/T1) PD5 ☐ 11	18 ☐ PB4 (MISO/PCINT4)	digital pin 12
digital pin 6 (PWM)	(PCINT22/OC0A/AIN0) PD6 ☐ 12	17 ☐ PB3 (MOSI/OC2A/PCINT3)	digital pin 11(PWM)
digital pin 7	(PCINT23/AIN1) PD7 ☐ 13	16 ☐ PB2 (SS/OC1B/PCINT2)	digital pin 10 (PWM)
digital pin 8	(PCINT0/CLKO/ICP1) PB0 ☐ 14	15 ☐ PB1 (OC1A/PCINT1)	digital pin 9 (PWM)

Digital Pins 11, 12 & 13 are used by the ICSP header for MOSI, MISO, SCK connections (Atmega168 pins 17, 18, & 19), Avoid low-impedance loads on these pins when using the ICSP header.

FIGURE 12.3

Atmega328 to Arduino I/O mapping. (From http://arduino.cc/en/Hacking/PinMapping168.)

Connections

Several connections need to be made to power the standalone ATmega chip. First, the reset pin is connected through a 10kΩ resistor to the power rail. Without this connection, the microcontroller might inadvertently "reboot." Next, *Vcc* and *GND* (pins 7 and 8) are connected to the power and ground rails respectively. On the other side of the chip, pin 20 (AVCC) is connect to the power rail, and pin 22 (GND) connects to ground (see the Figure 12.4).

295

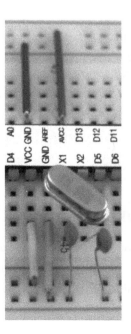

FIGURE 12.4

Breadboard with connections on pins 7, 8, 20, and 22.

For the standalone Arduino to function, it requires an external "heart-beat" or clock source. Amazingly, the tiny 16MHz clock crystal is capable of providing 16 million pulses every second to the chip. Connect the crystal (in either direction) to pins 9 and 10 on the ATmega328 chip. The legs of the crystal will likely be too far apart to place in adjacent holes, so angle the crystal as in Figure 12.5.

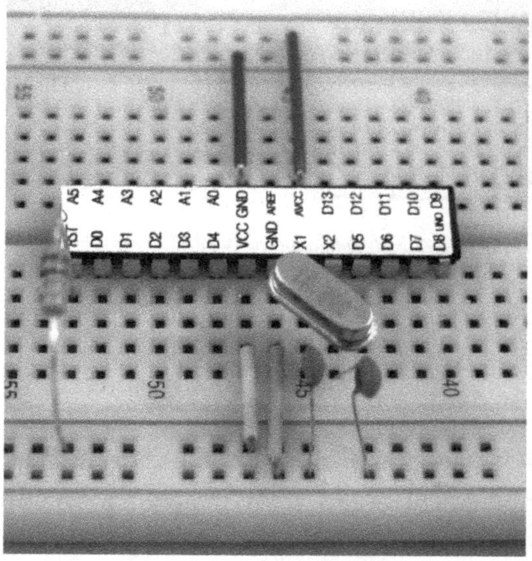

FIGURE 12.5

16MHz clock crystal connected to pins 9 and 10 (angled to accommodate wide pin spacing). 22pF ceramic capacitors connected to ground.

The pins on the crystal are connected through a pair of 22pF ceramic capacitors to ground. The capacitors help to stabilize the oscillation of the crystal against "insufficient capacitive load." The Atmel document *AVR042: AVR Hardware Design Considerations* provides more information including the following: "When using the clock option 'ext. crystal oscillator,' crystals with a nominal frequency from 400kHz and up can be used. For these standard "high" frequency crystals the recommended capacitor value is in the range 22–33pF."[4]

The complete solderless breadboard wiring of the ATmega328 chip can be seen in Figure 12.6. At this point, the chip is capable of providing the core functionality of an Arduino once an appropriate sketch has been uploaded to the device.

Burning a Bootloader to a Blank ATmega328

If you elect to purchase a "blank" ATmega328 sans bootloader, it will be necessary to upload a bootloader to the microcontroller. An Arduino UNO can be used for this purpose. The steps are detailed in an online Arduino tutorial and will be summarized in the following paragraphs.[5]

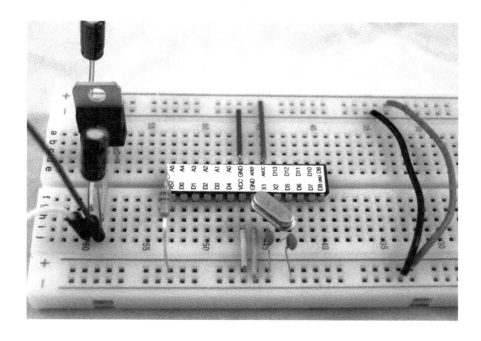

FIGURE 12.6

Solderless breadboard wiring of the ATmega328.

First, breadboard the ATmega328 microcontroller using the steps and diagrams in the previous section, but add the four new connections shown in Figure 12.7 (see reset (pin 0) and ATmega pins 17–19 connected to pins 10 and 11–13 on the Arduino).

Next, select "Arduino UNO" from the Tools→Board menu, select the appropriate serial connection that you usually use to program your Arduino board, and upload the sketch named ArduinoISP (available in Files→Examples) to the Arduino. Finally, select the Tools→Programmer→Arduino as ISP and select Tools→Burn Bootloader to upload the bootloader to the breadboarded ATmega328 microcontroller.

Programming Options

For most readers, the easiest method of programming the ATmega328 chip is to simply use an existing Arduino UNO. Be sure to unplug any power (USB or battery) that is applied to the Arduino and take note of the orientation of the existing ATmega328 chip in its socket. Use an IC chip removal tool (such as the one shown in Figure 12.8) to carefully remove the existing chip from the Arduino UNO and place it in a safe place such as some electrostatic dissipative foam.

Next, plug the new ATmega328 (with boot loader) in the empty socket of the Arduino. Be careful to insert the chip in the same orientation as the original, and avoid bending any pins. (You may need to bend the rows of pins slightly inward prior to inserting them into the empty socket.)

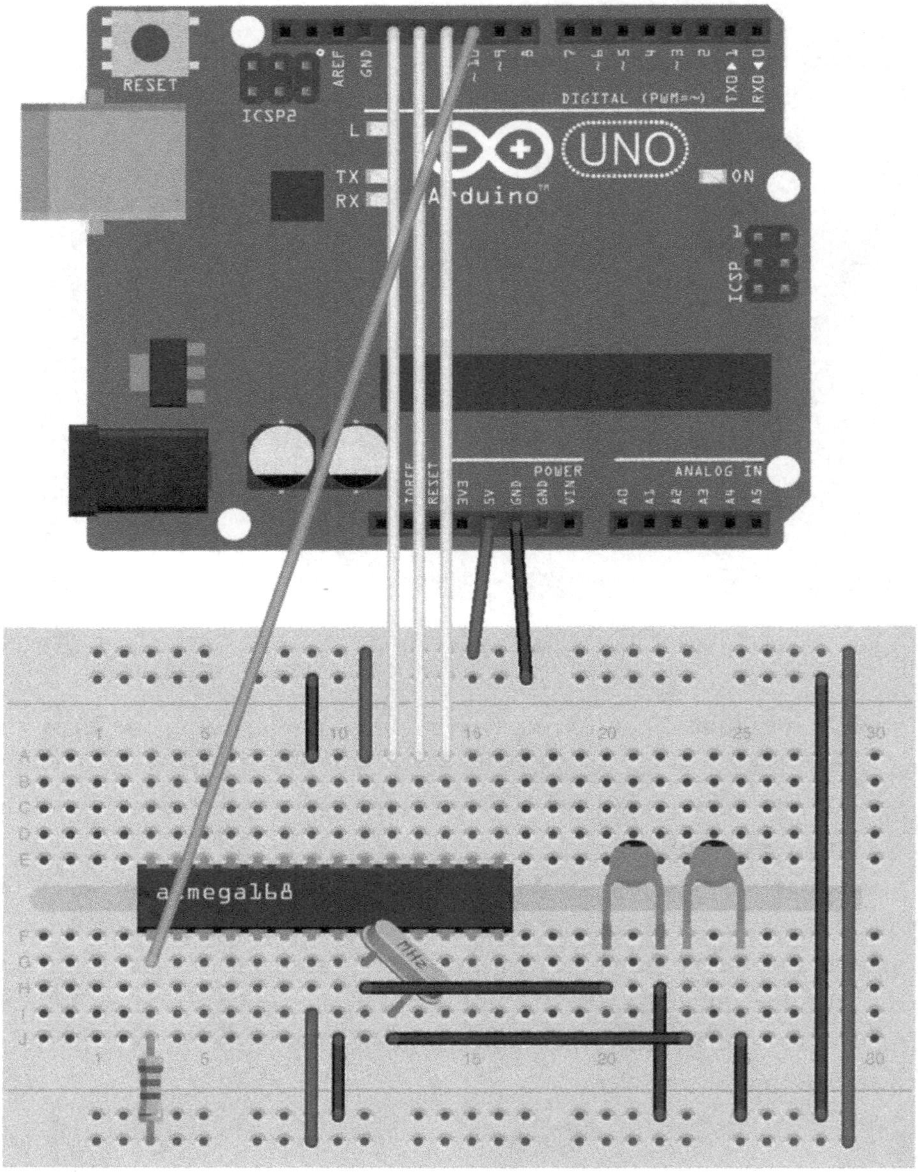

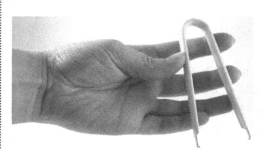

FIGURE 12.7

ATmega328 breadboard
setup with new
connections to reset pin 0,
and ATmega pins 17–19.

FIGURE 12.8

IC chip removal tool.

Assuming the chip has been preconfigured with a bootloader, your
new chip should now be ready to program as usual using the Arduino IDE.
Use a solderless breadboard to
create a mock-up of any circuits
you intend to connect to the
standalone Arduino, and use the
Arduino IDE to develop and
perfect your sketch. One you are
satisfied with the sketch, simply
reverse the process to use your

newly prepared ATmega328 in a project: unplug the Arduino USB connection and use the IC chip removal tool to remove the microcontroller. The chip is now ready to use in a standalone project with the minimal circuitry described in the first section of this chapter.

Other Programming Options

A *flash programmer* can be handy if you find yourself doing lots of standalone Arduino projects. A board, such LadyAda's USBTinyISP (see Figure 12.9), provides a USB connection and the necessary power, ground, and MOSI and MISO connections that are required to "flash" an ATmega chip.

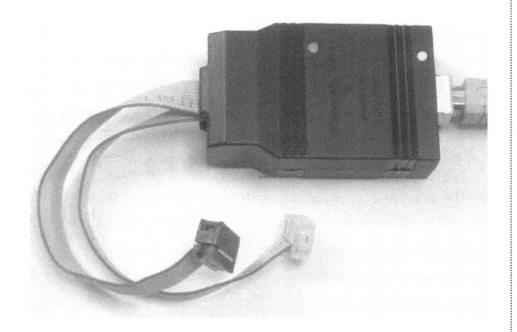

299

To use the breakout board, plug it into a solderless breadboard and make the connections shown in Table 12.2 (as detailed in Elliot Williams's *Make: AVR Programming*).[6] The ATmega chip can now be programmed with a USB cable

TABLE 12.2 ISP to ATmega328 Connections

ISP connector	ATmega connector
VCC	VCC (pin 7)
MOSI	RX1PB3 (MOSI/OC1B) pin 17
MISO	TXOPB4 (MISO) pin 18
SCK	PB5 (SCK) pin 19
RESET	(RESET) PC6 pin 1
GND	GND pins 8 and 22

just like a normal Arduino. Williams's book provides a wealth of information on AVR programming, and I recommend it to users who want to learn about the low-level details of AVR hardware.

A Demonstration Project

Now that the steps for creating a standalone Arduino have been detailed, it would be helpful to apply the concepts to a real-world application—a standalone version of the metronome project developed in Chapter 4. This project will use most of the circuits and code from that chapter with a few exceptions that will be described in the following paragraphs.

Rotary Encoder with Switch

I like the idea of minimalist design, so user input is handled by two components: a combination Rotary Encoder/Switch and serial 7-segment display. Although readers are encouraged to use any available components, which might consist of switches, potentiometer, and LEDs, the combination Rotary Encoder/Switch is convenient because it provides a rotary encoder and pushbutton on a single component. Figure 12.10 shows one approach to building a metronome with a minimal number of components.

The circuit and source code follows the design concepts that were detailed in previous chapters. The only difference is that the encoder and switch are contained in single physical component. Figure 12.11 shows the function of the pins on the encoder.

I elected to use the pin assignments shown in Table 12.3 to connect the rotary encoder, switch, and serial 7-segment display to the Arduino.

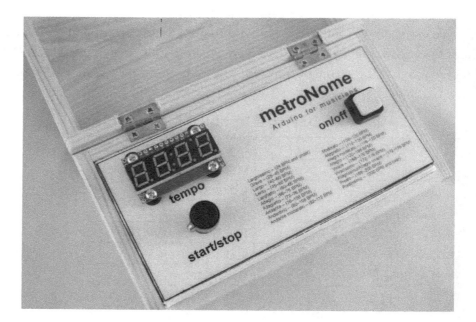

FIGURE 12.10

Photo of finished desktop metronome.

Complete Circuit

The entire circuit can be seen in Figure 12.12. For clarity, the ground rail is not shown. However, the ground of each component should form a common connection. One optional subcircuit not shown is an LM386 amplifier. The amplifier, as described in Chapter 3, can be used to drive the speaker to a higher level. Yet another option would be to utilize the circuits and code from Chapter 9 to provide synthesized (or sampled) output via an audio jack.

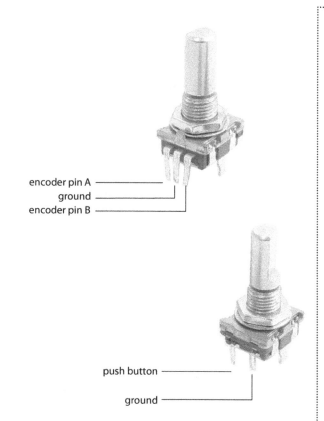

encoder pin A

ground

encoder pin B

push button

ground

FIGURE 12.11

Pin assignments on Rotary Encoder/Switch.

TABLE 12.3 Pin Assignments Showing Connection of Rotary Encoder and Serial 7-Segment Display to Arduino Pins

Component Pin	Arduino Pin
Encoder A	Pin 11
encoder ground	Ground
Encoder B	Pin 12
Serial 7-segment display vcc	+5V
Serial 7-segment display ground	Ground
Serial 7-segment display RX	TX
Speaker connection A	Pin 4 through 100Ω resistor
Speaker connection B	Ground
Encoder pushbutton	Pin 9

Code

The sketch utilizes the EasyButton and RotaryEncoder classes that were developed in Chapter 8 to handle user input. Those values are used to turn the metronome on and off and to adjust the speed of the metronome (see Listing 12.1).

301

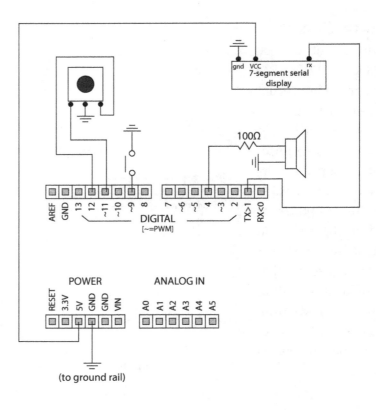

FIGURE 12.12

Complete metronome circuit.

Listing 12.1

```
void loop()
{
   int encoderPosition=rotary.trackShaftPosition();
   if(encoderPosition!=lastEncoderPosition)
   {
       beats_per_minute = encoderPosition;
       updateTempo();
       lastEncoderPosition=encoderPosition;
   }
   if(button.checkButtonPressed() == true && lastState != true)
   {
      //Button press detected
      lastState = true;
   }
   if(button.checkButtonPressed() == false && lastState !=
   false)
   {
      //Button release detected...
      lastState = false;
      //toggle the status of the metronome
      on=!on;

       if(on)
       {
          //Show that the metronome is on:
          printNumberToSerialDisplay(beats_per_minute);
          Serial.print("-");
       }else{
```

```
            printNumberToSerialDisplay(beats_per_minute);
        }
    }
  //Play a tone if the metronome is on.
  long current_time = millis();
  if((current_time - last_time >= delay_time) && on == true)
  {
      //Output the tone
      tone(speakerPin, frequency, duration);
      //Update last_time to current time
      last_time = current_time;
  }
}
```

7-Segment Serial Display

A 7-segment serial display is an attractive option for a desktop metronome. Fortunately, only three wires are needed to connect the display to an Arduino. Although it would be possible to use a nonserial 7-segment display, I have found the ease of use of the serial version to be well worth the marginal extra cost over the less expensive nonserial displays. In terms of code, a single function is used to write the current tempo to the display. The function is called during the *setup()* procedure and whenever the rotary encoder detects a tempo change (see Listing 12.2).

Listing 12.2 Displaying the tempo on the 7-segment serial display

```
void printNumberToSerialDisplay(int number)
{
  Serial.write(0x76);  //Clear the display
  Serial.print(number);
}
```

303

Note that the remainder of the code is similar to the metronome projects presented in Chapter 4 and involves setting up the pins and calculating tempo. The entire listing is available for download at the OUP website.

Finalizing the Project

Once you are happy with your solderless breadboard circuit and Arduino sketch, it is time to finalize the project using the steps detailed in Chapter 11. However, there are many modifications you might want to consider, such as handling multiple time signatures and emphasizing strong beats, adding a blinking LED (no sound) mode, providing audio or MIDI output jacks, or any number of other modifications. Although a homemade desktop metronome isn't the most glamorous project, there is a sense of satisfaction in creating a project from scratch that meets your exact needs. And you can't overestimate the value of the many new skills you will develop by bringing the project to fruition. Figure 12.13 shows one approach to soldering the circuit on stripboard.

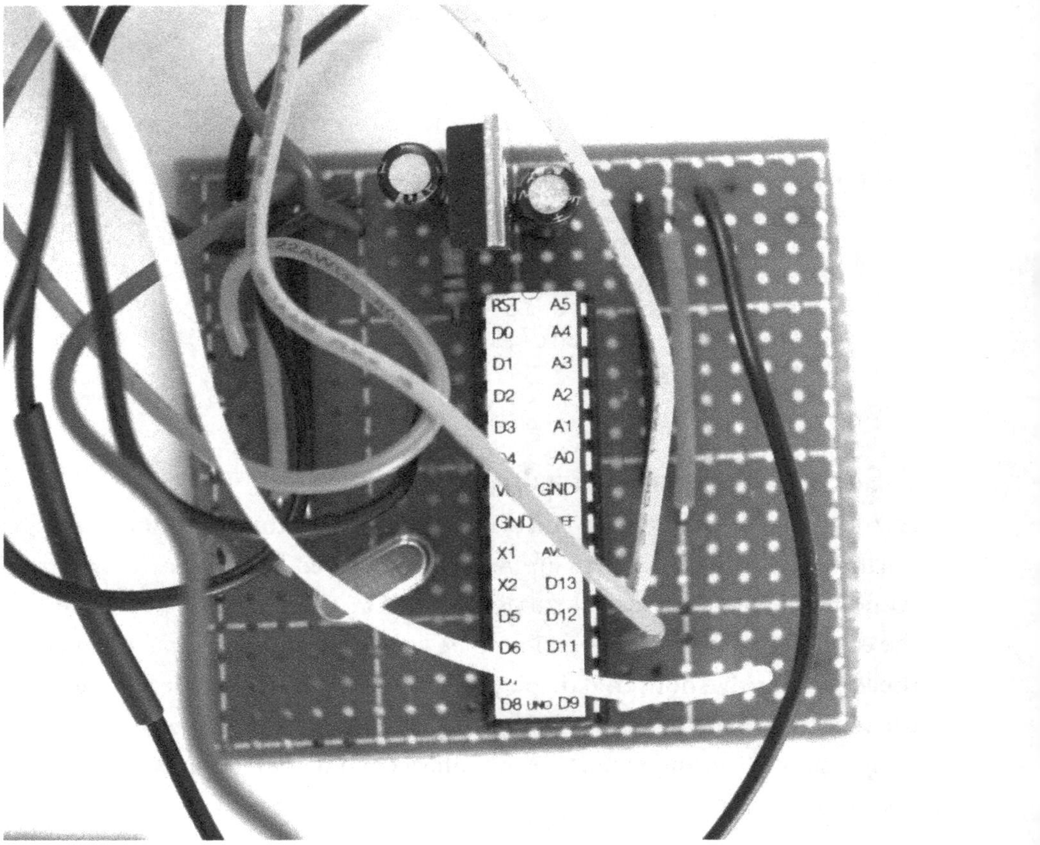

FIGURE 12.13

Soldered metronome circuit.

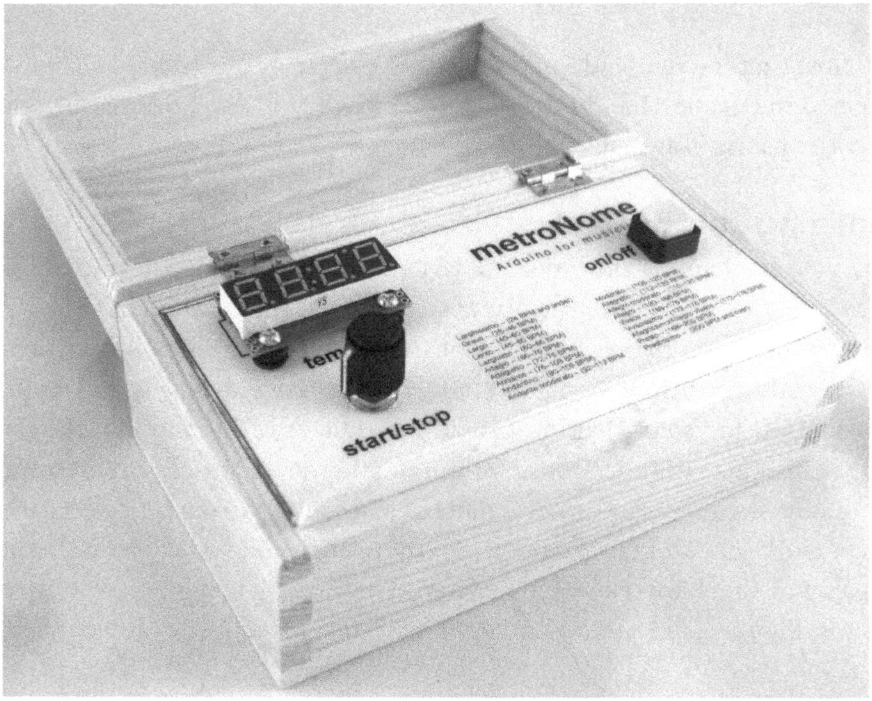

FIGURE 12.14

Another view of the finished metronome project.

There are lots of options for enclosures including purchasing a project enclosure, building your own box, or designing one using an online 3D printing service. I elected to use a low-tech solution, a box I purchased for $3 from a hobby store (see Figure 12.14). The box looks nice on my desk, but I can also imagine enclosing the project in something fun like a plastic toy dinosaur or other conversation piece.

MIDI Hand Drum Project

Overview

This chapter represents a milestone. The mini projects presented thus far have focused on developing a foundation of building blocks that will form the basis for any number of useful Arduino tools, but the projects in this section combine many of the building blocks in the form of fully functional and expressive musical instruments.

The goal is not to rehash building-block concepts but to focus on the opportunities and challenges that arise when projects become more complex. The projects in this section involve four primary concepts that will be of interest to many electronic musicians: live performance, direct digital synthesis, pattern sequencing, and real-time control. Demonstration videos for all of the projects are available at the OUP website, and readers are encouraged to view the demonstration videos to get a feel for how each instrument is used and to consider enhancements that can be tailored to individual preference before building any of the projects in this section.

There is a lot to cover in this section, so don't worry if some aspects of the sketches are unclear the first time you read the text. One of the great things about object-oriented programming is that you can use classes and libraries by more experienced programmers without understanding all of the inner workings of a class. As your programming chops grow you will be able to write your own C++ classes to share with other people. All of the code in this chapter is available for download, so have fun experimenting with the demonstration code as you learn to write more complex sketches.

Mongo: MIDI Bongo Drum

The Mongo drum is a MIDI drum that can be used to trigger a synthesizer or sounds in a Digital Audio Workstation. Although Mongo is an expressive instrument that is fun to play, the project utilizes a relatively small number of components so the circuitry is relatively easy to prototype and build.

The Mongo drum (see Figure 13.1) utilizes force-sensitive resistors (described in Chapter 6), as well as buttons, light emitting diodes, and a rotary encoder, which are described in the first section of the book. In addition to the hardware components, the project incorporates a simple yet robust firmware that enables a performer to play notes, edit note assignments, and store the settings in one of six storage banks in nonvolatile memory.

As with most of the projects in this book, three approaches to construction are possible: the project can be prototyped by connecting components to a solderless breadboard. A more permanent version can be achieved by soldering male headers to leads such that multiple components can be easily attached to the female headers on an Arduino or Teensy microcontroller. Finally, more advanced builders may wish to solder components to solderboard or create a printed circuit board (PCB) using the circuit designs available at the companion website. Note that Chapters 11 and 12 provide detailed instructions relating to creating permanent circuits on various types of solderboards.

13.1 MONGO DRUM

307

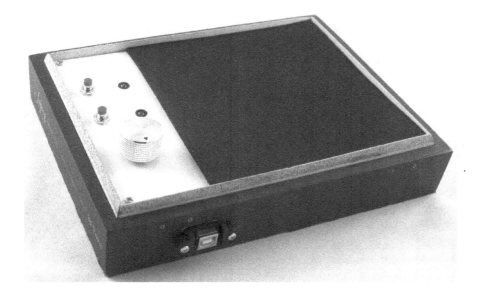

FIGURE 13.1

Finished Mongo drum.

Hardware

For the Mongo project I elected to incorporate a relatively inexpensive Teensy 2.0 microcontroller. The microcontroller, which is available for about $16 from http://www.pjrc.com/store/teensy.html, provides plenty of analog and digital inputs for the build and has the added benefit of being able to function as a plug-and-play USB Music Instrument Digital Interface. The design can be easily modified to incorporate an Arduino microcontroller with 5-pin DIN output port as described in Chapter 5.

Getting Started

It is advisable to start by mocking up the project on a solderless breadboard. This will provide an opportunity to ensure that components and software are functioning properly prior to committing the time and expense of soldering components to solderboard. It also provides an opportunity to consider alternate design strategies. For example, it might make sense to include a 5-pin DIN MIDI output port in addition to (or in lieu of) the USB MIDI interface provided by the Teensy 2.0 microcontroller. Another option might include using smaller (and less expensive) force-sensing resistors* that would be appropriate for a smaller form factor MIDI finger drum, or to simply use fewer force-sensing resistors.

The Mongo project utilizes the components shown in Table 13.1.

TABLE 13.1 Parts List for Mongo Project

QTY	Description	Notes	Approx. cost
2	LEDs	Use different colors	$0.35 each
2	Current limiting resistors	For use with LEDs	$.025 each
6	10KΩ resistors	For use with FSRs	$.025 each
1	Thru-hole rotary encoder	Knob is optional	$2.00
2	Thru-hole momentary push buttons		$0.50-$1.00
*6	1.5" Force-sensing resistors	With female connector	$8.00 each
6	2-pin headers	Used to connect FSRs	$0.25 each
1	Enclosure	Homemade or commercial	$5-20
1	Wide IC socket	For attaching Teensy to circuit	$0.40
MSCL	Solid insulated copper wire	22 AWG	-
1	Teensy 2.0 microcontroller		$16
1	Mini-B to Standard-B Panel Mount USB Adaptor	Optional	$5.50
1	Mouse pad	Used to cover and protect FSRs	$3.00
1	Veroboard or other solderboard		$3.00
1	⅛" marker board or similar material	Used to attach FSRs, momentary switches, LEDs, and encoder	-

*Although force-sensing resistors are relatively expensive, 2-pin headers are used to connect the leads to the circuit so the FSRs can easily be removed for use in other projects. Similarly, the Teensy is installed via an IC socket so it can be plugged in or removed as needed.

Making Connections

Force-sensing resistors form the backbone of this project. As described in Chapter 6, connect one of the leads of the FSR to the +5V output provided by the microcontroller. Attach the other lead to an analog pin on the microprocessor through a 10K resistor connected to ground (see Figure 13.2).

The other five force-sensing resistors are connected to additional analog ports on the Teensy 2.0 (see Figure 13.3).

Two momentary pushbuttons provide the ability to switch between performance and editing modes. As is described in Chapter 4, connect one side of the switch to one of the digital inputs on the microcontroller and attach the other side to ground (see Figure 13.4). Since the Mongo firmware utilizes

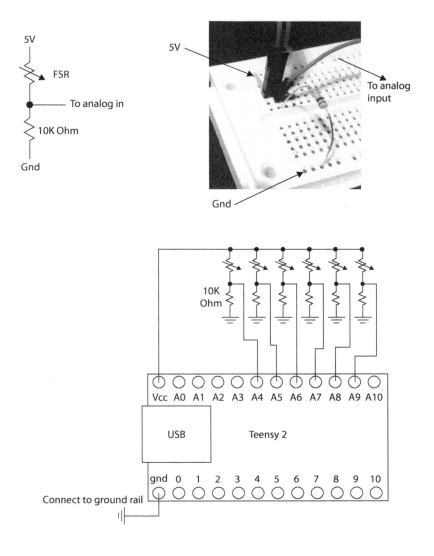

FIGURE 13.2

Force-sensing resister circuit.

309

FIGURE 13.3

Connecting 6 FSRs to the Teensy 2.0.

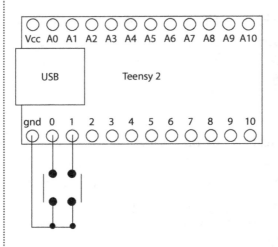

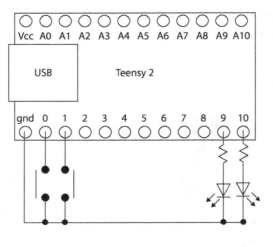

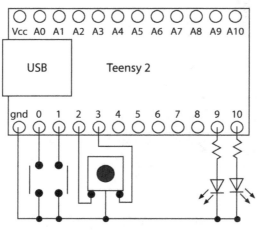

310

the *EasyButton* class that was developed in Chapter 8, it is not necessary to use a resistor in this application because the class sets up an internal pull-up resistor.

Two light-emitting diodes provide visual feedback indicating the state of the device. It is important to remember two things relating to LEDs from the discussion in Chapter 3: (1) LEDs are polarized and, as such, must be installed in the proper orientation (the flat side or short lead indicates the cathode that will be connected to ground); (2) it is also necessary to use a resistor to avoid "frying" the LED.

For this project I elected to use yellow and red LEDs to differentiate between the operating modes of the instrument. Connect the LEDs as shown in Figure 13.5.

The final hardware component is a rotary encoder that is used to select a MIDI note value for each of the performance pads. As with the switches used in this project, the Mongo firmware utilizes a custom rotary encoder class to track the status of the encoder. As described in Chapter 8, the *RotaryEncoder* class enables pullup resistors for each of the outer leads of the encoder, so it is not necessary to incorporate a resistor when connecting the encoder to the microcontroller. The rotary encoder is connected to the digital pins of the microcontroller as shown in Figure 13.6.

Developing the Mongo Firmware

My primary goal for the Mongo drum was to retain, as much as possible, the simplicity of a real hand drum while providing functions that would be useful

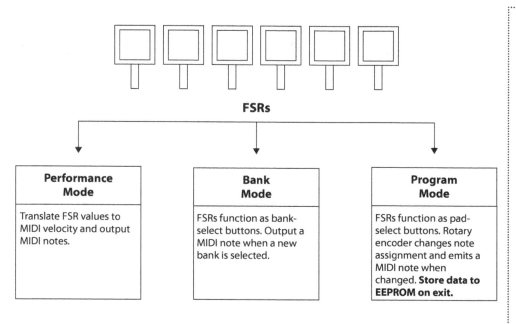

FIGURE 13.7

Diagram of the three modes of operation.

in performance. For this reason, I elected not to incorporate an LCD or an array of buttons that might be cumbersome to use in a live setting. In thinking through prospective design strategies, I realized that the force-sensing resistors could do double duty as interface switches, thereby simplifying the design and cost of the instrument.

The hand drum features three modes of operation. In *performance mode*, the force-sensing resistors function as touch-sensitive drum pads that are used to send MIDI Note-On messages to a computer or synthesizer. Performance mode is the default mode that is established when the unit is powered on via a USB cable.

A second mode, *bank select mode*, allows a performer to touch one of the performance pads to select from one of six banks of sounds. The program tracks the status of one of the momentary switches to detect when the device should enter (or exit) bank select mode.

The third mode of operation, *bank edit mode*, allows a performer to select and store a MIDI note to associate with each pad in a given bank of sounds. Bank edit mode automatically stores changes to internal nonvolatile EEPROM memory. Bank edit mode also provides an option for a user to reset the device to its default settings. Figure 13.7 illustrates the function of the three modes of operation.

The following paragraphs detail the design and function of the Mongo firmware. Although the program involves a fair amount of code, the underlying functionality can be broken down into discrete methods and classes that are easily understood. The code is available for download at the OUP website and can be used "as is" or modified to provide additional features.

Software Setup, Global Constants, and Variables

A number of constants and classes must be defined to handle the buttons, rotary encoder, and LEDs. Include statements are used to incorporate the *EasyButton* and *RotaryEncoder* classes as well as a new *TouchPad* class that will be described in a later paragraph. Your Arduino programming environment should come with a class titled EEPROM, which is used to read and write to nonvolatile flash memory:

```
#include <EEPROM.h>
#include <EasyButton.h>
#include <RotaryEncoder.h>
#include "TouchPad.h"
```

Several constants are used to signify the pins to which buttons and LEDs are attached to the microcontroller. Two instances of the *EasyButton* class are instantiated with these constant values, and two variables are defined to track the status of each button (see Listing 13.1).

Listing 13.1 Mongo constants

```
//Button and LED pins:
const int BUTTON_A=1; //TOP BUTTON
const int BUTTON_B=0; //BOTTOM BUTTON
const int LED_A=9;

const int LED_B=10;

EasyButton button_a;
EasyButton button_b;

//Variables:
boolean last_A_status = false;
boolean last_B_status = false;
```

An instance of the *RotaryEncoder* class is initialized in a similar fashion:

```
//Rotary encoder setup:
int status = 0;
int encoderPinA = 3;
int encoderPinB = 2;

RotaryEncoder encoder;
```

Constants are also defined to indicate the current mode of operation as well as numbers that will be useful when writing and retrieving data. They are also used to indicate pin assignments of the force-sensing resistors as well as pressure range and threshold. Integer variables are also defined to track the active bank and pad selection (see Listing 13.2).

Listing 13.2 Mongo mode and pad assignments

```
//Mode of operation constants
const int PLAY_MODE = 0;
const int BANK_MODE = 1;
const int PROGRAM_MODE = 2;
```

```
int currentMode=PLAY_MODE; //this variable indicates the
                           //current mode of operation

//Constants for storing data to EPROM
const byte EEPROM_ID = 0x99;
const int  ID_ADDRESS = 0;
const int  BASE_ADDRESS = 1;


//FSR constants:
const int NUM_PADS = 6;
const int NO_PAD_SELECTED = -1;
//Top row pin assignments
const int fsrA = 17;
const int fsrB = 15;
const int fsrC = 13;
//Bottom row pin assignments
const int fsrD = 16;
const int fsrE = 14;
const int fsrF = 12;

//Range values
const int minimum = 0;
const int maximum = 1000;
//Consider adding code for user to adjust the threshold
//value via the rotary encoder:
int THRESHOLD = 100;

//Variables to track the currently active pad and bank
int current_pad = 0;
int current_bank = 0;

byte MIDI_NOTES[6][6]={
  42, 46, 44, 35, 38, 49,  /*drums*/
  43, 45, 47, 48, 50, 54,  /*toms*/
  62 ,63, 64, 60, 61, 58,  /*conga*/
  65, 66, 67, 68, 69, 70,  /*timbale*/
  73, 73, 75, 76, 77, 78,  /*guiro*/
  37, 39, 51, 52, 57, 55}; /*cymbals*/
```

TouchPad Class

In order to simultaneously handle multiple force-sensing resistors, it is necessary to keep track of the status of the FSR to see if a note has already been emitted as a result of applying pressure to one of the pads. Without such a tracking mechanism, multiple notes would be emitted each time pressure is applied to a pad. A simple *TouchPad* class provides a mechanism for tracking the status of the pad as well as its pin assignment. The *TouchPad* class provides a more elegant method of accessing each touch pad—particularly when the pin assignments are not contiguous. For example, a simple array of *TouchPad* objects makes it easy to access each pad in a loop, even if the pins don't correspond to the indices of the array (see Listing 13.3).

Listing 13.3 Tracking the touch pads

```
//Create an array of TouchPad objects
TouchPad TouchPads[NUM_PADS];
.
.
.
//Loop through the pads
for(int i=0;i<NUM_PADS;i++)
{
   //Get the analog value of each pad
   val = TouchPads[i].getPadValue();
}
```

The *TouchPad* class consists of two data members that store the value of the pin assignment and MIDI Note-On status. A default constructor provides reasonable default values and "getter" and "setter" methods provide access to the data members (see Listing 13.4).

Listing 13.4 TouchPad class

```
#include <Arduino.h>
class TouchPad
{
  int m_pin;              //The analog pin to which the touch
                          //pad is attached
  boolean m_noteOn;       //The status of the pad (note on or
                          //note off)
  //Constructor
  public:
  TouchPad()
  {
    //establish defaults
    m_noteOn = false;     //default to a note off
    m_pin = 0;
  }
  //Setters and getters
  void setPin(int p)
  {
    m_pin = p;
  }
  void setNoteOnStatus(boolean note_status)
  {
    m_noteOn=note_status;
  }
  boolean getNoteOnStatus()
  {
      return m_noteOn;
  }
  int getPadValue()
  {
    return analogRead(m_pin);
  }
};
```

Moving back to the main program, an array of TouchPad objects is created and the *setup()* method initializes each of the *TouchPad* objects, establishes the output mode for each of the LED pins, calls a method to read data from EEPROM (more on this in a moment), and delays for 1s to allow the circuitry to stabilize prior to polling the status of the buttons (see Listing 13.5).

Listing 13.5 *setup()* function

```
/Create an array of TouchPad objects
TouchPad TouchPads[NUM_PADS];

void setup() {

  button_a.init(BUTTON_A, 20);
  button_b.init(BUTTON_B, 20);
  encoder.init(encoderPinA, encoderPinB, 20, 24, 0, 127);

  //set pin assignments
  TouchPads[0].setPin(fsrA);
  TouchPads[1].setPin(fsrB);
  TouchPads[2].setPin(fsrC);
  TouchPads[3].setPin(fsrD);
  TouchPads[4].setPin(fsrE);
  TouchPads[5].setPin(fsrF);

  //Set up LEDs
  pinMode(LED_A, OUTPUT);
  pinMode(LED_B, OUTPUT);

/* Load data from EPROM (this will flash yellow if
   data found, red if default values are stored
   to disk) */
  readDataFromEPROM();

  //Delay to stabilize the circuitry
  delay(1000);

}
```

Program Logic

Given that the hand drum will provide three modes of operation, it made sense to develop subloop functions to handle each of the three modes: performance, bank select, and bank edit. The main loop (see Listing 13.6) checks the status of the menu buttons via a method named *handleMenuButtons()* and calls the appropriate subroutine based on the value of the global variable named *currentMode*. The main loop also calls a method named *handleLEDs()* to update the values of the LEDs so that they correspond to the current mode of operation. The design of these functions is described in the following paragraphs.

Listing 13.6 Main loop

```
void loop()
{
    //handle lights and menu buttons
    handleLEDs();
    handleMenuButtons();

    //Check the current mode status and call the
    corresponding method
    if(currentMode==PLAY_MODE)
    {
        playMode();
    }
    if(currentMode==BANK_MODE)
    {
        bankMode();
    }
    if(currentMode==PROGRAM_MODE)
    {
        programMode();
    }
}
```

handleLEDs()

The *handleLEDs()* function (see Listing 13.7) simply checks the status of the current mode and turns the corresponding LEDs on or off. In this instance, the top LED is used to indicate bank select mode and the bottom LED indicates program mode.

Listing 13.7 handleLEDs function

```
void handleLEDs()
{
    if(currentMode==PLAY_MODE)
    {
        digitalWrite(LED_A, LOW);   //play mode on (lights off)
        digitalWrite(LED_B, LOW);
    }
    if(currentMode==BANK_MODE)
    {
        digitalWrite(LED_A, HIGH);  //bank select mode on
                                    //(top LED on)
        digitalWrite(LED_B, LOW);
    }
    if(currentMode==PROGRAM_MODE)
    {
        digitalWrite(LED_A, LOW);
        digitalWrite(LED_B, HIGH);  //program mode on
                                    //(bottom LED on)
    }
}
```

handleMenuButtons()

The *handleMenuButtons()* function (see Listing 13.8) provides the primary logic flow for the application. The function checks the status of each button and follows the logic of the following pseudo-code when a button is pressed.

If button A is pressed…

- If the current mode is bank mode go back to play mode
- If the current mode is play mode go to bank mode
- If the current mode is program mode store data and move to bank mode

If button B is pressed…

- If the current mode is program mode store data and go back to play mode
- Go to program mode if not already in program mode

The function changes modes as appropriate and the data storage method, *storeDataToEPROM()*, is called as necessary to store changes to nonvolatile memory (see Listing 13.8).

Listing 13.8 handleMenuButtons function

```
void handleMenuButtons()
{
  //========Button A: used to switch in and out of bank mode
  boolean a_status=button_a.checkButtonPressed();
  if(a_status !=last_A_status)
  {
    //Output only on press, not on release
    if(a_status==false)
    {
      if(currentMode==BANK_MODE)
      {
        currentMode=PLAY_MODE;
      }
      else if(currentMode==PLAY_MODE){
        currentMode=BANK_MODE;
      }

      if(currentMode==PROGRAM_MODE)
      {
        //exiting program mode...save work
        storeDataToEPROM();
        currentMode=BANK_MODE;
      }

    }
    last_A_status=a_status;
    delay(100);
  }
```

```
//Button B: used to switch in and out of program mode

boolean b_status=button_b.checkButtonPressed();
if(b_status!=last_B_status)
{
  //Output only on press, not on release
  if(b_status==false)
  {
    //Serial.println("Button B pressed");
    if(currentMode==PROGRAM_MODE)
    {
      currentMode=PLAY_MODE;
      storeDataToEPROM();
    }
    else{
      currentMode=PROGRAM_MODE;
    }
  }
  last_B_status=b_status;
  delay(100);
}
}
```

playMode()

The *playMode()* function contains a simple loop that calls a function named *handleFSR()* for each of the force-sensing resistors (see Listing 13.9).

Listing 13.9 playMode function

```
void playMode()
{
  //Loop through each pin and call the FSR handler
  for(int i=0;i<NUM_PADS;i++)
  {
    handleFSR(i);
  }
}
```

As is probably evident in Listing 13.10, the *handleFSR()* method polls each FSR via the associated instance of TouchPad, maps the value to an appropriate range and outputs a MIDI note as necessary. Note that the *map()* method provides a convenient way to scale the expected analog input values of approximately 0 to 1,000 to the smaller range that is used to represent MIDI velocity (0–127).

```
int midi_velocity=map(val, minimum, maximum, 0, 127);
```

handleFSR()

The *handleFSR()* function checks the status of the given *TouchPad* object. The methods emits a MIDI note providing that the value returned by *getPadValue()* is greater than the threshold constant and the method *getNoteOnStatus()*

returns false. The method emits a MIDI Note-Off message if the MIDI velocity is zero and *getNoteOnStatus()* returns true.

Listing 13.10 handleFSR function

```
void handleFSR(int index)
{
  //read FSR values, scale to midi velocity (0-127) and
  //output as MIDI notes
  int val=TouchPads[index].getPadValue();
  int last_value=0;

  //Scale the FSR value to a valid MIDI velocity range
  int midi_velocity=map(val, minimum, maximum, 0, 127);

  //===========Send a NOTE ON message if the given pad is
  //currently off
  if(val>THRESHOLD && TouchPads[index].
  getNoteOnStatus()==false)
  {

    TouchPads[index].setNoteOnStatus(true);

    //send a single note on for value greater than 0
    usbMIDI.sendNoteOn(MIDI_NOTES[current_bank][index],midi_
    velocity,1);
  }

  //===========Send a NOTE OFF message if the given pad is
  //currently on
  if(midi_velocity==0 && TouchPads[index].
  getNoteOnStatus()==true)
  {
    //send a single note off for velocity of 0
    usbMIDI.sendNoteOff(MIDI_NOTES[current_bank]
    [index],0,1);
    TouchPads[index].setNoteOnStatus(false);
  }
}
```

bankMode()

The *bankMode()* function (see Listing 13.11) tracks the status of each pad and sets the global variable named *current_bank* to the index of the selected pad. The method also emits a MIDI note represented by the first note in the MIDI_NOTES array to provide an aural clue as to the sound set that is associated with the bank. Note that the function *playMidiAlert()* provides a convenient method for outputting a consecutive Note-On and Note-Off message.

Listing 13.11 bankMode function

```
void bankMode()
{
  //poll FSRs to see if a new bank has been selected
  int val=0;
```

319

```
int last_bank=current_bank;
for(int i=0;i<NUM_PADS;i++)
{
  //Get the analog value of each pad
  val=TouchPads[i].getPadValue();

  //Set the index of the active bank if the given
  //pad reading is above the threshold
  if(val>THRESHOLD)
  {
    current_bank=i;
  }
}

//Provide audible feedback indicating the new note
//selection
if(current_bank!=last_bank)
{
  //Send a midi note on message followed by a midi note
  //off message
  playMidiAlert(MIDI_NOTES[current_bank][0], 100);
}
}
```

programMode()

The *programMode()* function is the most complex section of code in the Mongo firmware. The function calls the *playMode()* function so that pads can be played or auditioned during the editing process. *programMode()* also calls a helper function named *topRowPressed()* to see if a factory reset is necessary (see Listing 13.12).

Listing 13.12 programMode function

```
void programMode()
{
  //Call play mode so that pads can be played/auditioned
  //during the editing process
  playMode();

  //Check for factory reset
  if(topRowPressed())
  {
    factoryReset();
    flashLED(LED_A,10);
  }
```

The function then checks the value returned by *getPadValue()* and updates the variable current_pad to reflect the currently selected pad:

```
//poll FSRs to see if a new pad has been selected
int val=0;
for(int i=0;i<NUM_PADS;i++)
{
  //Get the analog value of each pad
  val=TouchPads[i].getPadValue();
```

```
  //Set the index of the active bank if the given pad
  //reading is above the threshold
  if(val>THRESHOLD)
  {
    current_pad=i;
    //set the encoder to match this value
    encoder.init(encoderPinA, encoderPinB, 20,
    MIDI_NOTES[current_bank][current_pad], 0, 127);
  }
}
```

The final section of code is responsible for polling the rotary encoder. The value for the currently selected pad is set to the value returned by the encoder class. The function also emits a MIDI note to provide an aural clue as to the currently selected sound (see Listing 13.13).

Listing 13.13 Reading the rotary encoder

```
//Get the value of the currently selected bank/pad
int note=MIDI_NOTES[current_bank][current_pad];

//Poll the encoder
int encoder_val = encoder.trackShaftPosition();
if(encoder_val != note)
{
    MIDI_NOTES[current_bank][current_pad] = encoder_val;
    playMidiAlert(encoder_val, 100);
    delay(300);
}
}
```

Storing Data

It is surprisingly easy to write and read data from EEPROM using the EEPROM class (which is made available by including the EEPROM.H header file). The function named *storeDataToEPROM()* demonstrates one approach. In this function, the *EEPROM.write()* method is used to store a byte representing the data ID to the first memory address in the device. When reading from EEPROM, a single byte can be read and checked against the value of the data ID to see if the data is valid.

The *write()* method takes an integer representing a memory location and a single byte representing the data to be stored to disk. Since bytes are used to store the values representing MIDI notes, it is easy to write the data. Note that larger data types require packing and unpacking of bytes and, thus, require additional steps to be stored and retrieved from EEPROM. The function is shown in its entirety in Listing 13.14.

Listing 13.14 storeDataToEPROM function

```
void storeDataToEPROM()
{
  //store the ID
  EEPROM.write(ID_ADDRESS, EEPROM_ID);
```

321

```
//loop through note array and store each item to EEPROM
int address=BASE_ADDRESS;
for(int bank=0; bank<6 ; bank++)
{
  for(int note=0;note<6;note++)
  {
    EEPROM.write(address, MIDI_NOTES[bank][note]);
    address++;
  }
}

flashLED(LED_B, 5);
}
```

The *readDataFromEPROM()* function is similar. This function tests the value of the first byte (located at ID_ADDRESS). If the byte is equal to the expected EEPROM_ID value, then the data are read from EEPROM. An unexpected value indicates that data have not yet been written, so the default values are written to nonvolatile memory via the *storeDataToEPROM()* function (see Listing 13.15).

Listing 13.15 readDataFromEPROM function

```
void readDataFromEPROM()
{
  //test for data ID byte:
  byte id=EEPROM.read(ID_ADDRESS);
  if(id==EEPROM_ID)
  {
    //read the data
    //loop through note array and load each item to EEPROM
    int address=BASE_ADDRESS;
    for(int bank=0; bank<6 ; bank++)
    {
      for(int note=0;note<6;note++)
      {
        MIDI_NOTES[bank][note]=EEPROM.read(address);
        address++;
      }
    }
    flashLED(LED_A, 5);

  }
  else{
    //No data found: write default data to EEPROM
    storeDataToEPROM();
  }

}
```

Helper Functions

We will conclude the discussion of the Mongo firmware by looking at three "helper" functions: *playMidiAlert()*, *flashLED()*, and *factoryReset()*.

playMidiAlert()

playMidiAlert() provides a convenient way to provide aural feedback when a user selects a new note value with the rotary encoder. The function simply outputs a MIDI Note-On message of the specified note value and velocity, delays for 50ms, and sends a corresponding Note-Off message to turn the note off. Since the function utilizes a delay, it should not be used in performance mode (see Listing 13.16).

Listing 13.16 playMidiAlert function

```
//Do not use in performance mode due to delay() function
void playMidiAlert(byte note, byte velocity)
{
    //Send midi note on:
    usbMIDI.sendNoteOn(note,velocity,1);
    delay(50);
    //Send midi note off:
    usbMIDI.sendNoteOff(note,0,1);
}
```

flashLED()

The *flashLED()* function provides visual feedback when data is read or stored to EEPROM. The function is similar to *playMidiAlert()*, but instead of sending MIDI values, the function blinks an LED a specified number of times (see Listing 13.17).

Listing 13.17 flashLed

```
void flashLED(int pin, int num_flashes)
{
  for(int c=0;c<num_flashes;c++)
  {
    digitalWrite(pin, HIGH);
    delay(100);
    digitalWrite(pin, LOW);
    delay(100);
  }
}
```

factoryReset()

The final helper function, *factoryReset()*, resets the values of the global MIDI_NOTES array. Note that only the first bank is shown in Listing 13.18.

Listing 13.18 factoryReset

```
void factoryReset()
{
    //Re-initialize sounds
    //bank 0
    MIDI_NOTES[0][0] = 42;
    MIDI_NOTES[0][1] = 46;
    MIDI_NOTES[0][2] = 44;
```

```
        MIDI_NOTES[0][3] = 35;
        MIDI_NOTES[0][4] = 38;
        MIDI_NOTES[0][5] = 49;
                  .
                  .
                  .
}
```

Building the Mongo Drum

As mentioned earlier in the chapter, the circuit for the Mongo drum can be created by using jumper wires to connect components on a breadboard. However, at some point you might want to create a more permanent version of the instrument. If you haven't done so already, be sure to read Chapter 11, Finalizing Projects, to learn about strategies for soldering circuits or creating your own custom printed circuit boards. Whatever method you choose, be sure to check your wiring and software before attempting to build the project using the steps outlined in the following paragraphs.

Circuit Design

There are many ways to approach a project like the Mongo drum, but for this project I elected to utilize a single circuit to house the microcontroller and a front panel to house the LEDs, switches, encoder, and FSRs. In a previous iteration of the project I used a small satellite board to house the buttons, LEDs, and rotary encoder, and that approach was also effective.

The primary function of the circuit is to house the Teensy 2.0 microcontroller and to provide connections between the analog and digital pins on the microcontroller with the force-sensing resistors, switches, LEDs, and encoder. The Teensy is relatively expensive, so I like the idea of having the option to use the microcontroller with other projects. For this reason, I used a socket instead of soldering the Teensy directly to the solderboard. This makes it easy to unplug the microcontroller for use in another project, and it also prevents damage that might occur by inadvertently overheating the Teensy during the soldering process. The force-sensing resistors are also expensive, so I purchased FSRs from a vendor that supplied an optional female plug. I soldered a pair of male header pins to the ends of a pair of copper leads and plugged the header pins into the female plug at the end of the FSR. The other end of the copper wire can be soldered directly to the appropriate location on the circuit.

Figure 13.8 shows one possible approach to laying out the Mongo circuit on stripboard. As was described earlier in the chapter, the FSRs connect to analog pins on the Teensy 2 and the rotary encoder, buttons, and LEDs are connected to digital pins. **As noted in the illustration, it is important to remember to drill out the copper stripboard holes in a column between the pins of the microcontroller to avoid a short circuit.** An oversized drill bit can be used to break the electrical connection without drilling all the way through the stripboard.

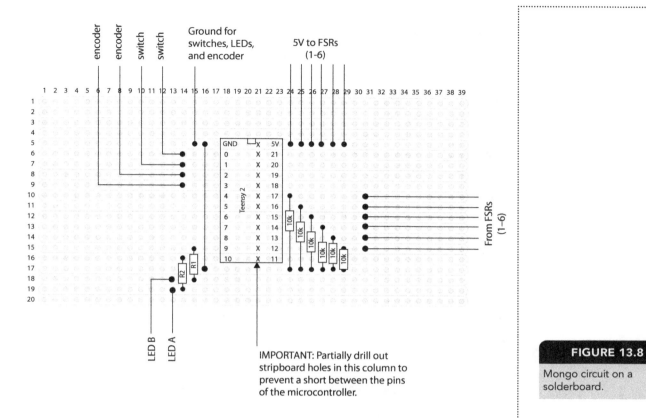

FIGURE 13.8

Mongo circuit on a solderboard.

Creating an Enclosure

In the first Mongo prototype I decided to create a custom enclosure for this project using 2 ½ × ¾" hardwood that is available at most home improvement stores. (Other options might include a cigar box similar to the one shown in Figure 13.1.) The first step is to cut the sides of the box to length. An *internal* dimension of 9 × 6" works well for this project, but be sure to add an additional 1½" to each side to account for the thickness of the wood.

Installing the Optional Panel Mount Adapter

Although optional, a USB panel mount adapter will provide a professional look to the project, and the best time to cut the hole for the panel mount is *before* you fasten the sides of the box. Measure your panel mount adapter to determine the size of the hole that is required, and use a pencil to mark the hole on the back of the box. I located the adapter on the back-right of the box, but any position will work as long as the internal USB cable can reach the microcontroller. Use a drill to remove most of the wood, and finish the hole with a coping saw or similar cutting tool.

Joining the Sides

I used a *mitre* joint to join the corners of the box, but a *half lap* or *butt joint* will also work. Advanced woodworkers will obviously want to consider a more elegant approach that might involve milling the wood and using attractive *dovetail* or *finger joints*.

Attaching the Bottom

For the bottom of the enclosure I used ¼" inch plywood. One strategy is to cut the plywood slightly larger than the box and use a router or plane and sanding block to trim away the excess. Use glue and brads to fasten the bottom of the box to the sides.

Adding Corner Posts and Circuit Base

You will want the top of the box to be inset so that the mouse pad is flush with the top, so cut four corner posts that are slightly shorter than the internal depth of the box. I used a value of 2¼" in order to leave about ¼" inch for the FSRs and mouse pad that will be affixed to the top (see Figure 13.9). Square dowels are available at most improvement stores and can be easily cut for corner posts.

Cut a length of scrap wood that is slightly larger than the bottom circuit and use wood glue to fasten the wood to the inside bottom of the enclosure. The wood will provide a base to which you can fasten the bottom circuit (see Figure 13.9).

FIGURE 13.9

Corner posts and circuit base.

Installing Components on the Face Plate

Assuming you created a box with an internal dimension of 9 × 6", cut another piece of ¼" plywood for use as the top panel. You will want to subtract about 1/16" from each dimension so the panel will comfortably fit the internal dimension of the box.

This would be a good time to sand all of the surfaces of the enclosure and apply your choice of stain and varnish. Although not essential, a nice finish will make your project look more professional and will help to protect the wood.

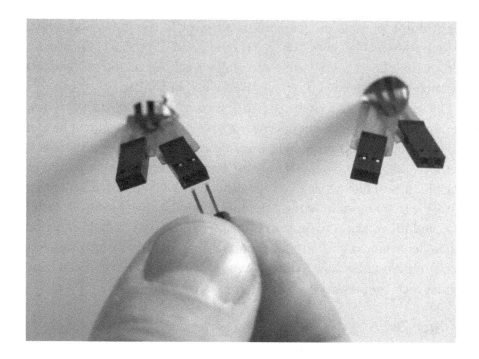

FIGURE 13.10

FSRs and holes for leads.

Before installing the FSRs, cut a piece of paper or clear plastic so that the sides are 6 ⅛ × 4⅞" and use a pen and ruler to mark the position of the force-sensing resistors. It is also helpful to mark the center of each FSR so that a dot can later be painted on the mouse pad to indicate the center of each FSR. Transfer the dimensions to the left side of the panel and drill three ⅜" holes that are centered between each column of FSRs (see Figure 13.10). The leads from each pair of FSRs can be threaded through the hole and connected via the male leads attached to the bottom circuit.

Painter's tape provides a simple method of attaching the FSRs to the panel. Carefully affix the tape to the sides of the FSRs. The weight of the mouse pad will help to hold the FSRs in position providing the pad is cut so that it fits snugly in the top inset.

Cut holes for through-hole components or a single hole if you use a control-panel subcircuit. Bolts and headers can be used to attach the subcircuit, or through-hole components can be attached directly to the top providing the material is a suitable thickness (less than or equal to about ⅛").

Finishing the Build

Once all of the components have been installed, it is time to test the unit. Download the code from the OUP website and compile and upload the software to the Teensy 2.0 as described in previous chapters. For this project, be sure to set the board type to "Teensy 2.0" and USB type to "MIDI" in the Tools menu of the Arduino programming environment prior to compiling and uploading code to the device. If all goes well, you should be able to connect the instrument to your computer via a USB cable and play virtual percussion in a sequencing application like Garage Band, Pro Tools, Cubase, or similar.

Debugging can be a challenge when a complex project doesn't work, but don't despair if the instrument doesn't work the first time you plug it in. Start by making a visual inspection of each wire and connection to see if there is a bad solder joint or if one or more leads have been inadvertently connected to the wrong pin. It is unlikely that all of the components are miswired, so a next step is to use the serial monitor in the development environment to check each FSR, button, and the rotary encoder. As described in Chapter 2, a multimeter can be useful in determining if a bad solder joint or other issue is creating problems in a circuit. You should be able to identify and fix any wiring issues if you methodically test each component and path in the circuit.

Moving On

Although there are a number of challenges presented in building an instrument like Mongo, the end result is an expressive instrument that will be a fun and useful addition to an electronic musician's toolkit. However, the real fun of working through the Mongo project is that it will open the door to your own creative design variations. Instead of FSRs, consider light-dependent resistors or infrared sensors. Alternatively, the project could be adapted to form the basis of a MIDI marimba or scaled down for a small finger drum built around two to four small FSRs.

In addition to exploring different sensors, consider how you might alter the underlying software. For example, touch-sensitive pads could provide a unique way to alter virtual synthesizer parameters such as filter cutoff or resonance, or the unit could provide a unique interface to algorithmic composition or pattern looping software. Yet another option might be to use the unit for touch-sensitive chord playback.

Stella Synthesizer Project

Stella Digital/Analog Synthesizer

The Stella Digital/Analog Synthesizer (see Figure 14.1) is a monophonic "retro" synth reminiscent of analog synthesizers by Moog and Korg. The synth utilizes the Mozzi sound synthesis library and features two tunable oscillators, resonant low-pass filter, and low-frequency oscillator that can be routed to modulate amplitude, filter cutoff, resonance, or frequency.

Although there are a minimal number of knobs and switches on the faceplate, a combination of rotary encoders and switches provides quite a bit of depth for sound synthesis and editing. As with many analog synthesizers, the Stella Synth is composed of four primary sections (see Figure 14.2) consisting of two oscillators, low-pass filter, low-frequency oscillator, and amplifier. Unlike analog synthesizers, all of the sounds are created and processed digitally using Tim Barrass's Mozzi sound synthesis library for Arduino.

Figure 14.3 provides a functional diagram of the unit. As is evident in the diagram, an oscillator switch toggles between six possible waveform editing modes, and an LFO switch routes the output of the LFO to five possible destinations.

The parts for the synthesizer are shown in Table 14.1. As with all of the projects in this book, be sure to use a solderless breadboard to experiment with the function of the unit before devoting time and money to a finalized version—many other possibilities exist in terms of the number of oscillators, LFO routing, integrating analog filters, and other possible enhancements.

FIGURE 14.1

Stella Synth.

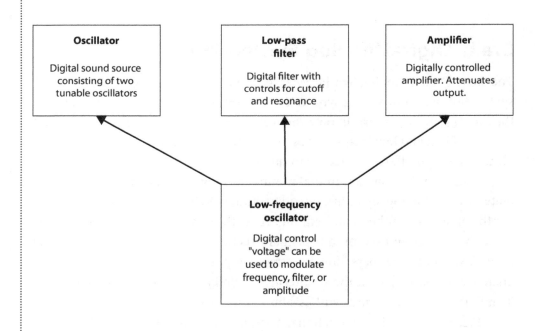

FIGURE 14.2

Stella Synth section diagram.

Front Panel

The components are mounted on inexpensive flashing material that can be purchased at most hardware stores. As described in Chapter 11, drawing software can be used to create layout guides for drilling and graphics for the front panel can be laminated to produce a professional look.

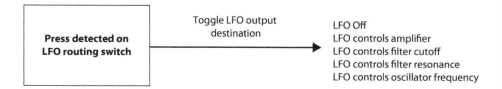

| Press detected on oscillator edit selection switch | Toggle between edit modes | OSC1: Select waveform
OSC1: Adjust octave offset
OSC1: Adjust tuning offset
OSC2: Select waveform
OSC2: Adjust octave offset
OSC2: Adjust tuning offset |

| Press detected on LFO routing switch | Toggle LFO output destination | LFO Off
LFO controls amplifier
LFO controls filter cutoff
LFO controls filter resonance
LFO controls oscillator frequency |

FIGURE 14.3

Stella synth functional diagram.

TABLE 14.1 Parts for Stella Synth

QTY	Description	Notes	Approx. cost
1	SPST switch for battery power		$1.00
5	Potentiometers (4 @10k, 1 @1M	Used for filter and LFO and amplitude	<$1.00 each
2	Rotary encoders with pushbutton	Also consider encoders and separate pushbuttons	$1.50–$3.50 each
1	Serial 7-segment display		$13.00
1	¼" mono audio jack		$1.00
1	Arduino UNO or standalone Arduino components	See Chapter 12 for standalone Arduino parts	$10.00–$25.00
1	Enclosure and faceplate	Homemade or commercial	$1–10
MSCL	Solid insulated copper wire	22 AWG	
1	Optional: MIDI 5-pin DIN and MIDI input components	See Chapter 5	$3
1	Optional: Solderable breadboard for creating "standalone" version of project		$2.00–$5.00
1	270Ω resistor and 100n capacitor	RC filter for audio output	<$0.50
1	LM358 op amp or similar	Used to buffer audio output	<$1.00

Circuitry

The electronics for the Stella Synth consist primarily of connections between components on the faceplate and respective pins on an Arduino. On the other hand, it is all too easy to create "spaghetti wiring" when so many components are in close proximity. One solution, which can be seen in Figure 14.4, is to tie ground connections from component to component on the faceplate. A similar approach can be used for +5V power connections from the Arduino. With this approach, only a single +5V and ground connection is needed to provide power to the entire faceplate. (Note that I elected to run separate connections to the 7-segment display so that it would be easier to disconnect should I want to use the unit in another project.)

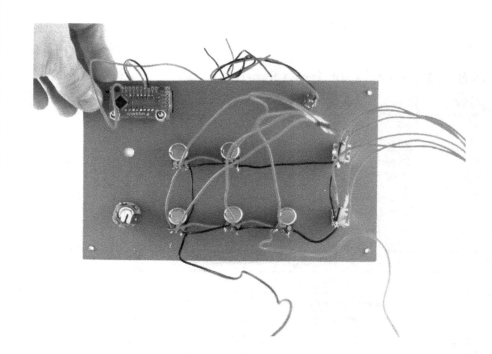

FIGURE 14.4

Using common ground connections to simplify wiring (back of Stella synth shown).

Audio output comes from a pulse-width modulation signal on pin 9 running through the circuit in Figure 14.5. I elected to use the pin assignments shown in Table 14.2 for the Stella Synth.

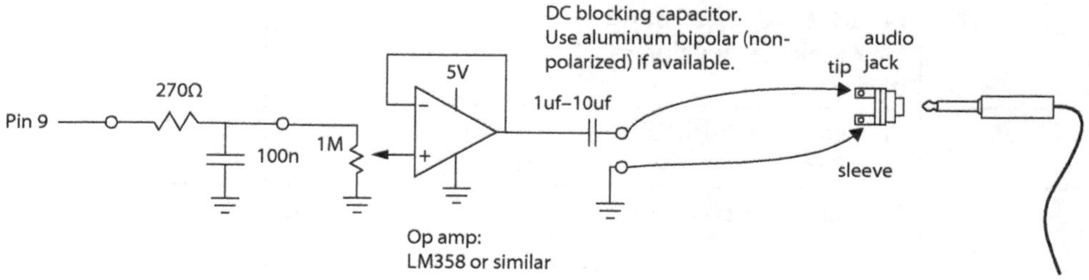

FIGURE 14.5

PWM output circuit.

TABLE 14.2 Stella Synth Pin Assignments

Component	Arduino UNO Pin
PWM output	9
Reserved for hi-fi audio output	10
Oscillator encoder A pin	2
Oscillator encoder B pin	3
Oscillator encoder pushbutton	4
LFO encoder A pin	5
LFO encoder B pin	6
LFO pushbutton	7
Low-pass filter cutoff	A0
Low-pass filter resonance	A1
LFO rate	A2
LFO Depth	A3
Amplitude level	A4
7-segment serial display	8 (using Software Serial library)
MIDI input	0 (RX)

Software: Encoders and Buttons

One small setback I experienced with the Stella Synth is that the convenience classes *EasyButton* and *RotaryEncoder* do not work with the Mozzi library. This is due to the fact that time functions including *millis()* are disabled by the library. A workaround was to create new versions of the classes, *EasyMozziButton* and *MozziEncoder*, to work with the library. The primary difference is that the new versions of the classes use Mozzi's *audioTicks()* function instead of *millis()*.

Another challenge is that, in the case of the oscillator encoder, one encoder is used to establish values for multiple editing operations. One approach would be to update the encoder with new values each time a new editing operation is selected, but a more elegant approach is to use a pointer. With a pointer, numerous rotary encoder objects can be created with different range values but *with the same pin assignments*. When a new editing mode is selected, all that needs to be done is to update the pointer to point to a new encoder object:

```
//These encoders handle oscillator editing
EasyMozziEncoder    wave1SelectionEncoder;
EasyMozziEncoder    wave1OctaveEncoder;
  .
  .
  .

//Set up a pointer to point at the current wave encoder
EasyMozziEncoder    * pOscEncoder;
pOscEncoder = &wave1SelectionEncoder;
```

```
//now call a method of wave1SelectionEncoder
pOscEncoder->trackShaftPosition();

//Now point to another encoder object
pOscEncoder = &wave1OctaveEcoder
```

Serial7Segment Class

The serial 7-segment display is easy to use, but a helper class makes it even easier and simplifies the logic of the main sketch. The class, which is available on the OUP website, takes a pointer to a SoftwareSerial object and provides convenience functions for outputting messages, setting the brightness, and clearing the display (see Listing 14.1). As I have mentioned numerous times in this book, C++ classes like *Serial7Segment* can be useful building blocks by encapsulating functionality into objects that are easy to use in other projects.

Listing 14.1 Serial7Segment class

```
#ifndef__SERIAL7SEGMENT
#define__SERIAL7SEGMENT

#include <SoftwareSerial.h>

class Serial7Segment
{
    public:
    SoftwareSerial* m_pSerialDisplay;
    Serial7Segment(SoftwareSerial* pSerial)
    {
        m_pSerialDisplay = pSerial;
        //start serial connection. Consider moving to an
        //init() method
        pSerial->begin(9600);
    };

    void printMessage(char *msg)
    {
        m_pSerialDisplay->write(0x76);   //Clear the display
        m_pSerialDisplay->print(msg);
    }

    void printMessage(int value)
    {
        m_pSerialDisplay->write(0x76);   //Clear the display
        m_pSerialDisplay->print(value);
    }

    void setBrightness(byte value)
    {
        m_pSerialDisplay->write(0x7A);   // Set brightness
                                         // command byte
        m_pSerialDisplay->write(value);  // brightness data
                                         // byte
```

334

```
    }

    void clearDisplay()
    {
        m_pSerialDisplay->write(0x76);  // Clear display
    }
};
#endif
```

Initialization of the Serial7Segment class can be seen in the following preamble section.

Preamble

As can also be seen in the synthesizer "preamble" in Listing 14.2, numerous variables are established to track the values of the potentiometers and for calculation of waveforms. One new class, *AutoMap*, is provided by the Mozzi library and provides a way to map inputs to a range of values in a way that is more efficient than the built-in *map()* function. *AutoMap* takes the anticipated range and scaling range as parameters. As with all of the examples in this chapter, enumerations are used as a convenience for handling oscillator editing, LFO routing, and waveform selection. The preamble is shown in its entirety in Listing 14.2.

Listing 14.2 Stella Synth preamble

```
#include <MozziGuts.h>
#include <Oscil.h> // oscillator template

//Table data
#include <tables/triangle_valve_2048_int8.h>
#include <tables/saw2048_int8.h>
#include <tables/sin2048_int8.h>

//Mscl. header files
#include <LowPassFilter.h>
#include <RollingAverage.h>
#include <mozzi_midi.h>
#include <AutoMap.h>
#include <SoftwareSerial.h>
#include "Serial7Segment.h"
#include "EasyMozziButton.h"
#include "MozziEncoder.h"
#include <MIDI.h>

MIDI_CREATE_DEFAULT_INSTANCE();

//LFO waveform
Oscil <SIN2048_NUM_CELLS, AUDIO_RATE> lfo(SIN2048_DATA);

//OSC1 waveforms:
Oscil<TRIANGLE_VALVE_2048_NUM_CELLS, AUDIO_RATE>
osc1a(TRIANGLE_VALVE_2048_DATA);
Oscil<SAW2048_NUM_CELLS, AUDIO_RATE> osc1b(SAW2048_DATA);
```

```
//OSC2 waveforms:
Oscil<TRIANGLE_VALVE_2048_NUM_CELLS, AUDIO_RATE>
osc2a(TRIANGLE_VALVE_2048_DATA);
Oscil<SAW2048_NUM_CELLS, AUDIO_RATE> osc2b(SAW2048_DATA);

//Enumeration to track active waveform
enum{triangle, saw};

//use #define for CONTROL_RATE, not a constant
#define CONTROL_RATE 128 // use powers of 2

//Set up 7-segment serial display which takes a pointer
//to an instance of SoftwareSerial.
#define DISPLAYPINTX   8
SoftwareSerial softwareSerial(11, DISPLAYPINTX);
Serial7Segment display(&softwareSerial);

//Pin definitions
#define MIDIINPIN       0
#define OSCENCODERA     2
#define OSCENCODERB     3
#define OSCPUSHPIN      4
#define LFOENCODERA     5
#define LFOENCODERB     6
#define LFOPUSHPIN      7
#define LPCUTOFF        A0
#define LPRESONANCE     A1
#define LFORATE         A2
#define LFODEPTH        A3
#define AMPLEVEL        A4

//Create an instance of a low pass filter
LowPassFilter lp_filter;

//Create button and encoder objects
EasyMozziButton  oscPushButton;
MozziEncoder     lfoEncoder;
EasyMozziButton  lfoPushButton;

//These encoders handle oscillator editing
MozziEncoder     wave1SelectionEncoder;
MozziEncoder     wave1OctaveEncoder;
MozziEncoder     wave1TuningEncoder;
MozziEncoder     wave2SelectionEncoder;
MozziEncoder     wave2OctaveEncoder;
MozziEncoder     wave2TuningEncoder;

//Set up a pointer that will point to the active wave
//encoder
MozziEncoder * pOscEncoder;

//Variables to track potentiometers
int ampLevel = 100;
int depth = 0;
int rate = 1;

//Globals for audio calculation
int osc1_wave_selection = triangle;
int osc1_octave_offset = 0;
int osc1_tune_offset = 0;
```

336

```
int osc2_wave_selection = triangle;
int osc2_octave_offset = 0;
int osc2_tune_offset = 0;
float current_osc1_frequency;
float current_osc2_frequency;
byte current_midi_note = 60;

//Tip: set note_on = true for testing sans MIDI input
boolean note_on = false;

//Set up auto map
AutoMap cutoffMap(0, 1023, 0, 255);
AutoMap resonanceMap(0, 1023, 0, 255);
AutoMap volumeMap(0, 1023, 0, 255);
AutoMap depthMap(0, 1023, 0, 5);
AutoMap rateMap(0, 1023, 0, 5000);
AutoMap cvToCutoff(0, 1275, 0, 255);
AutoMap cvToResonance(0, 1275, 0, 255);
AutoMap cvToAmplitude(0, 1275, 0, 255);

//Enumeration for oscillator editing
enum{osc1_wave, osc1_octave, osc1_tuning, osc2_wave,
osc2_octave, osc2_tuning};
int osc_selection;

//Enumeration for LFO editing
enum{lfo_off, lfo_amplitude, lfo_cutoff, lfo_resonance,
lfo_cutoff_and_resonance, lfo_frequency};
int lfo_selection;
```

Setup()

As is evident in Listing 14.3, the setup function sets up MIDI callback functions and calls the *MIDI.begin()* method, initializes the display, establishes default selections for the oscillator and LFO, initializes the Mozzi library, and initializes buttons and encoders.

Listing 14.3 Stella Synth Setup() function

```
void setup()
{
    //Set up MIDI
    MIDI.setHandleNoteOff(handleNoteOff);
    MIDI.setHandleNoteOn(handleNoteOn);

    //Start MIDI at standard baud rate of 31250;
    MIDI.begin();

    //Initialize display
    display.setBrightness(255);
    display.clearDisplay();
    display.printMessage("STEL");
    delay(1000); //Wait a second before starting

    osc_selection = osc1_wave;
    //Point to the selection encoder
```

```
pOscEncoder = &wave1SelectionEncoder;
lfo_selection = lfo_off;

startMozzi(CONTROL_RATE); // set control rate
setFrequencyFromMidiNote(current_midi_note);

oscPushButton.init(OSCPUSHPIN, 5000);
lfoEncoder.init(LFOENCODERB, LFOENCODERA,
        5, 50, 1, 100);
lfoPushButton.init(LFOPUSHPIN, 5000);

//Set up encoders for oscillator editing
wave1SelectionEncoder.init(OSCENCODERB, OSCENCODERA,
        50, 0, 0, 1);
wave1OctaveEncoder.init(OSCENCODERB, OSCENCODERA,
        50, 0, -4, 5);
wave1TuningEncoder.init(OSCENCODERB, OSCENCODERA,
        50, 0, 0, 100);
wave2SelectionEncoder.init(OSCENCODERB, OSCENCODERA,
        50, 0, 0, 1);
wave2OctaveEncoder.init(OSCENCODERB, OSCENCODERA,
        50, 0,-4, 5);
wave2TuningEncoder.init(OSCENCODERB, OSCENCODERA,
        50, 0, 0, 100);
}
```

Stella Synth Tasks

The remaining logic of the Stella Synth can be broken down into the following tasks:

- Responding to potentiometer changes
- Responding to oscillator selection button events
- Responding to oscillator encoder changes
- Responding to LFO selection button events
- Calculating samples in the *updateAudio() function*
- Responding to incoming MIDI data

Although there is quite a bit of code, the tasks can be organized into logical groups that are detailed in the following paragraphs.

Tracking Potentiometers

Unlike most Arduino sketches, most of the action happens in a function called *updateControl().*[1] Tim Barrass, the author of the library, provides the function as a way to minimize the timing impact of reading values in the main *loop()*. After all, a reduced number of input samples won't really matter for controllers like potentiometers.

The first part of *updateControl()* calls the *MIDI.read()* method and also reads the values of each pot using the AutoMap functionality to assign each value to its respective global variable (see Listing 14.4).

Listing 14.4 Reading potentiometer values

```
void updateControl()
{
    //Check for MIDI input
    MIDI.read();

    //==========READ THE POTENTIOMETERS
    int cutoff = mozziAnalogRead(LPCUTOFF);
    lp_filter.setCutoffFreq(cutoffMap(cutoff));

    int res = mozziAnalogRead(LPRESONANCE);
    lp_filter.setResonance(resonanceMap(res));

    ampLevel = mozziAnalogRead(AMPLEVEL);
    ampLevel = volumeMap(ampLevel);

    rate = mozziAnalogRead(LFORATE);
    rate = rateMap(rate);
    lfo.setFreq(rate);

    depth = mozziAnalogRead(LFODEPTH);
    depth = depthMap(depth);
        .
        .
        .
```

Handling the LFO

Next, *updateControl()* calculates a digital "control voltage" level and applies the voltage to frequency, cutoff, resonance, or amplitude depending on the current status of the LFO selection switch (see Listing 14.5). As with an analog synthesizer, the digital control voltage can be used to modulate synthesizer components. Note that a right-shift is used to quickly attenuate the voltage when it is used as a control source for frequency modulation in order to reduce the level to a more practical range. Many other routings and control-voltage manipulation are possible, so this section of code is a good place to add your own custom modulation features.

Listing 14.5 Handling LFO data

```
    //==========HANDLE THE LFO
    //Calculate control voltage amount
    long control_voltage = lfo.next() * depth;

    if(control_voltage && lfo_selection != lfo_off)
    {
        //Respond to control voltage depending on current
        //lfo selection
        if(lfo_selection == lfo_frequency)
        {
            int attenuated_voltage = control_voltage >> 1;
            //Update oscillators
            osc1a.setFreq(current_osc1_frequency +
                    attenuated_voltage);
            osc1b.setFreq(current_osc1_frequency +
                    attenuated_voltage);
```

339

```
                              osc2a.setFreq(current_osc2_frequency +
                              attenuated_voltage);
                              osc2b.setFreq(current_osc2_frequency +
                              attenuated_voltage);
                      }

                      if(lfo_selection == lfo_cutoff)
                      {
                              lp_filter.setCutoffFreq(cvToCutoff(control_
                              voltage));
                      }
                      if(lfo_selection == lfo_resonance)
                      {
                              lp_filter.setResonance(cvToResonance(control_
                              voltage));
                      }
                      if(lfo_selection == lfo_amplitude)
                      {
                              ampLevel = cvToAmplitude(control_voltage);
                      }


              }
```

Handling Pushbuttons and Encoder Movement

The final part of *updateControl()* checks the status of the buttons and calls an appropriate handler (which will be described in a moment). Similarly, a pointer to an encoder is used to track the position of the shaft and update the 7-segment display (see Listing 14.6). The final section of code overrides the current amplitude level to stop all sound if no MIDI notes are active.

Listing 14.6 Checking the status of buttons and rotary encoders

```
        //==========CHECK THE PUSHBUTTONS
        if(oscPushButton.checkButtonPressed())
        {
            oscSelectBtn();
        }
        if(lfoPushButton.checkButtonPressed())
        {
            lfoSelectBtn();
        }

    //Use a pointer to simplify oscillator editing
    int last_value = pOscEncoder->getValue();
    if(pOscEncoder->trackShaftPosition() != last_value)
    {
       //Call encoder change function
       onOscValueChange();
       //Display the value:
       display.printMessage(pOscEncoder->getValue());
    }

    //override amplitude settings if no note is currently
    //playing
```

```
if(note_on == false)
{
    ampLevel = 0;
}

}
```

Oscillator Button Selection Function

Oscillator selection is handled by a function named *oscSelectBtn()*. The function increments the active editing mode and outputs the results to the display. Note how the enumerations created in the preamble simplify the logic in this section of code (see Listing 14.7).

Listing 14.7 Handling button and rotary encoder events

```
void oscSelectBtn()
{
    osc_selection++;
    //Wrap around to first edit mode if necessary
    if(osc_selection > osc2_tuning)
    {
        osc_selection = osc1_wave;
    }

    //Update pointer and print display current edit mode
    switch(osc_selection)
    {
        case osc1_wave:
          pOscEncoder = &wave1SelectionEncoder;
          display.printMessage("OSC1");
          break;
        case osc1_octave:
          pOscEncoder = &wave1OctaveEncoder;
          display.printMessage("OCT1");
          break;
        case osc1_tuning:
          pOscEncoder = &wave1TuningEncoder;
          display.printMessage("TUN1");
          break;
        case osc2_wave:
          pOscEncoder = &wave2SelectionEncoder;
          display.printMessage("OSC2");
          break;
        case osc2_octave:
          pOscEncoder = &wave2OctaveEncoder;
          display.printMessage("OCT2");
          break;
        case osc2_tuning:
          pOscEncoder = &wave2TuningEncoder;
          display.printMessage("TUN2");
          break;
    }
}
```

341

LFO Selection Function

The function *lfoSelectBtn()* works in a similar way by incrementing the current selection and printing the results to the display (see Listing 14.8). Note that the frequency of the oscillators is reestablished at the end of the function. This prevents the LFO from leaving the oscillators on a random pitch when the operation mode changes from low-frequency pitch modulation to another mode.

Listing 14.8 LFO selection function

```
void lfoSelectBtn()
{
   lfo_selection++;
   //Wrap to first LFO edit mode if necessary
   if(lfo_selection > lfo_frequency)
   {
      lfo_selection = lfo_off;
   }

   //Display current LFO edit mode
   switch(lfo_selection)
   {
      case lfo_off:
         display.printMessage("OFF");    break;
      case lfo_cutoff:
         display.printMessage("CUT");    break;
      case lfo_resonance:
         display.printMessage("RES");    break;
      case lfo_amplitude:
         display.printMessage("VOL");    break;
      case lfo_frequency:
         display.printMessage("FREQ");   break;
   }

   //Reset frequency if changing from frequency modulation
   if(lfo_selection != lfo_frequency)
   {
      //Update oscillators
      osc1a.setFreq(current_osc1_frequency);
      osc1b.setFreq(current_osc1_frequency);
      osc2a.setFreq(current_osc2_frequency);
      osc2b.setFreq(current_osc2_frequency);
   }
}
```

Oscillator Value Change Function

There is only one more function to complete the Stella Synth event handling: *onOscValueChange()* is called in response to changes in the oscillator encoder. Values for the currently selected wave, octave, and tuning offset are gathered by polling the appropriate encoder. As with the other functions, a *switch()* statement is used for the underlying logic although a series of "if" statements could also be used (see Listing 14.9).

Listing 14.9 Oscillator value change function

```
void onOscValueChange()
{
   //Update global variables from encoder values
   switch(osc_selection)
   {
      case osc1_wave:
        osc1_wave_selection = wave1SelectionEncoder.
        getValue();
        break;
      case osc1_octave:
        osc1_octave_offset = wave1OctaveEncoder.getValue();
        break;
      case osc1_tuning:
        osc1_tune_offset = wave1TuningEncoder.getValue();
        break;
      case osc2_wave:
        osc2_wave_selection = wave2SelectionEncoder.
        getValue();
        break;
      case osc2_octave:
        osc2_octave_offset = wave2OctaveEncoder.getValue();
        break;
      case osc2_tuning:
        osc2_tune_offset = wave2TuningEncoder.getValue();
        break;
   }

   //Update frequency
   setFrequencyFromMidiNote(current_midi_note);
}
```

SetFrequencyFromMidiNote()

The function named *setFrequencyFromMidiNote()* is similar to a function that was described in Chapter 9. The function takes an *unsigned char* representing a MIDI note as a parameter and calculates a frequency in Hz. The function also uses the values for octave and tuning in the calculation, which enables the device to respond with an appropriate octave and tuning offset as set in the oscillator editor (see Listing 14.10).

Listing 14.10 setFrequencyFromMidiNote

```
void setFrequencyFromMidiNote(unsigned char note)
{
    // simple but less accurate
    current_osc1_frequency = mtof(note + (osc1_octave_
          offset * 12));
    current_osc2_frequency = mtof(note + (osc2_octave_
          offset * 12));

    //Add the tuning offsets...scale by 0.5 for more precise
    //tuning
    current_osc1_frequency += (float)osc1_tune_offset * 0.5;
```

343

```
current_osc2_frequency += (float)osc2_tune_
offset * 0.5;

//update the oscillators
osc1a.setFreq(current_osc1_frequency);
osc1b.setFreq(current_osc1_frequency);
osc2a.setFreq(current_osc2_frequency);
osc2b.setFreq(current_osc2_frequency);
current_midi_note = note;
}
```

Responding to Incoming MIDI Data

Incoming MIDI notes are handled by two callback functions, *handleNoteOff()* and *handleNoteOn()*, that are attached to the global MIDI object in the main *setup()* function. These functions are automatically called by the MIDI object as necessary when the *MIDI.read()* method is called in the *updateControl()* function.

Note-Off Messages

The Note-Off handler in Listing 14.11 is simple. Its job is to set the global amplitude level to zero and to toggle the global Boolean variable, *note_on*, to false as appropriate. However, one thing I noticed in testing the instrument is that some notes were inadvertently cut off when playing legato passages. The "if" statement ensures that the currently active note is not turned off if a previously played note is released after its initial attack.

Listing 14.11 *handleNoteOff()*

```
void handleNoteOff(byte channel, byte note, byte velocity)
{
    //Avoid turning off sound if another note is playing
    if(note == current_midi_note)
    {
        ampLevel = 0;
        note_on = false;
    }
}
```

Note-On Messages

Handling Note-On messages is slightly more complex. As is evident in Listing 14.12, the function updates the value of *current_midi_note*, a global variable, establishes the new oscillator frequency, and updates the display to show the incoming note value. Some MIDI streams utilize Note-On messages with a velocity of zero in lieu of Note-Off messages, so the function concludes by updating the *note_on* status and amplitude as necessary.

Listing 14.12 *handleNoteOn()*

```
void handleNoteOn(byte channel, byte note, byte velocity)
{
    current_midi_note = note;
```

```
setFrequencyFromMidiNote(current_midi_note);
note_on = true;
//Display the current MIDI note
display.printMessage(note);

//Some manufacturers use Note-On with velocity = 0 for
Note-Off
if(velocity == 0 && note == current_midi_note)
{
    ampLevel = 0;
    note_on = false;
}
}
```

updateAudio()

Tim Barrass, the author of the Mozzi library, does a wonderful job of creating extensible code using advanced C++ techniques such as class templates. However, one negative aspect of templates is that they make certain programming tasks, such as using a single pointer to access multiple derived classes, impractical. That is not a criticism of the library but one of the trade-offs that occurs with any design decision. In the case of the *Stella Synth*, it means that some extra "if" statements are required to retrieve a sample from the active oscillators. In this case, the *updateAudio()* function keeps all of the oscillators (including the inactive oscillators) in synch by calling the *next()* method for each oscillator object. Once a new sample has been calculated, the appropriate sample is assigned to the local variables *osc1_sample* and *osc2_sample* as shown in Listing 14.13.

Listing 14.13 updateAudio()

```
int updateAudio()
{
    //Update OSC1 waveforms
    char osc1a_sample = osc1a.next();
    char osc1b_sample = osc1b.next();

    //Update OSC2 waveforms
    char osc2a_sample = osc2a.next();
    char osc2b_sample = osc2b.next();

    //Grab the appropriate sample for processing
    char osc1_sample;
    if(osc1_wave_selection == triangle)
    {
        osc1_sample = osc1a_sample;
    }else{
        osc1_sample = osc1b_sample;
    }

    char osc2_sample;
    if(osc2_wave_selection == triangle)
    {
        osc2_sample = osc2a_sample;
```

345

```
    }else{
        osc2_sample = osc2b_sample;
    }

    //Combine the samples and attenuate, then multiply by
    //ampLevel and attenuate again

    int signal = (lp_filter.next((osc1_sample +
                    osc2_sample)>>1) *
                    ampLevel) >> 8;

    //return the processed sample
    return (int) signal;
}
```

If you are new to programming, the final section of code may be unintelligible.

```
int signal = (lp_filter.next((osc1_sample+osc2_sample)>>1) *
    ampLevel) >> 8;
```

However, the meaning becomes clearer if we break the line into smaller chunks. Start by looking at the code in the innermost parenthesis:

```
((osc1_sample+osc2_sample)>>1)
```

Here, the output sample from oscillators 1 and 2 are combined, and then the results are shifted to the right to keep the result in a valid range. The right shift is simply a quick way to divide by 2.

Moving to the next set of parenthesis, the results of the sum and shift are sent to the *next()* method of the low-pass filter:

```
lp_filter.next(sum of osc1 and os2 divided by 2)
```

Finally, the output of the filter (a processed version of the combined oscillator samples) is multiplied by the current amplitude level and the results are shifted eight times to the right to reduce the output once more to an appropriate range.

```
(filter out * amp level) >> 8 (right-shift by 8 is a fast way
to divide by 255)
```

Stella Synth in Action

Video and audio demonstrations for the Stella Synth are provided at the OUP website. It's a fairly complex sketch, but the results are well worth it in the form of a great sounding (and extensible) homemade synthesizer.

14.1 STELLA SYNTH

Enhancements

There are many enhancements to consider before finalizing the project to suit your tastes. For examples, the Mozzi library provides many waveform samples that could be substituted for the triangle and sawtooth waveforms used in this example. Another option might be to utilize an active low-pass filter by following the single-supply low-pass filter design in the LM358 (or similar) op amp datasheet. Yet another approach would be to provide a switch to toggle between external MIDI input and external voltage control. In this case, one of the analog input ports could be configured to scale the 0 to 5V voltage range to an appropriate frequency based on a variety of components such as a force-sensing resistor, photo cell, proximity sensor, or similar.

Conclusion

We have covered a lot of ground in this chapter, so don't be discouraged if some concepts like pointers or callbacks are not entirely clear. The beauty of C++ classes is that you can use libraries like *Mozzi* or *Serial7Segment* without knowing or understanding all of the inner details. You can still do some amazing things with an Arduino even if you are new to programming—and using libraries created by more experienced programmers is a great way to gain more experience. All of the source code from these projects is available for download at the OUP website, and I encourage you to download the code and begin exploring. Comprehension *will* grow as you experiment and revisit topics. And just like learning to play an instrument, there is nothing like hands-on practice to reinforce concepts.

Also keep in mind that challenging topics take time to master. Pianist Kenny Werner makes reference to the importance of patience as he describes the process of watching a sunrise in his book, *Effortless Mastery*:

> For the seeker, this sunrise is a metaphor, to have patience with each stage before it evolves into the next. The sun rose in its own time. It may be slow, but it always happens.[2]

347

Step Sequencer Project

The Step Sequencer project harkens back to the days of early analog synthesis when voltage-controlled sequencer modules were used to create hypnotic repeating patterns of notes. This digital version, which maintains the flavor of a "retro" synthesizer, provides several features including the ability to store sequences in nonvolatile memory and to edit the rate, number of steps, and transposition of each sequence. Of course, the digital underpinnings of the project make it easy to add additional features such as variable step length or MIDI output.

Hardware and Function

As with all of the projects in this book, I strongly encourage the use of a solderless breadboard to test and perfect circuits and code prior to spending the time and effort to create a permanent version of the project. There are a number of possible enhancements that could be incorporated, so the process of breadboarding will allow an opportunity to alter the project to suit your particular preferences.

One version of the completed project can be seen in Figure 15.1. The push button of a combination rotary encoder/switch is used to select one of four operation modes, and the encoder is used to select or alter notes while in edit mode. Two tactile switches (which are soldered to an LED subcircuit)

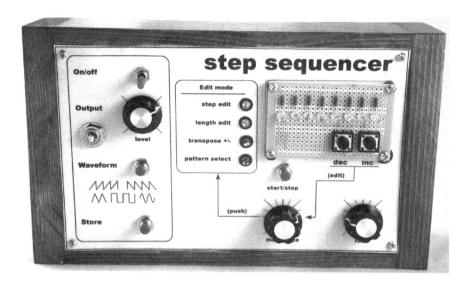

FIGURE 15.1

Step sequencer.

work in conjunction with the encoder for sequence editing. Three through-hole buttons provide the ability to select a waveform, store sequences to EPROM, or start and stop the sequencer. Finally, a 10k potentiometer is used to adjust the playback rate and a 1M potentiometer attenuates the audio output.

Getting Started

The primary parts that were used to make the step sequencer are listed in Table 15.1, but bear in mind that many substitutions are possible. For example, an additional through-hole switch could be substituted for the combination through-hole encoder/switch, or additional status LEDs could be configured to accommodate additional modes of operation.

TABLE 15.1 Primary Parts

QTY	Description	Notes	Approx. cost
12	LEDs	8 for step sequencer, 4 for mode status	$0.35 each
12	~330Ω resistors	For use with LEDs	$.025 each
1	10kΩ potentiometer	Used to control step rate	$1.00
1	1MΩ potentiometer	For adjusting output level	$1.00
1	Thru-hole rotary encoder with momentary switch	Knob is optional. Use to select operation mode and edit sequences.	$1.00
3–4	Thru-hole momentary switches	Use extra push button for mode selection if encoder with push button is not available.	$0.50–$1.00 each

(continued)

TABLE 15.1 Continued

QTY	Description	Notes	Approx. cost
4	LED mounting holders	For mounting status LEDs to panel	$0.25 each
1	SPST toggle switch	Used to connect or disconnect battery power for standalone operation	$1–2
1	¼" TS mono panel mount audio jack	Audio output	$1–2
1	Radio Shack multipurpose PC board with 417 holes	Used for LED sequence subassembly	$2.50
2	Tactile switches	Mounted to LED sub assembly. Used to select sequence step, transposition, etc.	$16
1	74HC595 Shift Register Adaptor	Used to connect multiple LEDs to Arduino	$0.75
1–2	Section of Veroboard	Used for shift register subcircuit. Optionally used for "standalone" Arduino circuit.	$1.00
Various	Solid insulated copper wire	22AWG hookup wire for LED subcircuit, etc.	
Optional	Parts for "standalone" Arduino	See Chapter 12	~10.00
Optional	Enclosure	Homemade, commercial, cigar box, etc.	
1	5 × 8 metal flashing from hardware store	Front panel	$0.50
1	LM358 (or similar) dual op amp	For unity gain buffer/ audio output	$1.00
MSCL	Parts for PWM output including DC blocking capacitor	See Chapter 9	$1.00–$2.00
MSCL	Nuts, bolts, and screws	For mounting LED subcircuit to front panel and (optionally) mounting panel to an enclosure	

Making Connections

The components on the front panel are connected to the Arduino pins using the assignments shown in Table 15.2.

A circuit diagram of the primary components can be seen in Figure 15.2. Note that the encoder and switches will be handled by the *EasyButton* and *RotaryEncoder* classes presented in Chapter 8, so internal pullup resistors will

TABLE 15.2 Pin Assignments

Pin	Component	Notes
D0	No connection	
D1	Encoder switch	Use encoder switch or separate pushbutton component
D2	Encoder: left	Used to lower pitch of a step
D3	Encoder: right	Used to raise pitch of a step
D4	Tactile switch 1	Selects previous step, length, pattern, or transposition
D5	Tactile switch 2	Selects next step, length, pattern, or transposition
D6	PWM	PWM Audio output
D7	Button 1	Sequence start/stop
D8	Button 2	Store (writes all sequences to EEPROM)
D9	Button 3	Wave toggle (selects waveform)
D10	Shift register: latch pin	See next section
D11	Shift register: data pin	See next section
D12	Shift register: clock pin	See next section
D13	No connection	
A0	Step edit LED	Mode status
A1	Length edit LED	Mode status
A2	Transposition edit LED	Mode status
A3	Sequence select LED	Mode status
A4	Potentiometer 1	Step rate
A5	No connection	

be configured for those components during initialization of the classes. The only unusual aspect of the circuit that has not been previously covered are the four status LEDs connected to analog ports A0–A3. Although those ports are usually used for analog input, they can also function as a standard digital output and, thus, are capable of driving an LED through an appropriate resistor. As you will see in a moment, the eight sequencer LEDs are connected via a shift register.

Shift Register

As is evident in the previous illustration, there aren't enough pins left to drive the sequence LEDs. There are several approaches to this problem, but one of the easiest methods is to use a Shift-Out Register such as the 74HC595. The IC can handle eight LEDs with just three connections consisting of data, latch, and clock lines (in addition to power and ground). The pinout for the shift register and connections to LEDs (through a current-limiting resistor) are shown in Figure 15.3.

Audio out: to LP filter, unity
gain buffer, and DC-blocking
capacitor (see Chapter 9)

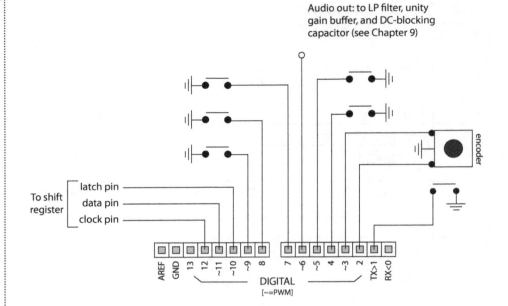

To shift
register

latch pin
data pin
clock pin

AREF GND 13 12 ~11 ~10 ~9 8   7 ~6 ~5 4 ~3 2 TX>1 RX<0

DIGITAL
[~=PWM]

encoder

POWER   ANALOG IN

RESET 3.3V 5V GND GND VIN   A0 A1 A2 A3 A4 A5

(to ground
rail)

rate pot

FIGURE 15.2

Schematic of primary
components.

Q1	1	16	Vcc (5V)
Q2	2	15	Q0
Q3	3	14	DS (data)
Q4	4	13	QE (ground)
Q5	5	12	ST_CP (latch)
Q6	6	11	SH_CP (clock)
Q7	7	10	MR (5V)
GND	8	9	Serial out (NC)

74HC595

FIGURE 15.3

74HC595 Pinout.

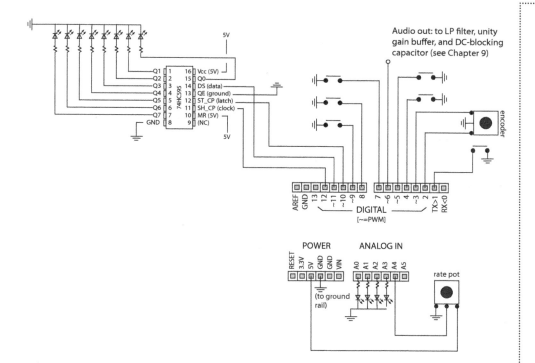

FIGURE 15.4

Complete Step Sequencer circuit.

The shift register is connected to the primary circuit as shown in Figure 15.4. We will look at the code for controlling the shift register in the next section.

Step Sequencer Software

As with all of the projects in this book, the sketch for the Step Sequencer project is available at the OUP website. Given that the code involving Direct Digital Synthesis output, encoders, switches, LEDs, and other components have already been covered in other chapters, we will focus on the underlying logic and organization of the Step Sequencer sketch.

StepSequence class

Two C++ classes, *StepSequence* and *StepSequencer*, provide much of the underlying logic of the sketch. As the name implies, the *StepSequence* class encapsulates the data members representing a musical sequence. As is evident in Listing 15.1, the step sequence class contains three data members: an array of notes, a byte to store the length of the sequence, and another byte to store the transposition. A class enumeration provides a convenient way to define a class-specific constant. In this case the constant is used to define the maximum number of notes in the sequence.

Listing 15.1 StepSequence.h

```
class StepSequence
{
    public:
    //use enumeration to define a class constant
    enum{max_notes = 8};
    private:
    byte m_notes[max_notes];
```

```
        byte m_length;
        byte m_transposition;
```

Constructor and reset() Method

In addition to the class constructor (which is used to initialize class variables to a default value), the class provides a convenience method, *reset()*, that initializes the sequence to a chromatic scale. Of course other options such as ascending fourths or random notes are possible (see Listing 15.2).

Listing 15.2 Constructor and reset() method

```
public:
    StepSequence()
    {
        m_length = max_notes;
        m_transposition = 0;
        //call reset() to initialize notes
        reset();
    };

    void reset()
    {
        //Initialize sequence to a chromatic scale
        for(int n = 0; n < max_notes; n++)
        {
            m_notes[n] = n + 30;
        }
    }
```

Getters and Setters

The remainder of the *StepSequence* class consists of getters and setters (Listing 15.3) that provide access to the notes of the sequence. Other than some basic error checking, the methods simply get or return the appropriate note, transposition, or sequence length.

Listing 15.3 Getters and setters

```
byte getNote(int _step)
  {
    if(_step >=0 && _step < max_notes)
    {
        return m_notes[_step];
    }
    return 0; //error
  }

  byte getTransposedNote(int _step)
  {
    return getNote(_step) + m_transposition;
  }
```

```
    byte getTransposition(){return m_transposition;};
    void setTransposition(byte trans)
    {
        m_transposition = trans;
    }

    void setNote(int _step, byte note)
    {
        if(_step >=0 && _step < max_notes)
        {
            m_notes[_step] = note;
        }
    }

    void setLength(byte _length)
    {
        if(_length <= max_notes && _length >0)
        {
            m_length = _length;
        }
    }

    byte getLength(){return m_length;};
    int getMaxLength(){return max_notes;};

};
```

StepSequencer class

A related class, *StepSequencer* is a *container class* that stores an array of *StepSequence* objects. As with the previous class, a class enumeration is used to define a class-specific constant. As is evident in Listing 15.4, the functionality of the class consists of keeping track of the currently active sequence (tracked by the *m_currentSequence* data member) and getting or returning values via several getter and setter methods. Although this functionality could also be handled in the main sketch, the use of a container class simplifies the logic of the main sketch. The class is shown in its entirety in Listing 15.4.

Listing 15.4 StepSequencer class

```
//Arduino for Musicians
//StepSequencer: A container class for StepSequence objects

#ifndef __STEPSEQUENCER
#define __STEPSEQUENCER

#include "StepSequence.h"

class StepSequencer
{
    public:
     //Use enumeration to define a class constant
    enum{max_sequences = 8};
```

355

```
private:
//Class data members:
int m_currentSequence; //index of currently active
                       //sequence
//This array stores the sequences
StepSequence m_sequence[max_sequences];

public:
//Public constructor and methods
StepSequencer()
{
    m_currentSequence = 0;
}

//"Getters" and "setters"
byte getNote(int _step)
{
    return m_sequence[m_currentSequence].getNote(_step);
}

byte getTransposition()
{
    return m_sequence[m_currentSequence].
        getTransposition();
}

byte getLength()
{
    return m_sequence[m_currentSequence].getLength();
}

byte getMaxLength()
{
    return m_sequence[m_currentSequence].getMaxLength();
}

int getCurrentSequence()
{
    return m_currentSequence;
}

void setNote(int _step, byte note)
{
    m_sequence[m_currentSequence].setNote(_step, note);
}

void setTransposition(byte transposition)
{
    m_sequence[m_currentSequence].setTransposition(trans
    position);
}

void setLength(byte _length)
{
    m_sequence[m_currentSequence].setLength(_length);
}
```

```
    void setCurrentSequence(int index)
    {
        if(index >=0 && index < max_sequences)
          m_currentSequence = index;
    }

    //Helper method
    void resetSequence(int index)
    {
        if(index >=0 && index < max_sequences)
          m_sequence[index].reset();
    }

    void selectPreviousSequence()
    {
      if(m_currentSequence > 0)
       m_currentSequence--;
    }

    void selectNextSequence()
    {
      if(m_currentSequence < max_sequences -1)
       m_currentSequence++;
    }
};

#endif
```

Program Logic

Other than the initialization that occurs in the *setup()* function, the functionality of the Step Sequencer is handled by the eight functions shown in the main loop (Listing 15.5). Note that an unsigned long, *current_time*, is incremented on each iteration of the loop and provides a rough timer that can be used to debounce switches and encoders. In addition to the user interface logic in the main loop, a timer callback handles playback (more on this later in the chapter).

Listing 15.5 Main loop

```
void loop()
{
    current_time++; //Increment "bogus" time for component
    //debouncing

    //Handle user interface
    handleModeButton();
    handlePitchEncoder();
    handleStepButtons();
    handleStartStopButton();
    handleStoreButton();
    handleWaveToggleButton();
    handleRatePotentiometer();
    handleLEDs();
}
```

Figure 15.5 provides an illustration of the tasks associated with each function in the main loop. A brief description of each function follows.

357

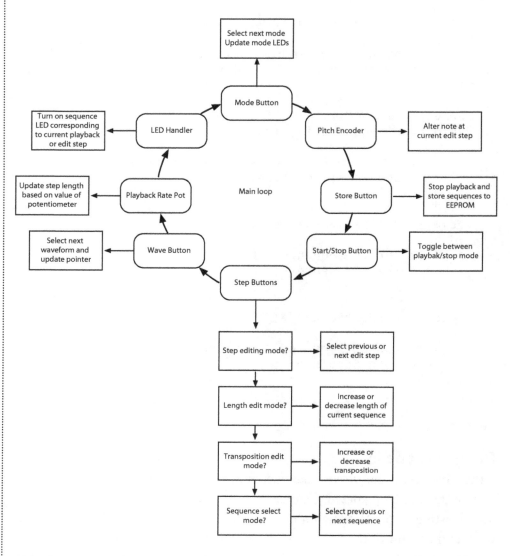

FIGURE 15.5

User interface logic.

handleModeButton()

Mode selection is handled by *modeButton*, an instance of the *EasyButton* class presented earlier in the book. When the function detects a button press, the current operational mode (stored in the variable *currentMode)* is incremented to the next mode. The modes, which range from *step_*edit to *sequence_*select, are enumerated at the top of the sketch:

```
//Mode enumeration
enum{step_edit, length_edit, transpose_edit, sequence_
select};
int currentMode = step_edit;
```

The enumeration simplifies the logic of toggling through the various modes (note the "if" statement that handles wrap around in Listing 15.6).

Listing 15.6 handleModeButton() function

```
void handleModeButton()
{
    //Track mode toggle button
    if(modeButton.checkButtonPressed(current_time)==true)
```

```
    {
        currentMode++;
        if(currentMode > sequence_select)
        {
            currentMode = step_edit; //Wrap around
        }
    }
    //Update the mode LEDs
    updateModeLEDs();
}
```

Also note that the function calls a helper function, *updateModeLEDs()*, to update the status of the LEDs to reflect the current mode selection.

handlePitchEncoder()

The function named *handlePitchEncoder()* tracks the position of the rotary encoder and is used to edit the pitch of the current step in the active sequence. If the function detects that the encoder has changed position, the new position is stored and an instance of the *StepSequencer* class is called to update the note at the index stored in *currentEditStep*. As with the mode handling function, *handlePitchEncoder()* calls a helper function, *handlePitchEncoder()*, to update the oscillator to reflect the new frequency (see Listing 15.7).

Listing 15.7 handlePitchEncoder()

```
void handlePitchEncoder()
{
    //Track pitch encoder:
    static int last_encoder_value = 0;

    int encoder_value=pitchEncoder.
    trackShaftPosition(current_time);
    if(encoder_value!=last_encoder_value)
    {
        last_encoder_value = encoder_value;
        sequencer.setNote(currentEditStep, encoder_value);

        //Update the oscillator with the new frequency
        //selection
        updateStepFrequency();
    }
}
```

359

handleStepButtons();

The functionality of the tactile switches (step buttons) is cumbersome, so *handleStepButtons()* (Listing 15.8) breaks the logic into two smaller functions.

Listing 15.8 handleStepButtons()

```
void handleStepButtons()
{
    //Break step button logic into smaller chunks
    handleLeftStepButton();
    handleRightStepButton();
}
```

Given that the code for the left- and right step button handlers is similar, we will focus on the function named *handleLeftStepButton()* (see Listing 15.9). Pseudo-code is as follows:

- *If the current mode is step edit:* decrease the edit step and update the pitch encoder to reflect the new step.
- *If the current mode is length edit:* decrease the sequence length unless the current length is one.
- *If the current mode is transposition edit:* subtract one from the current transposition.
- *If the current mode is sequence select:* ask the sequencer object to select the previous sequence and update the pitch encoder.

Although there are quite a few lines of code in Listing 15.9, it is relatively easy to follow the logic using the preceding pseudo-code.

Listing 15.9 *handleLeftStepButton()*

```
void handleLeftStepButton()
{
    if(stepLeftButton.checkButtonPressed(current_time)==true)
    {
        //Handle each of the three modes:
        //step_edit, length_edit, traspose_edit, and
        //sequence_select
        if(currentMode == step_edit)
        {
            if(currentEditStep > 0)
            {
                //Select previous step
                currentEditStep--;
                updatePitchEncoder();
            }
        }
        if(currentMode == length_edit)
        {
            if(sequencer.getLength() > 1)
            {
                //Decrese sequence length
                int new_length = sequencer.getLength()-1;
                sequencer.setLength(new_length);
            }
        }
        if(currentMode == transpose_edit)
        {
            //Decrease current transposition
            sequencer.setTransposition( sequencer.
            getTransposition()-1);
        }
        if(currentMode == sequence_select)
        {
```

```
                //Select previous sequence
                sequencer.selectPreviousSequence();
                updatePitchEncoder();
            }
        }
}
```

handleStartStopButton()

Sequence playback states are handled by the *handleStartStopButton()* function. A global Boolean variable, *playbackOn*, tracks the playback status and the function toggles between playback and stop when a button press is detected (see Listing 15.10).

Listing 15.10 handleStartStopButton()

```
void handleStartStopButton()
{
    //Toggle playback on/off
    if(startStopButton.checkButtonPressed(current_time)==true)
    {
        if(playbackOn == true)
        {
            playbackOn = false;
            //Update playback pitch
            updateStepFrequency();
        }else{
            playbackOn = true;
        }
    }
}
```

handleStoreButton()

Sequences can be stored to EEPROM when a user presses the store button. The button handler stops playback and calls two helper functions, *storeDataToEE-PROM()* and *blinkLED()*, which are used to store the data and to blink a "success" message, respectively (see Listing 15.11).

Listing 15.11 handleStoreButton()

```
void handleStoreButton()
{
    //Track store button:
    if(storeButton.checkButtonPressed(current_time)==true)
    {
        //Turn off playback
        playbackOn = false;
        //Store to EEPROM
        storeDataToEEPROM();
        //Bling an LED to show that data has been stored
        blinkLED(7, 8);
    }
}
```

StoreDataToEEPROM() and ReadDataFromEEPROM()

As with the Mongo Hand Drum project, the nonvolatile storage function relies on the EEPROM class to write data to EEPROM. The function starts by writing an identification byte to the address referenced by *ID_ADDR*. Once the initial byte has been written, a "for" loop is used to iterate through each sequence and the relevant data is stored in nonvolatile memory. Of particular note are the *prefix* increment operations (++*address*). Prefix increment means that the increment occurs *prior* to the variable's use as a function parameter and is necessary so the value of *address* is changed before the next byte is stored (see Listing 15.12).

Listing 15.12 storeDataToEEPROM()

```
void storeDataToEEPROM()
{
   EEPROM.write(ID_ADDR, EEPROM_ID);
   int address = ID_ADDR;
   for(int c = 0; c< StepSequencer::max_sequences; c++)
   {
       //Select the sequence with index c
       sequencer.setCurrentSequence(c);
       EEPROM.write(++address, sequencer.getLength());
       EEPROM.write(++address, sequencer.
       getTransposition());
       for(int n = 0; n < sequencer.getMaxLength(); n++)
       {
           EEPROM.write(++address, sequencer.getNote(n));
       }
   }
}
```

The process of reading data back from nonvolatile memory is similar. In this case the function checks for a valid identification byte and reads the data using a "for" loop. Note that default data are stored if a valid identification byte is not found (see Listing 15.13).

Listing 15.13 readDataFromEEPROM()

```
void readDataFromEEPROM()
{
   byte id = EEPROM.read(ID_ADDR);
   int address = ID_ADDR;
   if(id == EEPROM_ID)
   {
     //Read data
     for(int c = 0; c< StepSequencer::max_sequences; c++)
     {
         //Select the sequence with index c
         sequencer.setCurrentSequence(c);
         sequencer.setLength(EEPROM.read(++address));
         sequencer.setTransposition(EEPROM.read(
                     ++address));
         for(int n = 0; n < sequencer.getMaxLength(); n++)
```

```
            {
                sequencer.setNote(n,EEPROM.read(++address));
            }
        }
    }else{
        //No data found...write default data
        storeDataToEEPROM();
    }
}
```

handleWaveToggleButton()

Wave selection is handled by *waveButton*, another instance of *EasyButton*. When the handler detects a button press, the current wave (stored in the global variable *current_wave*) is incremented and the helper function *updateWaveSelection()* is called (see Listing 15.14). This is functionally similar to the way that an enumeration was used to clarify the underlying mode-of-operation logic. *updateWaveSelection()* assigns the global pointer *pOsc* to point to the current oscillator based on the value of *current_wave*.

Listing 15.14 handleWaveToggleButton() and updateWaveSelection()

```
void handleWaveToggleButton()
{
    //Track wave selection:
    if(waveButton.checkButtonPressed(current_time)==true)
    {
        //Select next waveform
        current_wave++;

        //Wrap around to sawtooth_wave if necessary
        if(current_wave > sine_wave)
        {
            current_wave = sawtooth_wave;
        }
        updateWaveSelection();
    }
}

void updateWaveSelection()
{
    //Update pOsc to point to the active wave
    switch(current_wave)
    {
        case sine_wave:
            pOsc = &sine;
            break;
        case sawtooth_wave:
            pOsc = &saw;
            break;
        case descending_sawtooth_wave:
            pOsc = &descending_saw;
            break;
        case pulse:
            pOsc = &pulse_osc;
            break;
```

```
            case triangle_wave:
                pOsc = &tri;
                break;
            default:
                pOsc = &saw;
    }
    //Update the oscillator with the new frequency selection
    updateStepFrequency();

}
```

handleRatePotentiometer()

The playback rate of the step sequencer is adjusted via a potentiometer attached to the analog A4 port. A global variable, *step_length*, determines the rate at which the steps advance, and the value returned by the *analogRead()* function is multiplied by 40 to scale the value to an appropriate range. The values returned from a potentiometer are likely to fluctuate, so the "if" statement in Listing 15.15 checks the current value against a "fudge factor" of three before updating the step length. Note that a *static int, last_pot_value*, retains its value between calls to the function. As mentioned previously, static variables can be a nice way of avoiding numerous global variables that might clutter and confuse the underlying logic of the sketch:

Listing 15.15 handleRatePotentiometer()

```
void handleRatePotentiometer()
{
    static int last_pot_val = 0;
    //Read rate potentiometer
    int pot_val = analogRead(ratePin);

    //Update the step length if it has changed
    if(pot_val < last_pot_val - 3 || pot_val > last_pot_val
    + 3)
    {
        step_length = (pot_val *40) +1;
        last_pot_val = pot_val;
    }
}
```

handleLEDs()

The function named *handleLEDs()* lights an LED corresponding to the current playback or edit step (see Listing 15.16). Its primary role is to call the helper function named *turnOnLED()*, which will be described in the next section.

Listing 15.16 handleLEDs()

```
void handleLEDs()
{
    //Light LEDs when current playback step changes
    static int last_playback_step = 0;
    if(playbackOn == true && playbackStep !=last_playback_
    step)
    {
```

364

```
        turnOnLED(playbackStep);
        last_playback_step = playbackStep;
    }

    if(playbackOn, == false)
    {
        if(currentMode == step_edit)
        {
            turnOnLED(currentEditStep);
            //updatePitchEncoder();
        }
        if(currentMode == length_edit)
        {
            turnOnLED(sequencer.getLength()-1);
        }
        if(currentMode == sequence_select)
        {
            turnOnLED(sequencer.getCurrentSequence());
        }
    }
}
```

Using the Shift Out IC: *turnOnLED()*

The shift register can be used to turn specific LEDs on or off. This is accomplished by setting individual bits of a number and using the *shiftOut()* function to write the data to the device. There are several things that must happen for this to work. First, the latch, clock, and data pins need to be configured as digital outputs in the *setup()* function (see Listing 15.17).

Listing 15.17 Setting the latch, clock, and data pins

```
pinMode(latchPin, OUTPUT);
pinMode(clockPin, OUTPUT);
pinMode(dataPin, OUTPUT);3
```

Next, individual bits of an integer are set or cleared to correspond to the status of one of eight LEDs. The *bitSet()* function provides a convenient way of setting and clearing individual bits:

```
int ledBit = 0;
bitSet(ledBit, led_number);
```

Finally, data is transferred by turning the latch pin low using the *digitalWrite()* function, and *shiftOut()* is used to send data to the shift register. Turning the latch pin high completes the operation (see Listing 15.18).

Listing 15.18 turnOnLED() function

```
//This function turns on one of 8 LEDs in the range of 0-7
void turnOnLED(int led_number)
{
    int ledBit = 0;
    bitSet(ledBit, led_number);
    //Pin low to avoid flicker
```

```
digitalWrite(latchPin, LOW);
//Shift out the bits:
shiftOut(dataPin, clockPin, MSBFIRST , ledBit);
//latch pin high to light LEDs
digitalWrite(latchPin, HIGH);
}
```

Playback

As with other direct digital synthesis examples in this book, audio playback is handled by a timer callback function, *ISR(TIMER1_COMPA_vect)*. As can be seen in Listing 15.19, the timer calls the oscillator *tick()* method to retrieve the current voltage level. Next, a static local variable named *time* is used to track the number of clock ticks that have occurred since the last step event. If the difference of *time* minus *last_time* is greater than or equal to *step_length*, the function advances the sequencer and stores the value in the local static variable named *last_time*. The function also resets the plackback step if the current step reaches the end of the sequence. In this way, the pattern plays repeatedly at the rate determined by the variable *step_length* (see Listing 15.19).

Listing 15.19 Timer callback function

```
ISR(TIMER1_COMPA_vect)
{
    //Set timer 0 to do PWM for desired voltage returned
    //from the oscillator
    OCR0A = pOsc->tick();
  //Static (local) variables to handle playback
  static unsigned long last_time = 0;
  static unsigned long time = 0;
  ime++;
  if(playbackOn == true)
  {
      if(time - last_time >= step_length)
      {
          playbackStep++;
          if(playbackStep >= sequencer.getLength())
          {
              playbackStep = 0;
          }
           pOsc->setMIDIFrequency(sequencer.
           getNote(playbackStep)+
                  sequencer.getTransposition());
          last_time = time;
      }
  }
}
```

Although the Step Sequencer sketch is fairly complex, the use of a number of small functions as well as the incorporation of the *Sequence* and *Sequencer* classes clarifies the underlying logic of the sketch. Another benefit of incorporating classes into the design is that the sketch is more extensible. For example, increasing the number of steps or adding variable step length would involve fairly small changes to the underlying classes.

Building the Step Sequencer

Once you have tested the project on a solderless breadboard you might want to consider creating a permanent version of the project. One approach is to create a faceplate utilizing inexpensive 5 × 8" flashing available at most hardware stores. Through-hole components can be attached to the faceplate, and male headers can be soldered to leads such that the components can be easily con-

FIGURE 15.6

Close-up of printed circuit board.

nected to an Arduino. Alternatively, a standalone version could be created using the concepts illustrated in Chapter 12. The ATMega328 microcontroller and related components can be affixed to stripboard or other type of solderboard. Yet another approach, which is the approach I used, is to create a bare-bones Arduino circuit using Eagle circuit-design software. I purchased 10 copies of the printed circuit board shown in Figure 15.6 for about $10.

Primary Circuit

Whether you utilize male headers for a "pluggable" design or solder a standalone version on stripboard, wiring of the front panel can be simplified by connecting ground leads from component to component. Figure 15.7 shows one approach.

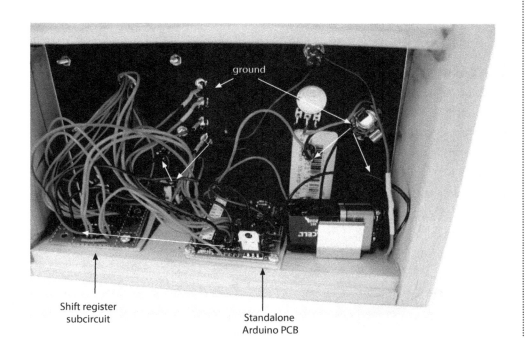

ground

Shift register
subcircuit

Standalone
Arduino PCB

FIGURE 15.7

Connecting ground from component to component.

LED Circuit

The sequence LED subcircuit can be soldered to solderboard and mounted on the front panel using standoffs, screws, and bolts, as shown in Figure 15.8. The solderboard shown in the illustration is from Radio Shack and worked well for this project because all of the LEDs could be connected to a single ground rail. In this version of the project I added an extra resistor to tone down the overall brightness of the LEDs. Although I like the "retro" look of multiple wires attached to the subcircuit, I elected to strip more material from the hookup wire and solder the wires to the back of the subcircuit in a second iteration of the project.

FIGURE 15.8

Sequence LED subcircuit.

Shift-Register Circuit

Stripboard or Veroboard is perhaps the most convenient way to create a subcircuit for the shift register. The circuit from Figure 15.3 can be applied directly to stripboard with the important caveat that *the stripboard column between pins on the IC must be scored or drilled to prevent a short circuit* (see Figure 15.9). I use an oversize drill bit to widen the holes without drilling all the way through the stripboard in order to break the electrical connection between holes on the stripboard. Connections are made by soldering hookup wire between the appropriate component and appropriate row on the stripboard.

Enclosure

I created an inexpensive enclosure by cutting lengths of wood and routing a small recess on the inside of the top and bottom pieces such that the face plate

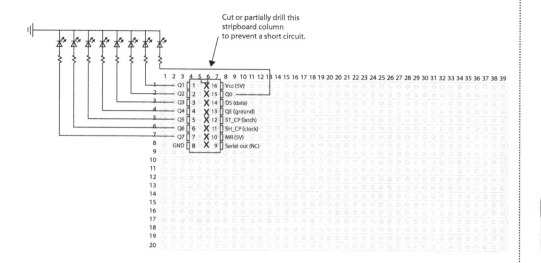

FIGURE 15.9

Stripboard shift register circuit.

would fit into the recessed area (see Figure 15.10). Wood glue was sufficient to make a strong joint between the sides of the box, and wood screws were used to attach the faceplate to the front of the box.

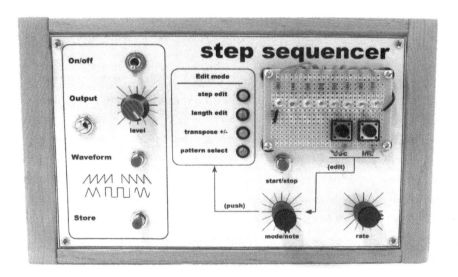

FIGURE 15.10

Enclosure.

369

Other Enhancements

Although there are some challenges associated with building the Step Sequencer project, the end result is a fully functional (and fun) music-making synthesizer. As I have stressed throughout the book, a good place to start is to use a solderless breadboard to connect the components to an Arduino and download the demonstration sketch from the OUP website. Exploring the software in this way will help you to get a feel for the form and function of the unit and to consider possible enhancements. For example, it might be useful to be able to edit the length of each step or to send MIDI notes (or respond to incoming MIDI timer messages). Ideally, the project will provide a useful foundation for your own creative endeavors.

Emöte MIDI Controller

Given the real-time performance potential of the many components described in this book, it was difficult to select a single project to demonstrate real-time control. For practical reasons, I elected to build a relatively simple yet powerful project based on the thumb joystick and pressure sensor presented in Chapter 6.

I have noticed that few keyboard manufacturers make instruments with X-Y controllers. This is unfortunate because I prefer using joystick controllers over separate pitch and modulation wheels (and I suspect that there are many readers who feel the same). This chapter details one approach to designing an X-Y real-time controller. In this sketch, the X-axis is used for pitch bend and the Y-axis for modulation, and a pressure sensor provides real-time expression control. The finished project is shown in Figure 6.1.

Although this project uses a Teensy microcontroller for MIDI output, very little retooling would be needed to adapt the project to the serial MIDI transmitter circuit from Chapter 5.

6.1 JOYSTICK MIDI CONTROLLER

Circuit

The circuit consists of an inexpensive thumb joystick and breakout, which can be found at many online sources including Adafruit and SparkFun. Breath control is handled by the Freescale Semiconductor MPX 5050GP Pressure Sensor described in Chapter 6. As is evident in Figure 16.2, only three connections are required to connect the joystick and pressure sensor to the Teensy microcontroller (in addition to 5V and ground). Additionally, two potentiometers are connected

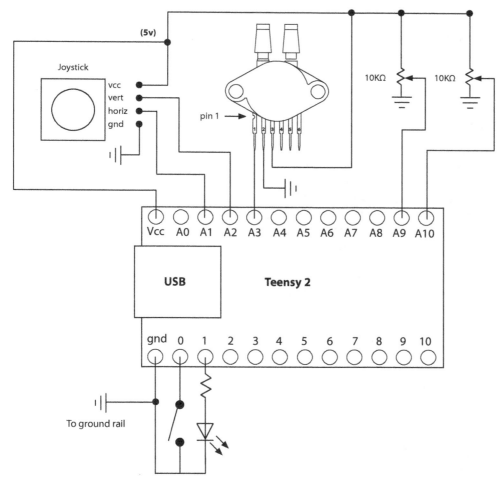

FIGURE 16.1

Emöte controller.

FIGURE 16.2

Emöte circuit.

to analog pins A9 and A10 to provide a way to adjust pressure sensitivity and range, and a SPST switch and LED are connected to the first two digital pins to provide a way to toggle breath control on and off.

Enclosure

The project was mounted in a RadioShack enclosure, but many other commercial or custom options would work. As previously described in the book,

I utilized drawing software to create the graphics for the faceplate which was then laminated and affixed to the removable top of the enclosure.

Code

The following paragraphs detail the code and underlying logic that form the basis for the project. As with the other projects in the book, be sure to experiment with the source code that is provided at the OUP website and extend or adapt the code for your own use.

Constants and Variables

As with most sketches, Listing 16.1 starts by defining several constants and variables. The sketch also makes use of two custom classes, *MidiBreathController* and *MIDIJoystick*, that will be described in the pages that follow.

Listing 16.1 Emote controller variables

```
#include "MIDIBreathController.h"
#include "MIDIJoystick.h"

MIDIBreathController bc;
MIDIJoystick js;

//Constants
const int joystickX = A1; //Joystick X
const int joystickY = A2; //Joystick Y
const int sensorPin = A3; //Pressure sensor
const int rangePin  = A9; //Pressure sensor range
const int sensitivityPin = A10; //Pressure sensor sensitivity
const int breathOnSwitch = PIN_D0;
const int breathOnLED = PIN_D1;

const int max_pressure = 100;
const int expression = 11;        //Controller number for MIDI
                                  //expression
const int midi_channel = 1;
const int modulation_CC = 1;

int centerY = 0;                  //The center Y position of
                                  //the joystick
int joystick_sensitivity = 3;     //Joystick sensitivity level
```

MIDI Breath Controller Class

MIDIBreathController is a convenience class consisting of a header file and .cpp source file. The class encapsulates the pressure sensor described in Chapter 6 into a convenient object that can be used in other projects. As is evident in Listing 16.2, the class contains several data members representing the sensor pin, MIDI channel, ambient pressure, and pressure range and sensitivity. The data member, *m_continuousController*, defaults to expression (MIDI Continuous Controller 11). Additionally, public methods are provided for tracking pressure and updating the range and sensitivity of the device.

Listing 16.2 MIDIBreathController.h

```
class MIDIBreathController
{
    private:
    int m_sensorPin;
    int m_MIDIChannel;
    int m_ambientPressure;
    int m_maxPressure;
    int m_sensitivity;
    int m_continuousController;

    public:
    MIDIBreathController();
    void init(int pin, int channel, int controller_number = 11,
                int max_pressure = 150, int sensitivity = 2);
    void init();
    void trackPressure();
    void updateSensitivity(int sensitivity);
    void updateRange(int range);
    int getAmbientPressure();
};
#endif
```

Listing 16.3 shows the "workhorse" method of the MIDIBreathController class, *trackPressure()*. This method compares the value returned by the sensor pin against the last value returned by the pin and outputs a MIDI Continuous Controller value if the value exceeds the given sensitivity value.

Listing 16.3 trackPressure()

```
void MIDIBreathController::trackPressure()
{
    static int lastSensorValue = 0;
    static int lastMidiValue = 0;

    //Read sensor
    int sensorValue = analogRead(m_sensorPin);

    //Map the value to a MIDI range of 0 to 127
    int midi_value = map(sensorValue, m_ambientPressure,
        m_maxPressure, 0, 127);

    //Constrain the number to a valid MIDI range so high
    //pressure values don't wrap around
    midi_value = constrain(midi_value, 0, 127);

    //Output the value if it changes more (or less) than
    //sensitivity value
    if((midi_value > lastMidiValue + m_sensitivity ||
        midi_value < lastMidiValue - m_sensitivity) &&
        midi_value != lastMidiValue)
```

```
    {
        usbMIDI.sendControlChange(m_continuousController,
                midi_value, m_MIDIChannel);

            //Store the value for next time
            lastMidiValue = midi_value;

    }
}
```

MIDI Joystick Class

As with the *MIDIBreathController* class, *MIDIJoystick* encapsulates the functionality of a joystick in an easy-to-use convenience class. Data members are provided to store the pin assignments, MIDI channel, Y-position, sensitivity, movement, and MIDI controller values. An "init" method provides an opportunity to assign values, and three tracking methods are provided to read the values returned by the joystick (see Listing 16.4).

Listing 16.4 MIDIJoystick.h

```
class MIDIJoystick
{

    private:
    int m_xPin;
    int m_yPin;
    int m_MIDIChannel;
    int m_centerY;
    int m_sensitivity;
    int m_controllerMod1;
    int m_controllerMod2;

    public:
    MIDIJoystick();
    void init(int yPin, int xPin, int channel, int
    controller_mod_1 = 1,
            int controller_mod_2 = 1, int sensitivity = 2);
    void trackJoystick();
    void trackModulation();
    void trackPitchBend();
};
```

Mapping Modulation Values (Y-Axis)

Although the joystick class is relatively simple, there are few challenges in converting the voltages returned by the joystick into meaningful MIDI values. Notably, the joystick returns X and Y values that are roughly in the middle of the possible range returned by the analog inputs (0–1,023). While it is easy to map this range to a valid pitch bend value, it is more awkward to scale the values for modulation. The strategy I used involves taking a reading when the initialization method is called in order to sample the "ambient" value of the Y-axis of the joystick (see Listing 16.5).

Listing 16.5 MIDIJoystick *init()* method

```
void MIDIJoystick::init(int yPin, int xPin, int channel, int
controller_mod_1,
                int controller_mod_2, int sensitivity)
{
    m_xPin = xPin;
    m_yPin = yPin;
    m_MIDIChannel = channel;
    m_controllerMod1 = controller_mod_1;
    m_controllerMod2 = controller_mod_2;
    m_sensitivity = sensitivity;

    //Get ambient reading of center Y:
    m_centerY = analogRead(m_yPin); //Get center of Y-xis
}
```

The center value of the Y-axis is used to adjust the offset of the joystick so that values above the center position are mapped to a MIDI range of 0 to 127. Similarly, values below the center Y position are also mapped from 0 to 127, but the mapping is inverted so more modulation is applied as the joystick moves towards the bottom of its range. The effect is that no modulation is applied when the stick is in its center Y position, but modulation increases when the stick moves away from the center in either direction. Other options might include using different MIDI controller messages on the positive and negative side of its range. The relevant code, which is in a method named *trackModulation()*, is called from the main *loop()*. In Listing 6.6, note how the "ambient" variable, *centerY*, is used to establish the zero position of the joystick, even though the value returned by *analogRead()* is approximately 500.

One other thing to note in this method is the use of the local static variable, *lastY*. Although the scope of this variable is limited to this method, the value of the variable is retained between calls. As mentioned previously in the book, static variables can be a nice choice when you don't want to clutter your code with global variables (see Listing 16.6).

Listing 16.6 Mapping Y values to modulation

```
void MIDIJoystick::trackModulation()
{
    static int lastY = 0;
    int joystick_y = analogRead(m_yPin);
    static int last_mod1 = 0;
    static int last_mod2 = 0;
    //Output modulation (continuous controller 1) if Y-axis
    //changes
    if(joystick_y < lastY - m_sensitivity ||
      joystick_y > lastY + m_sensitivity)
    {
        lastY = joystick_y;
        if(joystick_y >= m_centerY)
        {
            //Adjust the range so center value = 0:
            joystick_y = joystick_y - m_centerY;
```

```
                    //map the value:
                    int mod_wheel_amount = map(joystick_y, 0,
                    (1023 - m_centerY), 0, 127);
                    //Avoid clogging midi stream
                    if(mod_wheel_amount != last_mod1)
                    {

                        usbMIDI.sendControlChange(m_controllerMod1,
                        mod_wheel_amount, m_MIDIChannel);
                        last_mod1 = mod_wheel_amount;
                    }
            }else{
                //Looking at values from 0 to centerY-1.
                //Do reverse map
                int mod_wheel_amount = map(joystick_y,
                m_centerY, 0, 0, 127);
                //Avoid clogging midi stream
                if(mod_wheel_amount != last_mod2)
                {
                    usbMIDI.sendControlChange(m_controllerMod2,
                    mod_wheel_amount, m_MIDIChannel);
                    last_mod2 = mod_wheel_amount;
                }
            }

        //Store the current position of the joystick
        lastY = joystick_y;
    }
}
```

Mapping Pitch Bend (X-Axis)

Pitch bend is handled similarly, but there is no need to adjust for the center position of the joystick since this is how MIDI pitch bend is handled anyway: values above the midpoint raise the pitch, and values below the center point lower the pitch (see Listing 6.7).

Listing 16.7 Mapping the X-axis to pitch bend

```
void MIDIJoystick::trackPitchBend()
{
    static int last_x = 0;
    static int last_pitch_value = 0;
    //Read the joystick
    int joystick_x = analogRead(m_xPin);
    if(joystick_x > last_x + m_sensitivity ||
        joystick_x < last_x - m_sensitivity)
    {
        last_x = joystick_x;

        /*Scale the value returned by joystick.
          Note that pitch bend has 14-bit resolution
          (0-16383). Do a reverse mapping so up
          motion = sharp, down motion = flat.*/
```

```
        int pitch_bend_amount = map(joystick_x, 0, 1023,
            0, 16383);
        if(pitch_bend_amount != last_pitch_value)
        {
            last_pitch_value = pitch_bend_amount;
            usbMIDI.sendPitchBend(pitch_bend_amount,
            m_MIDIChannel);
        }
    }
}
```

Main loop()

Three things occur in each iteration of the main loop:

- The *trackJoystick()* method is called to handle pitch and modulation changes.
- The *trackPressure()* method is called if the breath-controller switch is on. (An LED is turned on or off depending on the status of the switch.)
- Breath controller sensitivity and range settings are read from two potentiometers via convenience functions, and the values are updated as necessary.

The three primary tasks of the main loop and related convenience functions are shown in Listing 16.8.

Listing 16.8 Main loop

```
void loop()
{
    //Track the joystick
    js.trackJoystick();

    //Track breath controller if BC switch is on
    if(!digitalRead(breathOnSwitch))
    {
        //Track breath controller
        bc.trackPressure();
        //Turn LED on
        digitalWrite(breathOnLED, HIGH);
    }else{
        digitalWrite(breathOnLED, LOW);
    }

    //Track the sensitivity and range pots
    trackSensitivity();
    trackRange();
}

void trackSensitivity()
{
    //Variable to store the sensitivity value
    static int last_sensitivity = 0;
```

```
        //Read the sensitivity pot
        int sensitivity_value = analogRead(sensitivityPin);

        //Map the value to a reasonable range
        sensitivity_value = map(sensitivity_value, 0, 1023, 0, 20);

        //update the sensitivity value if it changes
        if(sensitivity_value != last_sensitivity)
        {
            bc.updateSensitivity(sensitivity_value);
            last_sensitivity = sensitivity_value;
        }
}

void trackRange()
{
        //Variable to store the range value
        static int last_range = 0;

        //Read the range pot
        int range_value = analogRead(rangePin);

        //Map the value to a reasonable range
        range_value = map(range_value, 0, 1023, 50, 125);

        //update the range value if it changes
        if(range_value != last_range)
        {
            bc.updateRange(range_value);
            last_range = range_value;
        }
}
```

Conclusion

The emöte controller is a good example of a robust project that is relatively simple (and inexpensive) to build. An entirely new level of expressive control can be achieved for the price of a microcontroller and a handful of parts, and new forms of real-time control are only limited by your imagination. For example, photoresistors or force-sensitive resistors could provide an opportunity to respond to light and hand pressure, or capacitive sensing technology could be implemented to provide a way for performers to control a MIDI device with "touchless" proximity. The concepts described in this chapter can also be used to build more mundane devices for virtual mixing or patch and bank selection.

Conclusion

I n the 1990s I spent more than $1,000 dollars for a music-making computer with a clock speed of 8 million pulses per second. It is amazing to consider that for less than $5, I can now purchase a microprocessor with twice the clock speed and use it as the basis for any number of custom music-making tools. Not only is the technology less expensive and easier to use, a World Wide Web connects musicians, scientists, hobbyists, and tinkerers in a rich Maker movement—help, support, ideas, and documentation are just a few keystrokes away.

To be sure, there are many challenges associated with using new tools like Arduino, but facing them can be richly rewarded with an expanded palette of custom musical resources. It is my sincere goal that this book will provide a useful foundation for exploring the vast potential of Arduino and related products and that you will experience the joy that can come when technology is utilized to serve your artistic goals.

In some respects, Arduino represents a return to an essential element of the human spirit. It is not hard to imagine early man using sticks and reeds to make music, but in this age of master craftsmen and high-end electronics it is easy to forget that part of the joy of making music comes from creating the musical instruments. And Arduino represents a democratization of the process—powerful tools are now in the hands of everyday musicians.

Paul Griffiths, author of *A Guide to Electronic Music*, suggests that the electronic medium "has stimulated composers to consider music as a process rather than a form,"[1] and that sentiment fits perfectly with the music-making potential of the Arduino platform. New forms of synthesizer and computer control systems give rise to new creative explorations in a feedback loop that can be considered a form of "perpetual evolution," and this is another aspect of Arduino programming that I find so compelling. My music making is different now than it was before I started incorporating microcontroller technology, and that is no small thing. Noted historian Richard Taruskin discusses the role of technology in music production in his *Music in the Late Twentieth Century*, where he notes that samplers and sequencing programs have "affected virtually everyone's musical style."[2] Although traditionalists bemoan the loss of written music to a "resurgence of 'orality,'" microcontroller technology can move art in new and unexpected directions.

Not only is my approach to music making different, I would go so far as to suggest some cognitive benefits that come from incorporating programming languages into my workflow. Dr. John J. Medina, author of *Brain Rules*, discusses the work of Eric Kandel and states that "Kandel showed that when people learn something, the wiring in their brains changes. He demonstrated that acquiring even simple pieces of information involves the physical alteration of the structure of the neurons participating in the process."[3] Medina describes the process as "astonishing," and it is easy to envision how the process of learning and applying the language and logic of computers to music can open the door to new insights into the music-making process. As I mentioned earlier in the book, I have noticed some changes in my ability to organize musical materials and utilize formal processes. It's hard to know if the change is due to age and experience or something else, but intuition tells me that fluency with programming languages has had a positive impact on my musicianship.

It is fun to consider where music is heading. Not only have tools like Arduino democratized the process of making musical instruments and controllers, the Web has, to an extent, democratized the distribution of music and ideas. It is hard to guess the direction that music will take, but I have a feeling that a knowledge of programming and circuitry will be helpful to musicians in the twenty-first century. Just consider the technologies we already rely on to make music: analog-to-digital conversion, MIDI, wireless networks, and digital synthesis represent just a few of the many technologies that are used each day by modern musicians. Not only do existing technologies have new potential when combined with microcontroller technologies like Arduino, an understanding of the core competencies will provide a useful foundation for understanding and utilizing new technologies that may come into play in the future. Algorithmic composition, physical modeling, multimedia control systems, and gesture recognition are just a few of the concepts that may become more prevalent in the new century.

A primary goal in writing this book was to provide enough of a theoretical foundation in electronics and computer science to open the door for creative application of the concepts without overwhelming music practitioners with unnecessary minutiae. Ideally, the concepts will serve your creative pursuits, and you will experience the bliss that comes from learning and applying new things to the creative process. A final quote from Paul Griffiths is appropriate:

> It is true that the medium makes it only too easy to indulge in trick effects: bizarre juxtapositions of unrelated ideas, sudden shifts from the familiar to the unfamiliar, gradual disruptions of everyday sounds. Yet these devices can also, in the hands of a sensitive musician, give rise to the wonder which is not an insignificant part of our experience of electronic music. The wonder of new discovery, of having one's preconceptions overturned, is part of the excitement of the art.[4]

Appendix A

MIDI Control Changes

The following table, from the MIDI Manufacturers Association website, lists Control Changes and Mode Changes (status bytes 176–191).

TABLE A.1 Control Changes and Mode Changes

| Control Number (2nd Byte Value) | | | Control Function | 3rd Byte Value | |
Decimal	Binary	Hex		Value	Used As
0	0	0	Bank Select	0-127	MSB
1	1	1	Modulation Wheel or Lever	0-127	MSB
2	10	2	Breath Controller	0-127	MSB
3	11	3	Undefined	0-127	MSB
4	100	4	Foot Controller	0-127	MSB
5	101	5	Portamento Time	0-127	MSB
6	110	6	Data Entry MSB	0-127	MSB
7	111	7	Channel Volume (formerly Main Volume)	0-127	MSB
8	1000	8	Balance	0-127	MSB
9	1001	9	Undefined	0-127	MSB
10	1010	0A	Pan	0-127	MSB
11	1011	0B	Expression Controller	0-127	MSB
12	1100	0C	Effect Control 1	0-127	MSB
13	1101	0D	Effect Control 2	0-127	MSB
14	1110	0E	Undefined	0-127	MSB
15	1111	0F	Undefined	0-127	MSB
16	10000	10	General Purpose Controller 1	0-127	MSB
17	10001	11	General Purpose Controller 2	0-127	MSB
18	10010	12	General Purpose Controller 3	0-127	MSB
19	10011	13	General Purpose Controller 4	0-127	MSB
20	10100	14	Undefined	0-127	MSB

(continued)

TABLE A.1 Continued

Control Number (2nd Byte Value)			Control Function	3rd Byte Value	
Decimal	Binary	Hex		Value	Used As
21	10101	15	Undefined	0-127	MSB
22	10110	16	Undefined	0-127	MSB
23	10111	17	Undefined	0-127	MSB
24	11000	18	Undefined	0-127	MSB
25	11001	19	Undefined	0-127	MSB
26	11010	1A	Undefined	0-127	MSB
27	11011	1B	Undefined	0-127	MSB
28	11100	1C	Undefined	0-127	MSB
29	11101	1D	Undefined	0-127	MSB
30	11110	1E	Undefined	0-127	MSB
31	11111	1F	Undefined	0-127	MSB
32	100000	20	LSB for Control 0 (Bank Select)	0-127	LSB
33	100001	21	LSB for Control 1 (Modulation Wheel or Lever)	0-127	LSB
34	100010	22	LSB for Control 2 (Breath Controller)	0-127	LSB
35	100011	23	LSB for Control 3 (Undefined)	0-127	LSB
36	100100	24	LSB for Control 4 (Foot Controller)	0-127	LSB
37	100101	25	LSB for Control 5 (Portamento Time)	0-127	LSB
38	100110	26	LSB for Control 6 (Data Entry)	0-127	LSB
39	100111	27	LSB for Control 7 (Channel Volume, formerly Main Volume)	0-127	LSB
40	101000	28	LSB for Control 8 (Balance)	0-127	LSB
41	101001	29	LSB for Control 9 (Undefined)	0-127	LSB
42	101010	2A	LSB for Control 10 (Pan)	0-127	LSB
43	101011	2B	LSB for Control 11 (Expression Controller)	0-127	LSB
44	101100	2C	LSB for Control 12 (Effect control 1)	0-127	LSB
45	101101	2D	LSB for Control 13 (Effect control 2)	0-127	LSB

Control Number (2nd Byte Value)			Control Function	3rd Byte Value	
Decimal	Binary	Hex		Value	Used As
46	101110	2E	LSB for Control 14 (Undefined)	0-127	LSB
47	101111	2F	LSB for Control 15 (Undefined)	0-127	LSB
48	110000	30	LSB for Control 16 (General Purpose Controller 1)	0-127	LSB
49	110001	31	LSB for Control 17 (General Purpose Controller 2)	0-127	LSB
50	110010	32	LSB for Control 18 (General Purpose Controller 3)	0-127	LSB
51	110011	33	LSB for Control 19 (General Purpose Controller 4)	0-127	LSB
52	110100	34	LSB for Control 20 (Undefined)	0-127	LSB
53	110101	35	LSB for Control 21 (Undefined)	0-127	LSB
54	110110	36	LSB for Control 22 (Undefined)	0-127	LSB
55	110111	37	LSB for Control 23 (Undefined)	0-127	LSB
56	111000	38	LSB for Control 24 (Undefined)	0-127	LSB
57	111001	39	LSB for Control 25 (Undefined)	0-127	LSB
58	111010	3A	LSB for Control 26 (Undefined)	0-127	LSB
59	111011	3B	LSB for Control 27 (Undefined)	0-127	LSB
60	111100	3C	LSB for Control 28 (Undefined)	0-127	LSB
61	111101	3D	LSB for Control 29 (Undefined)	0-127	LSB
62	111110	3E	LSB for Control 30 (Undefined)	0-127	LSB
63	111111	3F	LSB for Control 31 (Undefined)	0-127	LSB
64	1000000	40	Damper Pedal on/off (Sustain)	≤63 off, ≥64 on	—

(continued)

383

TABLE A.1 Continued

Control Number (2nd Byte Value)			Control Function	3rd Byte Value	
Decimal	Binary	Hex		Value	Used As
65	1000001	41	Portamento On/Off	≤63 off, ≥64 on	—
66	1000010	42	Sostenuto On/Off	≤63 off, ≥64 on	—
67	1000011	43	Soft Pedal On/Off	≤63 off, ≥64 on	—
68	1000100	44	Legato Footswitch	≤63 Normal, ≥64 Legato	—
69	1000101	45	Hold 2	≤63 off, ≥64 on	—
70	1000110	46	Sound Controller 1 (default: Sound Variation)	0-127	LSB
71	1000111	47	Sound Controller 2 (default: Timbre/ Harmonic Intens.)	0-127	LSB
72	1001000	48	Sound Controller 3 (default: Release Time)	0-127	LSB
73	1001001	49	Sound Controller 4 (default: Attack Time)	0-127	LSB
74	1001010	4A	Sound Controller 5 (default: Brightness)	0-127	LSB
75	1001011	4B	Sound Controller 6 (default: Decay Time—see MMA RP-021)	0-127	LSB
76	1001100	4C	Sound Controller 7 (default: Vibrato Rate—see MMA RP-021)	0-127	LSB
77	1001101	4D	Sound Controller 8 (default: Vibrato Depth—see MMA RP-021)	0-127	LSB
78	1001110	4E	Sound Controller 9 (default: Vibrato Delay—see MMA RP-021)	0-127	LSB
79	1001111	4F	Sound Controller 10 (default undefined—see MMA RP-021)	0-127	LSB
80	1010000	50	General Purpose Controller 5	0-127	LSB
81	1010001	51	General Purpose Controller 6	0-127	LSB

| Control Number (2nd Byte Value) | | | Control Function | 3rd Byte Value | |
Decimal	Binary	Hex		Value	Used As
82	1010010	52	General Purpose Controller 7	0-127	LSB
83	1010011	53	General Purpose Controller 8	0-127	LSB
84	1010100	54	Portamento Control	0-127	LSB
85	1010101	55	Undefined	—	—
86	1010110	56	Undefined	—	—
87	1010111	57	Undefined	—	—
88	1011000	58	High Resolution Velocity Prefix	0-127	LSB
89	1011001	59	Undefined	—	—
90	1011010	5A	Undefined	—	—
91	1011011	5B	Effects 1 Depth (default: Reverb Send Level—see MMA RP-023) (formerly External Effects Depth)	0-127	—
92	1011100	5C	Effects 2 Depth (formerly Tremolo Depth)	0-127	—
93	1011101	5D	Effects 3 Depth (default: Chorus Send Level—see MMA RP-023) (formerly Chorus Depth)	0-127	—
94	1011110	5E	Effects 4 Depth (formerly Celeste [Detune] Depth)	0-127	—
95	1011111	5F	Effects 5 Depth (formerly Phaser Depth)	0-127	—
96	1100000	60	Data Increment (Data Entry +1) (see MMA RP-018)	N/A	—
97	1100001	61	Data Decrement (Data Entry -1) (see MMA RP-018)	N/A	—
98	1100010	62	Non-Registered Parameter Number (NRPN)—LSB	0-127	LSB

385

(continued)

TABLE A.1 Continued

| Control Number (2nd Byte Value) | | | Control Function | 3rd Byte Value | |
Decimal	Binary	Hex		Value	Used As
99	1100011	63	Non-Registered Parameter Number (NRPN)—MSB	0-127	MSB
100	1100100	64	Registered Parameter Number (RPN)—LSB*	0-127	LSB
101	1100101	65	Registered Parameter Number (RPN)—MSB*	0-127	MSB
102	1100110	66	Undefined	—	—
103	1100111	67	Undefined	—	—
104	1101000	68	Undefined	—	—
105	1101001	69	Undefined	—	—
106	1101010	6A	Undefined	—	—
107	1101011	6B	Undefined	—	—
108	1101100	6C	Undefined	—	—
109	1101101	6D	Undefined	—	—
110	1101110	6E	Undefined	—	—
111	1101111	6F	Undefined	—	—
112	1110000	70	Undefined	—	—
113	1110001	71	Undefined	—	—
114	1110010	72	Undefined	—	—
115	1110011	73	Undefined	—	—
116	1110100	74	Undefined	—	—
117	1110101	75	Undefined	—	—
118	1110110	76	Undefined	—	—
119	1110111	77	Undefined	—	—
Note:	Controller numbers 120–127 are reserved for Channel Mode Messages, which rather than controlling sound parameters, affect the channel's operating mode. (See also Table 1.)				
120	1111000	78	[Channel Mode Message] All Sound Off	0	—
121	1111001	79	[Channel Mode Message] Reset All Controllers (See MMA RP-015)	0	—
122	1111010	7A	[Channel Mode Message] Local Control On/Off	0 off, 127 on	—
123	1111011	7B	[Channel Mode Message] All Notes Off	0	—

386

Control Number (2nd Byte Value)			Control Function	3rd Byte Value	
Decimal	Binary	Hex		Value	Used As
124	1111100	7C	[Channel Mode Message] Omni Mode Off (+ all notes off)	0	—
125	1111101	7D	[Channel Mode Message] Omni Mode On (+ all notes off)	0	—
126	1111110	7E	[Channel Mode Message] Mono Mode On (+ poly off, + all notes off)		—
127	1111111	7F	[Channel Mode Message] Poly Mode On (+ mono off, +all notes off)	0	—

*Registered Parameter Numbers (RPN)

To set or change the value of a Registered Parameter:

1. Send two Control Change messages using Control Numbers 101 (65H) and 100 (64H) to select the desired Registered Parameter Number, as per the following table.

2. To set the selected Registered Parameter to a specific value, send a Control Change messages to the Data Entry MSB controller (Control Number 6). If the selected Registered Parameter requires the LSB to be set, send another Control Change message to the Data Entry LSB controller (Control Number 38).

3. To make a relative adjustment to the selected Registered Parameter's current value, use the Data Increment or Data Decrement controllers (Control Numbers 96 and 97).[1]

---

1 http://www.midi.org/techspecs/midimessages.php.

Appendix B

MMC Commands

MMC Command Structure

Byte (hexadecimal)	Decimal	Description
F0	240	F0 followed by 7F indicates Universal Real Time SysEx
7F	127	
Device ID	??	Specifies a particular device 7F (127) = all devices
06	6	MIDI Machine Control command
dd	??	Command (see Table 5.2)
F7	247	End of MMC message

Single-Byte MMC Commands

Command (hexadecimal)	Decimal	Description
01	1	Stop
02	2	Play
03	3	Deferred Play
04	4	Fast Forward
05	5	Rewind
06	6	Record Strobe (Punch In)
07	7	Record Exit (Punch out)
08	8	Record Pause
09	9	Pause
0A	10	Eject
0B	11	Chase
0C	12	Command Error Reset
0D	13	MMC Reset

Go To/Locate (multi-byte)

Command (hexadecimal)	Decimal	Description
F0	240	Universal Real Time Sys Ex header
7F	127	
id	??	ID of target device (7F = all devices)
06	6	Sub ID#1 = MMC Command
44	68	Sub ID#2 = Locate/Go To
06	6	number of data bytes that follow
01:		
hr		Hours and Type: 0yyzzzzz
		yy = Type: 00 = 24 fps, 01 = 25 fps, 10 = 30 fps (drop frame), 11 = 30 fps (non-drop frame)
		zzzzz = Hours (0–23)
mn		Minutes (0–59)
sc		Seconds (0–59)
fr		SMPTE frame number (0–29)
sf		SMPTE subframe number (0–99)
F7	247	EOX

Shuttle (multi-byte)

Command (hexadecimal)	Decimal	Description
F0	240	Universal Real Time Sys Ex header
7F	127	
id	??	ID of target device (7F = all devices)
06	06	Sub ID#1 = MMC Command
47	71	Sub ID#2 = Shuttle
03	03	number of data bytes that follow
sh sm sl		Shuttle direction and speed. Bit 6 of sh gives direction (0 = forward, 1 = backward)
F7	247	EOX

Source: Compiled from a list at: http://www.somascape.org/midi/tech/spec.html#rusx_mmcc.

Appendix **C**

Introduction to Bit Twiddling

This appendix provides a brief overview of common tasks involving bit shifting and manipulation. Although bit manipulation may not be necessary for most sketches, sketches involving Direct Digital Synthesis or other time-intensive tasks may require optimizations involving the direct manipulation of bits. For example, it is approximately 24 percent faster to directly set a bit than to call the built-in *bitSet()* function. Similarly, bit manipulation is typically required when working with the registers of a microcontroller or optimizing memory. For example, the status of 16 LEDs could be stored by setting or clearing the individual bits of a *single* 16-bit unsigned integer—a significant saving of memory when compared to storing the status in individual bytes.

Note that if efficiency is not a primary consideration, the Arduino environment provides functions for reading, writing, setting, and clearing individual bits as well as reading the low and high bytes of a word. The functions are clearly described in the Arduino documentation under the Bits and Bytes heading, so this appendix will be limited to the "pure C" equivalents that may be unfamiliar to many readers. It is also important to note that bit manipulation *only works with integral numbers*. It is not possible to utilize the concepts in this appendix on fractional types such as a *float*.

Right- and Left-Shift

The right-shift operator (>>) can sometimes be used in lieu of division—a notoriously slow operation on an Arduino. The right-shift shifts the operand on its left according to the number of bits following the operator. The following code snippet shows how an unsigned integer could be divided by two using the right-shift operator:

```
//Create a 16-bit unsigned integer with the maximum value
//(all bits set to 1)
uint16_t number = 0xFFFF;
//Divide the number:
number = (number >> 1);
```

Similarly, shift two places to the right to divide a number by four:

```
uint16_t number = 0xFFFF;
number = (number >> 2);
```

Left-shift works in a similar way, but the result is the given number is multiplied by a power of 2:

```
uint16_t number = 1;

number = (number << 1);//multiply by 2
number = (number << 4);//multiply by 4
```

The following sketch (Listing C.1), which is available for download at the OUP website, shows the effect of right- and left-shift on an unsigned 16-bit integer. In this case the effect is not cumulative because the result of the right- or left-shift is *not* assigned to the variable *number*—the result of the operation is passed to a function (not shown in Listing C.1) that prints the result in decimal, hexadecimal, and binary formats.

Listing C.1 Right- and Left-Shift (*printValue*() not shown)

```
//Arduino for Musicians
//Bit Twiddling: right- and left-shift

void setup()
{
  Serial.begin(9600);

  //Create a 16-bit unsigned integer with the maximum value:
  //(all bits set to 1)

  uint16_t number = 0xFFFF;

  //Print the number
  printValue(number);

  /*RIGHT SHIFT TEST
  See how right-shift effects the number:
  Note that the effect is not cumulative unless the number
  is assigned to the output of the shift operation (e.g. number =
  (number >> 1);
  Note how a right shift of 1 DIVIDES the number by 2, a
  right shift of 2 divides by 4, and so on.
  */

  Serial.println("RIGHT SHIFT TEST");
  Serial.println("Starting value: ");
  printValue(number);

  for(int shift = 1; shift < 16; shift++)
  {
    Serial.print("number >> "); Serial.println(shift);
    printValue(number >> shift);
  }
```

```
/*LEFT SHIFT TEST
See how left-shift effects the number:
left-shift of 1 multiplies by 2, left-shift of 2 multiples
by 4, and so on.
*/

number = 1; //Start with a value of 1

Serial.println("RIGHT SHIFT TEST");
Serial.println("Starting value: ");
printValue(number);
for(int shift = 1; shift < 16; shift++)
{
    Serial.print("number << "); Serial.println(shift);
    printValue(number << shift);
}
}
```

Output:

RIGHT SHIFT TEST
Starting value:
Decimal: 65535
Hexadecimal: FFFF
Binary: 1111111111111111

number >> 1
Decimal: 32767
Hexadecimal: 7FFF
Binary: 0111111111111111

number >> 2
Decimal: 16383
Hexadecimal: 3FFF
Binary: 0011111111111111

number >> 3
Decimal: 8191
Hexadecimal: 1FFF
Binary: 0001111111111111

number >> 4
Decimal: 4095
Hexadecimal: FFF
Binary: 0000111111111111

number >> 5
Decimal: 2047
Hexadecimal: 7FF
Binary: 0000011111111111

number >> 6
Decimal: 1023
Hexadecimal: 3FF
Binary: 0000001111111111

number >> 7
Decimal: 511
Hexadecimal: 1FF
Binary: 0000000111111111

number >> 8
Decimal: 255
Hexadecimal: FF
Binary: 0000000011111111

number >> 9
Decimal: 127
Hexadecimal: 7F
Binary: 0000000001111111

number >> 10
Decimal: 63
Hexadecimal: 3F
Binary: 0000000000111111

number >> 11
Decimal: 31
Hexadecimal: 1F
Binary: 0000000000011111

number >> 12
Decimal: 15

Hexadecimal: F
Binary: 0000000000001111

number >> 13
Decimal: 7
Hexadecimal: 7
Binary: 0000000000000111

number >> 14
Decimal: 3
Hexadecimal: 3
Binary: 0000000000000011

number >> 15
Decimal: 1
Hexadecimal: 1
Binary: 0000000000000001

LEFT SHIFT TEST
Starting value:
Decimal: 1
Hexadecimal: 1
Binary: 0000000000000001

number << 1
Decimal: 2
Hexadecimal: 2
Binary: 0000000000000010

number << 2
Decimal: 4
Hexadecimal: 4
Binary: 0000000000000100

number << 3
Decimal: 8
Hexadecimal: 8
Binary: 0000000000001000

number << 4
Decimal: 16
Hexadecimal: 10
Binary: 0000000000010000

number << 5
Decimal: 32
Hexadecimal: 20
Binary: 0000000000100000

number << 6
Decimal: 64
Hexadecimal: 40
Binary: 0000000001000000

number << 7
Decimal: 128
Hexadecimal: 80
Binary: 0000000010000000

number << 8
Decimal: 256
Hexadecimal: 100
Binary: 0000000100000000

number << 9
Decimal: 512
Hexadecimal: 200
Binary: 0000001000000000

number << 10
Decimal: 1024
Hexadecimal: 400
Binary: 0000010000000000

number << 11
Decimal: 2048
Hexadecimal: 800
Binary: 0000100000000000

number << 12
Decimal: 4096
Hexadecimal: 1000
Binary: 0001000000000000

number << 13
Decimal: 8192
Hexadecimal: 2000
Binary: 0010000000000000

number << 14
Decimal: 16384
Hexadecimal: 4000
Binary: 0100000000000000

number << 15
Decimal: 32768
Hexadecimal: 8000
Binary: 1000000000000000

Working with Individual Bits

Several *binary bitwise operators* provide the ability to perform Boolean algebra on individual bits. The operators return a result based on two arguments provided to the operator. It is important to note that bitwise operators are different than logical operators such as AND (&&) and OR (||). The bitwise operators are summarized as follows:

- Bitwise AND (&) returns a 1 in the output bit if *both* input bits are 1.
- Bitwise OR (|) returns a 1 in the output bit if *either* bit is 1 and returns a 0 if both input bits are 0.
- Exclusive OR (^) is the same as OR but returns *0 if both input bits are 1*.

Table C.1 summarizes the logic of the binary bitwise operators.

TABLE C.1 Results of Bitwise Operators

a	b	a & b (AND)	a ^ b (Exclusive OR)	a | b (OR)
0	0	0	0	0
0	1	0	1	1
1	0	0	1	1
1	1	1	0	1

A related *unary bitwise operator* called NOT (~) (also called the *ones complement operator*) takes a single operand and produces the *opposite* of the input bit. The NOT operator returns 1 if the input is 0 and returns 0 if the input bit is 1.

Although more could be said about binary operators, the overview of logic combined with the code snippets below should provide enough information to use and understand the function of the operators in common scenarios like the ones described in the following paragraphs.

Setting a Bit

A bit can be set as follows, where x represents the number of the bit—from 0 to 15 in a 16-bit number.

number |= (1 << x);

Code snippet:

```
Serial.println("BIT SET TEST: ");
Serial.println("Starting value: ");
printValue(number);

//Set the rightmost bit:
number |= (1 << 0);
printValue(number);
```

```
//Set the leftmost bit:
number |= (1 << 15);
printValue(number);
```

Output:

BIT SET TEST:
Starting value:
Decimal: 0
Hexadecimal: 0
Binary: 0000000000000000

Decimal: 1
Hexadecimal: 1
Binary: 0000000000000001

Decimal: 32769
Hexadecimal: 8001
Binary: 1000000000000001

Clearing a Bit

Individual bits can be cleared by inverting bits with the NOT operator and using AND to clear the given bit as in the next example. As with the preceding example, *x* represents the given bit:

number &= ~(1 << x);

Code snippet:

```
//Reset number so all the bits are set:
number = 0xFFFF;

Serial.println("BIT CLEAR TEST: ");
Serial.println("Starting value: ");
printValue(number);

//Clear the rightmost bit
number &= ~(1 << 0);
printValue(number);

//Clear the leftmost bit
number &= ~(1 << 15);
printValue(number);
```

Output:

Starting value:
Decimal: 65535
Hexadecimal: FFFF
Binary: 1111111111111111

Decimal: 65534
Hexadecimal: FFFE
Binary: 1111111111111110

Decimal: 32766
Hexadecimal: 7FFE
Binary: 0111111111111110

Toggling a Bit

The Exclusive OR bitwise operator can be used to conveniently toggle a given bit between states (0 or 1):

number ^= (1 << x);

Code snippet:

```
//Reset number so all the bitst are set:
number = 0xFFFF;
Serial.println("BIT TOGGLE TEST: ");
Serial.println("Starting value: ");
printValue(number);

//Toggle the rightmost bit:
number ^= (1 << 0);
printValue(number);

//Toggle the rightmost bit again
number ^= (1 << 0);
printValue(number);
```

Output:

Starting value:
Decimal: 65535
Hexadecimal: FFFF
Binary: 1111111111111111

Decimal: 65534
Hexadecimal: FFFE
Binary: 1111111111111110

Decimal: 65535
Hexadecimal: FFFF
Binary: 1111111111111111

Checking the Value of a Single Bit

It is sometimes helpful to look at the value of a single bit to determine if the bit has been set or cleared. The value of the given bit can be read as follows:

number & (1 << x);

Code snippet:

```
//Reset number so only the rightmost bit is set
number = 0x1;

Serial.println("BIT CHECK TEST: ");
Serial.println("Starting value: ");
printValue(number);
```

```
//See if rightmost bit is set:
boolean bit_status = number & (1 << 0);
Serial.print("Bit 0 value: "); Serial.println(bit_status);

//See if leftmost bit is set
bit_status = number & (1 << 15);
Serial.print("Bit 15 value: "); Serial.println(bit_status);
```

Output:

BIT CHECK TEST:

Starting value:

Decimal: 1

Hexadecimal: 1

Binary: 0000000000000001

Bit 0 value: 1

Bit 15 value: 0

Exploring the printValue() Function

Now that we have explored many of the important concepts relating to bit twiddling, it might be helpful to look at the *printValue()* function that was omitted from the preceding sketches. *printValue()* takes an unsigned 16-bit integer as a parameter and outputs the number in decimal, hexadecimal, and binary formats. Although the first two formats are easily handled by the *Serial.print()* method, the built-in implementation of binary printing is not adequate because not all bits are shown. As is evident in Listing C.2, the problem is easily handled by iterating through each bit of the parameter and outputting a "1" or "0" based on the value of the bit.

Listing C.2 printValue() function

```
//This helper function outputs a number in binary,
//hexadecimal, and binary
void printValue(uint16_t value)
{
    Serial.print("Decimal: "); Serial.println(value, DEC);
    Serial.print("Hexadecimal: "); Serial.println(value,
    HEX);
    Serial.print("Binary: ");

    /*
    The Serial.print(value, BIN) method does no always output
    all bits so use the following code to ensure that all
    bits are shown. Based on an example by Bruce Eckel in
    "Thinking In C++, Second Edition:"
    */
    for(int i = 15; i >= 0; i--)
    {
     if(value & (1 << i))
     {
```

```
      Serial.print("1");
    }else
    {
      Serial.print("0");
    }
  }

  //Provide some space between this output and the next
  Serial.println();
  Serial.println();
}
```

Conclusion

There is no question that bit manipulation is one of the more obtuse aspects of programming. However, in my estimation, the syntax is more confusing than the underlying logic. The code snippets in this appendix should provide a good foundation for understanding advanced code that you may find in books or on the Internet, and the examples should serve as a good starting point for situations where you need to squeeze some extra performance or memory out of your microcontroller.

Be sure to download the related sketches at the OUP website and experiment with the code. I also found it helpful to use the programmer mode of a software calculator (such as those provided by Windows and OS X) while writing this appendix—particularly when exploring the effect of right- and left-shift on a given number.

Sources

Catonmat.net. *Low Level Bit Hacks You Absolutely Must Know*. Online. Available: http://www.catonmat.net/blog/low-level-bit-hacks-you-absolutely-must-know/.

Eckel, Bruce. *Thinking in C++, Volume One: Introduction to Standard C++*, 2d ed. Upper Saddle River, NJ: Prentice Hall, 2000.

Eckel, Bruce. *Using C++*. Berkeley, CA: Osborne McGraw-Hill, 1990.

Notes

Preface

1. Chris Anderson, Makers the New Industrial Revolution (New York: Crown Publishing Group, 2012), p. 13.

Chapter 1

1. Elliot Williams, *Make: AVR Programming* (Sebastopol, CA: Maker Media, 2014), p. 249.
2. Dale Wheat, *Arduino Internals* (New York: Apress, 2011), p. 15.
3. Nicolas Collins, *Handmade Electronic Music: The Art of Hardware Hacking*, 2d ed. (New York: Routledge, 2009), p. XV.

Chapter 2

1. Chris Anderson, *Makers the New Industrial Revolution* (New York: Crown Publishing Group, 2012), p. 59.
2. Arduino, Serial. Online. Available: http://arduino.cc/en/Serial/begin.
3. Arduino, Reference. Online. Available: http://arduino.cc/en/Reference/.
4. Bruce Eckel, *Thinking in C++*, Vol. 1: *Introduction to Standard C++*, 2d ed. (Upper Saddle River, NJ: Prentice Hall, 2000), p. 156.
5. Perry R. Cook, *Real Sound Synthesis for Interactive Applications* (Natick, MA: A K Peters, Ltd., 2002), p. 4.
6. Bruce Eckel, *Thinking in C++*, Vol. 1: *Introduction to Standard C++*, 2d ed. (Upper Saddle River, NJ: Prentice Hall, 2000), pp. 143–144.
7. Ibid., p. 144.
8. Simon Monk, *Programming Arduino: Getting Started with Sketches* (New York: McGraw-Hill, 2012), pp. 56–57.
9. Arduino, String. Online. Available: http://arduino.cc/en/Reference/string.
10. Kyle Loudon, *C++ Pocket Reference* (Sebastopol, CA: O'Reilly, 2003), pp. 22–23.
11. Arduino, String. Online. Available: http://arduino.cc/en/Reference/StringObject.

Chapter 3

1. Charles Platt, *Make: Electronics* (Sebastopol, CA: O'Reilly Media, 2009), p. 41.
2. Ibid p. 12.
3. Robert T. Paynter and B. J. Toby Boydell, *Electronics Technology Fundamentals* (Saddle River, NJ: Prentice Hall, 2002), p. 30.
4. Forrest M. Mims III, *Getting Started In Electronics* (Niles, IL: Master Publishing, 2000), p. 66.
5. Robert T. Paynter and B. J. Toby Boydell, *Electronics Technology Fundamentals* (Saddle River,NJ: Prentice Hall, 2002), p. 25.
6. Ibid., p. 11.
7. Charles Platt, *Make: Electronics* (Sebastopol, CA: O'Reilly Media, 2009), p. 20.

8. Paul Scherz and Simon Monk, *Practical Electronics for Inventors*, 3d ed. (New York: McGraw-Hill, 2013), p. 42.

9. Ibid., p. 45.

10. Robert T. Paynter and B. J. Toby Boydell, *Electronics Technology Fundamentals* (Saddle River, NJ: Prentice Hall, 2002), p. 69.

11. Gordon McComb, *Robot Builder's Bonanza*, 4th ed. (New York: McGraw-Hill, 2011), pp. 382–383.

12. Charles Platt, *Make: Electronics* (Sebastopol, CA: O'Reilly Media, 2009), p. 76.

13. Simon Monk, *Hacking Electronics: An Illustrated DIY Guide for Makers and Hobbyists* (New York: McGraw-Hill, 2013).

14. Forrest M. Mims III, *Getting Started In Electronics* (Niles, IL: Master Publishing, 2000), p. 93.

15. Gordon McComb, *Robot Builder's Bonanza*, 4th ed. (New York: McGraw-Hill, 2011), p. 393.

16. Dennis Bohn, Pro Audio Reference. Online. Available: http://www.rane.com/digi-dic.html.

Chapter 4

1. Simon Monk, *Programming Arduino, Getting Started with Sketches* (New York: McGraw-Hill, 2012), p. 4.

2. Dale Wheat, *Arduino Internals* (New York: Apress, 2011), p. 174.

3. Paul Scherz and Simon Monk, *Practical Electronics for Inventors* (New York: McGraw-Hill, 2013), p. 790.

4. Michael Margolis, *Arduino Cookbook* (Sebastopol, CA: O'Reilly Media, 2011), p. 191.

5. Paul Scherz and Simon Monk, *Practical Electronics for Inventors* (New York: McGraw-Hill, 2013), p. 542.

6. Michael Margolis, *Arduino Cookbook* (Sebastopol, CA: O'Reilly Media, 2011), p. 193.

Chapter 5

1. MIDI Manufacturers Association, *Tutorial on MIDI and Music Synthesis from The Complete MIDI 1.0 Detailed Specification* (Los Angeles: MMA, revised 2006), p. 1.

2. MIDI Manufacturers Association, MusikkPraxis excerpts. Online. Available: http://www.midi.org/aboutus/news/interview_tw.php.

3. MIDI Manufacturers Association, Tutorial: History of MIDI. Online. Available: http://www.midi.org/aboutmidi/tut_history.php.

4. Paul Messick, *Maximum Midi* (Greenwich, CT: Manning Publications, 1998), p. 14.

5. MIDI Manufactures Association, *The Complete MIDI 1.0 Detailed Specification* (Los Angeles: MMA, revised 2006), p. 1.

6. Paul Messick, *Maximum Midi* (Greenwich, CT: Manning Publications, 1998), p. 18.

7. MIDI Manufacturers Association, MIDI Messages, Table 1—Summary of MIDI Messages. Online. Available: http://www.midi.org/techspecs/midimessages.php.

8. MIDI Manufacturers Association, *The Complete MIDI 1.0 Detailed Specification* (Los Angeles: MMA, revised 2006), p. 25.

9. Ibid., p. 26.

10. Paul Messick, *Maximum MIDI* (Greenwich, CT: Manning Publications, 1998), p. 21.

11. MIDI Manufacturers Association, MIDI Messages, Table 1—Summary of MIDI Messages. Online. Available: http://www.midi.org/techspecs/midimessages.php.

12. Brent Edstrom, *Musicianship in the Digital Age* (Boston: Thomson Course Technology PTR, 2006), p. 84.

13. MIDI Manufactures Association, *The Complete MIDI 1.0 Detailed Specification* (Los Angeles: MMA, revised 2006), p. 2.

14. Michael Margolis, *Arduino Cookbook* (Sebastopol, CA: O'Reilly Media, 2011), pp. 312–313.

15. MIDI Manufacturers Association, MIDI Electrical Specification Diagram & Proper Design of Joystick/MIDI Adapter. Online. Available: http://www.midi.org/techspecs/electrispec.php.

Chapter 6

1. Jeff Pressing, *Synthesizer Performance and Real-Time Techniques* (Greenwich, CT: A-R Editions, 1992), p. 187.

2. Interlink Electronics, FSR® Integration Guide (Camarillo, CA: Interlink Electronics, n.d.), PDF, p. 18.

3. Adafruit, Using an FSR. Online. Available: http://learn.adafruit.com/force-sensitive-resistor-fsr/using-an-fsr.

4. Get Touchy—Nintendo DS Touch Screen + Arduino. Online. Available: http://bildr.org/2011/06/ds-touch-screen-arduino/.

5. Mike Grusin, Thumb Joystick Retail. Online. Available: https://www.sparkfun.com/tutorials/272.

6. Paul Griffiths, *A Guide to Electronic Music* (New York: Thames and Hudson, 1980), p. 27.

Chapter 7

1. Sparkfun, Music Instrument Shield Quickstart Guide. Online. Available: https://www.sparkfun.com/tutorials/302.

2. waveHC Library. Online. Available: https://learn.adafruit.com/adafruit-wave-shield-audio-shield-for-arduino/wavehc-library.

3. Ginsingsound.com, GinSing Software Reference Guide. Online. Available: http://ginsingsound.com/23-online-docs/124-ginsing-software-reference-guide.

4. Ginsingsound.com, GinSing Programming Guide. Online. Available: http://www.ginsingsound.com/get-started-banner/16-public/instructions/32-progamming-guide-v10.

5. Arduino, SPI library. Online. Available: http://arduino.cc/en/Reference/SPI.

6. Excamera, Gameduino: a game adapter for microcontrollers. Online. Available: http://excamera.com/sphinx/gameduino/.

7. Hubert S. Howe, *Electronic Music Synthesis* (New York: W.W. Norton & Company, 1975), p. 84.

Chapter 8

1. Bruce Eckel, *Thinking in C++*, 2d ed., Vol. 1: *Introduction to Standard C++* (Upper Saddle River, NJ: Prentice Hall, 2000), p. 1.

2. Kyle Loudon, *C++ Pocket Reference* (Sebastopol, CA: O'Reilly, 2003), p. 68.

3. Michael Margolis, *Arduino Cookbook* (Sebastopol, CA: O'Reilly Media, 2011), p. 191.

4. Scott Meyers, *Effective C++: 50 Specific Ways to Improve Your Programs and Designs* (Reading, MA: Addison-Wesley, 1992), p. 63.

Chapter 9

1. Hal Chamberlin, *Musical Applications of Microprocessors* (Hasbrouck Heights, NJ: Hayden Book Company, 1985), p. 111.

2. Ibid., p. 329.

3. Delton T. Horn, *Music Synthesizers: A Manual of Design and Construction* (Blue Ridge Summit, PA: Tab Books, 1984), pp. 329–330.

4. G. Randy Slone, *TAB Electronics Guide to Understanding Electricity and Electronics* (New York: McGraw-Hill, 2000), p. 198.

5. Paul Scherz and Simon Monk, *Practical Electronics for Inventors*, 3d ed, (New York: McGraw-Hill, 2013), p. 640.

6. Michael Margolis, *Arduino Cookbook* (Sebastopol, CA: O'Reilly, 2011), p. 549.

7. Amanda Ghassaei, Arduino Audio Output. Online. Available: http://www.instructables.com/id/Arduino-Audio-Output.

8. Arduino, Port Manipulation. Online. Available: http://www.arduino.cc/en/Reference/PortManipulation.

9. André LaMothe, John Ratcliff, Mark Seminatore, and Denise Tyler, *Tricks of the Game—Programming Gurus* (Indianapolis, IN: SAMS, 1994), pp. 676–681.

10. Rugged Circuits, SineSynth. Online. Available: https://github.com/RuggedCircuits/Rugged-Audio-Shield-Library/blob/master/examples/SineSynth/SineSynth.ino.

11. Elliot Williams, *Make: AVR Programming* (Sebastopol, CA: Maker Media, 2014), p. 171.

12. Joe Wolfe, Note Names, MIDI Numbers and Frequencies. Online. Available: http://newt.phys.unsw.edu.au/jw/notes.html.

13. Bruce Eckel, *Thinking in C++*, 2d ed., Vol. 1: *Introduction to Standard C++* (Upper Saddle River, NJ: Prentice Hall, 2000), pp. 636–637.

14. Hal Chamberlin, *Musical Applications of Microprocessors* (Hasbrouck Heights, NJ: Hayden Book Company, 1985), pp. 532–533.

15. Martin Nawrath, lookup table. Online. Available: http://interface.khm.de/index.php/lab/experiments/arduino-dds-sinewave-generator/.

16. 13. Bruce Eckel, *Thinking in C++*, 2d ed., Vol. 1: *Introduction to Standard C++* (Upper Saddle River, NJ: Prentice Hall, 2000), p. 689.

17. Stephen Barras, MozziGutz.h. Online. Available: https://github.com/sensorium/Mozzi/blob/master/MozziGuts.h.

Chapter 10

1. Paul Scherz and Simon Monk, *Practical Electronics for Inventors*, 3d ed. (New York: McGraw-Hill, 2013), p. 303, fig. 3.51.

2. Simon Monk, *Programming Arduino: Getting Started with Sketches* (New York: McGraw-Hll, 2012), p. 217.

3. Amanda Ghassaei, Arduino Audio Input. Online. Available: http://www.instructables.com/id/Arduino-Audio-Input/.

4. Open Music Labs, ATmega-ADC. Online: Available: http://www.openmusiclabs.com/learning/digital/atmega-adc/.

5. Michael Margolis, *Arduino Cookbook* (Sebastopol, CA: O'Reilly Media, 2011), p. 549.

6. Atmel, Atmel 8-bit Microcontroller with 4/8/16/32KBytes In-System Programmable Flash ATmega48A; ATmega48PA; ATmega88A; ATmega88PA; ATmega168A; ATmega168PA; ATmega328; ATmega328P, p. 240.

7. Douglas Self, *Small Signal Audio Design*, 2d ed. (New York: NY: Focal Press, 2015), p. 727.
8. Paul Scherz and Simon Monk, *Practical Electronics for Inventors*, 3d ed. (New York: McGraw-Hill, 2013), p. 932.
9. Ibid., p. 930.
10. Elliot Williams, *Make: AVR Programming* (Sebastopol, CA: Maker Media, 2014), p. 141.
11. Open Music Labs, Arduino FHT Library. Online. Available: http://wiki.openmusiclabs.com/wiki/ArduinoFHT.
12. Ibid., FHT Functions.
13. Ibid., FHT Functions.
14. Simon Monk, *Programming Arduino Next Steps: Going Further with Sketches* (New York: McGraw-Hill, 2014), p. 214.
15. Gary Hill, PWM Sine Wave Generation. Online. Available: http://web.csulb.edu/~hill/ee470/Lab%202d%20-%20Sine_Wave_Generator.pdf.

Chapter 11

1. Ray Wilson, *Make: Analog Synthesizers* (Sebastopol, CA: Maker Media, 2013), p. 18.
2. Gordon McComb, *Robot Builder's Bonanza* (New York: McGraw-Hill, 2011), p. 417.
3. Kenny Werner, *Effortless Mastery* (New Albany, IN: Jamey Aebersold Jazz, 1996), p. 131.
4. Andrew Singmin, *Modern Electronics Soldering Techniques* (Indianapolis, IN: Prompt Publications Indianapolis, 2000), p. 13.
5. Ibid., p. 9.
6. Ray Wilson, *Make: Analog Synthesizers* (Sebastopol,, CA: Maker Media, 2013), p. 19.
7. G. Randy Slone, *Electricity and Electronics* (Hightstown, NJ: McGraw-Hill, 2000), p. 99.
8. Ibid., p. 100.
9. Chris Anderson, *Makers: The New Industrial Revolution* (New York: Crown Publishing Group, 2012), p. 93.

Chapter 12

1. Gordon McComb, *Robot Builder's Bonanza* (New York: McGraw-Hill, 2011), p. 202.
2. Charles Platt, *Make: Electronics* (Sebastopol, CA: O'Reilly Media, 2009), p. 155.
3. Arduino, ATmega168/328-Arduino Pin Mapping. Online. Available: http://arduino.cc/en/Hacking/PinMapping168.
4. Atmel, AVR042: AVR Hardware Design Considerations. Online. Available: http://www.atmel.com/Images/Atmel-2521-AVR-Hardware-Design-Considerations_ApplicationNote_AVR042.pdf, p. 12.
5. Arduino, From Arduino to a Microcontroller on a Breadboard. Online. Available: http://arduino.cc/en/Tutorial/ArduinoToBreadboard.
6. Elliot Williams, *Make: AVR Programming* (Sebastopol, CA: Maker Media, 2014), p. 31.

Chapter 14

1. Tim Barrass, Under the Hood. Online. Available: http://sensorium.github.io/Mozzi/learn/under-the-hood/.
2. Kenny Werner, *Effortless Mastery* (New Albany, IN: Jamey Aebersold Jazz, 1996), p. 116.

Conclusion

1. Paul Griffiths, *A Guide to Electronic Music* (New York: Thames and Hudson, 1980), p. 27.
2. Richard Taruskin, *Music in the Late Twentieth Century* (Oxford: Oxford University Press, 2010), p. 508.
3. John Medina, *Brain Rules* (Seattle, Pear Press, 2009), p. 56.
4. Paul Griffiths, *A Guide to Electronic Music* (New York: Thames and Hudson, 1980), p. 27.

Bibliography

Adafruit. *Using an FSR*. Online. Available: http://learn.adafruit.com/force-sensitive-resistor-fsr/using-an-fsr.

Adamson, Chris, and Kevin Avila. *Learning Core Audio*. Upper Saddle River, NJ: Addison-Wesley, 2012.

Allan, Alasdair. *iOS Sensor Apps with Arduino*. Sebastopol, CA: O'Reilly Media, 2011.

Analog Devices. *A Technical Tutorial on Digital Signal Synthesis*. Norwood, MA: Analog Devices, 1999.

Anderson, Chris. *Makers the New Industrial Revolution*. New York: Crown, 2012.

Anderton, Craig. *Electronic Projects for Musicians*. New York: Amsco, 1980.

Arduino. *Reference*. Online. Available: http://arduino.cc/en/Reference/

Arduino. *SPI Library*. Online. Available: http://arduino.cc/en/Reference/SPI

Arduino. *MCP3208*. Online. Available: http://playground.arduino.cc/Code/MCP3208

Arduino. From Arduino to Microcontroller on a Breadboard. Online. Available: http://arduino.cc/en/Tutorial/ArduinoToBreadboard

ATMEL, *Using the AVR's High-Speed PWM*. 8-bit AVR Microcontroller Application Note, 2003.

ATMEL, *8271GS Atmel 8-bit Microcontroller with 4/8/16/32KBytes In- System Programmable Flash*. [Datasheet Summary], San Jose, CA: Atmel, 2013.

ATMEL, *AVR042: AVR Hardware Design Considerations*. Application Note, 2013.

ATMEL. *Atmel 8-bit Microcontroller with 4/8/16/32KBytes In- System Programmable Flash*. San Jose, CA: Atmel, 2014.

Axelson, Jan. *Making Printed Circuit Boards*. New York: Tab Books, a division of McGraw-Hill, 1993.

Badger, Paul. *Capacitive Sensing Library*. Online. Available: http://playground.arduino.cc/Main/CapacitiveSensor?from=Main.CapSense

Banzi, Massimo. *Getting Started with Arduino*, 2d ed. Sebastopol, CA: Make: Books, an imprint of Maker Media, a division of O'Reilly Media, 2011.

Barker, Forrest L. and Gershon J. Wheeler. *Mathematics for Electronics*, 2d ed. Menlo Park, CA: Benjamin/Cummings, 1978.

Barrass, Tim. *Mozzi, an Introductory Tutorial*. Online. Available: http://sensorium.github.io/Mozzi/learn/introductory-tutorial/

Barrass, Tim. *Output Circuits*. Online. Available: http://sensorium.github.io/Mozzi/learn/output/

Barrass, Tim. *Under the Hood*. Online. Available: http://sensorium.github.io/Mozzi/learn/under-the-hood/

Barrass, Tim. *Writing a Mozzi Sketch*. Online. Available: http://sensorium.github.io/Mozzi/learn/a-simple-sketch/

B_E_N, *Data Types in Arduino*. Online. Available: https://learn.sparkfun.com/tutorials/data-types-in-arduino/defining-data-types

Bilder.org. *Get Touchy – Nintendo DS Touch Screen + Arduino*. Online. Available: http://bildr.org/2011/06/ds-touch-screen-arduino/

Bohn, Dennis. *Pro Audio Reference*. Online. Available: http://www.rane.com/digi-dic.html

Bowen, B.A. and R. J., A. Buhr. *The Logical Design of Multiple-Microprocessor Systems*. Englewood Cliffs, NJ: Prentice-Hall, 1980.

Bowman, James. *The Gameduino 2 Tutorial, Reference and Cookbook*. Pescadero, CA: Excamera Labs, 2013.

Catonmat.net. *Low Level Bit Hacks You Absolutely Must Know*. Online. Available: http://www.catonmat.net/blog/low-level-bit-hacks-you-absolutely-must-know/

Chamberlin, Hal. *Musical Applications of Microprocessors*, 2d ed. Hasbrouck Heights, NJ: Hayden, 1985.

Clendinning, Jen Piper and Elizabeth West Marvin. *The Musician's Guide to Theory and Analysis*, 2d ed. New York: W. W. Norton, 2011.

Collecchia, Regina. *Numbers & Notes: An introduction to musical signal processing*. Portland, OR: Perfectly Scientific Press, 2012.

Collins, Nicolas. *Handmade Electronic Music: The Art of Hardware Hacking*, 2d ed. New York: Routledge, 2009.

Cook, Perry R. *Real Sound Synthesis for Interactive Applications*. Natick, MA: A K Peters, 2002.

Coulter, Doug. *Digital Audio Processing*. Lawrence, KS: R&D Books, 2000.

cplusplus.com. *C++ Language*. Online. Available: http://www.cplusplus.com/doc/tutorial/

CTayor. *Music Instrument Shield Quickstart Guide*. Online. Available: https://www.sparkfun.com/tutorials/302

Cutcher, Dave. Electronic Circuits for the Evil Genius, 2d ed. New York: McGraw-Hill, 2011.

Davis, Bob. "Breaking the Arduino Speed Limit." *Nuts and Volts*. March, 2014. pp. 40–47.

Douglas-Young, John. *Complete Guide to Reading Schematic Diagrams*, 2d ed. West Nyack, NY: Parker, 1979.

Dratwa, Louis. "The Lost Art of Strip Board Prototyping." *Nuts and Volts*. June, 2013. pp. 48–53.

Eckel, Bruce. *Thinking in C++, Vol. 1: Introduction to Standard C++*, 2d ed. Upper Saddle River, NJ: Prentice Hall, 2000.

Eckel, Bruce. *Using C++*. Berkeley, CA: Osborne McGraw-Hill, 1990.

Eggleston, Dennis L. *Basic Electronics for Scientists and Engineers*. Cambridge, UK: Cambridge University Press, 2011.

Enders, Bernd and Wolfgang Klemme. *MIDI and Sound Book for the Atari ST*. Redwood City, CA: M&T Publishing, 1989.

Excamera. *Gameduino: a game adapter for microcontrollers*. Online. Available: http://excamera.com/sphinx/gameduino/

Faludi, Robert. *Building Wireless Sensor Networks*. Sebastopol, CA: O'Reilly Media, 2011.

Freescale Semiconductor. *Integrated Silicon Pressure Sensor On-Chip Signal Conditioned, Temperature Compensated and Calibrated*. MPX5050 Rev 11, 03/2010.

Ghassaei, Amanda. *Arduino Audio Input*. Online. Available: http://www.instructables.com/id/Arduino-Audio-Input/

Ghassaei, Amanda. *Arduino Frequency Detection*. Online. Available: http://www.instructables.com/id/Arduino-Frequency-Detection/

Ghassaei, Amanda. *Arduino Timer Interrupts*. Online. Available: http://www.instructables.com/id/Arduino-Timer-Interrupts/

Ghassaei, Amanda. *Arduino Vocal Effects Box*. Online. Available: http://www.instructables.com/id/Arduino-Vocal-Effects-Box/

Ginsingsound.com. *GinSing Programming Guide*. Online. Available: http://www.ginsing-sound.com/get-started-banner/16-public/instructions/32-progamming-guide-v10

Ginsingsound.com. *GinSing Software Reference Guide*. Online. Available: http://ginsing-sound.com/23-online-docs/124-ginsing-software-reference-guide

Griffiths, Paul. *A Guide to Electronic Music*. New York: Thames and Hudson, 1980.

Grossblatt, Robert. *Bob Grossblatt's Guide to Creative Circuit Design*. Blue Ridge Summit, PA: Tab Books, 1992.

Hantouch USA. *How it works: 4-Wire Analog-Resistive Touch Screens*. Online. Available: https://www.sparkfun.com/datasheets/LCD/HOW%20DOES%20IT%20WORK.pdf

Harbison, Samuel P., and Guy L. Steele Jr. *C: A Reference Manual*, 3d ed. Englewood Cliffs, NJ: Prentice Hall, 1991.

Henry, Thomas. *Build a Better Music Synthesizer*. Blue Ridge Summit, PA: Tab Books, 1987.

Henry, Thomas. "Build a MIDI to Logic Controller…the Easy Way." *Nuts and Volts* (October 2012): 32–37.

Henry, Thomas. "Getting Started with Matrix LED Displays." *Nuts and Volts* (May 2013): 42–47.

Hill, Gary. *PWM Sine Wave Generation*. Online. Available: http://www.csulb.edu/~hill/ee470/Lab%202d%20-%20Sine_Wave_Generator.pdf

Horn, Delton T. *Music Synthesizers a Manual of Design & Construction*, 2d ed. Blue Ridge Summit, PA: Tab Books, 1984.

Howe, Hubert S. *Electronic Music Synthesis*. New York: W.W. Norton, 1975.

Huber, David Miles. *The MIDI Manual*. Carmel, IN: Sams, A Division of Prentice Hall Computer Publishing, 1991.

Interlink Electronics. *FSR® Integration Guide*. Camarillo, CA: Interlink Electronics, 90-45632 Rev. D. PDF Document, n.d.

Jeans, Sir James. *Science & Music*. Mineola, NY: Dover, 1968.

Jung, Walt, ed. *Op Amp Applications Handbook*. Burlington, MA: Newnes, 2005.

Karvinen, Tero, and Kimmo Karvinen. *Make a Mind-Controlled Arduino Robot*. Sebastopol, CA: O'Reilly Media, 2011.

Knuth, Donald E. *The Art of Computer Programming*, Vol. 2—*Seminumerical Algorithms*. Reading, MA: Addison-Wesley, 1969.

Kuecken, John A. *How to Measure Anything with Electronic Instruments*. Blue Ridge Summit, PA: Tab Books, 1981.

Kurt, Tod E. *"WiiChuck" Wii Nunchuck Adapter*. Online. Available: http://todbot.com/blog/2008/02/18/wiichuck-wii-nunchuck-adapter-available/

LaMothe, Ratcliff, Seminatore & Tyler. *Tricks of the Game Programming Gurus*. Indianapolis, IN: Sams, 1994.

Lindley, Craig A. *Digital Audio with Java*. Upper Saddle River, NJ: Prentice Hall, 2000.

Loudon, Kyle. *C++ Pocket Reference*. Sabastopol, CA: O'Reilly Media, 2003.

Magda, Yury. *Arduino Interfacing and Signal Processing*. Yury Magda, 2012.

Manzo, V. J. *MAX/MSP/JITTER for Music*. New York: Oxford University Press, 2011.

Margolis, Michael. *Arduino Cookbook*. Sebastopol, CA: O'Reilly Media, 2011.

Mazurov, Oleg. *Reading rotary encoder on Arduino*. Online. Available: http://www.circuitsathome.com/mcu/programming/reading-rotary-encoder-on-arduino

McComb, Gordon. *Robot Builder's Bonanza*, 4th ed. New York: McGraw-Hill, 2011.

McComb, Gordon. "How to Make Professional Looking Control Panels and Enclosures: Part 2." *Nuts and Volts* (May 2013): 48–53.

McNamara, Brian. "The Luna Mod Simple, Addictive Sound Effects Looper." *Make* 26 (April 2011): 80–91.

Medina, John. *Brain Rules*. Seattle, WA: Pear Press, 2009.

Messick, Paul. *Maximum MIDI: Music Applications in C++*. Greenwich, CT: Manning, 1998.

Meyers, Scott. *Effective C++: 50 Specific Ways to Improve Your Programs and Designs.* Reading, MA: Addison-Wesley, 1992.

MIDI Manufacturers Association. *The Complete MIDI 1.0 Detailed Specification.* Los Angeles: The MIDI Manufacturers Association, 1996.

MIDI Manufacturers Association. MIDI Electrical Specification Diagram & Proper Design of Joystick/MIDI Adapter. Online. Available: http://www.midi.org/techspecs/electri-spec.php

MIDI Manufacturers Association. *MIDI Implementation Chart V2 Instructions.* Online. Available: http://www.midi.org/techspecs/midi_chart-v2.pdf

MIDI Manufacturers Association. *Summary of MIDI Messages.* Online. Available: http://www.midi.org/techspecs/midimessages.php

Mims, Forrest, M. III. *Getting Started in Electronics,* 4th ed. Niles, IL: Master Publishing, 2000.

Mims, Forrest, M. III. Workbook 2: *Digital Logic Projects: Workbook II.* Fort Worth, TX: RadioShack, 2000.

Mims, Forrest, M. III. *Volume I: Timer, Op Amp & Optoelectronic Circuits & Projects.* Niles, IL: Master Publishing, 2001.

Monk, Simon. *30 Arduino Projects for the Evil Genius.* New York: McGraw-Hill, 2010.

Monk, Simon. *Programming Arduino: getting started with sketches.* New York: McGraw-Hill, 2012.

Monk, Simon. *Hacking Electronics: An Illustrated DIY Guide for Makers and Hobbyists.* New York: McGraw-Hill, 2013.

Monk, Simon. *Programming the Raspberry Pi: Getting Started with Python.* New York: McGraw-Hill, 2013.

Monk, Simon. *Programming Arduino Next Steps: Going Further with Sketches.* New York: McGraw-Hill, 2014.

Murphy, Eva, and Colm Slattery. *Ask the Application Engineer—33 All About Direct Digital Synthesis.* Online. Available: http://www.analog.com/library/analogdialogue/archives/38-08/dds.html

Nierhaus, Gerhard. *Algorithmic Composition Paradigms of Automated Music Generation.* New York: Springer-Verlag, 2009.

Open Music Labs. *ATMega ADC.* Online. Available: http://www.openmusiclabs.com/learning/digital/atmega-adc/

Open Music Labs. *PWM DAC.* Online. Available: http://www.openmusiclabs.com/learning/digital/pwm-dac/

Open Music Labs. *Synchronizing Timers.* Online. Available: http://www.openmusiclabs.com/learning/digital/synchronizing-timers/

Pardue, Joe. "Fritzing With the Arduino—Part 2." *Nuts and Volts.* September, 2012. pp. 68–75.

Pardue, Joe. "Arduino Handheld Prototyper—Part 1." *Nuts and Volts* (July 2013): 68–73.

Pardue, Joe. "Arduino Handheld Prototyper—Part 2." *Nuts and Volts* (August 2013): 68–74.

Pardue, Joe. "Fritzingduino—Part 2." *Nuts and Volts.* June, 2013. pp. 67–72.

Pardue, Joe. "Arduino 101—Chapter 3: How an Arduino Program Works" *Nuts and Volts.* March, 2014. pp. 54–61.

Pardue, Joe. "Arduino 101—Chapter 4: Digital Input . . . Pushbuttons" *Nuts and Volts.* March, 2014. pp. 56–66.

Pardue, Joe. "Arduino 101—Chapter 6: Analog Input." *Nuts and Volts.* June, 2014. pp. 58–66.

Pardue, Joe. "The Arduino Classroom: Arduino 101." *Nuts and Volts.* January, 2014. pp. 52–60.

Paynter, Robert T., and B. J. Toby Boydell. *Electronics Technology Fundamentals.* Upper Saddle River, NJ: Prentice Hall, 2002.

Petruzzellis, Tom. *Electronic Games for the Evil Genius*. New York: McGraw-Hill, 2007.

PJRC. *Audio Library for Teensy 3*. Online. Available: https://www.pjrc.com/teensy/td_libs_Audio.html

PJRC. *Using USB MIDI*. Online. Available: https://www.pjrc.com/teensy/td_midi.html

Platt, Charles. *Make: Electronics*. Sebastopol, CA: O'Reilly Media, 2009.

Pressing, Jeff. *Synthesizer Performance and Real-Time Techniques*. Madison, WI: A-R Editions, 1992.

Rabiner, Lawrence R., and Bernard Gold. *Theory and Application of Digital Signal Processing*. Englewood Cliffs, NJ: Prentice-Hall, 1975.

Ragan, Sean Michael. "Optical Tremolo Box." *Make: Volume 25*, January 2013, pp. 97–103.

Roederer, Juan G. *Introduction to the Physics and Psychophysics of Music*, 2d ed. New York: Springer-Verlag, 1975.

Rugged Circuits. *Rugged Audio Shield*. Online. Available: http://174.136.57.214/html/rugged_audio_shield.html#SampleCode

Scherz, Paul, and Simon Monk. *Practical Electronics for Inventors*, 3d ed. New York: McGraw-Hill, 2013.

Self, Douglas. *Small Signal Audio Design*, 2d ed. New York: Focal Press, 2015.

Shields, John Potter. *How to Build Proximity Detectors & Metal Locators*. Indianapolis, IN: Howard W. Sams, 1967.

Short, Kenneth L. *Microprocessors and Programmed Logic*. Englewood Cliffs, NJ: Prentice-Hall, 1981.

Singmin, Andrew. *Modern Electronics Techniques*. Indianapolis, IN: Prompt Publications, an imprint of Sams Technical Publishing, 2000.

Slone, G. Randy. *Tab Electronics Guide to Understanding Electricity and Electronics*, 2d ed. New York: McGraw-Hill, 2000.

Slone, G. Randy. *The Audiophile's Project Sourcebook*. New York: McGraw-Hill, 2002.

Smith, Michael. *8-bit, 8000 Hz Audio Playback on a PC Speaker*. Online. Available: http://playground.arduino.cc/Code/PCMAudio

Sood, P. K. *Electronic Musical Projects*. New Delhi, India: BPB Publications, 2010.

Stein, Rob and John Day. *D/A Conversion Using PWM and R-2R Ladders to Generate Sine and DTMF Waveforms*. Online. Available: http://ww1.microchip.com/downloads/en/AppNotes/00655a.pdf

Taruskin, Richard. *Music in the Late Twentieth Century*. Oxford: Oxford University Press, 2010.

Texas Instruments. *More Filter Design on a Budget*. Application Report, 2001.

Thompson, Jon. "Advanced Arduino Sound Synthesis." *Make 35* (July 2013): 80–87.

Ward, Brice. *Electronic Music Circuit Guidebook*. Blue Ridge Summit, PA: Tab Books, 1977.

waveHC Library. Online. Available: https://learn.adafruit.com/adafruit-wave-shield-audio-shield-for-arduino/wavehc-library

Wheat, Dale. "Primer: Make and Use an Arduino." *Make 33* (January 2011): 62–70.

Wheat, Dale. *Arduino Internals*. New York: Apress (Springer Science+Business Media), 2011.

Williams, Elliot. *Make: AVR Programming*. Sebastopol, CA: Maker Media, 2014.

Wilson, Ray. *Make: Analog Synthesizers*. Sebastopol, CA: Maker Media, 2013.

Windell. *Quick and Dirty D to A on the AVR: A Timer Tutorial*. Online. Available: http://www.evilmadscientist.com/2007/quick-and-dirty-d-to-a-on-the-avr-a-timer-tutorial/

Winston, Lawrence E. *33 Electronic Music Projects You Can Build*. Blue Ridge Summit, PA: Tab Books, 1981.

Index